THE HUM

MW01026815

The International Committee of the Red Cross (ICRC) coordinates the world's largest private relief system for conflict situations. Its staff of 2,000 professionals, supported by 10,000 local employees, operates throughout the world. In recent years the ICRC has mounted large operations in the Balkans and Somalia. It also visits more detainees around the world than any other organization, including recently at Guantanamo Bay. Yet despite its very important role, its internal workings are mysterious and often secretive. This book examines the ICRC from its origins in the middle of the nineteenth century up to the present day, and provides a comprehensive overview of a unique organization, whose governing body remains all-Swiss, but which is recognized in international law and in other legal arrangements as if it were an inter-governmental organization. David Forsythe focuses on the policy making and field work of the ICRC, while not ignoring international humanitarian law. He explores how it exercises its independence, impartiality, and neutrality to try to protect prisoners in Iraq, displaced and starving civilians in Somalia, and families separated by conflict in the Israeli–Palestinian conflict.

DAVID P. FORSYTHE is Charles J. Mach Distinguished Professor and University Professor at the University of Nebraska, Lincoln. He has published extensively on different aspects of International Relations including *Human Rights in International Relations* (Cambridge, 2000), which has been translated into Arabic, Chinese, Turkish, Korean, and Bulgarian, and most recently, *Human Rights and Diversity: Area Studies Revisited* (edited with Patrice McMahon, 2004). He is also the general editor of the new edition of *The Encyclopedia of Human Rights*.

THE HUMANITARIANS

The International Committee of the Red Cross

DAVID P. FORSYTHE

CAMBRIDGE
UNIVERSITY PRESS

CAMBRIDGE UNIVERSITY PRESS
Cambridge, New York, Melbourne, Madrid, Cape Town, Singapore, São Paulo, Delhi

Cambridge University Press
The Edinburgh Building, Cambridge CB2 8RU, UK

Published in the United States of America by Cambridge University Press, New York

www.cambridge.org
Information on this title: www.cambridge.org/9780521612814

First published 2005

A catalogue record for this publication is available from the British Library

Library of Congress Cataloguing in Publication data
Forsythe, David P., 1941–
The humanitarians: the International Committee of the Red Cross /
David P. Forsythe.
p.   cm.
Includes bibliographical references and index.
ISBN 0 521 84828 8 (alk. paper) – ISBN 0 521 61281 0 (pb.)
1. International Committee of the Red Cross.   2. International Committee of the
Red Cross – History.   3. International relief.   I. Title.
HV568.F67 2005
361.7′7 – dc22   2005045782

ISBN 978-0-521-84828-2 hardback
ISBN 978-0-521-61281-4 paperback

Transferred to digital printing 2009

For
Pierre Boissier
and
Donald D. Tansley

The work of the ICRC is legendary.
> Jennifer Leaning, "When the System Doesn't Work: Somalia 1992," in Cahill, ed., *A Framework for Survival*, 105

There is at the center of the ICRC a type of conviction that we are the best in the world. That comes to us from our long history, and without doubt also from the success of our methods of work ... I have thus applied myself to try to contest that form of self-satisfaction, that institutional arrogance.
> Cornelio Sommaruga, former ICRC President, in Massimo Lorenzi, *Le CICR: le cœur et la raison*, 89

We're admired – we've won three Nobel Peace Prizes – but we're not liked.
> Urs Boegli, former Head, Washington Office, ICRC, quoted in *The New York Times*, 20 February 2002, A10.

Yet the International Committee itself remained a curious animal.
> Caroline Morehead, *Dunant's Dream*, 175

CONTENTS

In 1973 Pierre Boissier, an official of the ICRC and also at that time the Director of the now defunct Henry Dunant Institute, then supposedly the think tank of the Red Cross family, asked me to do some work for him as a research consultant. He was a wonderful and wise mentor, with a vast knowledge of humanitarian affairs. I later discovered that he had recommended me to others, and for certain positions, which shaped my professional life to a great extent. Among these positions was a stint as a consultant on humanitarian protection to Donald Tansley, head of the "Big Study" which led to the "Tansley Report" of 1975 on the reappraisal of the Red Cross Movement. On the basis of this foundation I was able to meet others and observe things which probably gave me a special niche for commenting on the ICRC as an informed outsider. I shall always be grateful for having encountered Pierre Boissier. It was a real tragedy that an accident cut short his life when he had so much to offer.

I am equally grateful to have worked for Don Tansley and to have experienced up close his caustic skepticism as he prepared to ruffle numerous Red Cross feathers. Being in Geneva more than twenty-five years after the publication of the Tansley Report, to which I made some contribution, I was amazed to see how much it had entered the history of the Red Cross Movement. Some of the changes being undertaken at the ICRC and the Red Cross Federation at the time of writing in 2004 had been recommended by us back in 1975. It is a pity that at least some of our ideas were not addressed with a greater sense of urgency then. But as Tansley was known to remark with tongue firmly in cheek, the Red Cross always moved with such amazing speed.

In any event, having followed the ICRC since the early 1970s, sometimes with special access and sometimes not, I wanted to make another attempt at a general overview. My first book on the ICRC tried to break new ground in looking at the field operations of the agency and its

policy-making process in Geneva.[1] As far as I am aware, that effort was
the first independent overview of the organization focusing not on legal
rules but on policy questions. Having collected interview findings and
other information for over thirty years, it seemed a pity not to review that
mass of material. Was anything of importance different about the ICRC
as we approach 2007 compared to 1977?

I write, like before, as a sympathetic but hopefully analytical observer.
Within some parts of the ICRC I am known as "a friend of the house,"
to quote one document I was not supposed to see. But a real friend does
not recoil from turning a critical eye toward some past events in the hope
that further reflection might prove beneficial. Some of my friends at the
ICRC, both back in the 1970s and again now, think I have been too critical.
Having read some of my drafts, one asked, "Why write a book if you are
going to be so critical?" That is certainly the wrong question. As Alex
de Waal has indicated, "Nobility of aim does not confer immunity from
sociological analysis or ethical critique."[2] It should also be said that many
of these interlocutors – but not all – continued to discuss interpretations
with me even when they thought I was being too critical – no doubt in
the hope that I would see the error of my ways.

Many ICRC loyalists still want every comment and publication to be
within the framework of advancing the reputation of the ICRC and the
respect for IHL. They disregard the warnings of former ICRC Acting
President Freymond, who noted that the ICRC did not like outside critiques, fearing that the organization would lose its status as a unique
organization; but he went on, defensiveness could slide into a belief in
infallibility.[3] While greatly sympathetic to the ICRC and humanitarian
values, as readers will discover if they stick with my account until the end,
I remain an outsider trying to observe with at least some academic detachment. The ICRC will only be fully effective – and fully respected – if it
confronts the controversial aspects of its record. My general theme is that
whereas in the past the ICRC was in fact not as independent and neutral
and effective as was often made out to be the case, in contemporary times
the ICRC is a very impressive agency.

Having had the good fortune at several junctures to live in Geneva, I
have supplemented the written record with a broad range of interviews
from the top of the organization to the bottom. I had discussions with

---

[1] *Humanitarian Politics: The International Committee of the Red Cross* (Baltimore: Johns
Hopkins University Press, 1977.)

[2] Quoted in David Rieff, *A Bed for the Night: Humanitarianism in Crisis* (New York: Simon
and Schuster, 2002), 116.

[3] Jacques Freymond, *Guerres, révolutions, Croix-Rouge* (Geneva: HEI, 1976), 57–8.

both Cornelio Sommaruga, ICRC President from 1987 to 1999, and Jakob Kellenberger, President from 2000, just as I had discussions with other presidents such as Marcel Naville, Alexander Hay, and Jacques Freymond (who was Acting President for a time). But I also interviewed a wide range of others, from newly appointed personnel to members of the Committee – the group of Swiss notables who comprise the highest policy-making organ of the organization. In formal session they comprise the Assembly. (So I use "the Committee" and "the Assembly" as synonyms, as compared to the organization as a whole – the ICRC.) At different times I talked a great deal with the various members of the Directorate, the highest rung of the professional staff who actually run the agency on a day to day basis: to use titles current in 2004, the Director-General, the Director of Operations, the Director of Resources and Operational Support, the Director of International Law and Movement Cooperation, and the Director of Communications. I also interviewed a number of persons outside the organization who were well informed about it, such as individuals in the Red Cross Federation, the American Red Cross, the US State Department, the US Department of Defense, and so on.

To all my interlocutors I express my gratitude for the time and insights given. Some of them were unusually open and helpful (and others decidedly not), but for reasons that should become obvious this is not the place to name names. I encountered at ICRC headquarters more than my share of what one colleague called "courteous stonewalling."[4] Some of these folks would make good Cardinals defending the secrets of the Vatican, and understanding the internal workings of the ICRC is probably similar to ferreting out Vatican decision making. This defensiveness by some high ICRC officials, who are very reluctant to speak candidly about personnel and the policy-making process in Geneva, has absolutely nothing to do with protecting the human dignity of victims of conflicts. This trait has everything to do with an irrational and sometimes dysfunctional tendency toward secrecy. Whether this mindless secrecy springs from Swiss society or ICRC organizational culture can be debated. No doubt the two are related.

But I want to emphasize that this book could not have been written without the candor and cooperation of many ICRC officials. I owe them a profound debt of gratitude. At an earlier stage I accompanied some ICRC delegations in the field to observe first hand how they conducted

---

[4] John F. Hutchinson, *Champions of Charity: War and the Rise of the Red Cross* (Boulder: Westview, 1996), 3.

detention visits, relief efforts, and the tracing of missing persons in trying circumstances. This obviously occurred with the cooperation of the organization. I also attended all four sessions of the 1974–77 diplomatic conference that adopted two protocols additional to the 1949 Geneva Conventions for victims of war. In the summer of 2004 senior levels of the organization reviewed a draft copy of the book manuscript, at my initiative, which gave their side a chance to raise comments, and gave me an opportunity to evaluate those comments. In light of their comments and any documentary evidence presented, sometimes I made changes in my draft but sometimes I did not. From my perspective, some of these brutal discussions were about the same as having dental work without a pain killer, but presumably the end justified the means. I should like to stress that all my interlocutors respected my academic freedom.

Some of my friends would prefer to see this book based entirely on documents rather than additional interviews. But the ICRC archives are closed for the more recent years (the last forty, to be exact). Moreover, some things are not written down in documents. Judgments about the relationship between the President and the Committee, or the President and the Director-General, are not going to rest primarily on documentary evidence. I am aware that some of my interpretations rest on information gained through interviews, and that interviewing is not an exact science. But it is not reliance on mere gossip either, since I try to cross-check my interview findings and to combine interviews with whatever documentary evidence I could come up with.

I write primarily for those interested in international humanitarian affairs – that is, interested in the fate of individuals in distress. From time to time I draw on more general literature from the social sciences and law, but this is not a book intended for theorists. Moreover, I have tried to write in a style not encumbered by academic jargon. Early drafts reflected what Jacques Meurant has referred to in a different context as "the zest of subjectivity."[5] In so far as these drafts indicated a personalized and (attempted) entertaining overview, I was persuaded to make the project more "scholarly." This change may entail some drawbacks. "The obvious explanation for the lack of appeal of written history [and political science] is the pedestrian way it is presented. Historical writing [and political science] is the preserve of academics whose language is often stuck in a

---

[5] "The International Committee of the Red Cross: Nazi Persecutions and the Concentration Camps," *International Review of the Red Cross* 271 (July–August 1989), 391.

thicket of subordinate clauses."[6] Nevertheless, I have provided as much documentation as I can and removed the more light-hearted observations, even if I fully admit that behind most "scholarly" studies in international relations lurks the inevitability of personal judgment.

It is no doubt the case that at the time of writing there is considerable wariness of American views about international relations, and at times in certain circles a clear anti-American feeling in Europe – including in Switzerland. This is a difficult time for an American author to take a close look at what has historically been a very Swiss organization. I understand this resentment. When the Swiss, both in the government and at the ICRC, dealt with Nazi Germany from 1942 to 1944, they were effectively surrounded by fascists and it was reasonable to think the independent existence of the country was in doubt. After all, the Nazis did have contingency plans for the invasion of Switzerland. By contrast, the United States refused to take in but a trickle of European Jewish refugees during this same time, although it was not under the same kind of external pressures and had plenty of room for them. Against this historical comparison, it can be annoying for Americans to pass judgment on Swiss difficult decisions in the 1940s. I can only say that I am trying to analyze the ICRC record with as much understanding as I can muster. Readers will find that I do not spare other actors like the United States when I analyze international relations (see my discussion about US treatment of "enemy" prisoners after September 11, 2001).

Writing in the mid-1990s, the British historian Geoffrey Best characterized my publications on the ICRC as "well rounded" and "a fair appraisal of the strengths and limitations" of the organization.[7] I hope his characterization will also fit this current effort. I suppose Swiss ultra-nationalists and most lawyers will no doubt be glad to learn I have almost – but not quite – said what I have to say about the ICRC.

Sometimes in the following pages I refer to the Red Cross Movement or to the Red Cross approach or the Red Cross tradition. I mean no disrespect to the Red Crescent and the organizations that use it, nor to the Red Shield of David and the Magen David Adom society that uses it in Israel. I use "Red Cross" sometimes as shorthand for a longer and more cumbersome term. Thus sometimes I refer to the Red Cross Federation as shorthand for the Federation of Red Cross and Red Crescent Societies (which at

---

[6] Michael Johnson, "Meanwhile: Linear Descendants of Conan the Barbarian," *International Herald Tribune*, 14 April 2004, www.iht.com/cgi-bin/generic_cgi?template= articleprint.tmplh&ArticleID=514736.

[7] Geoffrey Best, *War and Law since 1945* (Oxford: Oxford University Press, 1994), 380.

the time of writing excluded Magen David Adom – and the Palestinian Red Crescent for that matter). I have opted mostly for readability at the expense of legalistic accuracy. I offer my apologies in advance to anyone offended by my choice.

Likewise, I use "war" as a synonym for "armed conflict," even though some of my lawyer friends tell me that "war" is no longer a preferred term in international law.

I am grateful to the University of Nebraska, its Research Council, its Human Rights and Human Diversity Program, and its Political Science Department for research grants at various stages of this enterprise.

I am also grateful to the Center for Humanitarian Dialogue in Geneva, which in the fall of 2003 arranged a meeting at which experts in the Geneva area, including several from the ICRC, discussed my views and thus made a valuable contribution to subsequent revisions. In this regard Johanna Grombach Wagner deserves special thanks. Since she later went back to the ICRC, I should make clear that she bears no responsibility for the contents of what follows.

I am especially indebted to François Bugnion, whose knowledge of the ICRC and IHL is most impressive, and who took time from his pressing duties in the summer of 2004 to give me careful and extensive comments on the entire manuscript. I am also especially indebted to Bill Schabas, who read the entire manuscript with a fine eye for detail.

I benefited from comments on earlier versions of various chapters from several persons with no position at the ICRC: Adam Roberts, Tom Weiss, Larry Minear, Chris Joyner, John King Gamble, Peter Baehr, Brian Lepard, Danny Warner, Jean Freymond, Jurg Martin Gabriel, Lloyd Ambrosius, David Cahan, Jean Cahan, Joshua Mutuma Ruteere, and Barbara-Ann J. Rieffer. Eric Heinze and Caroline Lyznik helped with research. Jay Ovsiovitch provided many legal materials that I might have otherwise overlooked. Jordan Milliken, an experienced copy-editor, was of great assistance in preparing the final copy, especially in checking the French. Carrie Althoff also helped with manuscript preparation. I benefited from the critiques of several referees arranged by John Haslam of Cambridge University Press. Several of these pushed me into further revisions which markedly improved the manuscript.

As is customary, I alone am responsible for what follows.

David P. Forsythe
Lincoln, Nebraska
October 2004

ABBREVIATIONS

AI	Amnesty International
AP	Associated Press
ARC	American Red Cross
DIA	Defense Intelligence Agency
ECHO	European Community Humanitarian Office
GC	Geneva Convention
GONGO	Governmentally Organized Nongovernmental Organization
HRL	Human Rights Law
HRW	Human Rights Watch
ICC	International Criminal Court
ICRC	International Committee of the Red Cross
ICTY	International Criminal Tribunal for Yugoslavia
IHL	International Humanitarian Law
ILO	International Labor Organization
JAG	Judge Advocate General
MDA	Magen David Adom
MSF	Médecins Sans Frontières
NATO	North Atlantic Treaty Organisation
OCHA	Office for the Coordination of Humanitarian Affairs
UNHCR	United Nations High Commission on Refugees
UDHR	Universal Declaration of Human Rights
UNICEF	United Nations International Children's Emergency Fund
UNITAF	Unified Task Force (in Somalia)
UNOSOM	United Nations Operation in Somalia
UNPROFOR	United Nations Protection Force
UNRWA	United Nations Relief and Works Agency for Palestine Refugees in the Near East
UNSC	United Nations Security Council
WFP	Worlf Food Programme

INTRODUCTION

Yet the International Committee itself remained a curious animal.

Morehead, *Dunant's Dream*, 175

That the International Committee of the Red Cross (ICRC) remains poorly known attests to the past secrecy and poor communications policy of this important agency that was created in 1863. Despite ameliorative changes in recent years, it is still true to say that in any part of the world, save perhaps Geneva, one can complete a program of advanced study in international relations, even concentrating on international law and organization, and still be ill informed about the ICRC. One can find legal analyses of the Geneva Conventions and other parts of international humanitarian law (IHL – the law dealing with the protection of human dignity in armed conflict), and one can find histories of the evolution of this law. Both bodies of literature contain passing and hence superficial reference to the ICRC. The organization itself has published several accounts of its history and tasks, even if these are not fully candid. But until rather recently one could not find a substantial and significant body of work, in any language, made up of independent and analytical studies concerning what the agency did and how it took its decisions.

One eventually discovered an ICRC that was a private Swiss agency mandated by public international law to undertake certain tasks in war, such as visiting detainees and providing relief. But most outsiders knew very little about what it did or how. One found an organization of about 2,000 professionals, governed at the top by a group of Swiss notables serving in a volunteer capacity, that visited more detainees of various categories (e.g., prisoners of war, civilian detainees in war, detainees in civil wars, "political prisoners") than any other organization. Yet few knew of its efforts, policies, or results. One encountered a very discreet – at times in the past overly secretive – organization that officially coordinated the largest private relief program for conflict situations. There remained confusion, however, about where it fitted in the Red Cross family as well

1

as the larger world of private transnational actors. (See Annexes A, B, C, and D for an indication of ICRC relations with the Red Cross Movement, and for a comparison with some other public and private agencies.) Here was the "guardian" of international humanitarian law. But almost no one understood what was meant by that term.

There were ample reasons for the difficulty in fully understanding the ICRC, for it was an organization replete with paradoxes – and not only because it was, at its core, a private agency with public dimensions. This book will show that the organization displays liberal goals but pursues them through conservative means. That is, the welfare of individuals is the highest value in its mandate, but it proceeds slowly, cautiously, with minimal objectives, and mostly on the basis of the consent of public authorities. Further, it claims to be non-political but is inherently part of humanitarian politics. It professes impartiality and neutrality, but it calculates how to advance humanitarian policies that are in competition with other policies based on national and factional advantage. Also, it promotes IHL but downplays public legal judgments and emphasizes pragmatic – if principled – service. That is, it helps develop IHL mainly for others, while often emphasizing pragmatic, contextual morality itself.

Moreover, the ICRC is a product of, and is generally sustained by, western (Judeo-Christian) culture, although it tries to present itself as a secular Good Samaritan. Its roots are to be found in the notion of Christian charity, but it strives for non-denominational, non-sectarian humanitarianism. Still further, it is part of a universal movement stressing global humanity, but that movement is rent by nationalism, and the ICRC itself has not been immune to the siren call of Swiss nationalism. The ICRC (which remains all-Swiss at the top) has regularly competed with French, Russian, American, Swedish, and other national elements in the Red Cross Movement; and particularly during the Second World War the ICRC sometimes elevated Swiss nationalism over neutral humanitarianism. Finally, the organization has always had a limited humanitarian mandate, but over time it has expanded its activities enormously. Having started with a focus only on the wounded soldier in international war, the ICRC now concerns itself with much more, including some human rights issues that transcend conflict situations.

In a generous accounting, the ICRC has won four Nobel Peace Prizes: 1901, 1917, 1944, and 1963. The first went to the ICRC's founder Henry Dunant (and to the French peace activist Frédéric Passy); the last to the ICRC and the League – now Federation – of Red Cross and Red Crescent

Societies together. The ICRC was honored in its own right in 1917 and 1944 for its work in the world wars. No other organization has been so honored so many times, yet even in the West the ICRC is hardly well recognized or understood. One insightful observer referred to it as a "clannish sort of freemasonry," such were its secretive ways in the pursuit of doing good for individuals in conflicts.[1]

By the early twenty-first century renewed public and private concern with the fate of human beings in conflict situations brought the ICRC more attention. To take but two examples, one could not understand, report on, or make policy for situations like the failed state of Somalia, characterized by massive starvation during 1991–93, without considerable reference to the ICRC. Secondly, wars involving Iraq and Afghanistan between 1991 and 2003 brought ICRC protection efforts for prisoners back into the western press. ICRC visits to the captured Saddam Hussein in Iraq, or to prisoners held by the United States at Guantanamo Bay in Cuba, brought some renewed attention to the organization. Actually, some renewed press attention to humanitarian affairs had started years before, with large ICRC relief operations in Africa in the 1980s (Ethiopia, Angola), then in Asia (Thai–Cambodia border area, Afghanistan–Pakistan area).

As a French author noted, "'L'Humanitaire' has ... become at one and the same time, from the 1980s, a true phenomenon of society, at least in the countries of the [global] North, and a weighty factor in the game of international relations, with stronger reason since the end of the cold war."[2]

As a consequence, the ICRC's activity, budgets, and human resources expanded enormously after the Cold War. With humanitarian issues moving at least sometimes from the sidelines to center stage, the ICRC found itself the object of more attention. But much confusion about the agency remained. Even leading western journalists were not always accurate in their reporting on the ICRC in such situations.

By 2004 the ICRC was asking for voluntary budget contributions of 905 million Swiss francs, or about $730 million. In the immediately preceding years ICRC overall expenditures had been in the neighborhood of $600–650 million per annum. (For one point of comparison, in 2002 the US State Department alone spent about $600 million on public diplomacy.[3]

---

[1] I thank William Schabas for this insight.

[2] Philippe Ryfman, *La question humanitaire* (Paris: Ellipses, 1999), 9.

[3] Steven R. Weisman, "Bush-Appointed Panel Finds US Image Abroad Is in Peril," *New York Times*, 1 October 2003, A1.

For a second point of comparison, about $600 million was what the two leading candidates spent for advertising in the US presidential election of 2004.[4]) About 80–85% of this ICRC total budget was provided by governmental voluntary contributions. It employed over 800 persons at its Geneva headquarters, had about 1,200 expatriate professional staff in the field, and hired almost 10,000 local staff in the approximately eighty countries where it operated. The organization ran 200 offices in more than sixty delegations. In 2003 its largest field operations, measured by expenditure, were in Iraq, Israel and the Territories, Afghanistan, Ethiopia, Sudan, Democratic Republic of the Congo, Moscow Regional Delegation, Liberia, Colombia, and Angola.

In the larger International Red Cross and Red Crescent Movement, with the ICRC as founding agency, by 2004 there were 182 National Societies, with more than 97 million members and 300,000 staff members, helping more than 233 million beneficiaries around the world. Many persons who are officially members of, or active in, the Movement, however, have no clear understanding of the ICRC, its history, and its mandate.[5]

It was certainly not always clear to many observers what the ICRC did in the field, how and why. Some of those who took a new look at this old organization got the story, or parts of the story, wrong. Others got it right but focused on only small slices of the story. Still others continued to focus on legal rules rather than the actual protection of persons in conflicts. It remained difficult to find an independent and reasonably complete overview of ICRC decisions and actions in the last quarter of the twentieth century.

What the ICRC actually faced all too often in its humanitarian endeavors was finding the least worst choice that could be made in the context of well-armed brutality, with third parties refusing to commit to inconvenient policies. If third parties should become interested in a conflict's destructive nature, why would they risk blood and treasure to enforce humanitarian norms? If they were to engage, most of the time they would engage to deal with root causes and work for peace – not just for limits on the process of violence. To the extent that third parties would seriously engage at all, logic and experience suggests they would focus on

---

[4] Wire reports, *Lincoln Journal Star*, 1 November 2004, A11.

[5] Larry Minear and Peter Walker, "The Strategy for the Red Cross and Red Crescent Movement: A Review of the Evolving Partnership," unpublished report, 5 June 2003, commissioned by the Movement. This report found that individuals in the ICRC, Federation, and National Societies had little sense of identity with the Movement, as compared with the constituent unit within which they operated.

jus ad bellum, law regarding the justification of war, and not just *jus in bello*, legal limits on the process of war. So the ICRC was often left isolated from power centers in its concern for human dignity in conflicts.

All too often, the precise rules of international humanitarian law were what lawyers talked about in comfortable Geneva. Helping victims in Bosnia, Somalia, Rwanda, the Democratic Republic of the Congo, Sudan, East Timor, Kosovo, Sri Lanka, Colombia, Afghanistan, Liberia, Sierra Leone, and so on was often as far away from the details of humanitarian law as from Geneva. My focus, as before, remains on humanitarian policy as made in Geneva and as implemented on the ground. For this orientation, IHL is certainly a relevant factor – at least sometimes. But this is not a study of legal technicalities, legal logic, legal obligation. I am less interested in the letter of the law *per se*, and more interested in what actually happens to ICRC attempts to help victims caught up in conflict situations.

In writing this book about the ICRC I want to know what has changed, if anything, for the organization in the last quarter of the twentieth century, and what are its prospects in the twenty-first? What do we know for sure about the ICRC as an actor in international relations? How does it take its decisions, according to what considerations, with what results? How has it survived for so long, and even expanded, when other organizations – even highly regarded and reputable ones like Swissair – have floundered?[6] Without pretending to write a complete history or to cover all contemporary issues, I do try to answer these central questions.

Despite the recent expansion of budget and personnel, it is fair to ask if the world is in the process of making the ICRC anachronistic. After all, intergovernmental organizations like the United Nations and NATO, and private organizations like Amnesty International and Human Rights Watch, pay far more attention, with far more publicity, to victims of war and of similar conflicts than in the past. There are many public and private relief agencies, from the UN Office of the High Commissioner for Refugees, to UNICEF, to the World Food Program, to Oxfam, to World Vision. The UN has created an office to coordinate humanitarian assistance. There are global and regional international laws against torture and mistreatment of prisoners. UN and European agencies conduct prison

---

[6] This is actually an interesting comparison, despite the nature of the ICRC as humanitarian and Swissair as commercial. The latter was a highly regarded Swiss organization over considerable time that floundered and eventually went out of business because of poor decisions at the top. It did not adjust to its competition and did not develop proper internal procedures for appropriate policy making.

visits. Is the "Red Cross" vision of neutral humanitarianism in conflict situations *passé*? Is Red Cross neutral humanitarianism a form of "moral bankruptcy"?[7] Is the ICRC reliance on discretion out of date in a world in which there is much public criticism and debate about human rights and humanitarian affairs? Was its expansion of activity during the 1990s the dying gasp of an agency already in decline? Were its past mistakes, and above all its cautious approach to trying to protect human dignity, proving fatal?

Or, on the contrary, has the ICRC carved out for itself an enduring role that is important and complementary to other actors interested in human dignity in conflict situations? Has the end of the Cold War only highlighted the importance of the traditional roles of the ICRC? Has the agency demonstrated that it still does certain things better than others? Despite expanded attention to humanitarian issues by the United Nations and a bevy of non-governmental organizations, and despite growing attention to justice through criminal proceedings rather than to "charity" through Red Cross endeavors, is the ICRC likely to remain an important humanitarian actor in conflict situations in 2025 or 2050?

In Part One I provide enough history to give a foundation for later discussions. I try to highlight certain events and patterns relevant to contemporary analysis. It should be evident that these chapters do not purport to be a detailed and definitive history of the ICRC. I try to give a readable and interpretive historical introduction, mostly drawing on secondary sources. I do seek original interpretations from the mostly secondary material. I try to spot important developments based on history written by others, developments sometimes not fully drawn out by them. Sometimes I use my own original research in ICRC archives. My approach is roughly chronological, but at the same time thematic. The point is not just to describe, and certainly not to describe in comprehensive fashion, but to emphasize certain developments. If a historical situation was important for the evolution of the organization, or shows well its activity, I included it in my historical survey.

Those who want a more conventional and presumably definitive historical narrative are bound to be disappointed by what follows. I am not a historian, and I have not tried to do the historian's job with systematic archival material, but remain a political scientist with an awareness of the importance of history. No doubt there are historical episodes not covered

---

[7] See further Chr. Michelsen Institute, *Humanitarian Assistance and Conflict* (Bergen, Norway: C.M. Institute, 1997).

here that contributed to the ICRC's evolution. Space did not allow coverage of some interesting field work in places like Sri Lanka and Lebanon, among other places. But enough history is presented to give the crucial outlines of organizational development.

There is still something new and important to say about the period from 1859 to 1945, which I address in chapter 1. Chapter 2 summarizes the Cold War period, 1947–91, with much fascinating material about the organization's relief operations, detention visits, tracing of missing persons, and legal development work. I am especially interested in the ICRC during the first decade after the Cold War, which has not been covered systematically yet, and which I address in chapter 3. As I was completing this study in 2004, controversy erupted over US treatment of "enemy" detainees apprehended in its "war" on terrorism. So I decided to cover that episode as best I could, despite a lack of certain documentary evidence, since the ICRC was caught in the middle of that crisis.

After the Cold War, which is to say between 1991 and 2004, did the ICRC contribute to on-going wars and their war economies? Was the ICRC successful in carving out humanitarian space in the midst of conflict? Was its record better or worse than its record in previous eras? How does its record of humanitarian protection compare to other actors during this time, such as the UN Office of the High Commissioner for Refugees, or Doctors Without Borders? Was the ICRC naïve in its detention visits, easily manipulated by detaining authorities? How can we tell, given the discretion so favored by the organization and so approved by states? Did its relief, and its entire minimalist approach to human dignity, do anything but guarantee that victims would be adequately fed before being killed? What other protective tasks does the organization execute – such as the tracing of missing persons – and with what results? Did the organization place more emphasis on an integrated Red Cross Movement, compared to its go-it-alone orientation during much of the past?

In Part Two, I further draw out important points noted in ICRC history. My policy analysis begins in chapter 5, where I start with a discussion of the ICRC and peace. I then focus on certain ideas important to ICRC humanitarian protection: independence, neutrality, and impartiality. These principles, complex and sometimes misunderstood, greatly affect the decisions of the organization. They also serve as benchmarks for its evaluation. Even after all of this time, there remains debate about each. What is humanitarian protection, and is it different from assistance? What exactly is the difference between impartiality and neutrality? Can there really be neutral humanitarianism in conflict situations? How often has the ICRC yielded its independence to Swiss national interests as defined in Berne? Was the ICRC really the humanitarian arm of Swiss foreign policy?

Afterwards, in chapter 6, in one of the most difficult sections to research and analyze, I focus on ICRC structure and policy making, looking at the evolution and current status of the office of President, the Assembly, the Directorate, and the professional staff. (See Annexe E for the organizational chart of the agency.) The ICRC is still not fully transparent with regard to the exercise of influence inside the house. On the basis primarily of many interviews over many years, I address certain questions. How have these units of the organization interacted in the past to make policy in the name of the ICRC? How do they interact in the first decade of the twenty-first century? What can we say about the quality of the decisions that result from this interplay? Why has the ICRC appeared to be in a state of constant flux with regard to its policy-making process? Can we reasonably expect more of the same? Does the ICRC face a crisis about the quality of its staff? Is not the ICRC necessarily going to reopen the long debate about internationalizing its all-Swiss Assembly? Is the ICRC becoming too large and bureaucratic, sacrificing its flexibility in the field as a result? Is it a good idea to bureaucratize the Good Samaritan?[8] Is it like herding cats to emphasize creativity in the field but systematic management at headquarters? Is the ICRC characterized by civil war between the lawyers and the operations staff?

In chapter 7 I turn to IHL, with an emphasis on the role of the ICRC in developing, disseminating, and applying that law. Given the vast number of studies about the Geneva Conventions from 1949 and the two additional Protocols from 1977, I do not emphasize the technical details of IHL. Law professors have given us plenty of scholarship of that type. I want primarily to show the ICRC's role in contributing to the law as it now exists. I want to emphasize, despite the objections of many at the ICRC, that even without IHL, the organization would be doing more or less the same thing it does now. That is to say, contrary to all the emphasis by those with a legal bent who stress the Geneva or Red Cross legal tradition, most of what the ICRC does is based on moral reasoning and historical practice, and would largely continue without treaty law. One can see this most clearly in the organization's work in complex emergencies and domestic troubles and tensions, where IHL's application is contested. In

---

[8] I borrow the phrase from Tony Waters, *Bureaucratizing the Good Samaritan: The Limitations of Humanitarian Relief Operations* (Boulder: Westview, 2001).

these situations the ICRC acts basically the same as in war, minus appeals to IHL. Still, at least some of the time, it is better to have IHL than not, even if on a daily basis the ICRC may not emphasize the letter of the law. I also note some of the situations where the ICRC deemphasizes IHL because it is an impediment to actually helping victims.

Finally, in chapter 8, I present a general understanding of the contemporary ICRC – no easy task – and where it is likely headed in the future.

My general thesis, mentioned in the Preface, is that the ICRC in the past was not as independent, impartial, neutral, and effective as often pictured; but after about 1970, it has made great improvements. In other words, up until about 1970, the ICRC was a "totally unprofessional" organization,[9] but since that time it has become highly professional. In the last analysis, the ICRC today is a much more impressive organization than ever before, even if debate remains about some of its aspects.

---

[9] Written memo from a high ICRC official, 2004, in the possession of the author.

PART ONE

Historical analysis

1

The ICRC during its early years

The ICRC has always taken care not to go beyond the limits of that which risked alienating the good will of states to the detriment of tasks which they gave to it.

Boissier, *Histoire du Comité Internationale de la Croix-Rouge:*
De Solferino à Tsoushima, 23

The foundations of the International Committee of the Red Cross (ICRC) and the International Red Cross and Red Crescent Movement, and particularly the ICRC's humanitarian protection, are to be found in Calvinistic Geneva in the nineteenth century. What became the ICRC got its start between 1859 and 1869. Decisions during this time greatly shaped not just the ICRC and the larger Red Cross Movement, but the entire "Red Cross" approach to peace and war, to public authorities, and to scope and styles of Red Cross humanitarian action. Thereafter the ICRC remained enormously influential on these subjects.

It is a very complicated matter as to whether victims of war and victims of other struggles for power would have fared better in subsequent years through different decisions. What is clear is that the ICRC emerged as an important humanitarian actor in conflict situations and as "guardian" of a much revered – and much violated – international humanitarian law (IHL). The organization's provision of humanitarian relief, its visits to detainees, its efforts to restore family contacts, and its legal development work became fixtures of "man made" conflicts – first in Europe and then in the rest of the world.

Over time the ICRC managed to expand its humanitarian concern from international war to internal war and then to "internal troubles" beyond situations of war. Those benefiting from its concerns grew ever larger: sick and wounded combatants, captured combatants, civilians of all sorts, "political prisoners," those separated from relatives because of conflicts. Through dogged determination if not always accompanied by adequate resources, the ICRC led the international community into systematic concern for those affected adversely by an enemy. About one hundred years before the creation of Amnesty International (in London in 1961), the ICRC as a private organization was asking governments not to forget the human interest as they pursued their conflict-prone version of the national interest. It is a remarkable record of ingenuity and dedication to the cause.

There are parallels between the ICRC and what was first known as the Anti-Slavery Society. This latter private agency, established in London in 1839, prodded first Britain and then other states into practical and legal steps against the African slave trade and later all forms of slavery and slave-like practices. Both of these private actors sprang from European moralism, a type of international liberalism, in the mid-nineteenth century. Both focused on human dignity or individual welfare, either in war or as affected by the institution of slavery. If what is now Anti-Slavery International was the first modern human rights advocacy group, with considerable successes over time, the ICRC followed close behind with its different mandate and more discrete approach.[1]

The ICRC, despite its good works, is not free from controversy. As a Swiss private association it was obviously not immune from Swiss influences, the most pernicious of which was a strong Swiss nationalism made more dangerous because its existence went unnoticed for so long at ICRC headquarters. Other biases were probably inevitable, being pervasive in all western societies, such as demeaning attitudes toward non-whites and women. But Swiss nationalism proved the most damaging and the hardest to overcome. The organization, while stressing the limits of what National Red Cross Societies could do in conflicts, linked as they were to their governments, was for many years itself tied tightly to the Swiss Confederation – as the Swiss state is officially titled. Even as National Societies became quasi-governmental auxiliaries, and thus highly reluctant to deviate from prevailing orthodoxy in national public policy, so the ICRC in Geneva was from the very beginning closely linked to Berne as well as to the larger state system and its public law.

Among other things, the following pages seek to show that a number of ICRC traits, especially those of discretion and reluctance to publicly confront state wrong-doing, have deep roots in Swiss society. ICRC deference to public authority became especially dysfunctional in relation to its independent humanitarianism during the Second World War, when the

[1] At the time of writing, strangely enough, no scholarly history has been published about the Anti-Slavery Society.

Swiss Confederation kept a tight leash on the ICRC, lest Nazi Germany be unduly antagonized. A more general result of debatable ICRC attitudes and decisions, in part at least, is a very fragmented Red Cross Movement. If the ICRC has a remarkable record in caring for victims of war and other victims of power politics, its vision of the Red Cross Movement and Red Cross neutral humanitarianism is more open to debate.

The formative years: 1859–1869

In the middle of the nineteenth century the major European military powers in their great wisdom provided more veterinarians to care for horses than doctors to care for soldiers wounded in battle.[2] This was the inhumane situation that Henry Dunant discovered in 1859 when he happened upon the aftermath of the battle of Solferino, this murderous "one day tournament"[3] in what is now northern Italy. The Austro-Hungarian and French empires were much more interested in reasons of state (or actually in the prestige and power of the political elite that spoke for the state) than the fate of human beings who served the state – in this case its wounded soldiers. The weakness of the state opened the way for private "charity." Hence the early motto of the ICRC: *inter arma caritas.*

So Dunant, the adventuresome businessman from Geneva looking for special favors from French circles of power, and a "rank amateur"[4] in non-commercial matters of international relations, got sidetracked into organizing medical assistance to the wounded – with the help of mostly female locals. Thereafter his business entrepreneurship was largely supplanted by humanitarian entrepreneurship as he not only wrote about his experiences in *A Memory of Solferino* (1862), but also campaigned to create private societies to aid the wounded in war. In modern social science jargon, he became an idea entrepreneur. Ironically for an ICRC that was to become known for great discretion, if not secrecy, in its action,

[2] François Bugnion, *Le Comité International de la Croix-Rouge et la protection des victimes de la guerre* (Geneva: CICR, 1994), 7. A second French edition was published in 2000. An English edition was published in 2003. The author is an ICRC official. This is an indispensable source for understanding the ICRC, based on almost complete access to ICRC records. Because my personal notes stem from the first French edition, I have stuck with the pagination of that edition.
[3] Michael Ignatieff, *The Warrior's Honor: Ethnic War and the Modern Conscience* (London: Vintage, 1999), 118.
[4] *Ibid.,* 110.

Dunant was a firm believer in a powerful role for publicity and public opinion.[5]

The fact that similar ideas about making war more humane had already circulated, and were being rejuvenated, in other parts of the world does not detract from the creativity and energy which characterized Dunant. The middle of the nineteenth century in Europe and the larger western world was a period of reform and philanthropy.[6] Florence Nightingale (who saved many British lives in the Crimean war), Clara Barton (so instrumental in starting what became the American Red Cross), and Francis Lieber (who drew up a code of military conduct in the American civil war) all lived in the same era as Dunant, and all made major and lasting contributions to limiting the human costs of war.[7] Armed conflict was becoming less and less a chivalrous jousting contest for the few, and more and more a mass slaughter. Dunant was not the only one who noticed.

It might be argued that Dunant made the largest, most lasting, and most systematic contribution through his colleagues and successors in Geneva. Unlike most of the others, Dunant had an international vision with such appeal that it eventually led to a global movement that clearly impacted international relations, including especially international law. At the time of writing there are 182 National Red Cross or Red Crescent Societies in the world. Serious violations of international humanitarian law (the law designed to protect human dignity in armed conflict) now lead to universal jurisdiction by national authorities, under which jurisdiction states can hold individuals responsible for crimes even if the state has no direct connection to the crime. Serious violations of IHL also comprise part of the subject matter jurisdiction of the permanent International

---

[5] André Durand, *The International Committee of the Red Cross* (Geneva: ICRC, 1981), 4. The author was an ICRC official who first published his analysis in various issues of the *International Review of the Red Cross*.

[6] *Ibid.*, 9.

[7] For the era before Dunant see Henri Coursier, *La Croix-Rouge Internationale* (Paris: Presses Universitaires de France, 1962). The author was an official of the ICRC. See further Caroline Morehead, *Dunant's Dream: War, Switzerland and the History of the Red Cross* (New York: HarperCollins, 1999). John Hutchinson notes that Dunant was part of a wave of international moralism that swept especially Europe in the middle of the nineteenth century: *Champions of Charity: War and the Rise of the Red Cross* (Boulder: Westview, 1996), Part One. Certain German medical aid societies at that time were more developed and active than what became the ICRC in Geneva. See further Hutchinson, "Rethinking the Origins of the Red Cross," *Bulletin of the History of Medicine*, 63 (1989), 557–78. Propelling increased attention to medical neutrality and war was the fact that the British in the Crimean war of 1854–56 lost seven times more soldiers to sickness than to the battlefield; Philippe Ryfman, *La question humanitaire* (Paris: Ellipses, 1999), 32.

Criminal Court, the International Criminal Tribunal for Rwanda, the International Criminal Tribunal for Yugoslavia, and other courts like the special court in Sierra Leone.

Geneva, in the 1860s as today, being comprised to considerable extent of comfortably situated citizens possessing an international spirit of good works, and thus the money and leisure time to make that spirit count for something, proved receptive to Dunant's ideas. Dunant would ultimately draw upon what might be termed Genevan exceptionalism: the collective self-image, no doubt partially the product of Calvinism, that the citizens of Geneva constituted a special people with a positive role to play in the larger world.[8] Geneva, the birthplace of Jean-Jacques Rousseau, was sympathetic to his idea, expressed in *The Social Contract* much earlier (1762), that war was an interstate affair; and when soldiers ceased to be active instruments of the state, when in other words they became *hors de combat* by sickness, injury, or capture, they reverted to being individuals whose basic rights should be protected.[9]

In February 1863, the private Geneva Society of Public Utility created a permanent sub-committee: The International Committee for Aid to Wounded in Situations of War.[10] This was the embryonic ICRC, composed of five Geneva citizens, endorsing Dunant's strategic vision, which included a plan to legally neutralize medical personnel in war. Dunant, the visionary thinker, and especially Gustave Moynier, the more practical and systematic lawyer with obvious organizing talents (ICRC President 1864–1910), moved things ahead quickly.[11] The other Red Cross founding fathers – Théodore Maunoir, Louis Appia, and General Guillaume Henri Dufour – made their own contributions. Especially Dufour had

---

[8] According to one authority on these matters, certain ideas were prevalent in Geneva in the middle of the nineteenth century and affected Dunant: belief in the possibility of progress, an international outlook, a missionary spirit to do good in the world, acceptance of limitations on government including on military policy, a belief in human dignity. See François Bugnion, "Genève et la Croix-Rouge," in Roger Durand, ed., *Genève et la paix: acteurs, et enjeux, trois siècles d'histoire*, forthcoming.

[9] As noted in *ibid.*

[10] Jean-François Pitteloud, ed., *Procès-verbaux des séances du Comité International de la Croix-Rouge: 17 février 1863–28 août 1914* (Genève: Institut Henry Dunant et CICR, 1999), 17.

[11] Dunant was surely a different and difficult personality, and he was soon out of the Committee, but his ability to strategize was remarkable. From the start he wanted a movement made up of highly independent aid societies, understood by the public, with the support of European sovereigns, featuring an inter-governmental agreement to guarantee improved medical aid, focusing first only on international wars in Europe, but later taking on other conflicts. See Pitteloud, *ibid.*, 17–20.

good contacts and standing in the Swiss Confederation and in European
military circles.

The role of Dufour has been eclipsed by Dunant, and, for those few
in the know, by the key contributions of Moynier in building the ICRC.
But it was Dufour, twelve years before Solferino, who was the victorious
military leader in the Swiss civil war of the Sonderbund (1847), but who
insisted that the fighting be conducted according to humanitarian limits
to benefit women, the aged, religious officials, prisoners, and "above all"
the wounded.[12] Dunant and Moynier were building on ideas that Dufour
had already put into military practice (and that Rousseau had already
articulated).

In October of 1863 a conference of what would today be called government experts and interested private individuals decided to implement
Dunant's scheme, which constituted in effect the start of the Red Cross
Movement. The next step was to get the leaders of the Swiss Confederation to host a diplomatic conference, from which resulted in 1864 the first
Geneva Convention (GC) for the protection of victims of war, which was
immediately signed by twelve western states.

From one point of view, first there was action "in the field," or *sur place*,
then there followed legal codification of that action – or something close
to it. The moral imperative led law, not the other way around. The ICRC
has remained true to Dunant especially in the sense that it has become
known for creative and flexible action in the field, followed by attempts
to regularize the more successful of its actions in international law. From
the beginning law was secondary to practical action. Likewise in World
War I, first there was ICRC action for prisoners of war, then followed the 1929 Geneva Convention on that subject.[13] Law was to facilitate and ensure the repetition of the practical action that had already
occurred.

In this very early period of ICRC history, however, since the organization saw itself not as an actor in conflicts, but rather as a promoter of
national aid societies, legal development was a main ICRC activity. These
two trends were later to explain much about the ICRC. There was an
emphasis both on pragmatic action in the field, and on legal standards.

The 1864 GC may have been produced as much by reasons of state as
by humane concern. Signatory states were probably as concerned with

[12] Quoted in Bugnion, "Genève et la Croix-Rouge," 12 in the prepublication manuscript.
[13] True, the Hague Convention of 1907 already mentioned prisoners of war, but without
giving the ICRC special rights of visitation.

shoring up domestic support for war as an instrument of foreign policy, by providing better care for wounded soldiers in an age when news of battle was reaching the home front more quickly, as they were concerned with human welfare *per se*. These states were certainly concerned about private do-gooders getting in the way of military necessity.[14]

From the beginning the ICRC tried to protect the dignity of individuals caught up in conflicts while cooperating with states. On the one hand this is highly understandable, since one was initially talking about providing medical assistance in the midst of war. On the other hand this cooperation with states is highly paradoxical, since states can be one of the major threats to the human dignity of individuals. Even apart from the slaughter of war, states have killed millions by genocide and mass political murder in the twentieth century.[15] State power is Janus-like, able to protect human dignity or harm it. Given the negative aspects of state power, some private or civic society or advocacy groups adopt a confrontational approach, seeking to embarrass states into good behavior by exposing their shortcomings. The ICRC has long demonstrated a more discreet and cooperative approach. This orientation, while affected by the requirements of providing services on the ground, also has roots in Swiss society, as will be shown at the end of chapter 6.

Dunant and his colleagues

By the end of his life Dunant, though born into a family of high standing, was no longer part of the Swiss establishment. He had failed financially, there was the hint of scandal in that failure, and to some he was an eccentric idealist and religious crank.[16] Ironically, by 1867 he became *persona non grata* in his own organization – the ICRC. But his colleagues and successors in the organization were indeed establishment figures. The events during

---

[14] Hutchinson, *Champions of Charity*. Compare Martha Finnemore, *National Interests and International Society* (Ithaca: Cornell University Press, 1996). He stresses what she omits entirely, namely state interest in humanitarian affairs as a way of maintaining war as a viable institution.

[15] R. J. Rummel, *Death by Government: Genocide and Mass Murder Since 1900* (New York: Transaction, 1997).

[16] It has been said, somewhat tongue in cheek, that many of those who gravitate to humanitarian organizations seem to be "misfits or mystics." Quoted in David Rieff, *A Bed for the Night: Humanitarianism in Crisis* (New York: Simon and Schuster, 2002), 274. Dunant was both. His colleagues and successors at the ICRC were not. See also Hutchinson, *Champions of Charity*.

1846–48 in Switzerland and Europe, which liberalized electoral politics in favor of more democratic and bourgeois elements, may have pushed these conservative, upper-class personalities like Moynier into social work rather than holding national office in Berne. But they remained part of the broad governing class, especially in Geneva. Early ICRC leaders may have had their factional differences with those who governed in Berne, but they were certainly supportive of the Swiss state and great believers in the role of public law – national and international. They no more thought of overtly challenging Swiss authorities or others who governed than they thought of inviting Catholics, or German-speakers, or females to join them.

How could ICRC leaders challenge states, or differ very much from the Swiss state, when certain ICRC members were part of the state? Several ICRC members were part of the Confederation's official delegation to the 1864 Geneva diplomatic conference that produced the first Geneva Convention for protection of war victims. There was no practice then of seating non-state delegations as observers at diplomatic conferences. Double membership in the ICRC and Swiss public agencies thus has a long history. Many members of the ICRC's Assembly represented the Swiss state, or a canton or city, while serving on the ICRC between 1864 and more modern times. (To cite a later and notable example, ICRC President Max Huber was an official legal advisor to the Swiss Confederation, specifically its foreign ministry or Department of Political Affairs.) For a long time Committee members saw no contradiction between ICRC humanitarianism and especially Swiss nationalism. Things would change in this regard only after the Second World War.

The International Red Cross Movement

Liberal ends (focusing on human dignity or individual welfare as highest priority) and conservative means (proceeding cautiously and slowly on the basis of state consent) are evident not just in the ICRC's history but in the evolution of the larger Red Cross Movement (which used to be called the International Red Cross). As noted, initial ICRC efforts to create a string of national aid societies in 1863 were approved by states. Not just the ICRC but all Red Cross agencies have been linked to, and historically deferential to, states. This has been especially true since the 1880s when the Italian model of things became accepted as the proper course of action at the national level. Before then, national aid societies had been part of civil society – that is, fully private, although mostly drawn from establishment social circles. But starting in Italy, these private societies to aid the war wounded became true auxiliaries of state military establishments and thus quasi-public.[17]

For virtually all Red Cross Societies, and not just those in totalitarian states, full independence or autonomy from states is thus a myth. In fact, in the United States during the First World War, a citizen was convicted of treason not for criticizing the government but for being insufficiently charitable toward the American Red Cross.[18]

Moreover, governments speaking for states that are parties to the Geneva Conventions for Victims of War have always attended the International Red Cross Conferences. This situation shows the confusion of "the Movement" as well as leading to "inconvenient" debates in the Conference.[19] In 1991 the 26th Red Cross Conference scheduled for Budapest had to be cancelled altogether, such was the maneuvering of states over the question of whether a Palestinian delegation should be seated at the Conference. It is no wonder that after World War II, some officials in the British Foreign and Colonial Office thought that the British government had no business being represented in Red Cross Conferences.[20]

In the penultimate meeting of the Red Cross network, the Red Cross Conference, governments still attend and vote. The Conference cannot possibly take a position on putatively humanitarian matters in a strictly impartial, independent, and neutral way when governments – which have many and varied interests – are present and voting. How can governments be independent of "politics"?

It is true that there may be some advantage, at least sometimes, in involving governments in various Red Cross discussions. Since states vote on Conference resolutions, in principle the ICRC can refer to these resolutions as a kind of quasi-public international law authorizing the organization to undertake a particular activity. It is not clear in the practice of the ICRC, however, whether the agency often finds such an appeal to Conference decisions effective. And sometimes the ICRC will deemphasize Conference resolutions which, in its judgment, might impede its practical work.[21]

---

[17] Hutchinson, *Champions of Charity*, 176.

[18] *Ibid.*, 271–5.   [19] Coursier, *La Croix-Rouge Internationale*, 76.

[20] Geoffrey Best, "Making the Geneva Conventions of 1949: The View from Whitehall," in Christophe Swinarski, ed., *Studies and Essays on International Humanitarian Law and Red Cross Principles* (Dordrecht: Martinus Nijhoff Publishers, 1984), 12.

[21] The Conference adopted a resolution regarding political detainees in 1921, but subsequently the ICRC decided to base its overtures not on this resolution but on its own Statutes and traditions. See further André Durand, *History of the International Committee of the Red Cross: From Sarajevo To Hiroshima* (Geneva: Henry Dunant Institute, 1984), 282.

The complicating fact remains that states – with their great sensitivity
to power politics and status – play a large role in the Red Cross network.
It was only in 1986 that the Movement stipulated that a single delegation
to the International Red Cross Conference could not represent both a
state and its Red Cross Society, such were the close bonds up to that time
between the two – and such was the habitual violation of the principle of
Red Cross independence from "politics."[22]

Summary

In 1859–69 a small start was made in trying to protect some victims in
armed conflict. To use an oxymoron, a small start was made in humanizing war. Reasons of state had been combined with humanitarianism to
produce incremental gain for some victims of war – at least on paper. *A
Memory of Solferino* in 1862 and the first Geneva Convention for Victims
of War in 1864 did not change the world in any appreciable way – at least
not right away. Certainly a spirit of universal humanitarianism did not
sweep all before it. Nationalism, militarism, conflict, and war all continued largely as before. A discredited Dunant was forced out of the Geneva
committee by Moynier. Only much later was he "rediscovered" and "rehabilitated," although never by Moynier, and named co-winner of the first
Nobel Peace Prize in 1901.[23] Even at the time of this prize, one heard
the argument that Dunant should not have been selected because: (1)
he did not work directly for peace, and (2) making war more humane

[22] Some at the ICRC insist that states belong in the Red Cross Conference because they
have ratified the Geneva Conventions and have pledged to respect the rules of the Movement. This is a truly legalistic argument. In the Conference, many states have brought
their strategic and ideological concerns with them, adversely affecting Conference deliberations. This was true of the East and the West during the Cold War, of Arabs and
Israelis during their long struggle, and so forth, as per the cancellation of the 1991
Conference.

[23] Upon Dunant's death in 1910, Paul des Gouttes, secretary to the ICRC President, and
in effect recording secretary for the Committee, indelicately recorded the view that
"This death has caused an emotion out of proportion with the role played by Henry
Dunant." The minutes also note that the Committee has kept a file on Dunant and
the 1868 legal judgment against him and his co-administrators in the failure of Crédit
Genevois, the business affair that tarnished Dunant's integrity. Pitteloud, *Procès-verbaux*,
696, minutes of Committee meeting of 10 December 1910. Gustave Moynier had carried on a feud with Dunant, an animosity that was continued by the son, and Committee Member, Adolphe Moynier. Committee politics were not always very charitable. In
general see Jean de Senarclens, *Gustave Moynier: le bâtisseur* (Genève: Editions Slatkine,
2000).

perpetuated the institution of war.[24] The subject of the Red Cross and peace is addressed further in chapter 5.

The ICRC arranged for two persons wearing an arm band with a red cross on a white background to observe the war in Schleswig-Holstein in 1864.[25] The effort from Geneva was decidedly meager. Other aid societies were more active in the field in this conflict. The persons sent indirectly by the ICRC largely observed and reported back to Geneva. But this ICRC presence in war, along with the newly minted Geneva Convention of 1864, presaged much that was eventually to follow. Properly to evaluate the ICRC, one has to look not so much at its immediate effort in any one situation, but at the cumulative result of that effort decades later. The ICRC often accepts slow and incremental change over a long time, rather than walking away in protest.

Beyond the original vision: 1870–1919

War creates as well as destroys.[26] In international relations war often performs elective and legislative functions, producing new hegemonic or dominant states and new roles for various actors. The trauma of war frequently leads to new arrangements to reduce its horrors. One can trace the outlines of ICRC history mostly through wars and other major conflicts.

Expanding the vision

After the Austro-Prussian war, the Franco-Prussian war of 1870–71 saw relatively expanded humanitarian activity based from Geneva. The ICRC began to move – at least in a crab-like way – toward a direct protection role. Moynier and others began to consider that the Committee in Geneva was going to have to play a much more active role if humanitarian action

---

[24] Ivar Libaek, "The Red Cross: Three-Time Recipient of the Peace Prize," Nobel Museum, www.nobel.se/peace/articles/libaek.

[25] The ICRC at that time did not see itself as taking a direct role in conflicts, so it created a "Geneva branch" of itself to send out the delegates: Hans G. Knitel, *Les Délégations du Comité International de la Croix-Rouge* (Geneva: Henry 1967). The ICRC has long shown both a legal and a pragmatic dimension. Even at this early time the Committee, and especially General Dufour, was highly sensitive about the appearance of neutrality for representatives in the field. Thus they were careful to send one person to Denmark, another to Germany, to guarantee a neutral image. Pitteloud, *Procès-verbaux*, 27.

[26] See further Robert Gilpin, *War and Change in World Politics* (Cambridge: Cambridge University Press, 1981); and Lewis A. Coser, *Functions of Social Conflict* (Glencoe, IL: Free Press, 1964).

in war was going to be anything more than disorganized and nationalized do-goodism. The Geneva Committee could not achieve much by being only a rearguard mailbox and storage depot for national aid societies. It was the Franco-Prussian war that first pushed the ICRC beyond its original vision.[27]

Did the 1864 Geneva Convention make much difference in that war? What one historian said of the laws and customs of war in an earlier period pertained as well in 1870–71: "It must not be imagined that those laws and customs made more than an occasional and limited difference to what actually happened in war."[28] Particularly on the French side, the Geneva Convention of 1864 was hardly known, and the various medical efforts were badly organized.[29] The private associations that had been formed to help the war wounded were each doing their own small thing, mostly acting to help only co-nationals. German generals could hardly expect French voluntary aid workers to operate behind German lines, and vice versa for French generals. One saw at this early date the use of ambulances marked with the Red Cross for transport of weapons. In fact, the Red Cross idea almost perished during the Franco-Prussian war. Another meeting of the International Red Cross Conference was not held until 1880. The ICRC only tried to update the 1864 Convention in 1906. In the meantime the ICRC had become more of an actor in the field, rather than only a supportive mechanism for the action of national aid societies. Permanent Swiss neutrality meant that the all-Swiss ICRC in Geneva might be able to take humanitarian action that other aid societies could not.

The Franco-Prussian war also saw repeated an interesting paradox displayed by the ICRC: legalism combined with creative pragmatism.[30] Under the terms of the 1864 Geneva Convention and its own rules of operation, the ICRC was snared in a legal dilemma: it could not provide assistance to prisoners of war. It was only supposed to get others to deal with the war wounded. The demands of humanity were clearly otherwise, in that non-wounded but detained combatants were in need. So the ICRC created a separate agency in Basel, supposedly independent of the ICRC

---

[27] Boissier, *Histoire du Comité*, 356.

[28] Geoffrey Best, *Law and War since 1945* (Oxford: Oxford University Press, 1991; 1997 edn), 20.

[29] See Pitteloud, *Procès-verbaux*, 109.

[30] My interpretation is based on facts presented in Bugnion, *La protection*, 36–43; and Pitteloud, *Procès-verbaux*, 97. Recall also, as per Knitel, *Les Délégations*, that the ICRC sent two delegates to Schleswig-Holstein, but officially not in its own name. There was attention to rules, but pragmatic concern about how to do what needed to be done.

in Geneva and marked by a green cross, but in fact organized and directed behind the scenes by the ICRC. The ICRC paid considerable attention to rules, but at the same time found a creative and pragmatic way to respond to a humanitarian problem. The ICRC also wanted to act through the agency at Basel to enhance its own image of absolute neutrality.[31] It was not just in the twenty-first century that the ICRC manifested both a legal culture and an operations culture sometimes disdainful of such legalisms. It is also clear than notions of an almost absolute neutrality loomed large in Committee decisions.

Modesty but determined independence

One of the early characteristics of the Committee persisted, however. Despite increased action by itself, it was still not always assertive, and certainly not very assertive about what came to be called the Red Cross Movement. Clearly it was content with decentralized – one could even say fragmented – efforts. The problem was surely not an expansive and overbearing ambition. Consider the words of Dunant at the first meeting of what became the ICRC on 17 Feburary 1863, laying down the guidelines of the Movement: "leaving always to each country . . . to each town even, the freedom to set itself up under the form that it will prefer, and exercise its action in this or that manner which pleases it."[32] To one historian, this reflected a naïve faith in Geneva in some sort of hidden hand of humanitarian spirit that would make everything right among aid societies.[33] The organization was *in some ways* quite modest, unwilling to centralize and control. The Founding Five had not intended to become an authoritative body. Moynier wanted to "guide" but not "govern" developments.[34] The initial vision was of a decentralized network that relied heavily on national customs and traditions.[35] When in the 1880s the Russians proposed to create a more authoritative ICRC with the right to dictate to National Societies during time of conflict (and to overtly

---

[31] Pitteloud, *Procès-verbaux*, 97 Likewise, when Appia wanted to go and observe things in the Franco-Prussian theatre of war, the ICRC gave him permission but no official status, supposedly again to protect the neutrality of the Committee. *Ibid.*, 101–3. It is doubtful that a non-Swiss Committee would have been so fixated on such an absolute notion of neutrality.

[32] *Ibid.*, 17.

[33] See further Hutchinson, *Champions of Charity*, 134: the ICRC often assumed that "enlightened opinion would be on their side."

[34] Morehead, *Dunant's Dream*, 123.   [35] Bugnion, *La protection*, 18; see also 20.

challenge governmental policies), the ICRC was opposed.[36] The organization believed in both decentralization (which is a very Swiss view, Swiss federal authorities being relatively weak) and deference to the nation-state. Most National Societies also opposed the Russian initiative, not wanting to be dominated by the ICRC.

As will be shown, however, the ICRC persistently maneuvered to protect its position as the guardian of IHL and a fully independent unit of the Red Cross Movement specializing in conflict situations. The ICRC was repeatedly more assertive about protecting its independence than about ensuring an integrated and efficient Red Cross Movement. Or, ICRC initial views of the Red Cross Movement and then assertiveness in behalf of its independence contributed to a highly fragmented Red Cross Movement.

The more positive interpretation of these things is that the ICRC well understood how closely National Societies were linked to their governments, and thus how little independent influence they could exercise in behalf of all victims in need. The more critical interpretation is that the ICRC was so interested in protecting its independent position, as a derivative of Swiss nationalism, that it failed to see the damage it was doing in blocking a unified Red Cross Movement. This critical view raises the counter-factual historical question: Why not team with the Russians in the 1880s and create a Red Cross Movement in which the ICRC would be the supra-national Red Cross authority in conflict situations? Why not work to wean National Red Cross Societies toward maximum autonomy from their governments? Why not promote a Red Cross Movement that was fully private, rather than quasi-public? (We will eventually find some efforts in this direction in contemporary times.[37])

Some, especially in National Societies and their governments, might say that it was good that the Committee in Geneva lacked the ambition to centralize and control. It was not just some leaders in the more active, richer National Societies who found it annoying to contemplate following the lead of the ICRC in conflict situations. But the fact that no one was clearly in control of Red Cross action in war certainly led to difficulties, which persist in modern times. Even in the twenty-first century, any

---

[36] Boissier, *Histoire du Comité*, 449.

[37] Slightly later in 1907 the Committee notes with suspicion the creation of the International Society of the White Cross to enhance the physical and moral health of peoples. The ICRC is skeptical about what this new organization is up to, decides not to openly criticize or fight it, but thinks that the new group wants to bask in the glow of ICRC accomplishments. It is clear that the Committee is suspicious of rivals. Pitteloud, *Procès-verbaux*, 670–1.

number of persons are confused by what is encompassed by the phrase "the international Red Cross." It refers in fact to an often disjointed and uncoordinated network of actors, and this condition stems to considerable degree from the early vision of the ICRC. "The Red Cross" professes the principle of unity, but it is anything but a unified movement. The Red Cross family was, and often still is, a dysfunctional family.[38]

The emblem

"Red Cross" fragmentation was much in evidence in certain respects during the violence in the Ottoman Empire in the 1870s. The Turkish society for aid to war wounded started using the Red Crescent symbol rather than the Red Cross in 1876. One could certainly understand why a historically Islamic society would not want to use the cross. True, the red cross on a white background was the reverse of the Swiss national flag. The Swiss national flag, in turn, borrowed from the flag of the canton of Schwyz. So some might be inclined to say that all of this showed a basically secular rather than religious development. The ICRC sometimes tried to downplay, for the best of reasons, its religious origins. It worked for human dignity in conflicts without regard to religion or – concerning communist states – official atheism.

But it was a fact that Dunant was an evangelical and fundamentalist Christian, and the origin of the Geneva committee was steeped in notions of Christian charity and good works.[39] Dunant saw himself, in his own words, as "an instrument in the hands of God."[40] "The founders were themselves guided by their religious feeling."[41] Red Cross charity derived from Christian charity. The New Testament biblical character of the "Good Samaritan" permeates the official history of the ICRC.[42] One ICRC author said of Max Huber, ICRC President in the 1930s and 1940s, that his "reflections [were] stamped with a high evangelical idealism – for it was in the teaching of the Gospels, and especially in the parable

---

[38] This disunity was eventually spelled out for all to see in the Tansley Report of 1975: *Agenda for Red Cross* (Geneva: Henry Dunant Institute, 1975).

[39] Morehead says (*Dunant's Dream*, 51) that the original Red Cross ideas "had no religious overtones." But see Hutchinson, *Champions of Charity*, and Coursier, *La Croix-Rouge Internationale*. But see Boissier, *Histoire du Comité*, with reference to Moynier, 344.

[40] Pierre Boissier, "Henry Dunant," *International Review of the Red Cross*, 161 (August 1974), 411.

[41] Durand, *The ICRC*, 48.

[42] Max Huber, *Le bon samaritain* (Neuchâtel: Editions de la Baconnière, 1943).

of the good Samaritan, that Max Huber found the sources of his inspira-
tion."[43] That parable was still a lodestar for ICRC President Sommaruga –
a self-described practicing Catholic[44] – in the 1990s.

Paul Grossrieder, a former Director-General of the ICRC, writes that
after Dunant the other founding fathers of the organization were not
driven by religious motivation.[45] And it is true that Gustave Moynier, in
declining on behalf of the ICRC an invitation to attend a meeting of faith-
based groups in Austria, said in 1898, "our committee does not belong in
the category of religious societies."[46]

However, it is clear that Christianity, in Geneva and in the West in
general, as a general orientation and background condition, contributed
to the rise and perseverance of the ICRC and the Red Cross Movement.
The heritage of Christianity and Christian charity and Calvinistic good
works contributed greatly to western culture, which is more supportive
of the Red Cross idea than most other cultures. Even today, most of the
funding for the ICRC comes from governments that are western, which
is a grouping defined in part by a Christian heritage. The fact that Henry
Dunant was an evangelical Christian prone to conflicts with the Calvinistic
establishment of Geneva, and that Gustave Moynier was neither, does not
detract from the general role that Christianity (including Calvinism) has
had in supporting various humanitarian organizations that transcend a
morality of family networks only.[47]

In any event the ICRC, while concerned about a proliferation of
emblems, deferred to the *fait accompli* by Turkish parties regarding the
emblem.[48] (It was to do so again in the 1920s when the Iranian aid society
started using the Red Lion and Sun as its emblem. The question of Israel
and the Red Shield of David used by Magen David Adom is addressed in

[43] Durand, *From Sarajevo*, 282.
[44] Massimo Lorenzi, *Entretiens avec Cornelio Sommaruga* (Lausanne: Favre, 1998), 84.
[45] See his "Humanitarian Action in the Twenty-First Century: The Danger of Setback," in
Kevin M. Cahill, ed., *Basics of International Humanitarian Missions* (New York: Fordham,
2003), 3–17.
[46] Pitteloud, *Procès-verbaux*, 606, as recorded by the Committee secretary, E. Odier on
1 December 1898.
[47] On African culture as oriented to the extended family rather than universal humanitarian movements, see the African scholar Ali A. Mazrui, "The Red Cross and Politics in
Africa," quoted in David P. Forsythe, *Humanitarian Politics: The International Committee
of the Red Cross* (Baltimore: Johns Hopkins University Press, 1977), 240–1. The footnotes
immediately following that section are relevant to this discussion.
[48] See further François Bugnion, *L'emblème de la Croix-Rouge: aperçu historique* (Geneva:
CICR, 1977).

chapter 7.) Faced with a conflict between the desire to promote a universal humanitarian movement and a desire to maintain one clear emblem, the ICRC finally opted for the former. It was primarily states like Turkey, Persia (Iran), and Egypt that were responsible for the proliferation of neutral emblems recognized in public international law. The ICRC found it necessary to defer. The result for the Red Cross Movement was unfortunate, as neither the ICRC nor the Movement was able to assert the necessary independence to arrive at another solution. It was not always a good thing for the Movement to be so dominated by states or so tied to public international law. The proliferation of Movement emblems reflected the fragmentation of the Movement.[49]

It was only in 1875 that the Geneva Committee itself added the phrase "Red Cross" to its official name. There were to be no official rules – or Statutes – for the Movement until 1928. The seven official principles of the Red Cross (humanity, impartiality, neutrality, independence, voluntary service, unity, universality) were not adopted until 1965, although the ICRC used certain principles in the recognition of National Societies by early 1901.[50] So the matter of the emblem in the 1870s symbolized Movement fragmentation and lack of firm control from the center. Whether the strength of various nationalisms permitted any other outcome is an interesting "what if" question.[51]

Toward World War I

Aside from the matter of the emblem, the violence to the east of Geneva in the 1870s saw only meager and mostly unsuccessful efforts by the ICRC.[52] It was asked to send relief to the Balkans but was not in a position to do so. The organization did dispatch three persons to Montenegro in 1875,

---

[49] Had the ICRC led the Movement into adopting some new and independent emblem(s), the Movement would have wound up using one or more emblems not recognized as neutral in international law. Whether such a situation would have compelled states to change the law is an interesting "what if" question. But National Societies were almost always under the control of their governments, so such discussion is highly academic.

[50] Pitteloud, *Procès-verbaux*, 618–19.

[51] Later private networks, like Amnesty International, developed a clearly defined and more authoritative center, even while accommodating diverse sections around the world. AI manifests centrally defined mandates and policies, while allowing for national and subnational initiatives and energy. See Jonathan Power, *Like Water on Stone: The Story of Amnesty International* (Boston: Northeastern University Press, 2001). AI is normally independent of the nation-state. National Red Cross Societies are normally not.

[52] This paragraph draws on Bugnion, *la Protection*.

but they were able to achieve virtually nothing in humanitarian terms. Given the thinking and technology of the times, it is hardly surprising that the agency played little role in the Russo-Japanese war of 1904. In the Boer war, also far from Geneva, the ICRC mostly contented itself with calling on the fighting parties to formally adhere to the 1864 Geneva Convention, although it did send some money to various aid societies[53] – that being still the primary way the Committee involved itself in various conflicts. The ICRC was in no position to try to ameliorate the British concentration camps for civilians in that war, camps which led to the death of about 25,000, mostly women and children.[54] The organization was again involved in minor ways in Balkan instability during 1912–13.

Surely it is stretching things a bit to conclude that the Red Cross network had provided impressive means to deal with victims of war in the years leading up to the First World War.[55] The ICRC was certainly dedicated to its cause, at least in an inconsistent way, but already by 1871 the ICRC could be termed conservative and defensive rather than boldly creative.[56] One sees this especially well in the organization's reluctance to take on various issues in the Spanish-American war.[57] So the ICRC showed some modest concern about a disintegrating Ottoman Empire, but not in a declining Spanish Empire even though the latter was also European. Pre-1914, and despite what had happened in the Franco-Prussian war, it still saw itself primarily as an actor with only moral influence, whose role was to encourage states and national aid societies to act directly for victims of war.

In the Greek-Turk conflict just before the First World War, Committee Member Edouard Naville wanted more ICRC representatives in the field to check on how aid operations were transpiring; he was unhappy with

---

[53] Pitteloud, *Procès-verbaux*, 615.

[54] Thomas Pakenham, *The Boer War* (London: Weidenfeld and Nicolson, 1979). Similar camps were used by the Spanish in Cuba and the Americans in the Philippines during the Spanish-American war and immediately thereafter, but without similar mortality rates. The ICRC was apparently not involved with any of them. I am indebted to the historian Peter Maslowski for help on these points.

[55] Bugnion, *La protection*, 57   [56] *Ibid.*, 65.

[57] Pitteloud, *Procès-verbaux*, 609–10. Interestingly, the ICRC declined a Spanish request to help negotiate the release of Spanish soldiers captured by Filipino insurgents, saying the matter fell outside the mandate of the organization. Pitteloud, *Procès-verbaux*, 609–10. On some other matters in the Spanish-American war, Moynier told Clara Barton in the United States, who was personally close to President William McKinley, to work something out regarding the Philippines. It was clear that Moynier did not want to project the organization into the various humanitarian matters of the Spanish-American war.

the Committee providing Swiss francs to various aid societies in a *carte blanche* process.[58] But in August 1914, "The ICRC had no administrative staff."[59] This showed that even after the Franco-Prussian war, as well as after the dispatch of various ICRC members to conflicts in the Balkans, the ICRC in Geneva still had very little capacity for independent action on the ground. It encouraged others to act for victims of war, and sent money to other organizations, but it was still not a major and consistent field actor itself.

It was in the First World War that the ICRC became a highly active neutral intermediary among belligerents, and more identified with visits to detainees rather than only with medical aid to war wounded. The ICRC started off associated with the idea of promoting medical assistance to wounded combatants by others under the notion of medical neutrality, and it wound up, largely because of the First World War, increasingly associated with detention visits carried out by itself.

Interestingly, the ICRC got into the business of reporting on prisoners of war not by focusing on Geneva law but by the Hague Regulations of 1907.[60] The ICRC, drawing on the Hague norms, tried to stop various reprisals against POWS and to ensure various types of relief to them. Its detention visits, however, had no grounding in general international law, being the product of *ad hoc* agreements with the belligerents, starting with France and Germany.[61] And, one can only speculate as to the course of subsequent events if the ICRC had continued, as it did early on, to go public with its POW reports, instead of giving them discreetly to involved governments. An official ICRC historian passes over this subject quickly when he writes with regard to such reports that they were "published and offered for sale, a custom that was later dropped."[62] In his long history there is no further discussion of this important matter. ICRC discretion today about detention visits, regardless of the type of situation or prisoner,

---

[58] Pitteloud, *Procès-verbaux*, 710–11.   [59] Durand, *From Sarajevo*, 35.

[60] Compare Bugnion, *La protection*, as cited below, with Georges Abi-Saab, "The Specificities of Humanitarian Law," in Swinarski, ed., *Studies and Essays*, 277. The former stresses ICRC efforts to stop reprisals against prisoners, whereas the latter stresses the provision of relief to prisoners.

[61] Bugnion, *La protection*, 102–11. He notes that the ICRC archives are not completely informative regarding all the details on this subject matter in this period.

[62] Durand, *From Sarajevo*, 78. Bugnion, *La protection*, 106, says the ICRC publicized the results of its prison visits in order to reassure families and the public, and also thus break the circle of reprisals and counter-reprisals. But he does not explain the reasons for the later change in ICRC policy on this matter of publicity. See 706.

is not mandated by any written provision anywhere in public international law but is entirely the product of ICRC practice.

In "the Great War" the ICRC for the first time gave considerable attention to civilians, especially detained ones, and not just fighters *hors de combat*. Yet the drastically limited legal and material resources at its disposal meant that all efforts were small scale. As was to be generally the case with conflicts until the 1970s, the ICRC entered the Great war with no strategic planning.[63] It was to react to humanitarian need on an *ad hoc* basis. Given the biases of the times in Geneva and lacking a strategic plan, it was not really impartial in impact. The organization gave more attention to the western front than to the eastern front of the Austrian–Italian confrontation.[64]

As will be shown, in most major conflicts an evaluation of the ICRC leads to a mixed conclusion: there were disappointments and failures combined with some successes and advances. Did the 1864 Geneva Convention (revised in 1906) and related humanitarian activity between 1859 and 1914 greatly humanize war? One knowledgeable historian wrote with characteristic brevity and insight, "It did not take long after the first of August 1914 for wisdom to appear to have been on the sceptics' side."[65] From the brutalizing of Belgium through the horrors of trench warfare to the use of poison gas on both sides, chivalry was not exactly the dominant value – even among "Christian" nations.

Yet this same author provides an accurate and more encouraging summary: "The fundamental humanitarian principles of protecting the sick and wounded, and of treating prisoners decently, survived the war intact, strengthened, indeed, by so many millions of people's becoming acquainted, in the course of so prolonged a war, with the work of ambulances and hospitals on the one hand, the predicaments of POWs and their families on the other. The ICRC and the national Red Cross societies came out of the war raised in reputation and regard."[66]

A problem emerged for the ICRC but was swept under the rug, with unfortunate results later in World War II. When on 18 February 1918, the ICRC issued its public appeal for the belligerents not to use poisonous gases, two members of the Committee, Gustave Ador and Edouard Odier, did not sign the statement because they were at the same time officials

---

[63] Bugnion, *La protection*, 93, 94. It could be said that the only actor in the First World War that had a strategic plan was Germany, in the form of the von Schlieffen plan, which saw a quick offensive victory over France, and it failed.
[64] *Ibid.*, 95.   [65] Best, *Humanity in Warfare*, 46.   [66] *Ibid.*, 52.

of the Swiss Confederation.[67] They believed that Swiss neutrality precluded their taking a policy position on this question in the name of the ICRC. Thus their position at the top of the ICRC was compromised by their dual position in the Confederation. This system of dual memberships, in the Committee and the Swiss state, was not addressed by the Committee at that time. Later conflicts of interests from dual membership were to prove still more serious, as shown at the end of this chapter.

A leading authority on ICRC history believes that the First World War did more to shape the modern organization than any other conflict.[68] Partly on the basis of its efforts for detainees, carried out by forty-one delegates and through 524 visits,[69] even though highly incomplete and unsystematic,[70] it won the Nobel Peace Prize in 1917. National Red Cross Societies were mentioned specifically in Article 25 of the Covenant of the League of Nations. This was either a reflection of a certain preferred position for Red Cross agencies among social actors, based on performance in the Great war, or a reflection of the fact that Henry P. Davison, President of the American Red Cross, was extremely close to Woodrow Wilson, and thus in a position to get his future hopes written into the Covenant. ("The Red Cross" was not to be mentioned in the Charter of the United Nations in 1945.)

Important changes: 1920–1939

The years 1920–39 manifested a number of major changes for the ICRC. In the aftermath of the Great War, the ICRC began to inquire more systematically into the conditions for detainees beyond situations of international war. Already in the early phases of the instability within the Ottoman Empire, the ICRC had added internal war to international war as part of its self-devised mandate. In Russia after 1917 the organization again devoted considerable efforts to the victims of civil war.

In that situation, however, we should note that the ICRC spent considerable time helping Swiss citizens in Russia at the request of the Swiss Confederation. Because Berne asked it to do so, Geneva gave priority to quasi-consular functions benefiting Swiss citizens living in the Soviet Union. These functions had little to do with individuals in distress because of war or similar conflict. As a result, the small ICRC necessarily paid less

---

[67] Durand, *From Sarajevo*, 90.   [68] Bugnion, *La protection*, 128.
[69] Knitel, *Les Délégations*, 43.   [70] Bugnion, *La protection*, 109.

attention to those detained in connection with the Russian civil war. No doubt Soviet authorities came to see the ICRC as a *de facto* arm of the Swiss state, the latter being clearly hostile to the new Soviet state.[71] Here again we see that the close ties between the ICRC and the Swiss Confederation did not always enhance the neutral status and work of the agency.

In Hungary from 1919 the ICRC sought to visit those detained in situations short of even civil war – hence to visit political or security prisoners. Those "detained by reason of events" – a wonderful phrase invented by the ICRC to lessen controversy about the nature of situations characterized by ICRC detention visits – could arise from domestic troubles and tensions.[72]

There was a logic of expansion to these ICRC concerns. If prisoners of war morally mattered in international armed conflict, why not detained combatants in internal wars; and why not other "political enemies" when detained? Were not all of these detainees in potential danger and thus in need of a humanitarian intermediary when in the hands of an adversary? Was not one of the main roles of the ICRC – and a persistently unpopular one – that of being an advocate for "the enemy" when *hors de combat?* After all, how many people in a nation – or some other political grouping – profess solidarity with the enemy?[73] Hence the ICRC's moral imperative to protect detained "enemies" transcended the categories of conflict so beloved by states with their fixations on the murky notion of state sovereignty and domestic jurisdiction.

---

[71] Jean-François Fayet and Peter Huber, "La mission Wehrlin du CICR en Union Soviétique (1920–1938), *International Review of the Red Cross*, 849 (March 2003), 95–118. This is a very important article, showing how Swiss nationalism caused the leaders of the ICRC to depart from neutral humanitarianism in conflicts. See further Amnon Sella, *The Value of Human Life in Soviet Warfare* (London: Routledge, 1992).

[72] Jacques Moreillon, *Le Comité International de la Croix-Rouge et la protection des détenus politiques* (Geneva: Institut Henry Dunant, 1973). This remains the most authoritative work on the early years of ICRC efforts for political prisoners, although there is no English edition. However, the situation in Hungary in 1919 was very close to that of an internal armed conflict. See Durand, *From Sarajevo*, 133. The dividing line between internal war and internal troubles is not always crystal clear. It is interesting to speculate if the bourgeois ICRC got involved in protecting political prisoners in Hungary because the Bela Kun communist government was detaining bourgeois and other "counter-revolutionary" elements. Note the message from the ICRC delegate in Budapest, recorded in Durand, *From Sarajevo*, 133, advising Geneva that in the interests of a neutral image "it would be wise to cut down our activities in favour of the bourgeois and the counter-revolutionaries." Later the ICRC visited communist detainees in Hungary imprisoned by the anti-communist government of Admiral Horthy.

[73] See further Durand, *The ICRC*, 5.

Thus, even as the ICRC became better known for work with prisoners of war in World War I, it was in the process of expanding its focus to include all prisoners of *conflict*, including where traditional notions of war were said not to apply.

The organization was also involved in coping with refugees uprooted by major transformations in Russia and Central Europe. Particularly in dealing with the mass flight of civilians in the wake of the Russian and Hungarian political revolutions, the ICRC found that it was too small to manage things by itself.[74] Here already in Europe in the aftermath of the First World War we see something that occurs again later – the proliferation of public and private agencies seeking to cope with mass migration. The ICRC was joined by Herbert Hoover's American Relief Association, the first Save the Children agency (based in Britain), and eventually the Nansen Refugee Office of the League of Nations, among others.[75] We analyze aspects of this evolution pertaining to refugees in subsequent chapters.

The Red Cross Movement

Another important change occurring in this era affected the overall structure of the Red Cross Movement. Because the First World War was the war to end all wars, and since henceforth international relations would be characterized only by peace-loving democratic states, the Federation – originally the League – of Red Cross Societies was created under the driving force of the American Red Cross and its leader, Henry P. Davison.[76] He expected the ICRC to yield gracefully to new "realities." His "reality" was that victorious National Red Cross Societies would form the Federation so as to control all Red Cross action in international affairs. After all, in the First World War the Americans had deployed four times as many volunteers in the American Red Cross as the government had deployed soldiers in the US expeditionary force.[77] No doubt the ICRC seemed to Davison to be very small and quite *passé*. He

---

[74] Bugnion, *La protection*, 150.

[75] See further Ryfman, *La question humanitaire*, 40–1.

[76] "The Soviet Red Cross was probably the first to propose formally the creation, after the war, of an international Federation of Red Cross Societies," Durand, *From Sarajevo*, 141. So at least in this one area the US and the USSR saw eye to eye. Neither was a strong supporter of the ICRC.

[77] Ryfman, *La question humanitaire*, 39.

wanted to create "a real international Red Cross"[78] by replacing the mono-national ICRC.

Earlier in its history the ICRC had been willing to consider some sort of international Red Cross council featuring representatives from the various National Societies. This group, which would have existed in addition to the Red Cross Conference, was seen however as a largely honorific body, with the all-Swiss ICRC remaining in charge of day-to-day humanitarian work.[79] This point notwithstanding, after the Great war the ICRC resisted American claims to leadership via the Federation, just as the ICRC had maneuvered to block earlier proposals that would have moved the organization to Paris and introduced broad French influence. Moynier and others had long fought to keep the all-Swiss ICRC in an independent and predominant position in the evolution of things,[80] even as they did not wish to implement a tightly centralized scheme. As long as it was regarded as the guardian of international humanitarian law and the preeminent Red Cross actor in conflict situations, it did not often involve the National Societies in planning and policy making after 1914. After recognition, the relationship was mostly *ad hoc*, driven by momentary needs in conflicts. Some members of the ICRC's Assembly paid lip service to the idea of close and systematic interaction with the National Societies, but reality was mostly otherwise from the First World War to the end of the Cold War. Swiss aloofness or unilateralism was hard to overcome. The ICRC only stressed the need for a tighter relationship between it and the National Societies under the press of the move toward the Red Cross Federation in 1920.[81] Even then, the ICRC's stated concern for an integrated movement was more rhetoric than reality.

Davison formally got a Federation, but in several ways it remained the ugly duckling of the Red Cross family – at least for some decades. It started with only five members. For a time some important National Societies, like those in the Nordic countries, did not belong. The ICRC clearly saw the new Federation as a threat to its existence,[82] and thus deployed its considerable diplomatic skills to limit the Federation's authority and mandate. In the last analysis the well-established and well-connected ICRC managed to preserve its domain of humanitarian protection in conflict

---

[78] Durand, *From Sarajevo*, 147.   [79] See Hutchinson, *Champions of Charity*.
[80] Hutchinson, *ibid.*, is very clear on this matter.   [81] *Ibid.*, chapter 6.
[82] François Bugnion, "The Standing Commission of the Red Cross and Red Crescent: Its Origins, Role and Prospects for the Future," in Liesbeth Lignzaad, *et al.*, eds., *Making the Voice of Humanity Heard* (Leiden and Boston: Martinus Nijhoff Publishers, 2004), 43.

situations, leaving the Federation with the arguably less glamorous work of coordinating Red Cross responses to natural – and eventually industrial/technological – disasters. According to a British historian, the general outcome was that "the League could all too easily have the appearance of a pushy, Americanized, cuckoo in the Red Cross nest."[83]

But events from 1920 were to leave the ICRC with a considerable organizational problem: the Red Cross Movement was to have two heads, which sometimes did not speak to each other, at least not in friendly and cooperative tones, as well as many arms in the form of the growing number of National Societies. The Red Cross Federation, the loose union of all National Societies, was a controversial addition to the Red Cross network. It was not initially approved by the Red Cross Conference and was created in violation of the Red Cross principle of universality – since under American pressure the National Societies of the defeated belligerents were excluded. Nevertheless, American power talked, and the ICRC was forced to accept the new organ as a *fait accompli.*

When in 1928 the first Statutes of the Movements patched together this new, often quarrelsome family, a close reading of the Statutes revealed that the ICRC took instructions neither from the Conference nor from any other Red Cross party – and certainly not from the Federation. Despite the new Movement Statutes, the ICRC remained fully independent within the Red Cross Movement on the basis of its own Statutes. An innovation was the creation of the Red Cross Standing Commission, primarily to serve as a mediator between the ICRC and the Federation – or an arbitrator if those two agencies agreed to submit a dispute to it, which they never did.[84] According to a somewhat acerbic historian, "This [1928] agreement has often been hailed as a great step forward in the development of the Red Cross, but it seems more accurate to regard it as a sedative that those involved gladly swallowed to relieve the pains of rebirth."[85] Subsequent revisions of the various Statutes only reaffirmed the point of ICRC independence and Movement fragmentation. The Federation existed, but the ICRC lost very little.

After the 1920s the ICRC did have a somewhat more complicated relationship with the National Societies. But this did not really trouble the organization very much, because for a long time it continued to keep the National Societies at considerable distance concerning its thinking and

[83] Best, *Humanity in Warfare,* 82.
[84] See especially Bugnion, "Standing Commission," 41–59.
[85] Hutchinson, *Champions of Charity,* 345.

policies. Ad hocery continued to be the predominant mode of interaction between the ICRC and the various National Societies.

For similar reasons, the ICRC also maneuvered to block a powerful International Relief Union in the inter-war years even though it was advocated by certain Red Cross officials.[86] ICRC opposition, though presented in a Judas embrace, stemmed from two considerations. If the mandate of the new relief organization was to include relief in armed conflict, the ICRC's traditional role would be greatly reduced. To add insult to injury, the new relief organization was projected to rely heavily on the Red Cross Federation for operational capacity. The ICRC was greatly relieved when much private and governmental consideration of this Relief Union effectively came to naught.

Field record

As was true of almost every era, the inter-war years produced field work that was to affect the future of the ICRC – even if much of this effect was not evident at the time. The ICRC was active on a small scale in the leading crises of that period – the Italian invasion of Ethiopia and the Spanish civil war, and to a lesser extent in East Asia.

It is worth noting in passing that when dealing with what a government might regard possibly as either internal war or troubles, the ICRC insisted on trying to act first via the National Red Cross Society – normally an appendage of the state. And so it was in the early 1920s when the ICRC wanted to get involved in the violent dispute, featuring considerable detention, over the future of Ireland. The organization contacted the British Red Cross which, consistent with its devotion to the British government, told the ICRC that there was no war of any type within the United Kingdom and furthermore no other reason for Geneva to concern itself with events in Ireland.[87] Protecting British jurisdictional claims rather than advancing neutral humanitarian protection was the priority of the British Red Cross. This is the same ICRC approach that proved so fruitless in the next decade when dealing with German political detainees, as we shall see. The ICRC, however, did manage some access to Ireland – but certainly not because of any help from the British Red Cross.

---

[86] See especially John Hutchinson, "Disasters and the International Order: Earthquakes, Humanitarians, and the Ciraolo Project," *International History Review*, 22 no. 1 (January 2000), 1–36; and Hutchinson, "Disasters and the International Order–II: The International Relief Union," *International History Review*, 23 no. 2 (June 2001), 253–504.

[87] Durand, *From Sarajevo*, 226–7.

Regarding the Italian invasion of Ethiopia, one finds a few creative ICRC delegates in the field struggling against impossible odds to instill humanitarian considerations into this war of imperial conquest against an impoverished people. The organization was not allowed to operate on the Italian side. Such was the conservatism of its tactics that even in the face of intentional Italian bombing of Red Cross facilities, the ICRC stuck to its policy of discreet overtures rather than public protests. The fact that the very highest levels of the organization also decided not to make a public protest against the Italian use of poison gas, even though it had made such a protest about the use of gas during World War I, raised serious question about whether ICRC headquarters was more interested in good relations with Rome than the defense of victims in Ethiopia. It was sometimes said that some important ICRC officials saw the European fascists as a barrier to the Soviet communists.[88] After all, this view was prevalent in many European circles then, including in parts of the Vatican.[89] It was also said that Rome perhaps used the issue of the gender orientation of one of the ICRC delegates in Ethiopia as pressure on the organization to remain discreet about Italian brutalities in Ethiopia.[90]

As for the Spanish civil war, some in the ICRC correctly saw that what was happening on the Iberian peninsula foretold what was going to happen later on a larger scale: the bombing of cities from the air, reprisals and atrocities against individuals, complete disregard for elemental principles of humanity.[91] The ICRC made a greater effort in Spain than in Ethiopia and had more to show for it at the end of the day. The Spanish civil war lasted longer than the Italian conquest of Ethiopia, and Europe – including the ICRC – took more interest in the former than in the latter. An outstanding ICRC delegate, Marcel Junod, who had been active also in Ethiopia, was dynamic and dogged, showing what individual initiative could accomplish in the field.[92]

Ultimately the ICRC fielded ten delegations on both sides of the bloody conflict, arranging prisoner exchanges, caring for displaced children, ameliorating the conditions of prisoners and hospital patients. It is hard, however, not to conclude that given what the Spanish were doing to each other, and given what their respective patrons were doing – the Soviets

[88] See Morehead, *Dunant's Dream*.
[89] See further John Cornwell, *Hitler's Pope: The Secret History of Pius XII* (New York: Viking, 1999).
[90] Morehead, *Dunant's Dream*, 305–16.
[91] See Hugh Thomas, *The Spanish Civil War* (London: Penguin Books, 1974).
[92] Marcel Junod, *Warrior without Weapons* (Geneva: ICRC, 1982; reprint from Jonathan Cape Publishers, 1951).

on the side of the Republicans, and the Germans and Italians on the side of the Franco fascist rebels – what the ICRC accomplished was marginal to the overall conduct of the war.[93] This was civil war, even if internationalized, and the existing Geneva Conventions were said not to apply legally. As Marcel Junod was later to write about all of his experiences between 1933 and 1945, "How could we not have felt the tragic hiatus between our weak powers and the magnitude of the drama unleashed all around us?"[94]

But the ICRC's humanitarian work in Spain, important to the individuals it touched, also fed into the growing effort to humanize civil as well as international war. What might be marginal in the 1930s became more significant later. In 1949 Common Article 3 was added to the Geneva Conventions, legally regulating civil wars via written law. In 1977 Protocol II to those Geneva Conventions extended Common Article 3 into a short treaty covering certain civil wars. At the turn of the next century, some officials were successfully prosecuted in international criminal courts and then incarcerated because of their foul deeds inside Bosnia and Rwanda and Yugoslavia (Kosovo). The application of IHL to the internal armed conflicts of later years had important precedents in ICRC efforts in the Spanish civil war. Once again, a long time frame is required to evaluate the overall importance of ICRC action.

Given the communications technology of the times, which affected the practical applications of the principles of humanity and impartiality, the ICRC was not a player when Japan invaded Chinese Manchuria in the mid-1930s. In fact, the ICRC seemed content to take note of the conflict and made little effort to act independently for the (mostly Chinese) victims of that conflict; it underestimated the importance of events in that part of the world.[95] The organization, operating out of a small villa on the west bank of Lake Geneva, with a tiny staff and budget, was far more active in Spain than in all of East Asia in the 1930s.

Could the ICRC defer to or rely on National Societies in East Asia? The Japanese Red Cross had accepted, with logistically impressive results, the idea of Red Cross medical services as early as the Russo-Japanese war at the turn of the century.[96] Thus the notion of "Red Cross work" was definitely not limited to Europe, laying to rest debates over the evolution of the Movement by Dunant, Moynier, and others. In fact, as early as 1863,

---

[93] This interpretation is confirmed by Best, *Humanity in Warfare*, 58–9.
[94] Junod, *Warrior without Weapons*, 311.   [95] Bugnion, *La protection*, 157.
[96] Hutchinson, *Champions of Charity*, chapter 5.

the ICRC founding fathers had decided to build up activity in Europe in international war, leaving to a later time both geographical and functional expansion.[97] From the beginning the ICRC showed, at least sometimes, a penchant for strategic calculation in humanitarian endeavors. Yet the Japanese Red Cross showed that the application of Red Cross ideas would not be tightly controlled from Geneva.

The Japanese National Society followed the Japanese military into China in the 1930s. But that National Society had already showed, even before the national triumphs of communism and fascism in Europe, how the idea of the Red Cross could be completely nationalized and thus made to violate principles of impartial humanitarianism and independence from power politics. In the land of the rising sun, as in many if not most other places, fanatical patriotism trumped global humanitarianism.

Headquarters

In 1923 the ICRC admitted to membership in the Assembly, in the person of Max Huber, its first non-Genevan. In this same year it admitted its first Catholic in the person of Giuseppe Motta. It had admitted its first woman, Marguerite Cramer, in 1918. It remained, and remains, all white. It was essentially a very amateur organization, with a group of Swiss at the top in the Assembly who did not always read the reports submitted to them or attend the few meetings scheduled, and who were supported if not led by a tiny if dedicated professional staff. It often operated in areas far from Geneva by consulting with the Swiss government and finding a Swiss businessman or other Swiss citizen in the area of concern and deputizing him (always a him) to undertake some humanitarian action – without training and often without much instruction. Huber, President from 1928 to 1945, was often in ill health and away from Geneva. In his absence, Carl Burckhardt, another conservative Swiss-German, often played a very large role. (See chapter 6 for more details about ICRC personnel over time.)

A controversial Nobel Peace Prize: World War II

The ICRC was not, in fact, in good shape for the Second World War. In 1939, the ICRC administrative staff consisted of three persons.[98] As an ICRC author stated much later, "The ICRC was not sufficiently well equipped to tackle the vast humanitarian problems which were about to

---

[97] Durand, The ICRC, 10–11.   [98] Durand, From Sarajevo, 413.

emerge in the course of the war."[99] It is remarkable in retrospect that it was able to achieve as much as it did. The ICRC is very good at counting things, and a statistical summary of its activity in World War II is impressive: 11,000 detention visits; 445,702 tons of relief delivered, valued then at 3,400 million Swiss francs; 30 million persons registered and aided in one way or another.[100] Its accomplishments were mostly due to improvisation by its small but dedicated staff and a mobilization of committed volunteers. Its work was more focused on the European theatre of war compared to the Asian.

Overview

In matters covered by IHL, and where reciprocity prevailed, the ICRC was able to achieve much. This was true, for example, regarding detention visits to Allied prisoners of war held by the Nazis, and vice versa. But the ICRC record was much different regarding prisoner of war matters – and other humanitarian issues – between the Nazis and the Soviet Union. ICRC efforts were also greatly restricted by Japanese policies.

In the view of one scholar on these matters, the Second World War demonstrated that if the ICRC was dealing with a regime that manifested little inclination toward liberalism – featuring the fundamental worth of the individual – then the organization could accomplish only so much.[101] If for the moment we assume this is true, we find that Germany and Japan during World War II were basically illiberal nation-states highly prone to abusing "enemies."[102] The German record in particular was somewhat ameliorated by its legal obligations under existing IHL, since a curious German sensitivity to legal rules persisted in the Nazi era, leading to reciprocity with the western Allies but not the Soviets. The Wehrmacht was, relatively speaking, perhaps less abusive overall than the SS, at least partly because of notions of military honor.

---

[99] Jacques Meurant, "The International Committee of the Red Cross: Nazi Persecutions and the Concentration Camps," *International Review of the Red Cross*, 271 (July–August 1989), 380. "Not well equipped" should be understood in a very broad sense.

[100] The official source is ICRC, *Report of the International Committee of the Red Cross on Its Activities during the Second World War* (Geneva: ICRC, 1948), 3 vols. and annexes. For the abridged version, see ICRC, *Inter Arma Caritas: l'œuvre du Comité International de la Croix-Rouge pendant la Second Guerre Mondiale* (Geneva: CICR, 1947; English 2nd edn 1973).

[101] Best, *Humanity in Warfare*, 60.

[102] We take up a fuller discussion of the various reasons for applying IHL in chapter 7.

On the Soviet side, most historians have found that Moscow was persistently indifferent to humanitarian affairs. One author, however, concluded that Moscow was prepared to respect the 1929 Geneva Convention concerning prisoners of war, even though it had never ratified that legal instrument, and even though some of its military orders mandated no surrender but rather a fight to the finish. It may have been the case that Soviet treatment of German POWs was superior to German treatment of Soviet POWs.[103]

It is worth noting that the Swiss state was clearly hostile to the USSR during the Second World War, allowing grievous and sometimes fatal assaults on Soviet citizens who had managed to find a harsh refuge in Switzerland. This state of affairs led to a Soviet effort to damage, if not destroy, the ICRC after the war, since the ICRC was closely aligned with Berne. Indeed, some key leaders in Berne were also members of the ICRC Assembly.[104]

Be all that as it may, the ICRC demonstrated during the Second World War, as had been true for the organization from its very start, more persistence and commitment to humanitarian values than adequate material and human resources. Its maximum number of delegates during the war never topped 150, whereas at the start of the twenty-first century its personnel just at the Geneva headquarters alone numbered about 800, with some 2,000 professionals in its service overall, not counting another 8,000–10,000 local staff recruited for logistical support. The organization did mobilize thousands of volunteers during the Second World War.

From time to time the ICRC was highly creative. For example, in order to try to enlist the cooperation of the Soviet Union regarding detention visits to prisoners of war, it even departed from the principle of the all-Swiss nature of its staff, offering to Moscow the possibility of Swedish delegates if that would prove more agreeable.[105] It did not.

At other times the organization was severely hindered by the policies of the parties. For example, the ICRC agreed to have its delegates accompanied by Japanese officers during the organization's detention visits to Allied prisoners of war held in Japan.[106] Japan had long objected to prisoner interviews without witnesses. The ICRC was left with a procedure in the POW camps that did not exactly encourage fact finding and truth

---

[103] Sella, *Human Life.*   [104] *Ibid.* Also see Fayet and Huber, "La mission Wehrlin."

[105] Bugnion, *La protection*, 215; Durand, *From Sarajevo*, 510. Sweden was the Protecting Power of the USSR.

[106] Bugnion, *La protection*, 220; Durand, *From Sarajevo*, 526.

telling about camp conditions and treatment. Its only alternative was to forego the visits. However, Japanese authorities were responsible for this situation.

Its efforts for prisoners of war, interned foreign civilians, and assistance to the civilian population, as well as its attempts to trace missing persons, earned it in 1944 its second Nobel Peace Prize (third if you count Dunant's in 1901).

In places like Greece under Nazi (and Italian) occupation, the ICRC in cooperation with other actors like the Swedish Red Cross engaged in heroic endeavors to benefit the civilian population.[107] The case of occupied Greece, in fact, demonstrated much about the ICRC. It could be of great service when the controlling powers, in this case the British Navy, allowed humanitarian relief to go forward. It magnified its efforts by teaming with a competent National Society (Swedish). The relief ultimately originated from the West because of a combination of humanitarian and strategic motivations (London felt the need to facilitate relief lest relations be soured with the United States where the Greek lobby was influential). Apart from relief, the ICRC was helpless to prevent the atrocities that were carried out by almost all of the parties involved (Germans, Greek communist resistance fighters, Greek nationalist fighters on the right, etc.). When it came to massacres, the ICRC was mostly a scorekeeper for the historical record rather than a force that could prevent or ameliorate terrible things. Still, the relief record was impressive.

The issue of the German Holocaust, however, damaged the ICRC. The more one examined the issue, the more damage one found. More than one observer believes that the ICRC's record on this one subject "has haunted it ever since."[108] Given the information that already exists, this section will content itself with main developments and interpretations, with further information provided in chapter 5 when ICRC independence is discussed further.[109]

The Holocaust

In 1933 the ICRC began contacting the German Red Cross about the concentration camps. Given that the German Red Cross was thoroughly

[107] Mark Mazower, *Inside Hitler's Greece: The Experience of Occupation, 1941–1944* (New Haven: Yale University Press, 1993, 1995), especially 47 and 337.
[108] Morehead, *Dunant's Dream*, xxxi.
[109] The essential work is by Jean-Claude Favez, *The Red Cross and the Holocaust* (Cambridge: Cambridge University Press, 1999, based on a 1988 French edition).

Nazified, and that the head of the German Red Cross, Ernst Grawitz, was a major figure in pseudo-medical experiments on the Jews and other "enemies of the state," this ICRC effort in 1933 and thereafter was naïve, legalistic, and pedantic. To leave the question of the concentration camps to the German Red Cross was legalistic escapism *par excellence*.[110] President Huber and certain staff persons were highly regarded in moral and legal circles, but there is scant evidence they were clever strategic thinkers about humanitarian policy. Even an extremely dedicated ICRC official characterizes the ICRC orientation to the German Red Cross as ultra cautious.[111]

The ICRC apparently did not consider de-recognizing the German Red Cross in its Nazi form, despite the latter's eventual participation in genocide and other bestiality. Such an approach would obviously cause conflict with the rest of the Nazi state and might jeopardize ICRC activities that were allowed in Nazi territory. (Such an approach would also raise questions about the legitimacy of Red Cross Societies in other totalitarian states, as in the Soviet Union or later in China, where the Society was fully part of the repressive state. Such an approach would have raised still further questions about the legitimacy of other Red Cross Societies in such places as racially segregated America or South Africa, where the principle of impartial humanity was violated in important but less drastic ways.)

As a relevant aside, it should be noted that the ICRC was able to make several visits to political detainees in neighboring Austria before the Anschluss of 1938. Also relevant is the commentary of an official ICRC historian who remarked that it was the organization itself that did not vigorously pursue the possibility of more systematic detention visits in Austria.[112]

Dealing directly with the Nazi government, the ICRC was able to effectuate several unsystematic camp visits up to 1936.[113] The ICRC never achieved systematic and meaningful access to the Nazi camps. Once again an ICRC historian concludes that "the ICRC does not appear to have tried to continue such visits in a systematic way."[114] For a time the ICRC tried mailing relief parcels into the camps, which worked for a time and even allowed the organization to document prisoners by means of return receipts. But the limited effort was at least partially abandoned in the wake

---

[110] See further especially Meurant, "Nazi Persecutions," 381. His essay is, in part, a book review of Favez, *Holocaust*.

[111] "Fort prudente," Bugnion, *La protection*, 238.   [112] Durand, *From Sarajevo*, 282.

[113] See Bugnion, *La protection*, 245 and *passim*. Also Favez, *Holocaust*; and Meurant, "Nazi Persecutions."

[114] Durand, *From Sarajevo*, 287.

of reports about some of the relief going to non-humanitarian purposes. At the very end of the war when the Nazi regime was clearly on its last legs, the ICRC negotiated access for its delegates into various camps where they remained in effect hostages themselves – able to supervise incoming relief but prevented from leaving until the Allied liberation of the camps.[115] A number of lives were saved and much good was done at this stage.[116] Again, as with the German Red Cross, the ICRC effort *vis-à-vis* the Nazi government can be generally characterized by lack of dynamism and passion. It is perhaps intermittently persistent. It is certainly discreet.

There is no evidence uncovered in the ICRC archives thus far of overt anti-Semitism. Indeed, once the ICRC discovered that some European Jews in countries under Nazi control could escape arrest and/or deportation by being on a list of those registered for emigration to Palestine, ICRC delegates helped many Jews so to register.[117] There is also precious little evidence in the archives of ICRC anguish or urgency over knowledge, at least from mid-summer of 1942, about genocide in the heart of "developed" Europe. There is little remarkable creativity in ICRC overtures to Nazi leaders on this question of official genocide. President Huber and his alter ego Jacob Burckhardt never went to Berlin to take up the question of the camps with the highest Nazi officials. Is it possible that a legal orientation combined with Swiss prejudices caused the ICRC to show more concern for Soviet prisoners of war, admittedly badly treated by the Germans, than to the extermination of the Jews?

Beyond the core system of Nazi concentration camps, work camps, and death camps, the ICRC compiled a much better record of responding to German persecution of the Jews. In places like Hungary, ICRC delegates like Friedrich Born – acting with only slight instruction from Geneva – did much to interfere with German efforts to deport Jews to a genocidal fate.[118] This raised the question of whether the difference in effort and result stemmed from the difference between core and periphery of Nazi rule, or the difference in individuals. Was it that the Nazis were unalterably committed to genocide in the core of the Third Reich itself but not able to firmly effectuate that policy on the edges of Nazi control? Or was it that Huber and Burckhardt and others at ICRC headquarters lacked the

[115] Drago Arsenijevic, *Otages volontaires des SS* (Paris: Editions France Empire, 1974, 1984).
[116] Claude Mossé, *Ces Messieurs de Berne, 1939–1945* (Paris: Stock, 1997), alleges that the ICRC did not place its delegates in the concentration camps in 1944 until Berne gave the organization the green light to do so. But this is a controversial source.
[117] Durand, *From Sarajevo*, 438.
[118] Arieh Ben-Tov, *Facing the Holocaust in Budapest* (Geneva: Henry Dunant Institute, 1988).

passion and ingenuity of the delegates in Hungary? Huber after all was a deeply conservative intellectual known for illiberal musings. Moreover, his family – and he himself – led a Swiss firm that not only produced weapons but also used Nazi slave labor in its German subsidiary.[119] Burckhardt was also conservative, operated easily in German and pro-German circles, and compiled a most ambiguous record on "the Jewish question."[120]

Attention has been directed to a meeting of the ICRC Assembly on 14 October 1942 when it decided not to approve a public appeal dealing in part with the Holocaust. The outlines of the issue can be reviewed here, with more details covered later when ICRC independence is discussed more fully.[121]

By that October the ICRC had reliable information about some sort of German genocide. The Assembly had before it a proposal about a public appeal to all belligerents, reminding them of certain humanitarian principles. The draft proposal, vaguely worded, covered four subjects.[122] It was not, therefore, an explicit appeal to the Germans alone about their treatment of Jews, Roma, homosexuals, and other victims of the death camps.[123] From prior discussions and then the initial comments made by Assembly members in the debate, it appeared that a majority was in favor of a public statement.

The President of the Swiss Federal Council that year, Philippe Etter, also a member of the ICRC Assembly, having been alerted to likely action from that body by a carefully constructed system of oversight (that is covered in chapter 5), spoke out against any public statement. His position reflected the Confederation's policy of accommodating the Nazis. Switzerland, like

[119] Morehead, *Dunant's Dream*, 704–5. Jean Ziegler, *The Swiss, the Gold, and the Dead: How Swiss Bankers Helped Finance the Nazi War Machine* (London: Penguin, 1997, 1998), 61–2. Favez, the Swiss historian, notes that Huber sometimes spoke approvingly of authoritarian states and was not a man of decisive action; *Holocaust*, especially 283–4.

[120] Favez considers Burckhardt a philosophical conservative who long overrated Nazi power and chances of victory – views he shared with many other members of the Swiss establishment: *Holocaust*, especially 284–5. Morehead sees Burckhardt as one who viewed the fascists as a bulwark against the communists: see *Dunant's Dream*, 311.

[121] My account is based on ICRC archives: procès-verbal of Assembly meetings, 1942–47, vol. 18, organized by dates of meetings; supplemented by other archival sources such as staff PTT consultations with Assembly members regarding a public protest, found in G.85/127, CR73/8-/24.

[122] ICRC Archives; Dossier CR 73; Carton 50, Fourth Draft, 16 September 1942, covering the subjects of: the effects of aerial bombardment on the civilian population; the effects of economic blockade on the civilian population; the fate of those civilians of various nationalities who were detained, deported, or taken hostage; and treatment of prisoners of war.

[123] Morehead is not correct on this point.

other European neutrals such as Sweden and Spain and Portugal, adjusted their neutrality to the ebb and flow of the war. At this time of the war when German power was expanding, the neutrals accommodated that power in various ways. Swiss policy during this period was to tilt toward the Nazis through such matters as cooperative banking[124] so as to guarantee Swiss independence and forestall any thoughts in Berlin about an invasion of Switzerland. The Swiss state also adopted refugee policies at least partly with an eye to not antagonizing its fascist neighbors.[125]

President Etter did not want the ICRC to run the risk of offending Nazi sensitivities with a public statement – regardless of how mild, vague, and balanced such a statement might be. ICRC Assembly members ultimately deferred to the wishes of President Etter, probably a majority of them against their better judgment. The ICRC therefore caved in to Swiss national interests as defined in Berne, sacrificing the independence and humanitarian values of the organization.[126] The main ICRC defense of its actions related to the German Holocaust in the core of the Third Reich was twofold. First is the argument that had it spoken out over the concentration camps, which were not covered by IHL, the ICRC would have jeopardized its ongoing access to Allied prisoners of war held by the Nazis.[127] André Durand, the official historian, says that the ICRC saw no point in a frontal confrontation with Nazi Germany regarding political detainees; rather, the organization sought to exploit whatever openings for humanitarian action might arise.[128]

Second is the argument that, given the demonstrated commitment of the Nazis to their genocide after early 1942, a public statement by the

---

[124] Adam Lebor, *Hitler's Secret Bankers: How Switzerland Profited from Nazi Genocide* (London: Simon and Schuster, 1997, 1999); Jean Ziegler, *The Swiss, the Gold, and the Dead: How Swiss Bankers Helped Finance the Nazi War Machine* (London: Penguin, 1997, 1998). The latter is more carefully presented than the former. Swiss banking circles cooperated with the Nazis long after there was any credible threat of invasion of, or even significant Nazi pressure against, Switzerland. See Stuart E. Eisenstat, *Imperfect Justice: Looted Assets, Slave Labor, and the Unfinished Business of World War II* (New York: Public Affairs, 2003). See also Alan Cowell, "Switzerland's Wartime Blood Money," *Foreign Policy*, 107 (Summer 1997), 132–44, and his bibliography.

[125] Jean-François Bergier, "Switzerland and Refugees in the Nazi Era," December 1999, www.uek.ch. This is part of a draft report commissioned by Swiss Federal authorities in response to controversies about Swiss policies during the Nazi era. See also Elizabeth Olson, "Commission Concludes that Swiss Policies Aided the Nazis," *New York Times*, 23 March 2002, A4, covering release of the final report.

[126] Recall that the organization did as Berne had requested with regard to servicing Swiss citizens in the Soviet Union in the inter-war years, even though this required the ICRC to depart from a strictly impartial humanitarian focus in conflict situations.

[127] Meurant, "Nazi Persecutions."   [128] Durand, *From Sarajevo*, 556.

ICRC stood no chance of changing German policy.[129] On this second point Morehead seems to suggest otherwise,[130] as have others. This second guessing is not persuasive. Not only did the fanatical Hitler regime continue devoting resources to the death camps even when the regime was on its last legs. Also, the Allied governments did publicly protest unspecified Nazi brutalities in December 1942 – with no effect.[131]

But this debate misses a crucial point, involving how and why the ICRC remained silent. Faced with the worst humanitarian crisis of the war, the ICRC not only remained silent but also allowed Swiss national interests to trump the independent humanitarian judgment of the organization. The ICRC needed to protect its reputation as an independent humanitarian agency that was dynamic in its efforts. Faced with a new and egregious German policy of genocide in 1942, the ICRC did not rise to the challenge with new creativity and determination. Rather, it deferred to Berne, whose priority on this matter was not offending Nazi Germany.

With great prescience, several Assembly members (Mr. Micheli, Mme. Frick-Cramer, Mme. Odier, Mr. Boissier), speaking in advance of President Etter at the 14 October meeting, said that if the ICRC did not issue the public statement under consideration, its future work would be tainted. But they, too, deferred to the Swiss President in the last analysis.[132]

The historian Michael Beschloss has written that the United States did not respond appropriately to "the historical gravity of the Holocaust" and that its history would have been brighter had it done so.[133] The same could be written of the ICRC.

---

[129] See Meurant, "Nazi Persecutions"; the Sommaruga letter in the same source; and Bugnion, *La protection*, 253.

[130] *Dunant's Dream*, 551. But compare her front matter, xxx–xxxi.

[131] If one wants to speculate, it might have been possible that a broad public condemnation of German policies toward those in the concentration camps before the late fall of 1941 might have deterred the Holocaust. Nazi policy toward the Jews and other targets of persecution involved restrictions and/or forced emigration, but not genocide, from 1933 until late 1941 and early 1942. Christopher R. Browning, *The Origins of the Final Solution: The Evolution of Nazi Jewish Policy, September 1939–March 1942* (Lincoln: University of Nebraska Press, 2004). A strong response by outsiders – not just by the small and mostly unknown ICRC alone – might have affected an uncertain German policy. But after the Wannsee conference of early 1942, it is almost certainly the case that the ICRC could not have very much affected the course of the Holocaust. It could only have protected its own reputation for integrity.

[132] ICRC President Huber, absent because of sickness, and having been non-committal during earlier discussions about a public statement, rather than exercising leadership sent a message saying he would support whatever a unified Assembly approved. Burckhardt, as noted, was opposed to a public appeal.

[133] Michael Beschloss, *The Conquerors: Roosevelt, Truman and the Destruction of Hitler's Germany 1941–1945* (New York: Simon and Schuster, 2002), 65.

Later, the then ICRC President Sommaruga, being personally appalled at what had happened,[134] would say repeatedly that the entire western world failed to respond adequately to the Holocaust and the ICRC was part of that failure.: "j'ai dit clairement que l'Holocauste était la faillite claire et nette de toute un civilisation. La civilisation occidentale avait complètement failli; et la Croix-Rouge était partie de cette civilisation. Quant au CICR, il regrettait les erreurs et les omissions possibles de la Croix-Rouge de cette époque."[135] But even that statement was seen by some as an effort to deflect criticism from the organization by broadening the group of those negligent.

In writing of the United Nations' failure to stop genocide in Rwanda in 1994, Michael Barnett wrote of the effort by UN officials to democratize the blame, to minimize their responsibility.[136] The game was often played the same way at the highest levels of the ICRC.

---

[134] Interviews, Geneva. See also Sommaruga's statement of 19 March 1988, approved by the ICRC Assembly, directed to Favez upon publication of his book, reprinted in *International Review of the Red Cross*, 271 (July–August 1989), 394–7. "Your work makes it clear that the ICRC did not sufficiently grasp the unprecedented nature of the tragedy taking place and thus failed to readjust its priorities accordingly," 395. But this letter accuses Favez of not documenting what the ICRC knew and when, and finds numerous other faults with Favez's work. The tone of the letter seems hyper-critical of Favez and defensive of the organization.

[135] Quoted in Massimo Lorenzi, *Le CICR, le cur et la raison* (Lausanne: Favre, 1998), 114. Note the phrase, "possible errors and omissions."

[136] Michael Barnett, *Eyewitness to a Genocide: The United Nations and Rwanda* (Ithaca: Cornell University Press, 2002), 154.

2

The ICRC during the Cold War

> While there are some signs of change in the right direction, there is still a
> great need for the ICRC to "open the windows" ... On the whole, the ICRC
> seems to have blurred the differences between the discretion which their
> work requires and an obsession with needless secrecy.
>
> Tansley, *Final Report: An Agenda for Red Cross*, July 1975, 114

The Cold War years presented various challenges to the ICRC. Under concerted criticism not only from communist but also from certain western democratic circles, the ICRC staved off unwanted changes in its composition and mandate mainly through its performance in various conflicts – in Palestine and Hungary, for example. It also played its traditional role in helping to further develop international humanitarian law. By the middle of the Cold War, the organization was engaged broadly in complex ways not only in the Global South but also in Europe – not only in "developing areas" but also in Greece and Northern Ireland. There was clearly a need for its traditional roles during the Cold War, even if the ICRC was slow to anticipate some needed changes at headquarters as well as in the field.

Its controversial performance in the conflict in Nigeria during 1967–70 led to important changes in Geneva. There were other opportunities for striking change, as in response to the 1975 Tansley Report on the Re-appraisal of the Red Cross, or at the 1974–77 diplomatic conference that produced two protocols additional to the 1949 Geneva Conventions. But the ICRC embraced change only slowly, frequently when anticipated negative outcomes left little choice but to change.

At best, IHL presented a very mixed picture in terms of application, as evidenced by the fate of both combatant and civilian victims of war in places like Korea, Vietnam, and Israeli occupied territory in the Middle East. The Red Cross Movement remained highly fragmented.

Despite evident difficulties, paradoxically enough, the continuing nature of international relations and some ICRC changes after the Nigerian conflict combined to leave the organization in an enhanced condition at the end of the Cold War. This was due primarily to continued excellence by its committed delegates in the field, as well as to improved strategic planning and structures of decision making at headquarters. It was also because neither the United Nations nor any other organization developed in such a way as to eliminate the need for the humanitarian protection that the ICRC provided.

1946–1966: doing good and satisfying critics

Despite its 1944 Nobel Peace Prize the ICRC emerged from World War II concerned for its future existence. It was certainly criticized in various circles for its record on the Holocaust. Leaders of the Swedish Red Cross, among others, saw the ICRC immediately after the Second World War as too stodgy to cope with threats to human dignity. They wanted to internationalize the ICRC's Assembly. Count Folke Bernadotte of Sweden, head of the Swedish Red Cross, later to be assassinated while serving as a UN mediator in the Middle East, was a prominent critic of the mono-national Assembly of the ICRC before changing his mind.[1] During World War II he had led a daring raid into German territory to rescue Swedes (and thereby compromised the Red Cross principle of impartiality by acting for one nationality only). Later he worked for the UN while continuing to use the Red Cross emblem (and thereby compromised the Red Cross principle of independence). He regarded the all-Swiss ICRC as too cautious, but came to believe an internationalized ICRC Assembly would create insurmountable problems in decision making during the Cold War.

Mixed in with his criticisms of the ICRC were his own personal ambitions, which were not small, and the ambitions also of some of his co-nationals who wanted the Swedish Red Cross to become a power center – if not *the* power center – in the Red Cross Movement. So after the Second World War the Swedes followed in the footsteps of the French, Russians, and Americans in trying to substitute for Swiss influence at the center of the Red Cross Movement. From the view of Sweden, to some the Switzerland of northern Europe, why should Swedish neutrality take a back seat to Swiss neutrality? As is frequently the case, policy debates were affected by egos, individual and collective. Struggles for power and status within the Red Cross Movement were not always very charitable.[2]

[1] See Folke Bernadotte, *Instead of Arms* (London: Hodder and Stoughton, 1949). And Ralph Hewins, *Count Folke Bernadotte, His Life and Work* (London: Hutchinson and Co., 1949).
[2] For a concise review of maneuvers within the Red Cross Movement immediately after the Second World War, including the remark about the uncharitable nature of Movement

To compound ICRC difficulties, most communist governments gave it little or no cooperation during the Cold War, seeing the organization – not entirely incorrectly – as a bourgeois organization of the liberal West. After the Second World War Soviet leaders initially suggested the USSR might not show in meetings to further develop IHL, and Moscow's policy was to damage an ICRC that was closely linked to a hostile Confederation.[3] Certainly from 1939, if not before, the Soviet Union had given the ICRC the cold shoulder.[4] ICRC high officials never met with Soviet high officials until the Gorbachev era, when President Alexander Hay and Director-General Jacques Moreillon met with Foreign Minister Eduard Shevardnaze. Aside from some aspects of the 1956 Hungarian crisis and the 1962 Cuban missile crisis, explained below, the Soviets never cooperated with the ICRC in meaningful ways on humanitarian protection during the Cold War proper.

As for the emerging communist power in East Asia, the Chinese government in Beijing after 1949 hardly saw humanitarianism as a top priority. Mao Tse-sung supposedly told the western journalist Edgar Snow that he was thankful for Japanese atrocities in China; they showed the weakness of the Nationalist Party (Kuomintang) in China and thus paved the way for communist victory.[5] Whether this story is true or not, it became patently clear that the People's Republic of China, like other communist states, was not a champion of individual welfare – its utopian ideology of personal liberation notwithstanding. The statement above attributed to Mao is consistent with a dominant trend in communist thinking,

---

politics, see Geoffrey Best, *War and Law since 1945* (Oxford: Oxford University Press, 1994), 86 and *passim*. For a classic analysis of how policy developments are affected by individual egos and motivation, see Harold Lasswell, *Psychopathology and Politics* (Chicago: University of Chicago Press, renewed edition in 1986).

[3] In addition to Best, *Humanity in Warfare*, see Amnon Stella, *The Value of Human Life in Soviet Warfare* (London: Routledge, 1992, 110); and Jean-François Fayet and Peter Huber, "La mission Wehrlin du CICR en Union Soviétique (1920–1938)," *International Review of the Red Cross*, 849 (March 2003), 95–118.

[4] Best, *Humanity in Warfare*, 83–4. According to this view, the Soviets became disenchanted with the ICRC when Moscow developed the conclusion that the organization had been soft in responding to fascist atrocities in the Spanish civil war. When the Soviets invaded Finland in 1939, and the ICRC contacted Moscow in an effort to play its usual roles, there was no reply. But even from 1917, relations between the ICRC and the Soviets had never been more than frigidly correct. Relations between the organization and the USSR may have been better than between Berne and Moscow, but that is not saying much. When the Confederation voted against admitting the Soviet Union to the League of Nations, this cannot have helped an ICRC that was no doubt seen by Moscow as in the pocket of Berne. See Fayet and Huber, "La mission Wehrlin," and Sella, *Human Life*.

[5] Interviews, Beijing, 2001.

that what matters is the triumph of the proletariat in the long run, not what happens to various individuals along the way. The Czechoslovak effort to create communism with a human face, and hence with certain individual rights, was of course crushed by the Soviet invasion of 1968.

Only toward the end of the Cold War did the ICRC manage to carry out significant activities in a communist-controlled area. There was a very large ICRC relief program in Hun Sen's Cambodia from 1979 while the former Khmer Rouge member was a proxy for communist North Vietnam (covered below). There were traditional detention visits involving China and North Vietnam in their 1979 border war, where each recognized the applicability of the Third GC from 1949. There were also detention visits in communist Poland in the 1980s when European communism was on its deathbed (covered below).

On the other side of the East–West divide, American moralism, as personified by Secretary of State John Foster Dulles by 1953, seemed to rule out neutrality in the Cold War between western democratic capitalism and "eastern" authoritarian socialism. Yet the Americans and their allies continued to support the ICRC, and to try to use it for their purposes in places like Korea, far more than the communist coalition.

The ICRC responded to this challenging situation immediately after the Second World War in three ways.

The 1949 Geneva Conventions

First, the organization played its usual role in helping to produce the four Geneva Conventions of 12 August 1949 for victims of war. That is to say, in close cooperation with the Swiss Confederation that called the diplomatic conference, it served as a drafting secretariat to produce material for Red Cross and state evaluation. The ICRC proposes, but states dispose. Just as the 1906 Geneva Convention had been based on changing wartime needs since 1864, and just as the 1929 Geneva Convention on Prisoners of War had built on experience from World War I, so the four interlocking Geneva Conventions of 1949 were to reflect learning from the previous years. The ICRC, while not acting as an open and dynamic lobby, drew on its considerable experience to produce draft texts that reflected what it hoped to achieve. In the international relations of the late 1940s, dominated by a western club of small membership that was not plagued by North–South relations, more than a few ICRC new ideas made it into the final documents.

The 1949 Geneva Conventions were to prove, along with the 1948 Universal Declaration of Human Rights (UDHR), one of the two main moral pillars for international relations after 1945. Michael Ignatieff has remarked that the 1948 Universal Declaration was "part of a wider reordering of the normative order of postwar international relations, designed to create fire walls against barbarism."[6] The 1949 Geneva Conventions were a major part of this reordering, reaffirming and developing the notion that belligerents should not be barbarians. The 1948 UDHR codified thirty basic principles for human rights in peace. The 1949 Geneva Conventions for Victims of War (plus eventually the 1977 Additional Protocols), through their more than 600 articles, codified humanitarian values in armed conflict. The ICRC certainly made an important contribution to what remains the core of contemporary IHL through its drafting process leading to the 1949 Conventions. The process was relatively rapid as global negotiations go, and the inhibiting struggles over state power and status were mild compared to what was to transpire when two additional protocols were added in 1977. (Further details will be covered in chapter 7.)

Palestine, 1948–1950

Secondly, the ICRC got deeply involved in the conflict over the disposition of British Palestine – not only because of humanitarian motivation, but also quite consciously to prove to the world that it was still a viable institution.[7]

In the previous chapter we noted that the ICRC had frequently acted to protect its position in the Red Cross Movement and the larger system of international relations – resisting French and American attempts to take over leadership of the Movement, opposing Russian attempts in the nineteenth century to centralize the Movement, making sure the still-born International Relief Union did not encroach on its mandate or strengthen the Federation. Of course all of these efforts to preserve the Geneva-based, all-Swiss ICRC could be justified – some would say rationalized – in terms

---

[6] *Human Rights as Politics and Idolatry* (Princeton: Princeton University Press, 2001), 5.

[7] Dominique-D. Junod, *The Imperiled Red Cross and the Palestine–Eretz-Yisrael Conflict 1945–1952* (London: Kegan Paul International, 1996). This book relies in part on a number of internal ICRC documents, and its publication was not free from controversy. The author worked at the ICRC for fifteen years. She later converted to Judaism and moved to Israel. She started the book with the cooperation of the ICRC, but their relations became testy in later stages of the project.

of guaranteeing humanitarian protection to victims of conflict as linked to mono-national decision making and permanent Swiss neutrality.

The ICRC saw the clash of Arab and Zionist aspirations in Palestine as a place to prove itself and fight off demands for radical change in its composition and role. The organization was involved in small ways in the conflicts of the 1940s in South Asia, Indonesia, Southeast Asia, and southeastern Europe, but its strategy was to emphasize Palestine. Whether the ICRC's approach violated the principle of impartial attention to all victims within its mandate is an interesting question.

The ICRC's impact on the conflict for control of western Palestine during 1948–49 (eastern Palestine having been transformed into what is now Jordan in 1947) was, like most of its impact in most wars to that time, marginal to the basic evolution of the conflict. Those with a critical bent could note that neutral zones "protected" by the Red Cross flag did not hold very long. Atrocities, including attempts at ethnic cleansing of areas, occurred. Humane principles and the rules of war were breached as often as, or more than, they observed. This was a war for national identity and existence, which meant that often there was little room for charity toward individuals. According to the organization's head of delegation in the conflict, Jacques de Reynier, ICRC field personnel did not even initially know the geography or languages of Palestine (save for English).[8]

A balanced account would surely note, however, that the ICRC – on the basis of eighteen persons and eight vehicles – negotiated a number of cease fires for the benefit of the wounded and others. The organization eventually provided a considerable amount of medical assistance important to the operation of hospitals, and also provided valuable relief to some 500,000–750,000 Palestinian refugees until the United Nations took over that work via the United Nations Relief and Works Agency (UNRWA) during 1949–50.[9] Detention visits and particularly the repatriation of prisoners of war went relatively smoothly. Some ICRC delegates showed uncommon valor. Two delegates suffered permanently

---

[8] Jacques de Reynier, *1948: à Jerusalem* (Neuchâtel: Editions de la Baconnière, 1969). Statements of fact in this section are based on this account, unless noted otherwise.

[9] Max Petitpierre, "A Contemporary Look at the International Committee of the Red Cross," *International Review of the Red Cross*, 119 (February 1971), 63–81 (reproduced as monograph, Geneva: ICRC, 1971). The author was a member of the ICRC Assembly and formerly a high Confederation official in charge of Swiss foreign policy for about two decades. He was one of the leading personalities in Swiss politics at that time. See also Rony E. Gabbay, *A Political Study of the Arab–Jewish Conflict: The Arab Refugee Problem* (Geneva: Librairie Droz, 1959).

incapacitating injuries from boldness in the line of duty, and three others underwent prolonged treatment for exhaustion. No doubt thousands of lives were saved or otherwise bettered. This was the first armed conflict in which the ICRC had extensive and direct contact with Arab parties.

D.-D. Junod alleges that the ICRC tilted toward the Arab side.[10] Accusation of bias for those who are intermediaries in the Arab-Israeli conflict is nothing new. On the one hand, a close reading of Junod leads to the conclusion that she does not back up her allegations with compelling evidence. On the other hand, a close reading of the memoir by Jacques de Reynier, ICRC head of delegation for the duration of this early phase of the conflict, finds that he manifested considerable sympathy for the Palestinians. He did, after all, investigate the massacre at Deir Yassin, where the Zionist Stern Gang killed over 200 Arab civilians before turning the area over to mainstream Zionist organizations – the same organizations that hampered de Reynier's efforts to get to the scene of the massacre. Ethnic cleansing, and official cooperation with it, is nothing new. But de Reynier also praises certain Jewish officials and policies in his book.

The ICRC record in the first Arab-Israeli war did not prevent a long and partially cooperative relationship between the organization and Israel in the succeeding years – especially after 1967 (covered below), although one would have to characterize ICRC–Israeli relations much of the time as delicate and conflicted. Events linked to the Holocaust no doubt played a role in producing that complex relationship.

In any event, the push to internationalize the ICRC Assembly began to lose steam. The ICRC showed in the struggle for western Palestine that once again it could do considerable good for victims on both sides of the fighting.

Red Cross Statutes

Thirdly, in its effort to secure its position in post-1945 international relations, the ICRC spent considerable time and energy on the revision of the Statutes of the Red Cross Movement. We noted in the previous chapter that the initial Statutes of the Movement had been adopted by the Red Cross Conference only in 1928, after the creation of the Federation. To make a long story short, when the Movement Statutes were revised at the Toronto Red Cross Conference in 1952, not much changed. This was a

---

[10] Junod, *Imperiled Red Cross.*

victory for the ICRC, which maintained its status, according to the new Movement Statutes, as "an independent institution governed by its own statutes."[11] The ICRC's separate Statutes continued to specify that it was a Swiss private organization, whose policy-making Assembly was made up of coopted Swiss citizens, and with an unchanged mandate.[12]

Meanwhile, other ICRC field activities continued to be important to the evolution of the organization.

Korea, 1950–1953

During the Korean war (1950–53), the organization may have tilted toward the US-UN side by some heavy-handed pressure on North Korea. True, the North Korean communists were not cooperative in the least regarding detention visits to the prisoners of war they held. And the ICRC, under the conservative and nationalist Paul Ruegger, was diligent in exploring various diplomatic avenues to try to secure Pyongyang's consent for such visits.[13] But by announcing publicly at one point that the organization had dispatched personnel to East Asia in preparation for those traditional visits, without first securing the consent of North Korea, this probably betrayed ICRC frustration with a recalcitrant and brutal communist party.[14]

Even more to the point, during the Korean war there were communist allegations that the US-UN side was engaging in biological warfare. Washington and New York rejected these allegations, and the United States proposed that a responsible third party such as the ICRC or the World Health Organization, *inter alia*, carry out an on-site investigation.[15] The ICRC did not object to the use of its name in US resolutions submitted in the UN Security Council without the agreement of the other side. Then the ICRC immediately proposed to China and North Korea that it organize and conduct precisely such an investigation. This public démarche by the organization made it seem that the ICRC was acting in tandem with US policy. Rather than launching a discreet démarche to the communist side to see what role it might play in the controversy, the ICRC went

---

[11] *International Red Cross Handbook* (Geneva: ICRC, 1994).
[12] *Ibid.*   [13] Ruegger is discussed in some detail in chapter 6.
[14] See further, William L. White, *The Captives of Korea: An Unofficial White Paper on the Treatment of War Prisoners* (New York: Scribner, 1957, reprinted, Westport, CT: Greenwood Publishers, 1979).
[15] Milton Leitenberg, "New Evidence on the Korean War Biological Warfare Allegations," Woodrow Wilson International Center for Scholars, Cold War International History Project, www.kimsoft.com.2000/germberia.htm.

public with a proposal that fitted exactly with what Washington wanted. The ICRC never received a reply from Beijing or Pyongyang.[16]

Hungary, 1956

What the ICRC set out to do strategically in Palestine – namely, help victims of armed conflict while refurbishing its own reputation – it largely succeeded in doing in Hungary during 1956. Responding to the Soviet invasion of Hungary, the organization showed that it could act quickly and with efficiency within the constraints eventually imposed by Soviet authorities and their protégés in Budapest.[17] The ICRC, quick to respond to Hungarian requests for assistance early in the uprising against communism, dispatched industrious delegates to work in the Hungarian capital and reached agreement with the Red Cross Federation that the latter would concentrate on Hungarian refugees mainly in Austria while the ICRC focused on Hungary itself.

Backed by more than thirty National Societies, the ICRC got convoy after convoy of relief into Hungary during the harsh winter of 1956–57. The Soviet Union may have charged very high duties on much of this material, but they let it get through – no doubt aware that Red Cross relief was helping Moscow care for a restive population that was much in the western eye. The Soviets and their local protégés were much less cooperative when it came to ICRC requests to see prisoners, although this can hardly be said to be a failure by the organization.[18] In this crisis the ICRC and the Red Cross Movement as a whole emerged with high honors.

French Algeria, 1954–1962

At more or less the same time the ICRC responded in its usual way to another situation that touched parts of Europe deeply, the

---

[16] At precisely this time the Swiss Confederation, despite renewed proclamations of "super neutrality" in the Cold War, was quietly cooperating with the US in applying economic sanctions against the communist coalition. Jurg Martin Gabriel, "Switzerland and the European Union," paper presented at the CUNY European Union Studies Center, New York, 30 November 2000, http://web/gc.cuny.edu/Eusc/activities/paper/gabriel.htm. Given this mindset in Berne, and given that ICRC President Paul Ruegger was extremely close to, if not actually a part of, the Berne political establishment, it seems clear that the ICRC leadership favored the West somewhat during the Korean war. Given Confederation policies, the ICRC's close ties to Berne impeded its being accepted in the communist world as a neutral actor.

[17] ICRC, *Report on the Relief Action in Hungary* (Geneva: ICRC, 1957). See further Isabelle Voneche Cardia, *Hungarian October* (Geneva: ICRC, 1999).

[18] Compare Morehead, *Dunant's Dream*, 584.

Algerian-French war of 1954 to 1962. Notable in this brutal conflict was
an ICRC report on prisoners detained by the French that documented systematic torture. When the report was leaked to the French press (5 January
1960, *Le Monde*), probably by a French official, the uproar was so great in
France, and its salutary effect so evident regarding the reduction of French
abuse of Algerian prisoners, that the ICRC in Geneva discussed the merits
of greater use of publicity to protect victims of war.[19] The French military
had created a clandestine torture bureau, and the leaked ICRC report led
to its rapid demise. But in the end conservatism prevailed in Geneva,
and the ICRC retained its traditional policy of discretion – reporting the
results of detention visits only to the detaining party in situations claimed
to be internal war, and giving that detaining power ample time to make
ameliorative changes.

In this case the ICRC had shown, among other things, how important
were its detention visits even when "civilized" western democracies were
the detaining powers. Western "civilized" powers were not always very
civil toward their colonial subjects. In the previous chapter we noted that
the British, Americans, and Spanish all ran harsh concentration camps in
their "colonial" wars.

(Some state policies designed for these colonial areas later influenced
events in Europe. The British, for example, developed certain interrogation techniques in places like Aden and Cyprus that they then used in
Northern Ireland. And the ICRC found itself coping with the conditions
of detention in both regions. For example, eventually the organization
was allowed by London to visit members of the Provisional Irish Republican Army and other detainees connected to "the troubles" in Northern
Ireland. The British never agreed that it was faced with an internal armed
conflict in that area, but it did agree to an ICRC presence as a neutral
humanitarian intermediary. Northern Ireland was one of those places
where the fight continued in detention. Some IRA prisoners of the British
gave ICRC delegates a very hard time. The prisoners did not want the
British to profit from ICRC visits; they did not want the British to gain
a reputation for humane detention policies. So some IRA prisoners were
antagonistic toward the ICRC.[20])

---

[19] Interviews, Geneva.
[20] Interviews, Geneva, London, Dublin. British brutal interrogation in places like Aden
    shocked early leaders of Amnesty International: see Kirsten Sellars, *The Rise and Rise
    of Human Rights* (Phoenix Mill: Sutton Publishing Ltd, 2002), chapter 5. She says that in
    Aden the British government was able to keep some aspects of detention and interrogation
    secret even from the ICRC delegate there, André Rochat.

Cuban missile crisis, 1962

Then there was the Cuban missile crisis of 1962.[21] Given the gravity of the situation, which presented the prospect of strategic nuclear war, the leadership of the ICRC let it be known in UN circles that Geneva might be prepared to assist in a resolution of the crisis. Against that background Secretary-General U Thant mentioned to the protagonists that various forms of international supervision could be brought into play to verify agreements reached among Cuba, the United States, and the USSR. As far as the ICRC was concerned, discussion soon centered on its role in verifying that no weapons were on board Soviet vessels bound for Cuba. UN teams, not the ICRC, would supposedly be involved in verifying the dismantling of Soviet missile sites in Cuba.

In response to a démarche from U Thant, ICRC President Léopold Bossier gave tentative approval, and the Assembly eventually gave fuller approval, to an exceptional use of the ICRC name and its contacts and resources. It was finally agreed that the organization would act beyond its traditional mandate to provide inspectors who would report to the UN. (The United States wanted the inspectors to be Swiss.) The ICRC was never a mediator on the substantive issues of the crisis, but rather was to be a source of neutral inspectors regarding Soviet ships in international waters. While this arrangement proved officially acceptable to all parties, especially the Soviets, it soon became evident that Moscow did not foresee the actual operation of the scheme. It became clear that the Soviets were going to shift policy and cease the introduction of missile parts into Cuba. (They also adopted policies that made it unnecessary for the UN to bargain with Cuba over verification within Cuban territory.) Ultimately all verification of agreements was done by national means.

While the ICRC was prepared to play an exceptional role in the Cuban missile crisis, whose evolution to strategic nuclear war would have made much traditional ICRC work meaningless, it did not in fact have to do so. After the crisis, some inside and outside the organization foresaw an expanded notion of good offices or mediation for the ICRC. But this view did not ultimately prevail. The members of the Assembly who objected to the broader role at the time of the crisis lost in the short term but prevailed in the long run. The organization stuck with its traditional mandate in

---

[21] See further U Thant, *View from the UN* (Garden City, NY: Doubleday and Co., Inc., 1978), 180–90; and Thomas Fischer, "The ICRC and the 1962 Cuban Missile Crisis," *International Review of the Red Cross*, 842 (June 2001), 287–309. With regard to the ICRC, the latter seems more accurate and comprehensive than the former.

general. Later the ICRC would be drawn into broader negotiations from time to time, as on the subject of negotiations in the wake of hijacked aircraft in the Middle East, and as on the matter of "the Red Cross" facilitating peace negotiations in El Salvador. But the ICRC wound up, sometimes on the basis of negative experiences, reiterating that it was an intermediary primarily concerning humanitarian protection of victims of conflict.

On the one hand the UN request in 1962, with the approval of Washington and Moscow, and with the eventual deference of Cuba, showed the ICRC's reputation for integrity and principled conduct. It seemed that even Moscow manifested some confidence in the ICRC – or at least would consider a role for the ICRC as a way to extricate itself from a supremely dangerous confrontation. To some, these events put to rest questions about the staying power of the organization after World War II. On the other hand, a number of skeptical ICRC officials were never too impressed by the course of events. They believed that the Soviet Union never intended actually to implement a process involving an ICRC role, but rather was using discussions about the organization to buy time for its decision making. Moscow, while mostly rejecting cooperation with the ICRC on practical protection matters around the world pertaining to detention visits and relief, nevertheless agreed to diplomatic use of the ICRC name to extricate itself from catastrophic confrontation with a minimum of loss of face. The episode did show the pragmatic flexibility of the ICRC and its ability, not without internal opposition however, to adjust its mandate temporarily in exceptional ways as broad considerations of humanity seemed to require.

1967: snapshot of broad engagement

The year 1967 shows how complex the ICRC mandate is, and how entangled in conflicts the organization can become on a very broad scale. In 1967 the ICRC found itself: thrashing about in the Nigerian civil war in ways that were to change the house over time; making a public protest about the use of poison gas in Yemen; taking remarkable strides in dealing with non-war detainees in Greece under military rule; and beginning its long effort to bring the Fourth Geneva Convention to bear in territories captured by Israel in the Six Day war. With the exception of the Yemeni case, the ICRC engagements that started in 1967 went on for some time. As with many historical dates, 1967 is simply a benchmark. The Nigerian case is so important to the history of the ICRC that it merits extended analysis.

Nigeria, 1967–1970

Just when the 1962 missile crisis, on top of the 1956 Hungarian crisis, seemed to put the final nail in the coffin of those who wanted radical change at the ICRC, the Nigerian civil war (1967–70) once again called into question the role of the organization. In World War II for the most part, the ICRC operated in secure rear areas after the fog of war had cleared, visiting detainees and providing various types of assistance in occupied territory and the like. In the Nigerian conflict, as in Palestine but with much greater media scrutiny, the ICRC was expected to act in the midst of conflict while the fighting still raged. It was a foretaste of the growing humanitarian expectations particularly in the West, expectations that were to resurface in places like Bosnia and Somalia in the 1990s. It was also a precursor to the widespread manipulation of humanitarian issues by fighting parties.

Two major questions arose out of the Nigerian civil war for the ICRC. First, was it too amateurish at the top, lacking strategic vision as a result? Second, was it too restricted by its vision of neutrality to be able to take the steps needed actually to protect persons in dire straits? These questions went to the heart of the ICRC, and Red Cross neutral humanitarianism, as it existed in the 1960s and as it had existed for a long time.

As for the first question, the time of the Nigerian war was a time of weakness throughout the ICRC but especially at the top. President Samuel Gonard, who had suffered a stroke, resigned in early 1969, having failed to deal adequately with the conflict. The Assembly then elected a former banker, Marcel Naville, who also was to go down in history as one of the more forgettable ICRC officials. He was not able to assume his duties at the ICRC immediately, so one of his Vice Presidents, Jacques Freymond, became Acting President.

Freymond was a distinguished historian who wrote about the need to correct ICRC amateurism.[22] But ironically, Freymond as a full-time academic and part-time ICRC official was an amateur in the world of diplomacy, despite his expertise in diplomatic history. He might go down in history as one of the better thinkers at the top of the ICRC, and he achieved progress on a number of protection matters while Acting President, but he was not a professional diplomat or "aid worker" and thus most fundamentally he was an amateur humanitarian.

His strong point was probably his intellectual ability to cut directly to the heart of a complicated problem. Amateur status aside, he turned out

---

[22] Jacques Freymond, *Guerres, révolutions, Croix-Rouge: réflexions sur le rôle du Comité International de la Croix-Rouge* (Geneva: HEI, 1976).

to be an effective interlocutor with governments in places like Greece, the Middle East, and Southeast Asia. His weaknesses were lack of patience and tendencies toward authoritarian decision making. He was used to running the Graduate Institute of International Studies (HEI) of the University of Geneva, where he was Director, in an authoritarian and highly personalized manner. HEI was accurately known as his personal fiefdom in the tradition of European feudalism. In Geneva HEI was often known as *l'Institut Freymond*.

Whatever his contributions to the ICRC, and they were many, he failed to provide successful leadership during the first half of 1969. In particular, in part because of his personal style, he failed to get the Assembly to deal with the Nigerian conflict in a systematic and well-considered way. After failing to persuade his colleagues on the Assembly of the wisdom of reconstituting that body into a smaller group of five to seven professional humanitarians, he resigned in protest. Some of his ideas were later implemented in various ways, and it could be said of him that on a number of issues he was proven right in the long term. (Chapter 6 below traces the declining role of the ICRC Assembly and by 1998–2002 the transfer of much policy making within the organization to a much smaller group of professional humanitarians – which is what Freymond sought in the late 1960s.) As one of his ardent supporters was known to say, he was not wrong but rather right too soon.

In general, the top level of the ICRC delegated matters in Nigeria almost completely to its temporary delegate August Lindt, who was brought into the organization specifically to deal with the crisis from the summer of 1968. Among other positions Lindt had been UN High Commissioner for Refugees, and he was therefore an experienced diplomat with knowledge of Africa. Before that he was known among other things as a courageous individual prepared to challenge the rest of the Swiss elite during the Nazi era if they took Swiss accommodation of the Nazis too far. He was thus a dynamic and principled man. As a partial reflection of his dynamism, the ICRC delivered 120,000 tons of nutritional and medical assistance during the conflict, while operating forty-five medical teams, fifty-three first aid stations, and five hospitals; the total cost to the organization at that time was about 600 million Swiss francs; fourteen persons working for the ICRC paid with their lives.[23]

---

[23] Petitpierre, "A Contemporary Look," 71 and *passim*.

Lindt, however, was said to be so arrogant and brusque as to offend African sensitivities. Other allegations arose during his tenure.[24] He was eventually declared *persona non grata* by Lagos.

For an ICRC delegate to be kicked out of a country for policy reasons is, possibly, not always a bad thing. It is worth debating whether it should happen more often, and we revisit this issue in the concluding chapter. It shows assertiveness for humanitarian causes and draws attention to recalcitrant parties. But in this case Lindt may have become a liability to the organization. If one is going to push to the maximum for the benefit of war victims, one has to know how to do it in a legally defensible way, as well as how to calculate a desirable impact on the target actor.

ICRC headquarters, despite having some knowledgeable persons on the ground in Nigeria (e.g., Georg Hoffmann), never fully understood the various issues in the conflict and never developed a clear and viable strategic vision for its management. Lindt had no meaningful instructions or supervision. The members of the Assembly were not *au courant* about many specifics, and they had no real CEO and professional bureaucracy on which to rely – although Roger Gallopin carried the title of Director-General.[25] Despite its successes in Palestine, Hungary, and elsewhere, the ICRC in the late 1960s was still a very amateurish organization.

---

[24] According to John de St. Jorre, *The Nigerian Civil war* (London: Hodder and Stoughton, 1972, 239), ICRC delegates in Nigeria during the time of Lindt were known for their high living and night life. A novel written by a former ICRC official seemed to suggest (p. 149) that Lindt was a flamboyant womanizer with a taste for African women: Laurent Marti, *Bonsoir mes victimes* (Geneva: Labor and Fides, 1996). Marti said in a preface that his contents were based on historical figures and events. At other times and in other places, like Israel and Somalia, ICRC male delegates were said to socialize extensively with local women and be known for considerable night life. The organization seemed to have no personnel policies restricting or regulating such social interaction. Historically, some delegates were drawn to the ICRC because of the lure of adventure in exotic places. Interviews, Geneva, Washington, Jerusalem. See further chapter 4, section on Somalia.

[25] One of the best treatments is by Thierry Hentsch, *Face au blocus: la Croix-Rouge Internationale dans le Nigeria en guerre (1967–1970)* (Geneva: HEI, 1973). Hentsch for a time was an assistant to Freymond at the HEI. Freymond was the director of this academic study, and it seems the book reflects Freymond's thinking as much as Hentsch's. The latter obtained access to documents not available to others. Under the prevailing regime at the time, the ICRC archives were closed. But special friends of the organization, like Hentsch, arranged to publish works on the basis of material denied to others. The ICRC finally changed the rules regarding access to its archives. But bits of the old system persisted. Officials of the ICRC like François Bugnion could publish material informed by ICRC archival material within the "last forty years." The archives remained closed to outside researchers for that shifting period. One simply had to wait to gain access in order to test in-house interpretations.

The ICRC lurched from day to day, crisis to crisis, whipsawed by various forces: public relations agents hired by the fighting parties (the most effective of which was Biafra's agent, Markpress News Feature Service), European public opinion (which was largely pro-Biafra), some important National Red Cross Societies like the Swedish one (also largely pro-Biafra), and the British and US governments (that tilted toward Lagos, while France tilted toward Biafra). One result was justified concern about the ICRC process of policy making. Administrative changes were eventually to be made (covered in chapter 6). The Nigerian civil war definitely showed weakness at the top of the organization.

As for the second question about ICRC strategy for humanitarian action, particularly among French Red Cross officials active in the conflict, the ICRC seemed too wedded to the rules of the Geneva Conventions and also too cautiously concerned about proceeding on the basis of agreement by the fighting parties. Bernard Kouchner was to found Doctors Without Borders (Médecins Sans Frontières, MSF), and somewhat later Doctors of the World (Médecins du Monde), because of his dissatisfaction with the ICRC over the issue of getting food relief into Biafra. For them, Biafra was a modern Solferino, shocking the conscience and calling for bold new action.[26]

Kouchner, like others including not a few ICRC officials, was deeply troubled about the extent of civilian starvation in rebel-held areas. But unlike the ICRC, which could not make up its collective mind in any systematic way over time about what to do, Kouchner was clearly in favor of trying to deliver relief whatever the fighting parties, and particularly the Federal side in Lagos, might say. The fact that the French government supported Biafran independence, if only to oppose the influence of the Anglo-Saxons through the Federal side, may partially explain why the French Red Cross acted so independently of the ICRC and with so little regard to Federal sensitivities. But the Nordic National Societies also acted at times without regard to what Lagos might think. So the Red Cross Movement had its more revolutionary elements, pushing the ICRC to act in ways not sanctioned by IHL and without full and clear agreement by both fighting parties. The ICRC was at least sometimes concerned about appearing timid relative to other Red Cross and religious relief agencies.

---

[26] See further Jean-Christophe Rufin, *L'aventure humanitaire* (Paris: Gallimard, Collection Découvertes-Histoire, 2001, 2nd edn). Some French observers date the first century of international humanitarian action from Solferino in 1859 to Biafra in 1967.

At times the ICRC proceeded with relief flights into Biafra, "at its own risk" in the words of Lagos, mixing its planes with flights running weapons to the rebels, and thus contributing indirectly to the rebels' fighting ability. But after one of the planes on loan to it was shot down by Federal fighter aircraft with loss of life, the ICRC reverted to the more cautious position that, according to the principles of humanitarian law, Lagos had the right to supervise relief flights to inspect for contraband. The 1949 Conventions did not cover civil wars in detail, but reasoning by analogy to what was said about international war, the ICRC finally decided that prudence was the best course after all. To act against the wishes of Lagos was said by Geneva to be acting against the principle of neutrality. But by then the ICRC was on the sidelines. Lindt was finished, having paid insufficient attention to the logic of the GCs. International relief operations were being mostly handled by a consortium of churches (Joint Church Aid), with whom the ICRC had been competing for a central role regarding relief into Biafra, along with some others like the French Red Cross.

After the fact, ICRC headquarters realized that Biafran leaders had manipulated the relief issue to build support for their cause in western circles. One of the best "weapons" they had, in order to draw attention to their secessionist efforts, was the media image of starving children. Biafran leaders would not agree to balanced or Lagos-inspected relief schemes that would cut off that image. They also wanted to use relief shipments to contribute to weapons delivery. Thus Biafran leaders profited from the specter of mass starvation supposedly caused by the Federal side, and for a time they counted on the reluctance of Lagos to attack the night-time weapons flights for fear of hitting Red Cross planes in the process. Kouchner was apparently not concerned with any of this, believing that the needs of civilians trumped any other "political" consideration. But the ICRC, which helped negotiate the Geneva Conventions for victims of war, and which was given special rights under that law, was eventually – if belatedly – concerned about its role in the next war if it flouted the principles of IHL in the Nigerian war. It also finally reviewed the point that unarmed relief workers were at the mercy of those with guns on the ground – or in this case, in the air.

Kouchner was to argue initially, via the development of MSF, that a relief agency could openly contradict public authorities and still be oper-ative in conflict situations. MSF was to argue that neutrality depended on commitment to principle – such as the right to medical assistance regard-less of "political" allegiance. This position was similar to several human rights groups like Amnesty International, who argued they should be seen as impartial and neutral because of their commitment to the Universal Declaration of Human Rights, even though they publicly contradicted governments' policies.[27]

The ICRC finally, if belatedly, decided in the Nigerian war that it should stick – at least most of the time – with its traditional approach, built on discreet cooperation with public authorities. This, the ICRC in effect said, was part of the meaning of Red Cross neutrality. If the fighting parties could not agree on a relief scheme, and guarantee security to the ICRC, the organization could not proceed. The collapse of the Biafran secessionist movement in 1970 "solved" that particular problem, but debate about ICRC neutrality was to persist.

Yemen, 1967

At the time the Nigerian civil war was getting underway in 1967, ICRC delegates in Yemen found themselves in the proximity of an aerial gas attack by Egyptian forces that were involved in the Yemeni civil war. Unlike in Ethiopia in the 1930s, but like during World War I, the ICRC made a public protest. The use of poison gas was not repeated in the Yemeni conflict.[28]

Greece and political prisoners, 1967–1974

As noted in the previous chapter, the ICRC began visiting those detained by reason of involvement in internal troubles and tensions in 1918.[29] The International Conference of the Red Cross had endorsed this activity at its London meeting in 1939, and again in other years. Events in Greece provided a new and important chapter in this aspect of the ICRC's work.

In April of 1967 a group of military officers overthrew the elected government in Athens; brutal repression followed.[30] The ICRC delegate at

---

[27] See further Ann Marie Clark, *Diplomacy of Conscience: Amnesty International and Changing Human Rights Norms* (Princeton: Princeton University Press, 2001).

[28] ICRC, *The ICRC and the Yemen Conflict* (Geneva: ICRC, 1964).

[29] In addition to the previously cited book by Jacques Moreillon, see Jan Egeland, *Humanitarian Initiative against Political "Disappearances"* (Geneva: Henry Dunant Institute, 1982).

[30] See Roland Siegrist, *The Protection of Political Detainees: The International Committee of the Red Cross in Greece (1967–1971)* (Montreux: Corbaz, 1985); and David P. Forsythe, *Humanitarian Politics: The International Committee of the Red Cross* (Baltimore: Johns Hopkins University Press, 1977), 76–86.

the time, who was neither young nor dynamic, was eventually replaced,[31] and the organization – benefiting from the governmental links of the conservative leadership of the Greek Red Cross – progressively became more assertive in challenging the detention policies of the Greek junta. In the context of international pressure brought to bear on Athens, the ICRC was able to obtain in 1969 a written agreement from the junta giving the ICRC extremely broad access to detention centers, including places of alleged torture like local police stations. The junta was under intense public pressure from certain European states which were members of the Council of Europe, some states in NATO, parts of the US Congress, and private human rights groups like Amnesty International. The ICRC, on the basis of this one-year contract, became in effect a daily supervisor of Greek military and police forces in Greece.

The interplay of the ICRC's humanitarian concerns with the junta's strategic calculations was well understood in Geneva:

> The government intended to make use of the ICRC to improve its credit internationally and it hoped to limit the risks which it ran by opening its prisons and police stations. The ICRC, on its side, knew that it could be reproached for lending itself to a political manoeuvre and that at best its naivete would arouse smiles, but it hoped, thanks to the concession it had wrested from the government, to ensure greater protection for the victims. What was decisive was the quality of the delegates' work, their humane qualities and the tact with which they attenuated their daring.[32]

After this one-year period, however, the junta failed to renew the accord and the ICRC became marginal to the fate of detainees under military rule (which lasted until 1974). Two factors accounted for this drastic change. First, the ICRC had been vigorous in trying to implement the accord, which resulted in considerable friction with Greek authorities bent on continuing brutal repression. The ultra-nationalists in the Greek government tired of the ICRC presence. The assertive second head of ICRC delegation, Roland Marti, was recalled to Geneva before he was declared *persona non grata* by the junta.[33] Second, the prospect of continuing international pressure was reduced. The US Executive Branch normalized relations with the junta in the name of national security, Greece

---

[31] Marti, *Bonsoir mes victimes*, confirms the interpretations in Forsythe, *Humanitarian Politics*. See also Siegrist, *Political Detainees*.

[32] Jacques Freymond, "Humanitarian policy and pragmatism," *Government and Opposition*, 11 (Autumn 1976), 419.

[33] Siegrist, *Political Detainees*, 123.

being perceived as supremely important to the southern flank of NATO during the Cold War. Also, what is now the European Union declined to apply collective economic sanctions on the junta, given both the Cold War and the legally binding nature of trade agreements in place. Moreover, Athens both denounced the European Convention on Human Rights and withdrew from the Council of Europe. Thus the junta did not feel the need, given changing international developments, to tolerate further an assertive ICRC.

There was no question that the ICRC, after a somewhat slow start, had worked diligently to protect all political prisoners in Greece regardless of their ideological orientation. Interviews with a few former detainees after the fall of the junta led to mostly good marks for the organization.[34] The lessons to be learned from this episode for the ICRC's protection of political detainees are not so clear. Is it better to have a written agreement or leave matters to the shifting possibilities of changing conditions? Is it better to maximize the challenges to state authority, by including supervision of police stations, or proceed less ambitiously so as not to antagonize the ultra-nationalists?

Middle East territories, from 1967

Israel's capture of the West Bank and eastern Jerusalem from Jordanian control, Gaza from Egypt, and the Golan Heights from Syria, led to prolonged and complicated involvement by the organization.

The ICRC, with the support of virtually all states, maintained that the Fourth Convention (GC) from 1949 was legally applicable to these areas as occupied territories captured in armed conflict. Occupied territory meant foreign territory. Such a position led to the conclusion that the territories did not belong to Israel, since international law generally proscribed acquisition of foreign territory by military force.

Israel, wanting to maintain the freedom to consider various outcomes for these territories, maintained that one should leave open the question of the applicability of the Fourth GC. Israel argued that since the West Bank and eastern Jerusalem, which were of great importance to certain religious sects in Israel, were not legally part of Jordan, these territories were legally unique and not covered by the wording of the Fourth GC. Parts of the West Bank were also important to Israel's security, and as a location for affordable housing close to population centers. (Israel had no

---

[34] *Ibid.*, 126–9.

comparable argument for not applying the Fourth GC to Gaza and the Golan Heights.)

It was thus impossible for the ICRC to take a stand on the Fourth GC, written primarily for humanitarian reasons, without also affecting the "political" bargaining position of the protagonists in the conflict over the West Bank and Jerusalem. Israel did promise to apply the humanitarian principles of the Fourth GC, even if – in its view – IHL was not in full legal force.[35]

In general between 1967 and the end of the Cold War, the ICRC was able to carry out detention visits to inhabitants of the territories detained by Israel. There were periods when the ICRC was barred from detainees or certain categories of detainees.[36] With regard to detainees undergoing interrogation, an especially dangerous time for prisoners, the ICRC eventually agreed with Israel that: (1) the organization must be notified of detention within a specified time; and (2) ICRC representatives could see the person without witnesses a certain time after that arrest (originally four weeks, later negotiated down to three weeks and finally over much time to fourteen days). There was thus a period of time in which the detainee was under the full and unsupervised control of the Israelis. The ICRC made the judgment that this was the best (or least worst) arrangement it could secure, given particularly its conclusion that important parties like the United States were simply not going to pressure Israel on the issue of treatment of detainees. At least the organization could see the detainee after interrogation, without witnesses, and discreetly protest to Israel about any concerns it had.

It eventually became known that the Israelis applied what they termed moderate physical pressure to many such detainees in an effort to extract

[35] See further, from a vast and uneven literature: Pierre-Yves Fux and Mirko Zambelli, "Mise en œuvre de la Quatrième Convention de Genève dans les territoires palestiniens occupés: historique d'un processus multilatéral (1997–2001)," *International Review of the Red Cross*, 847 (September 2002), 661–97; Adam Roberts, "Prolonged Military Occupation: The Israeli-Occupied Territories since 1967, *American Journal of International Law*, 84 no. 1 (January 1990), at 44; Eyal Benvenisti, *The International Law of Occupation* (Princeton: Princeton University Press, 2004); and Ilan Peleg, *Human Rights in the West Bank and Gaza: Legacy and Politics* (Syracuse: Syracuse University Press, 1995). In 2003 Israel's Prime Minister Ariel Sharon created an uproar in that country when he referred to certain territories under Israel's control as occupied. This event reflects the fact, noted in this text, that one could not separate IHL for occupied territory from "the politics" of the protagonists. There was little if any neutral humanitarian space on this issue.
[36] Article 126 (2) of the Third GC allows for the interruption of ICRC visits for "imperative military necessity . . . as an exceptional and temporary measure." The comparable article in the Fourth GC is 143 (3).

information supposedly affecting their security. Such tactics were similar to what the British used against IRA and other detainees suspected
of illegal activity in Northern Ireland: sleep deprivation, hooding, confinement in uncomfortable positions, making loud noises near the ears,
violent shaking of the body, and so on. (The United States was later to use
similar tactics in dealing with detainees linked to its "war" against terror.)
The ICRC protested such tactics *vis-à-vis* Israeli authorities and issued a
number of public statements indicating ICRC disagreement with unspecified detention practices.[37] The ICRC was confirmed in its view about the
larger context, as the United States did not pick up on ICRC statements
or significantly pressure the Israelis to change their policies. Some policies did change, for whatever reason. For example, by 1986 Israel ceased
the more arbitrary of its administrative detentions, although the general
practice was still employed. Israeli courts over time constrained some of
the interrogation practices used against prisoners.

At other times, such as the Arab uprising against occupation starting
in late 1987 called the first intifada, high Israeli officials openly called for
mistreatment of Arabs who were opponents of Israeli occupation. The
Israelis instituted harsh detention policies in general in an effort to defer
opposition to its presence in the territories. The ICRC protested such
Israeli policies in its traditional discreet way. It issued special publications
from time to time.

Occasionally Arab detainees died in Israeli captivity.[38] It fell to the
ICRC to contact the family and return the body. Such events were not
common, as they reflected a failure of Israeli policy. The official Israeli
policy was to deal with detainees short of fatal abuse. In deciding to stay
in the territories under conditions imposed by Israel, the ICRC took into
account the willingness of Israel to allow a certain measure of cooperation
with the organization, cooperation not always duplicated by other states –
particularly communist ones. The ICRC also noted the policy – not always
duplicated by other states in the Arab and Islamic worlds – of trying to
limit the range of pressure against detainees.

---

[37] For a clear statement of ICRC criticism of Israeli policies in the territories, see its report,
Five Years of Activity 1981–1985 (Geneva: ICRC, 1986), 34–8. See also *International Review
of the Red Cross*, 286 (January–February 1992), 85–6.
[38] For an example after the Cold War, see ICRC press release 95/14, "Israel and the Occupied
Territories: Death of a Palestinian Detainee," 30 April 1995. It is clear from this statement
that the ICRC is protesting Israel's treatment of detainees, but without giving the details
of this particular incident, and without charging Israel with war crimes under the Fourth
GC. Thus, the style of this statement is typical of the organization.

Other issues arising under the Fourth GC showed a similar pattern. The ICRC publicly stated that the building of Jewish settlements in the territories, the Israeli use of collective punishments, the destruction of Arab houses as punishment, the expulsion of Arabs from the territories, and the seizing of Arab lands and resources without compelling military necessity, *inter alia*, all violated the Fourth GC. But given the lack of effective outside pressure on Israel, there was little or no change in the policies of the Jewish state on most of these questions.[39]

(After the Cold War, when Israel erected a security fence that cut deeply into what were widely considered to be Palestinian lands, the ICRC clearly stated that this wall violated the Fourth GC pertaining to occupied territory.[40] The organization, while condemning Palestinian attacks on Jewish civilians, concluded that the fence violated the occupying power's responsibility to the welfare of the occupied people, since the fence deprived many Palestinians of access to land and other economic opportunities. The issue was also litigated at the International Court of Justice, but that Court's advisory opinion of July 2004, while supporting the ICRC's position, failed to alter Israeli basic policy on the question.[41] Israeli court judgments, on the other hand, did bring about some changes in the wall's contours, even as the wall itself was ruled acceptable.[42])

The ICRC not only was keenly aware of the absence of effective restraining pressure on Israel, but also was aware that various Arab and other parties were using the Fourth GC for *realpolitik* reasons in their continuing effort to weaken Israel. Some of the Arab or Islamic parties like Iraq and Iran, who frequently criticized Israel harshly for its humanitarian record in the territories, gave the ICRC decidedly less than perfect cooperation in such situations as the First Persian Gulf war during 1980–88. The Saddam Hussein government, a persistent and active critic of Israel with reference to IHL, used poison gas on Iraqi Kurds in 1988. It failed to meet many of its obligations under IHL during

---

[39] See the clear example, after the Cold War, from the ICRC statement in the UN General Assembly on 13 November 1997 during the emergency special session of that organ, reproduced on the ICRC homepage. By early 2004, the ICRC had about 250 public statements recorded on its web page regarding Israel and the territories. Not all these statements were critical of Israel; some of the statements were critical of attacks on Israel.

[40] ICRC Press Release No. 04/12, 18 February 2004.

[41] ICJ, "Legal Consequences of the Construction of a Wall in the Occupied Palestinian Territory," General List No. 31, 9 July 2004, www.icj-cij.org/icgwww/idocket/ imwp/ imwpframe/htm.

[42] Among numerous sources see CBS, "Court Orders Israel Fence Change," www.cbsnews.com/stories/2004/07/01/world/main62694.shtml.

armed conflicts in 1991 and again in 2003. Iran, another vocal and active critic of Israel, denied ICRC access to many Iraqi prisoners of war, especially those of Shi'ite belief that Iran sought to turn against the Saddam Hussein government which was based on support from Sunni elements. Some of these Iraqi Shi'ites, under Iran's encouragement and influence, physically assaulted an ICRC delegate who was seeking to interview them.[43]

The ICRC felt obligated to continue its presence and work in the territories taken in 1967 despite continuing Israeli violations of humanitarian norms. It did publish its views rather extensively, even if in a low-key, non-flamboyant style, and it did take into account the wishes of those who were victimized under the occupation and who wanted the ICRC to stay engaged. Among many actions, the ICRC organized family visits to those detained by the Israelis, and distributed food and medical assistance to the civilian population under occupation. The ICRC came to be highly respected, especially by Palestinian parties. These parties knew that the ICRC was making a good-faith effort to lessen the hardships of occupation, in keeping with the terms of the Fourth GC.[44] On occasion the ICRC received favorable press in Israel, as when it organized the repatriation of Israeli military personnel held in Lebanon.

Southeast Asia as magnifying glass

In a summary historical chapter such as this one, one cannot begin to do justice to all of the details of the ICRC's humanitarian work during the Cold War. One can, however, use a region to demonstrate the organization's major efforts at humanitarian protection – in the form both of attention to detention visits and of attempts to provide relief. One can also see that other decisions – such as whether to comment on bombing policies – can be part of humanitarian protection.

Vietnam, 1954-1975

This conflict showed indeed that humanitarian law could be hugely ineffective. According to former Acting President Freymond, reflecting only slight overstatement, "the balance sheet of this long and terrible war for

---

[43] Interviews, Geneva.   [44] Interviews, occupied territories.

Vietnam is singularly negative for one who considers it from the point of view of humanitarian law."[45]

The ICRC had been involved in a minor way during the First Indochina war that saw the defeat of French colonial forces in 1954. This phase of the struggle (1945–54) between France and communist Vietnamese parties occurred during a period when the organization was downsizing after World War II. The ICRC thought small during this era, and its emphasis was on Palestine as noted above. Consequently its impact on Southeast Asia was slight. The ICRC had few delegates on the ground in this phase of the war; they concentrated primarily on prisoner matters. The budgetary situation of the Geneva headquarters ruled out large-scale relief operations. In an all too familiar pattern, the delegates worked assiduously but received only minimal cooperation from the fighting parties, especially from the communist side. Moreover, the fact that ICRC delegates were dependent on the French side for communications and transport certainly compromised the neutral image of the ICRC. Beyond questions of image, in substance the organization sometimes deferred to French sensitivities rather than assertively challenge certain French policies. The actual behavior of the ICRC in Southeast Asia (and Korea) in the early 1950s cast serious shadows over the organization's claims to independence and neutrality.[46]

The ICRC remained involved when the United States replaced France in trying to create a non-communist regime in the south of Vietnam, despite the 1954 Geneva Accords and their call for national elections throughout one Vietnam. As in other conflicts, National Red Cross Societies did not fully – or sometimes even marginally – coordinate their activities with the ICRC. First the French and then the American Red Cross did their own thing in the south, even though there existed on paper during some stages of the war a coordinated Red Cross program in South Vietnam.[47] In 1966 the Vietnamese Red Cross in the south

---

[45] Freymond, *Guerres, révolutions, Croix-Rouge*, 94.

[46] Florianne Truninger, "The International Committee of the Red Cross and the Indochina War," *International Review of the Red Cross*, 303 (November–December 1994), 564–94. The author was given access to ICRC archives, closed at that time, being chosen by the organization to write an official history. See also Jean-François Berger, *L'action du Comité International de la Croix-Rouge en Indochine (1946–1954)* (Montreux: Corbaz, 1982).

[47] See further Georges Willemin and Roger Heacock, *The International Committee of the Red Cross* (Dordrecht: Martinus Nijhoff Publishers, 1984), 146.

teamed with the government in Saigon, the American Red Cross, and the Federation to eliminate the ICRC from some humanitarian relief programs.[48]

There is ample literature documenting the brutality of the American phase of the Vietnam war – brutality by all fighting parties.[49] Enemy wounded were often intentionally killed, civilians were displaced, political prisoners were abused, military attacks were imprecise, civilian leaders were assassinated, supposedly civilian journalists became combatants from time to time. Even with the best of intentions, the irregular nature of much of the war often made it difficult for combatants to identify true civilians. There was prolonged disagreement over whether this was an international armed conflict, or whether it was essentially an internal armed conflict within one Vietnam – although with obvious participation by outside states. So there was even disagreement over which humanitarian rules applied. The various protagonists lied about their policies and tried to minimize their humanitarian obligations. Training in the Geneva Conventions was meager to non-existent.

An aroused nationalism pushed for minimizing even the most egregious violations of the laws of war by one's own side, as in the American response to the My Lai massacre. First the military tried to cover up the 1968 massacre, and then, when unofficial information compelled some penal response, President Nixon, responding to domestic public opinion, pardoned the one lower-ranking soldier who was convicted – even though he had been responsible for the killing and other abuse of large numbers of unresisting and non-threatening civilians. The North Vietnamese massacre of civilians during the battle of Hue was, if anything, even more morally repugnant in that it stemmed from official policy rather than soldier frustration, and there was no attempt by Hanoi even at a pretense of criminal justice. The ICRC was a weak barrier to such powerful nationalistic forces.

---

[48] Freymond, *Guerres, révolutions, Croix-Rouge*, 151–2.

[49] In addition to the standard literature, now voluminous, a book published at the end of 2001 gives a close-up and memorable view of the nature of this brutal and dehumanizing war: John Laurence, *The Cat from Hue: A Vietnam war Story* (New York: Public Affairs, 2001). Other publications long after the war confirm, for example, the brutality and wanton behavior of many US military forces: see John Kifner, "Ex-GI's tell of Vietnam Brutality," *New York Times*, 29 December 2003, reprinted in the *International Herald Tribune*, www.iht.com/cgi-bin/generic.cgi?template = articleprint.tmplh&ArticleId=123026. This is not to suggest that the behavior of other fighting forces was more humane.

With increased US bombing of the north in the late 1960s came increased numbers of US prisoners of war held by the People's Republic of Vietnam. Despite repeated overtures, the ICRC never was able to persuade Hanoi to respect its obligations under the Third Geneva Convention of 1949, and in particular to grant access to the ICRC in order to monitor the conditions of detention of downed pilots. We now know that Hanoi violated in practice many of the standards it had accepted in legal theory. US prisoners of war were brutally treated before being released in 1973 as the result of inter-state bargaining.

It is of more than passing interest that when Hanoi and Washington reached agreement in 1973 on the conditions for the withdrawal of US military personnel from the south, an exchange of prisoners was possible. In the south, the ICRC had arranged with the United States and South Vietnam to give a special detention status to North Vietnamese and Viet Cong prisoners captured with their weapons visible. Thus, even if not in uniform, these combatants were obviously just that – combatants, and thus under humanitarian principles entitled to a special regime of detention when *hors de combat*. The ICRC, drawing on its experience in Algeria (1954–62), where the French had adopted a similar policy, thus helped Washington and Saigon to distinguish open combatants – even if not in uniform – from terrorists and saboteurs, and from other "political prisoners" who employed violence clandestinely or just fell victim to Saigon's suspicions. The United States and Saigon did not afford the informal combatants POW status, especially the Viet Cong, but did allow ICRC visits. Thus in the 1973 bargaining, it was possible to arrange a reciprocal trade of prisoners. In the midst of brutality, the ICRC did help carve out some humanitarian space for irregular but open combatants *hors de combat*. And this humanitarian space did contribute to a negotiated end to the US military presence.[50]

Beyond prisoner matters, the ICRC was not very vigorous in raising questions about the US bombing of the North, and whether the bounds of military necessity were exceeded through the striking of essentially civilian targets or excessive "collateral damage." Later, ICRC officials were to note, in carefully crafted prose, that the ICRC had only raised public question about the bombing in 1972, when the most active US phase of the fighting was almost over, and long after the escalation of bombing from 1967 to

---

[50] Freymond vigorously criticized the ICRC for its inconsistent and weak attention to political prisoners held by South Vietnam: *Guerres, révolutions, Croix-Rouge*, 91.

1969.[51] It could be reasonably argued that the ICRC was not entirely balanced or neutral – difficult to achieve, of course – in dealing with the United States and North Vietnam during this period.

True, the ICRC was the guardian of IHL that focused on victims, and it was not the guardian of the Hague law that focused on means and methods of warfare. So a legalist might say that the ICRC was not the guardian of the law covering aerial warfare. But the Hague tradition had no modern guardian, and both traditions of international law had the same goal – to limit the destruction of war by protecting as much human dignity as military necessity allowed. The two traditions were effectively combined in the two Protocols of 1977. So some would be inclined to say that the ICRC should have raised more questions about the US bombing, especially since the ICRC had raised persistent question about damage to civilians from aerial attack since the 1930s.

The ICRC was involved in many other ways in the Vietnam war before the conflict's denouement in 1975, but it never obtained much cooperation from Hanoi on any issue. Thus the ICRC's experience in the American phase of the Vietnam war was similar to the French phase, in the sense of Geneva never gaining meaningful acceptance on the communist side. It was only during the Chinese–North Vietnamese border war in 1979 that the ICRC was accepted as neutral intermediary for detention visits by both Hanoi and Beijing, in keeping with the Third GC of 1949. Then, the organization was able to carry out its normal visits. Whether this was because, in the ideological view of Hanoi, there could be neutral humanitarian space between two communist protagonists, but no neutrality in a communist–capitalist struggle, is very difficult to say.

Cambodia, 1979–1980

In 1979 the ICRC started a relief operation in Cambodia that was to prove as expansive as it was complicated.[52] Cambodia had been, in effect, a collective victim of the war in Vietnam. Its weak neutralism had been

---

[51] François Bugnion, "Droit de Genève et droit de La Haye," *International Review of the Red Cross*, 844 (December 2001), 901–22, especially at 917.

[52] This section draws heavily on information in William Shawcross, *The Quality of Mercy: Cambodia, Holocaust, and Modern Conscience* (New York: Simon and Schuster, 1984). See also Fiona Terry, *Condemned To Repeat? The Paradox of Humanitarian Action* (Ithaca: Cornell University Press, 2002), 114–54. And see L. Mason and R. Brown, *Rice, Rivalry, and Politics: Managing Cambodian Relief* (South Bend, IN: University of Notre Dame Press, 1983).

exploited by North Vietnamese forces, which used Cambodian territory for military purposes. This in turn led to a US invasion, which resulted in the fall of the weak neutralist monarchy at the hands of some pro-western military officers, which in turn led to the triumph of the brutal agrarian communist radicals known as the Khmer Rouge. When Vietnamese forces pushed Pol Pot's Khmer Rouge out of Phnom Penh in 1979, in part because of the latter's alignment with China, the ICRC tried to create a new humanitarian space in order to work for civilians impoverished and otherwise endangered by brutal policies and interstate conflict. Hanoi realized it needed the help of outside agencies to care for the society it had just taken over. The ICRC used this opportunity to develop its most important relief program with any communist state during the Cold War.[53]

On the basis of conflicted consent from the new Hun Sen government in Cambodia during 1979, the ICRC and UNICEF mounted a large joint relief operation in the devastated country. Other aid agencies, notably Oxfam, ran separate programs under different, more discriminatory rules. For example, Oxfam relief to areas still under Khmer Rouge control was forbidden. The ICRC and UNICEF held firm that this was a violation of the principle of impartiality, a principle absolutely central to their relief. A further problem involved Cambodian civilians caught between Khmer Rouge areas and the Thai border. The Thai government was not consistently sympathetic to their plight, to put it mildly, at times not wanting to get involved in complications from two hostile parties that had external backers. In some ways the Khmer Rouge was a proxy for China, and the Hun Sen government in Phnom Penh was a proxy for North Vietnam.

The ICRC and UNICEF were trying to provide almost every conceivable type of assistance in a devastated land while lacking the full support of the key governments. Needless to say, the remnant of the Khmer Rouge was not very cooperative either. Finally a deal was brokered that both facilitated joint ICRC–UNICEF relief and resolved the refugee problem on the Thai border. By this time the ICRC found itself with its largest relief program ever mounted to that time. The once small private agency in Geneva was now operating on a par with major intergovernmental agencies like UNICEF, the Office of the UN High Commissioner for Refugees, and the World Food Programme. From early August to the end of 1979, some 34,428 tons of food worth about $16 million was provided.[54] In the first six

---

[53] Bugnion, "The Activities," 215.
[54] ICRC, *Annual Report 1979* (Geneva: ICRC, 1980), 40.

months of 1980, the ICRC–UNICEF team oversaw the delivery of about 60,000 tons of seed rice and another 30,000 tons of foodstuffs.[55] By the end of 1980 the ICRC alone foresaw expenditures in the area of Cambodia and Thailand topping $36 million.[56]

Questions can be raised about some of the compromises made by the ICRC (and UNICEF) in quest of providing relief to Cambodian civilians. Certainly, considerable relief went to fighting parties. This demonstrates one way in which the ICRC contributed to continuing violence. In addition, public authorities proved corrupt, as relief was sold for profit by various parties, and the Hun Sen government displayed less than determined commitment to get the relief goods out of the warehouses in Phnom Penh and into the hands of civilians. In its determination to respond quickly to civilian distress, the ICRC (and UNICEF) had agreed with the Hun Sen government that it would forego its normal supervision of relief. The government alone was in charge of relief distribution. This was a major mistake.

According to William Shawcross, the ICRC was slow and deficient in organizing medical relief for refugees in Thailand. In general, there were many complaints about lack of organization and systematic action by the ICRC–UNICEF team. Of course this team had no authority over the UNHCR, the World Food Programme, Oxfam, or any of the other almost one hundred private relief agencies active in that conflict situation.

On the other hand the ICRC showed remarkable persistence both concerning food relief in Cambodia, including areas held by the Khmer Rouge, and concerning the forced repatriation of Cambodians who had sought sanctuary in Thailand. The organization's François Bugnion and François Perez were determined and clever during the early stages of bargaining with parties in 1979. They insisted on impartial attention to civilians both under the control of the government and under control of the Khmer Rouge, despite being actively and intentionally undercut by Oxfam on this issue. ICRC delegate Francis Amar became *persona non grata* in Thailand because of his determined protests against forced repatriation of refugees to a still dangerous Cambodia. The ICRC decided on a "cross-border operation" from Thailand into areas of Cambodia held by the Khmer Rouge – which means that the government of Cambodia, which claimed sovereignty over the territory, was not informed about the relief

---

[55] ICRC, *Annual Report 1980* (Geneva: ICRC, 1981), 35.   [56] *Ibid.*, 36.

operation in advance. (The ICRC exercised this type of cross-border operation in Ethiopia/Eritrea as well.) According to Shawcross, the ICRC was
consistently more forceful than UNICEF in dealing with public authorities. According to Fiona Terry, the ICRC, but not other relief agencies,
withdrew from certain operations when their "political" impact exceeded
their humanitarian content.

Major relief operations are almost always chaotic at the start, especially
in failed states lacking effective government and adequate infrastructure.
No doubt the ICRC made a number of policy errors. Still, the ICRC gets
high marks for creativity, persistence, and determined action.

Political prisoners in South America

The situation of political prisoners in Greece from 1967 to 1974, covered
above, while illustrative of continuing ICRC efforts for that type of victim
of conflicts, was not, of course, the full story. Many other situations manifested widespread and sometimes brutal conditions for those "detained
by reason of political events." In the final chapter we pay some attention to Nelson Mandela and detainees in the Republic of South Africa
during the apartheid era. Here we note that in the 1970s and 1980s in
particular, many countries in South America were characterized by "the
national security state" featuring overthrow of democracy and severe
repression of those viewed as threats to the military's view of security
requirements.

No one or two cases can capture all the details of ICRC work for
security prisoners in Paraguay, Uruguay, Brazil, Colombia, and so on,
not to mention the somewhat different "political" factors in places like
El Salvador, Nicaragua, and Guatemala in Central America. But one
can still say something about this work through sketches of Chile and
Argentina.

Chile

As the numerous historical accounts indicate, on 11 September 1973, the
leader of the Chilean armed forces, General Augusto Pinochet, organized a
violent coup that successfully took control of the government in Santiago
from the democratically elected leftist president, Salvador Allende. In
the subsequent state of siege, Pinochet declared a metaphorical war on
civilians who were viewed as part of the subversive left and engaged in a

series of arrests, detentions, and "disappearances."[57] By 20 September, the ICRC obtained the permission of the military government to visit most places of detention – with the notable exception of military detention and interrogation centers. By the end of the year, ICRC delegates had made 114 visits to 61 places of detention, meeting several thousand detainees held by military authorities.[58]

The humanitarian objectives of the ICRC soon became intertwined with certain strategic calculations of the military government, when, exactly one year after the coup, the Chilean authorities asked the ICRC to supervise the release of a number of detainees on condition that those released be forced to live in exile.[59] The organization was thus faced with the decision of whether or not to play an active role in the implementation of the policies of the military government. Based on experience with the Greek junta, however, it was well understood in Geneva that humanitarian concerns must be balanced with the military government's strategic calculations. In the end, the ICRC cooperated in helping the Chilean government implement the "release program." While seeking further access, the ICRC helped many of these detainees leave the country, with the Central Tracing Agency in Geneva helping to prepare the necessary travel documents.

Gradually, the ICRC was able to expand its access to previously off-limits military installations, using its normal procedure of interviews without witnesses. There were, however, certain detention and interrogation centers that remained closed to ICRC personnel throughout, and in June 1974 several scheduled visits to military detention centers were interrupted because the required authorizations were not renewed.[60] By 1976, however, the organization had basically achieved full access, which was a certain progress. But by this time the Pinochet regime had essentially eliminated those persons high on its list of "subversives" and could afford to relax its repression and allow more thorough scrutiny of detention by the ICRC.

The decrease in number of detainees during 1975 to 1976 prompted the ICRC to adapt its strategy by progressively reducing the size of its delegation in Chile. By the end of 1975, there were only fifteen delegates

[57] For a concise and prize-winning treatment from a voluminous literature, see Darren G. Hawkins, *International Human Rights and Authoritarian Rule in Chile* (Lincoln: University of Nebraska Press, 2002).

[58] ICRC, *Annual Report 1973* (Geneva: ICRC, 1974), 33–4.

[59] ICRC, *Annual Report 1974* (Geneva: ICRC, 1975), 45.   [60] *Ibid.*, 43.

left – half the number at the beginning of the year.[61] This adjustment in strategy was further compounded by a major structural adjustment in 1977 when the staff of the Chilean delegation was integrated with the regional delegation of the "Southern Cone." This reduced the presence in Chile to two delegates – a doctor and an administrative secretary, with six locally recruited assistants.[62]

While successfully gaining access to detention centers and overseeing the release of several hundred detainees throughout the tenure of the military government, a persistent problem remained that of disappeared persons. This problem was raised by ICRC President Alexander Hay in face to face meetings with General Pinochet in 1976, with lists of the missing handed directly to the dictator. Some 900 names of missing persons were presented to the Chilean authorities on two separate lists. Despite the fact that the Chilean government provided information that led to the solving of 119 of these cases, the matter was never fully resolved.[63]

Conditions in Chile seemed to be improving when in April 1978 a government act proclaimed the end of the state of siege. Under Decree 2.191 of this act, amnesty was granted for all serious crimes committed between 11 September 1973 and 10 March 1978. This "amnesty law," however, came as a mixed blessing. While its coverage was extended to opponents of the Pinochet regime and allowed several hundred leftist political prisoners to be released from Chilean jails, the careful observer will note that it was meant to apply equally (if not primarily) to members of the military government – including Pinochet – who himself committed human rights atrocities during the state of siege. In this way, the Pinochet regime prevented its own criminality from being (domestically) legally challenged.[64] Owing to these developments, the ICRC closed its permanent delegation to Santiago in October, leaving only a liaison office with a locally recruited secretary.[65] The organization continued to carry out periodic visits to detainees from its office in Buenos Aires, Argentina.

The issue of missing persons continued to be pursued after the withdrawal of ICRC personnel from Santiago in 1978 – mostly by the Central Tracing Agency – as a new list of "disappeared" was submitted

---

[61] ICRC, *Annual Report 1975* (Geneva: ICRC, 1976), 9.
[62] ICRC, *Annual Report 1977* (Geneva: ICRC, 1978), 25.   [63] *Ibid.*, 26.
[64] Richard A. Falk, "Assessing the Pinochet Litigation: Whither Universal Jurisdiction?" in Stephen Macedo, ed., *Universal Jurisdiction: National Courts and the Prosecution of Serious Crimes under International Law* (Philadelphia: University of Pennsylvania Press, 2004), 103.
[65] ICRC, *Annual Report 1978* (Geneva: ICRC, 1979), 43.

to Chilean authorities.[66] But the government provided little information, and by November 1984 the state of siege was resumed. This prompted the reopening of the Santiago office in 1985, which pursued the usual visits to detention centers, but also took a slightly different and new strategy, which was to try and pressure the government to ratify the Additional Protocols to the Geneva Conventions. While it was highly unlikely that ratification would be forthcoming, the hope was that simply bringing up the issue would help to disseminate knowledge of IHL among police and military personnel.[67] It is not known whether this strategy helped to improve conditions for detainees, or resulted in any changes in behavior on the part of authorities, though Chile did eventually ratify the Protocols in April 1991, shortly after the end of military rule in 1990.

Overall, however, the resumption of the state of siege was accompanied by the usual game of cat and mouse between the Chilean authorities and the ICRC. In particular, Chilean authorities persistently denied visits by the ICRC to detainees held incommunicado, citing a law that allowed such detentions without visits for up to ten days. After much frustration, an unusual event took place in June 1989 when Chile's Supreme Court, despite the law to the contrary, adopted and transmitted a resolution to civilian and military authorities in support of the ICRC's attempts to gain access to these detainees. This proved to be a significant turning point, as less than a year later Pinochet handed over the presidency to the rightfully elected Patricio Aylwin Azocar, having failed in his bid to gain popular ratification for his rule.

Argentina

A similar military coup occurred in neighboring Argentina in March 1976, when the elected president Maria Martinez de Peron (the third wife and vice-president of the venerated President Juan Domingo Peron) was overthrown by the military, which subsequently exercised power through a junta composed of three service commanders. As in Chile, the coup was followed by similar atrocities against perceived opponents of the resulting "national security state," whereby political prisoners were abducted, tortured, "disappeared," and oftentimes killed in atrocious ways.[68] *Unlike*

---

[66] *Ibid.*, 44.   [67] ICRC, *Annual Report 1985* (Geneva: ICRC, 1986), 43.

[68] Among many sources see especially Iain Guest, *Behind the Disappearances: Argentina's Dirty War against Human Rights and the United Nations* (Philadelphia: University of Pennsylvania Press, 1990), which, despite its extensive coverage of Argentina detention, inexplicably fails to cover the ICRC.

in the case of Chile – where the ICRC was able to negotiate access to most places of detention within a matter of weeks – the first visits to detention centers in Argentina did not take place until January 1977, some nine months after the coup.[69] Again as in Chile, it ultimately took the organization about three years to gain more or less systematic access to Argentine places of detention,[70] by which time the brutal junta had eliminated its most "dangerous opponents."

After its initial series of visits beginning in January 1977, the ICRC obtained an agreement with the junta for the continuation of visits to detainees, which the Argentine authorities initially refused to honor. It was only after Alexander Hay personally intervened and wrote to the "leader" of the junta, General Jorge Rafael Videla, that visits were resumed. But the visits did not resume until December 1977, almost a full year after the initial visits took place.[71] While these visits were continued into 1978, it was only after this time that the organization negotiated the release of significant numbers of detainees, which was followed by yet another interruption of visits between December 1978 and February 1979.[72] As one account suggests, such tactics intended to frustrate the work of the ICRC were part of a broader plan of deception that also included the transfer of detainees immediately prior to scheduled visits, the use of death threats against the detainees if they disclosed too much during interviews, and the scheduling of bogus interviews with supposed detainees who were actually junta "collaborators."[73] By 1981, the frequency of the interruptions of detention visits led to the organization's decision to carry out only one complete visit a year to each place of detention, followed by shorter sporadic visits to only some of the detainees, including what were called "emergency" visits.[74] This same year, paradoxically, several hundred detainees were released allowing a further decrease of the ICRC's work in this field.[75]

Another analogy to the Chilean experience was the problem of disappeared persons. As in Chile, the ICRC delivered lists of missing persons to the Argentine authorities that totaled some 2,500 persons between 1977

[69] ICRC, *Annual Report 1976* (Geneva: ICRC, 1977), 26; ICRC Annual Report 1977, 25.
[70] ICRC, *Annual Report 1979*, 35.   [71] ICRC, *Annual Report 1977*, 25.
[72] ICRC, *Annual Report 1978*, 44; ICRC, *Annual Report 1979*, 34.
[73] *Nunca Más: The Report of the Argentine National Commission on the Disappeared* (New York: Farrar Straus Giroux, 1986), 190.
[74] ICRC, *Annual Report 1981* (Geneva: ICRC, 1982), 31; ICRC, *Annual Report 1982* (Geneva: ICRC, 1983), 53.
[75] ICRC, *Annual Report 1981*, 31.

and 1979. Again as in Chile, the activities of the ICRC were marginal to the fate of most of the disappeared. It later became evident that the junta had become proficient at simply denying that they had any knowledge that certain people were missing. When questioned, authorities would insist that they had no evidence of the whereabouts of these individuals and that they were not under arrest. Despite such assertions, some of these people eventually turned up in detention centers, while some missing children even turned up in the custody of government officials who had registered them as their own children.[76] The continued frustrations in the ICRC's work on disappeared persons were also in no small part due to a law issued by the government, according to which persons missing for a certain period of time could be considered dead, thus providing an excuse for the authorities' indifference.[77] In the end, the fate of most of these disappeared persons was never ascertained and most are now presumed to have been killed.

Despite the elaborate deception schemes by the Argentine authorities, the ICRC continued to visit detainees, inquire about the disappeared, and negotiate the release of many detainees until the fall of the junta in 1983. The systematic release of detainees began taking place in 1982, and by the end of that year the number of security detainees still held had decreased dramatically. By the end of 1983, this number had decreased to only a few hundred.[78] By this time, the junta had fallen and the ICRC found itself cooperating with the Argentine National Commission on the Disappeared, under the government of Raoul Alfonsin, to deal with the remaining questions that lingered about prisoners never accounted for during the junta's brutal rule. As such, the years 1983 and 1984 saw the gradual release of most detainees. As documented by the ICRC, "Almost all the 122 persons imprisoned for offenses against State security, who were still detained at the end of the previous year, were gradually released; of the people arrested before the civilian government came into power following the elections in October 1983, only about 15 were still in prison by the end of 1984."[79] When military rule ended, the ICRC could boast notable success in securing the release of detainees they had accounted for, particularly given the initial problems obtaining access to detention centers and the considerable obstructionism on the part of Argentine

---

[76] *Nunca Más*, 257.   [77] ICRC, *Annual Report 1979*, 35.
[78] ICRC, *Annual Report 1983* (Geneva: ICRC, 1984), 35.
[79] ICRC, *Annual Report 1984* (Geneva: ICRC, 1985), 39.

authorities. Talk of successes in the area of the disappeared, however, was noticeably muted.

If the Pinochet regime killed 6,000 civilians, the Argentine junta may have killed 30,000. For the ICRC, it may have been the case that the Argentine junta, seeing the work of the organization in Chile, expanded the rather new process of making persons "disappear." By not accepting responsibility for persons in detention, by claiming no knowledge, the junta made it more difficult for the ICRC to provide minimal humanitarian protection. Unhappily, ICRC diligence in Chile may have led to expanded forms of brutal repression in Argentina.

Comparing Poland

Brief mention can also be made of the situation in Poland in 1981, in which the ICRC gained access to large numbers of prisoners interned but not charged under a decree of martial law by the government of Wojciech Jaruzelski. This was the only time during the Cold War that the ICRC was able to carry out extensive visits to political detainees under a European communist regime. Acting in conjunction with the Red Cross Federation, which itself was somewhat unusual, the ICRC exercised its normal visits until July 1982, when the period of martial law ended. Despite its requests, the organization was never able to extend its visits to those charged with or convicted of crimes against state security. After a general amnesty was declared in 1984, the ICRC shut down its office for detention visits in Poland.

Summary of political prisoners

During the Cold War the ICRC may have conducted prison visits to political detainees in sixty to seventy countries in any given year. This is more or less the same number of countries in which Amnesty International was reporting, between 1961 and 1991, that torture was employed against detainees. The sketches of Greece, Chile, Argentina, and Poland, while obviously not replicating each situation, give an impression of how the ICRC attempted to deal with the pervasive humanitarian problem of political detention on a global scale. The situation in South Africa was certainly one of the more interesting and salient chapters in the ICRC's effort to protect political prisoners. It is covered in the final chapter as part of a summary evaluation of the ICRC.

Aside from field operations

The ICRC used its field record in conflicts during the Cold War era to enhance its reputation for dedicated, responsible, and mostly well-considered humanitarian action – Nigeria aside. Complicated, however, were ICRC relations with the rest of the Red Cross world as well as with states in the development of IHL.

The Tansley Report

In the early 1970s the ICRC, along with other components of the Red Cross Movement, agreed to a review of Red Cross affairs by a multinational team of mostly "outsiders," funded by a consortium of private donors. The ICRC was not enthusiastic about these developments. In a later book by two authors, one of whom was an ICRC staff member, there is this passage: "These discussions led . . . to setting up the Tansley Commission [*sic*], which the ICRC, as jealous as it may be of its independence and conscious of the particular nature of its mission and status, could not afford not to associate itself."[80] This passage, however stilted the prose, captures the reality that the ICRC was not eager for a reappraisal of the Red Cross Movement since that might well call into question the agency's record of leadership. But the organization did not feel it could openly resist an independent review.[81]

In 1973 the International Red Cross Conference created an *ad hoc* evaluation committee, led by a Finnish Red Cross official (Kai Warras), to oversee the reappraisal process. Donald Tansley, a Canadian development official, was chosen to head a small study team. Tansley proceeded in a systematic and fully independent manner to confirm what dissatisfied parties suspected: that the Red Cross Movement was not in great shape and could benefit from numerous changes. As one author observed, Tansley dared to be critical.[82]

---

[80] Georges Willemin and Roger Heacock, *The International Committee of the Red Cross* (Boston: Martinus Nijhoff, 1984), 145.

[81] Once in existence, the Tansley team received exceptional cooperation from the ICRC.

[82] See further Morehead, *Dunant's Dream*, 631. She says, in an overstatement, that the Tansley report "sank," 632. She also says that Tansley seemed to reserve his greatest criticism for the ICRC, 631. Actually, Tansley held the ICRC in high regard, especially compared to other units of the Movement. See also Rezso Sztuchlik and Anja Toivola, *What Was the Impact of the "Tansley Report"?* (Geneva: Henry Dunant Institute, 1988). "We, like the majority of persons consulted, think that most of the findings and many of the recommendations of the Tansley Report are still valid today," 22.

On the surface, the ICRC responded to the 1975 Tansley Report with pro forma thanks and a long list of reasons why most of his recommendations could not be implemented.[83] For example, Tansley stated boldly that the Movement needed a new emblem that could symbolize unity and bypass states' *realpolitik* debates about Israel and Magen David Adom. But at that time the organization was not prepared to take any significant initiatives on that subject. The ICRC Assembly refused to endorse a plan for change presented by the Directorate.[84] It was only decades later that the ICRC tried to break the *realpolitik* logjam regarding the emblem (covered in chapter 7).

Beneath the surface, however, the ICRC set in motion some important changes in reaction to the Tansley Report. That report had presented – in public and convincing fashion – some facts that the ICRC could not really ignore while remaining a credible leader in the Red Cross world. (Tansley was finally honored at the 2000 Red Cross Conference in Geneva for his contributions. That it took a quarter of a century for this recognition was further confirmation of his point that the Red Cross Movement acted with glacial swiftness.)

From the ICRC perspective, perhaps the most important change that was to emerge over the next couple of years was an effort to improve relations between the organization and the National Red Cross Societies. The Tansley Report had shown both the weakness of many such National Societies and the lack of consistent and helpful ICRC relations with them. As noted in previous chapters, once recognized by the ICRC, National Societies went their own ways with little connection to the founding agency. As a result, many National Societies – especially in the Global South – could not provide the ICRC with reliable help in conflict situations. The organization very slowly began to rectify matters during the Presidency of Alexander Hay (1976–1987). Hence, stimulated by Tansley, the ICRC began to see itself less as a completely autonomous actor, and more as part of a relatively more integrated Movement. This was an old issue but at long last the ICRC, embarrassed by Tansley, began to take the question of integrated effectiveness more seriously. The ICRC treated Tansley like Freymond: it rejected his ideas at the time, but implemented many of them over time.

---

[83] *The ICRC, the League, and the Tansley Report* (Geneva: ICRC, 1977). The response to Tansley was very positive by former ICRC Acting President Freymond (see *Guerres, Révolutions, Croix-Rouge*), but by the mid-1970s Freymond had resigned from the Committee. Our last chapter below notes some renewed attention to the Tansley Report by the ICRC thirty years after its publication.

[84] Interviews, Geneva.

It has to be added, however, that the ICRC was partly motivated in these new endeavors by its continuing friction with the Red Cross Federation. Building better relations with National Societies was not only a way for the ICRC to develop better national partners for humanitarian protection, but also a way to wean those National Societies from full loyalty to the Federation at the expense of the ICRC.

The Tansley Report had both documented and deplored the ICRC–Federation conflict. But that conflict for leadership of the Movement was to continue in rather virulent form for several more decades. The two Geneva-based agencies might have their ups and downs in mutual relations, and they might even sign "peace treaties" *inter se* (as they were called in some internal ICRC documents), but the Federation would continue to be headed much of the time by Presidents and Secretaries-General who wanted to expand their prestige and range of action at the expense of the ICRC. The ICRC was equally determined to protect its independence and traditional mandate, as it had done since the founding of the Federation after the First World War. The ICRC continued to think, with some reason, that the multinational and weak Federation could not provide proper humanitarian protection.

In East Africa, for example, the ICRC judged that the Mengistu government of Ethiopia was trying in 1986 to use Red Cross relief to help lure civilians away from rebel-held areas in Eritrea, and thus to isolate rebel fighters who – as usual – sought the cover of civilians for their secessionist operations. The ICRC felt it could not participate in such a civilian relocation scheme because of its profound impact on the basic maneuvers of the fighting parties. For the ICRC, governmental guidelines about relief compromised its neutrality in major ways. So either it decided to pull out of relief operations in Ethiopia, or it was asked to leave by the government, depending on who one talked to.[85] The Federation then agreed to provide Red Cross relief in Ethiopia on governmental terms already rejected by the ICRC. The Federation was primarily interested in getting a piece of the relief action in the midst of conflict in Ethiopia, regardless of Red Cross unity and neutrality. Privately ICRC officials were furious with the Federation.[86]

Whatever the balance sheet on ICRC–Federation relations during the Cold War, the Tansley Report did lead to gradual change at the ICRC on the question of closer relations with National Societies. This change was

---

[85] See the careful wording in ICRC, *Annual Report 1986* (Geneva: ICRC, 1987), 21.
[86] Interviews, Geneva.

to have important consequences after the Cold War, as we will see in later chapters.

Perhaps the second most important change at the ICRC in the wake of the Tansley Report was its move – albeit very slowly – to increase openness. Parts of the ICRC were shocked at Tanlsey's frontal assault on the closed and stuffy nature of the organization. But even a later President of the ICRC, Cornelio Sommaruga, was to deplore the arrogant and smug nature of many ICRC officials who considered themselves better than the rest as the high priests of humanitarianism.[87] In the mid-1970s Tansley had the audacity to say publicly that the ICRC should "open the windows." A more open ICRC would have better relations with other Red Cross actors, so the question of openness was related to the question of ICRC links to the National Societies and the Federation.

It took some time, but finally the ICRC realized the accuracy of the Tansley Report on this point. If the ICRC was closed, aloof, and not well known, it could not be supported. Secrecy had become dysfunctional. ICRC secrecy was as much the product of Swiss society as it was a logical aspect of the nature of its work. Had complete secrecy really been logically necessary, the ICRC would not have become so dysfunctional. It was not maximizing its potential as part of the Red Cross Movement. Despite its small size, it was trying to do too much by itself in too secretive a manner.

Key ICRC officials also saw that more openness was a way to oppose efforts to internationalize the top of the ICRC. If the ICRC consulted regularly with a broader range of personalities and organizations, there might be less reason to talk about internationalizing the Committee. So, as on the issue of relations with National Societies, the ICRC eventually saw that what Tansley was suggesting for reasons of efficiency was also in the organization's more narrow self-interest.

A decade after the Tansley Report, the ICRC started a series of consultations with leading diplomats and other experts in international relations. Many ICRC officials made a concerted effort to discuss issues frankly with "outsiders." True, other ICRC officials retained a more traditional Swiss aloofness. One could go through the motions of consulting but not really be interested in the dialogue. After all, as noted above, President Sommaruga found in the 1990s that some of the organization's aloofness had not been fully laid to rest.

---

[87] Massimo Lorenzi, *Le CICR, le cœur et la raison: entretiens avec Cornelio Sommaruga* (Lausanne: Favre, 1998), 89.

Perhaps the greatest defect of the Tansley Report was its failure to compel the ICRC to improve its muddled pronouncements on the meaning of humanitarian protection – which includes assistance (and which is explained more fully in the following chapter). Tansley was a pragmatic public official, not a theorist. Given that the ICRC and other Red Cross actors mostly talked about protection and assistance as two different things, Tansley operated on that premise and assigned duties to his staff accordingly. One person was given the portfolio of assistance, another of protection. The two young study team members proceeded with their assignment to evaluate each. The result was a failure ever to address the relationship between the two. The outcome was not only an important conceptual failure but an unfortunate practical problem as well.

Because Tansley was Canadian, the more paranoid ICRC officials thought he was in league with certain Canadians in the Federation to have the latter take over all assistance roles in the name of the Red Cross, even in conflict situations, leaving the ICRC with a much reduced role concerning detention visits only. This erroneous view stemmed in part from the fact that the Tansley Report addressed the subject of protection largely in terms of development of law and detention visits, with only passing reference to assistance by the ICRC. Red Cross assistance by the Federation in natural disasters got much more attention. Just as the organization used the term "ICRC" to refer to both the entire organization and the top Assembly, to the evident confusion of all, so it referred to protection as both separate from assistance but also including assistance. While the ICRC created this confusing situation, the Tansley team should have done better in sorting out this confused rhetoric – a confusion that affects things even now.[88]

The Additional Protocols of 1977

From 1968 there arose a movement to pay attention once again to the further development of IHL. This move came not from the ICRC but from the United Nations. The 1968 UN Conference on Human Rights in Teheran asked the UN Secretariat to prepare studies about improving "human rights in armed conflict." Because of the nature of its origins, this initiative was to be concerned as much with *realpolitik* as with war victims. The ICRC might see IHL as a means to regularize improved humanitarian

---

[88] The reader will recall that the present author was a consultant on protection for the Tansley team.

protection for victims of war, but states might very well see IHL as another policy instrument to advance their primary policy concerns – concerns that might not prioritize the well-being of victims.

Newly independent states of the Global South were unhappy about being bound by the 1949 law that they had had no influence in creating. In the 1970s these numerous states of the Global South, usually backed by the communist bloc, sought to use IHL to weaken Israel and white-ruled South Africa and colonial Portugal in particular, and to benefit what they regarded as "national liberation movements." At the same time these states sought to protect themselves from burdensome legal guidelines regulating how they dealt with secessionist movements in their own territories.

Some further details about the Additional Protocols and their negotiation are dealt with in chapter 7. Here we note simply that by 1977, on the basis of a four-year off-and-on negotiating process, two Protocols were added to the 1949 Geneva Conventions. The first pertained to international armed conflict. The second became the first treaty on internal armed conflict, supplementing the general provisions of Common Article 3 from 1949. The first protocol occasioned much controversy about when the law applied, to what kind of actors, and whether certain individuals such as mercenaries were to benefit from its terms when *hors de combat*. Lurking behind such legal controversies were *realpolitik* considerations stemming from the Arab-Israeli conflict in particular and the North–South conflict in general. The second protocol was seen as a threat to state sovereignty particularly by those states fearful of national unrest and secessionist movements. Ironically, partially because of the role of the Pakistani delegation, it too was approved by the diplomatic conference.

Despite such problems and controversies, by 2004 both protocols had been formally accepted by a large number of states: Protocol I by 161 states, and Protocol II by 156. Formal acceptance, however, was not the same as conscientious application. The United States has not yet formally accepted Protocol I because of concerns both by the Pentagon about infringements on military necessity, and by those friendly toward Israel and worried about implications in the Middle East. Yet even the United States eventually accepted that large parts of Protocol I codified customary international law binding on all. It is said that during the Persian Gulf war of 1991 for the liberation of Kuwait from Iraqi control, US commanders paid considerable attention to Protocol I despite US non-ratification.[89]

---

[89] Interviews, Geneva, Washington.

However, what one historian said in the mid-1990s about Protocol II could be said of both Protocols: IHL "continued to be, in various respects, disappointingly ineffective."[90] Numerous warring parties continued to make civilians the object of attack, and to mistreat combatants upon their capture.

Toward the end of the Cold War there was talk at the United Nations of a New International Humanitarian Order, perhaps paralleling a New International Economic Order and the New International Information Order. All suffered the same fate: oblivion. A private grouping of independent persons comprised the Independent Commission on International Humanitarian Issues. This body, including the Federation official Henrik Beer, paid much attention to norms in armed conflict, as well as to practical social problems affecting persons in both peace and war. A follow-on Independent Bureau for Humanitarian Issues proved short lived, failing to provide significant follow-up. The ICRC retained its central position in international humanitarian affairs.[91]

Conclusion

By the time the Soviet Union decided to give up its control over Eastern Europe in the late 1980s, and then imploded in 1991, the ICRC had not only survived the Cold War but solidified its status as a unique organization whose humanitarian contributions were not fully duplicated by any other actor. True, the UN had progressively taken an increasing interest in the plight of individuals in wars and what were called complex emergencies. (The latter were never defined precisely but included situations that involved the breakdown of public order threatening human security.) True, dynamic private human rights groups like Amnesty International and Human Rights Watch paid much attention not only to human rights narrowly defined but also to humanitarian law and diplomacy.

Nevertheless, particularly concerning detention visits, no agency duplicated the role of the ICRC on a global basis. This was so despite the fact that the Council of Europe established an agency to inspect detention conditions under the European Convention on Torture, modeled on the ICRC's experience and approach.[92] In 2002 the UN created a similar

---

[90] Best, *Humanity in Warfare*, 74.

[91] See further *Winning the Human Race? The Report of the Independent Commission on International Humanitarian Issues* (London: Zed Books, 1988).

[92] See further Malcolm D. Evans, *Preventing Torture: A Study of the European Convention for the Prevention of Torture and Inhuman or Degrading Treatment or Punishment* (Oxford: Oxford University Press, 1998).

agency for global detention visits under the first optional protocol to the UN Convention Against Torture. This UN agency was a sub-committee of ten persons, reporting to the UN Committee Against Torture. As of 2004, only three states had ratified this optional protocol, far short of the fifty states needed to bring the inspection system into legal force. Thus there remained ample reason for broad ICRC work for detainees.

As for relief, the road had not been smooth for the ICRC. Various National Red Cross Societies, the Red Cross Federation, Doctors Without Borders, Oxfam, and various religious or secular relief agencies like the consortium Joint Church Aid in Nigeria had all challenged the ICRC's basic role and operating style regarding assistance in conflict situations. UN agencies like the UNHCR, UNICEF, and the World Food Programme often played a large role in relief operations. Still, at the end of the Cold War the organization remained the titular manager for the largest private relief operation in the world for conflicts.

The ICRC also retained some importance in the development of IHL, and especially in tracing activities.

3

The ICRC after the Cold War

> The humanitarian organizations have not emerged unscathed from the
> [Balkan] conflict in which so many men, women and children have per-
> ished. Is there still any point in trying to mitigate man-made chaos by
> humanitarian aid? No idle question, for former Yugoslavia provides an
> especially edifying and indeed exemplary instance of the juxtaposition of
> barbarous conduct on the one hand, bravery and useless heroism on the
> other. In these conditions humanitarian aid has to contend with the most
> abject political conduct and the inexhaustible indifference of governments.
>
> Mercier, *Crimes sans Châtiment*, 1

It hardly seemed possible that the end of the Cold War would usher
in such humanitarian catastrophes. Optimism, however, was to meet a
cruel fate in the wake of the collapse of European communism and the
implosion of the Soviet Union. President George H. W. Bush went to
the United Nations General Assembly in the fall of 1991 and proclaimed
that a New World Order had arrived. The trigger was not just the collapse of Soviet-led communism. There was also the liberation of Kuwait
from Iraqi control earlier that year, and then shortly thereafter the UN
Security Council characterized the ramifications of domestic repression
by Saddam Hussein as a threat to international peace and security. All
of this made western triumphalism, centered on human dignity, seem
credible.

But it quickly became evident that many parts of the globe presented a New World Disorder. After the 1991 events in the Persian
Gulf and northern Iraq, conflicts in the Balkans, Somalia, Chechnya,
Angola, Mozambique, Sierra Leone, Rwanda, former Zaire, Cambodia,
East Timor, Afghanistan, Iraq again, and other places posed grave humanitarian challenges. Indeed, some persons would even long for the stability
and prudence imposed by the forty-year global conflict between democratic capitalism and authoritarian socialism, backed as the two sides were
by massive nuclear arsenals. It became a very close call as to whether the

96

world was better or worse off after the Cold War, especially in those parts of the world where local hostilities could more easily rise to the surface once the loose bipolar power structure of the Cold War was gone.

The ICRC, which had already undertaken numerous changes from about 1970 on, which will be more clearly explained in chapter 6, faced important decisions about its role in the world. It was to find itself in the vortex of unspeakable atrocities and was to see its staff intentionally murdered, its vehicles and facilities attacked, its emblem disregarded as a source of neutral humanitarianism, its discreet requests and its public protests often ignored. Brave new talk by governments, especially by the United States, about a New World Order was not often backed by brave new deeds to guarantee the human dignity of "others." This left the ICRC isolated, frustrated, and all too often targeted.

Yet, as had happened before, a certain humanitarian progress went hand in hand with tragedy. We saw that the First World War, for all of its slaughter, had firmly established the ICRC and the Red Cross Movement on the world stage. And we saw that the Second World War, despite its massive destruction, had led to the 1949 Geneva Conventions – which included new legal provisions especially for the civilian population and for internal war – and eventually to the 1977 Additional Protocols.

The collapse of communism – as the functional equivalent of the Third World War – brought some humanitarian progress. In places like the Persian Gulf and Kosovo, several belligerents fought "modern wars" with a bevy of military lawyers trained in international humanitarian law.[1] In these and other places journalists became more familiar with the ICRC and IHL. UN major organs like the Security Council, and UN functional or specialized agencies like the UNHCR and UNICEF, became even more involved with humanitarian law and policy. New courts were created for war crimes and other aspects of international criminal justice. Under the pressure of events and facing increased competition from more numerous humanitarian actors, the ICRC and the Red Cross Federation finally improved their cooperation. At least relative to their past, they saw the necessity of a more integrated Movement that drew more systematically on the resources of National Red Cross and Red Crescent Societies.

---

[1] According to Wesley Clark, supreme NATO commander in the 1999 bombing of Serbia because of Kosovo, modern wars are characterized by great attention to international law, great attention to the media, and great attention to allies: see his *Waging Modern War: Bosnia, Kosovo, and the Future of Conflict* (New York: Public Affairs Press, 2002).

An overview

Given the rash of violent conflicts after the Cold War, one might be forgiven for thinking that the humanitarian problems were more evident than the humanitarian progress.[2] Many of the conflicts were, at their core, internal or the result of failed states. In these atrocious situations in places like Somalia, Liberia, and former Zaire, few of those with weapons had ever heard of the Geneva Conventions and Protocols. Fighting forces were usually irregular, without much discipline or training. Often public purpose was obscure, replaced by unvarnished personal ambition and/or greed over the spoils of natural resources. In these "deconstructed" conflicts, notions of military honor, neutrality, and distinctions between combatant and civilian all paled into insignificance. Particularly in the Balkan wars from 1992 to 1999, and even more so in Rwanda during 1994, systematic attacks on civilians were one of the principal objectives of a fighting party, not just a matter of unfortunate collateral damage. The calculated intent was to persecute, to abuse, to forcibly displace, and to kill noncombatants. In such conflicts, agreed-upon humanitarian space tends to disappear.

Physical security became a major issue for the ICRC. By the late 1990s ICRC field operations around the world encountered about 120–150 attacks per year. They were overwhelmingly intentional, whether politically or commercially motivated. In 1996 alone, six field workers were killed in Chechnya and three in Burundi. This reality, plus the nature of abuse directed at local victims, caused the ICRC in 1993 to open a special office dealing with delegate stress. In the mid-1990s, about 20% of delegates returning to headquarters showed serious signs of stress impacting negatively on work and family.[3]

In Baghdad, Iraq, in October 2003 the ICRC headquarters building was intentionally attacked, with loss of life. Slightly earlier, an ICRC vehicle, clearly marked with the legally neutralized emblem, was intentionally attacked from close range with loss of life. Those carrying out the

---

[2] Among the helpful overviews are: Adam Roberts, *Humanitarian Action in War* (London: Adelphi Paper No. 305, Oxford University Press, for the Institute for Strategic Studies, 1996); *Humanitarian Assistance in Conflict*, Report prepared for the Norwegian Ministry of Foreign Affairs (Bergen, Norway: Chr. Michelsen Institute, 2 June 1997); Simone Delorenzi, *ICRC Policy since the End of the Cold War* (Geneva: ICRC, 1999); Larry Minear and Thomas G. Weiss, *Mercy under Fire: War and the Global Humanitarian Community* (Boulder: Westview, 1995).

[3] This paragraph is based on internal ICRC documents, in the possession of the author.

attacks most likely saw ICRC activity as contributing to the welfare of the Iraqi people, which *ipso facto* contributed to what the US-led coalition forces were trying to achieve: a satisfied Iraqi nation willing to accept a post-Saddam government which was greatly influenced by the United States.

In most of these attacks on ICRC personnel, however, no political group claimed responsibility. Arrests were not made. The perpetrators were never held legally accountable. It was difficult to know for sure the motives and objectives of the attackers.

After the October attack in Iraq, the US Secretary of State telephoned the ICRC President, urging the organization not to pull out its remaining expatriate personnel. The United States wanted the ICRC to stay, mostly because its staying would indicate that the security situation was not so dire. In Iraq in 2003, a US occupation without the parallel work of the ICRC and/or the UN was a more fragile occupation. Thus for both the United States and its opponents, the ICRC presence had strategic implications. The fact that the ICRC saw its presence in terms of neutral humanitarianism made little difference to those prone to stress the strategic implications of that presence. There was almost no objective humanitarian space for the ICRC in the midst of occupied Iraq. The major protagonists defined that presence in terms of power politics.[4]

The ICRC suspended a constant expatriate presence in Iraq in late October 2003, being unable to guarantee physical security. Much as in Chechnya and Somalia somewhat earlier, the ICRC based its expatriate presence in a nearby country, moving its specialized personnel into the conflict area for short, specific tasks. Local partners, at least relatively less prone to become targets, remained on the ground in the core conflict area.

Such dilemmas resurrected the old debate about neutral versus "political" or solidarity humanitarianism. Already in places like Bosnia and

---

[4] The ICRC was probably attacked for the same reason the UN headquarters had been attacked some weeks earlier, leading to the death of Sergio de Mello, the Special Representative of the UN Secretary-General in Iraq, among others. No matter how much the UN or the ICRC might try to signal that they were separate from the US-led coalition forces, for example by not fortifying their in-country headquarters, their work for the Iraqi people dovetailed with US objectives. In working for humane conditions for the Iraqi people, the ICRC inherently contributed to the US strategic objective of a stable Iraq under a new regime. Those carrying out the attacks most likely wanted chaos, disorder, insecurity – at least for a period sufficient to rid the country of foreign occupation before a new pro-western regime was secure. Probably for these same reasons, the head of CARE in Iraq was kidnapped by unknown persons in the fall of 2004.

Somalia, where attacks on civilians and disregard for neutral third parties like the ICRC or UN personnel were rampant, the old argument was made again that "neutrality was a form of moral bankruptcy." It followed that the only truly moral course of action was to choose sides – to forcibly oppose those carrying out atrocities and violating international law. This was essentially the same debate that had arisen back in the late 1960s at the time of the Nigerian civil war, when in particular some French and Scandinavian circles of opinion wanted to end Biafran civilian suffering via solidarity with the Biafran side, even if this violated nice notions of neutrality.

After the Cold War, as at the end of the Nigerian–Biafran conflict, the ICRC wound up almost always on the side of traditional conceptions of neutrality.[5] One should say "almost always" because on a few occasions the ICRC has participated in "cross-border" relief operations which are characterized by relief actions without the advance consent of public authorities: in the Horn of Africa in the 1980s, the Thai–Cambodian border area during 1979 to 1980, and the Iran–Iraq border area during their war in 1980–88. (It seems that the ICRC conducted at least one cross-border relief operation in the French-Algerian war of 1954–62.)[6]

The ICRC created a new office in Brussels, headquarters of both the European Union, a major donor, and NATO. NATO officials spoke at ICRC headquarters in Geneva, and ICRC delegates even participated in NATO military exercises, along with the more usual training courses in the laws of war. But this close interaction did not signal a new form of "solidarity humanitarianism" by the ICRC, attaching itself to the superior military coalition after the Cold War. Rather, given that the EU was a major donor, and that the organization and NATO found themselves acting in close proximity in places like Bosnia – and later in Kosovo and Afghanistan – there was a concerted effort to make sure that all actors understood each other. There was an effort especially to differentiate between neutral humanitarianism as practiced by the ICRC, and intergovernmental, and

---

[5] The prominent journalist David Rieff also came down on the side of neutral humanitarianism, even though he had earlier advocated solidarity or politicized humanitarianism. Wrongly, he attributes the model of neutral humanitarianism to the agency Doctors Without Borders, whereas in fact the historical model for neutral humanitarianism is the ICRC. He apparently does not care for the ICRC because of its record on the German Holocaust. See his *A Bed for the Night: Humanitarianism in Crisis* (New York: Simon and Schuster, 2002).

[6] Interviews, Geneva.

sometimes coercive, "humanitarianism" or humanitarian intervention as practiced by NATO.[7]

For those advocating a more "politicized" humanitarianism, however, there was usually an absence of political will on the part of outside states to either start or sustain a "politicized" humanitarian intervention. Given the thinness of moral solidarity across national borders, outside states with the putative military muscle to stop the abuses of non-combatants were mostly reluctant to put their military personnel in harm's way in the absence of expedient reasons. They never intervened in Rwanda to stop a genocide that killed almost a million persons. In Somalia, a relatively few American casualties proved sufficient to end the experiment in coercive nation and state building. In Bosnia, it took the tragedy of the Srebrenican massacre to goad NATO into coercive action against the Serbs. Even that brief display of muscle, through high-altitude air strikes presenting little prospect of casualties to NATO pilots, which led to the negotiated peace at Dayton in late 1995, did not result in systematic and persistent pressure on Serb leaders. At the time of writing, the Bosnian Serb leaders General Ratko Mladic and Radavan Karadic have remained free, despite indictment by the prosecutor of the International Criminal Tribunal for Yugoslavia. Western states were not eager to introduce their troops in the Darfur region of the Sudan in 2004 to stop what US Secretary of State Colin Powell had called genocide.

Beyond the central question of whether neutral humanitarianism could survive after the Cold War, other debates arose that challenged the ICRC's traditional activities. Did humanitarian relief to the civilian population actually prolong wars and violent crises, freeing the fighting parties from social duties and thus allowing them to concentrate their resources on combat? When the ICRC hired private security forces or paid locals to deliver relief in dangerous areas, did this contribute to a war economy?

---

[7] Thierry Germond, "NATO and the ICRC," *NATO Review*, 45 (May/June 1997), 30–2. For a critique of how "humanitarian aid and diplomacy" as practiced by the United States and other states endangered more independent actors such as Doctors Without Borders or the ICRC, see Edward Giradet, "A Disaster for Humanitarian Relief," *International Herald Tribune*, 2 August 2004, www.iht.com/articles/532107.html. This article was written after five MSF workers were intentionally killed in Afghanistan, leading that organization to suspend its operations in that country. Giradet critiqued states, especially the United States, for pursuing strategic and intelligence goals under the banner of "humanitarian aid." One of the most egregious examples of misnomers occurred during the Reagan Administration when Washington referred to its non-lethal aid to the contras in Central America as "humanitarian." The contras were a fighting force trying to overthrow the Sandinista government in Nicaragua.

Did the ICRC presence lead to a culture of dependency and undermine both self-reliance and sustainable development? Did independent ICRC action conflict with, or duplicate, the work of other humanitarian actors whether public (the UN) or private (many NGOs)? Should the ICRC remain discreet given the intentional and heinous treatment directed to civilians and detained fighters?[8]

As in previous eras, we can chart the evolution of the ICRC through a brief review of some of its major engagements.

The 1991 Persian Gulf war and northern Iraq

When Iraq invaded Kuwait on 2 August 1990, the ICRC already had delegates in Baghdad. The organization had been trying to play its traditional role as a neutral intermediary in the armed conflict between Iraq and Iran (1980–88), as well as in the aftermath of that conflict. The ICRC had also undertaken other activities in the area, including a cross-border operation along the Iran–Iraq border for the benefit of civilians on the Iraqi side. The fact that the ICRC undertook this humanitarian relief action without the advance consent of Iraq did not impede relations between them. Iraq was to cooperate with, or ignore, the ICRC depending on shifting calculations of its national interests. No evidence has surfaced suggesting that the cross-border operation loomed large in Baghdad's subsequent decision making. In fact, because of new tensions after 2 August, Iraq turned to the ICRC to help repatriate Iranian prisoners of war left in limbo since 1988, as Iraq sought to patch up relations with Iran. In 1990 Saddam Hussein suddenly decided to repatriate most of the remaining Iranian POWs, and sought a coordinating role for the ICRC. Both sides had held on to captured enemy combatants long after the cessation of active hostilities, in violation of the Third Geneva Convention of 1949. There followed in the fall of 1990 a mutual exchange of POWs through the ICRC totaling more

---

[8] From the voluminous literature covering such questions and debates, several sources merit citation: Fiona Terry, *Condemend to Repeat? The Paradox of Humanitarian Action* (Ithaca: Cornell University Press, 2002); Larry Minear, *The Humanitarian Enterprise: Dilemmas and Discoveries* (Bloomfield, CT: Kumarian Press, 2002); Mary Anderson, *Do No Harm: How Aid Can Support Peace – or War* (Boulder: Lynne Rienner, 1999); Alex de Waal and Rakiya Omaar, *Humanitarianism Unbound? Current Dilemmas Facing Multi-Mandate Relief Operations in Political Emergencies* (London: African Rights, 1994); Mark Duffield, "The Political Economy of Internal War," in Joann Macrae *et al.*, eds., *War and Hunger* (London: Zed Books, 1994); John Prendergast, *Frontline Diplomacy: Humanitarian Aid and Conflict in Africa* (Boulder: Lynne Rienner, 1996).

than 78,000, although tens of thousands of Iraqis were still left in Iranian hands.[9]

Immediately after Iraqi military forces moved south into Kuwait, the ICRC took the public position that this was indeed an international armed conflict to which the bulk of IHL applied. While the rest of the world had no difficulty with this stand, Iraq never accepted it – claiming that Kuwait was an internal Iraqi province. On this and certain other issues the ICRC tried to achieve a change in Iraqi policy by communicating via other parties with whom the agency had good relations and who might have the ear of high Iraqi officials – parties such as the Palestine Liberation Organization, Algeria, and Jordan. This effort was to no avail. During the duration of the Iraqi occupation of Kuwait, which the UN Security Council as well as the ICRC considered to be occupied territory subject to the Fourth Geneva Convention, the ICRC was denied access there.

It thus quickly became evident that the ICRC's link to the Fourth GC concerning occupied territory was a liability in dealing with Baghdad, so the organization did not press legal arguments on that subject. The UN Security Council was to call repeatedly on Iraq to respect IHL. The ICRC, however, shifted to a pragmatic line and tried to secure humanitarian cooperation with Baghdad that avoided explicit reference to the Geneva Conventions and Protocols – even though what the ICRC requested in its diplomacy was in keeping with the contents of IHL. This is yet another case of reference to IHL being a hindrance to the practical field efforts of the ICRC.

The Iraqi move south created a civilian exodus from Kuwait, mostly into Jordan. Since Jordan was not at war, a legalist might say that this was of no concern to the ICRC but rather was a problem for Jordan, the Jordanian Red Crescent, and the Red Cross Federation. But the latter actors were overwhelmed by the sudden rush of massive proportions, and so the ICRC cooperated with the Jordanian Red Crescent, not to mention with other actors like Doctors Without Borders, to provide emergency relief to "war refugees" there. While the ICRC helped construct one tent city, population 30,000, the Federation helped elsewhere.

---

[9] Unless otherwise noted, this section is drawn from Christophe Girod, *Tempête sur le désert: le Comité International de la Croix-Rouge et la Guerre du Golfe 1990–1991* (Brussels: Bruylant, 1994). The author was an ICRC official. Although this is supposedly a personal narrative, it was written at the initiative of the ICRC. It could not have been published, and the author remain with the ICRC, without the *de facto* cooperation of the organization. It uses internal ICRC documents. Since the ICRC archives are closed to outsiders for a forty-year period, it is impossible fully to cross-check this version.

As was true historically, the unity of the Red Cross Movement was a problematic side show to the war. In the fall of 1990 that unity was non-existent, not only in Jordan but elsewhere. The Indian Red Cross, for example, acted in tandem with the Indian government to deliver relief supplies to Iraq, but without advance notice to the ICRC, supposedly the lead Red Cross agency in conflicts. Later, the ICRC arranged an accord with the Federation to specify duties among the units of the Red Cross Movement, so that progressively into early 1991 the overall Red Cross presence in the conflict area was more coordinated. But in March 1991, the Federation negated that accord, launched its own appeal for charitable funds, and was only dissuaded from this independent course of action by the negative reactions of various National Societies. As had been true in the past, the ICRC had to negotiate almost as much with its Red Cross "partners" as with the belligerents. Donors no doubt were not impressed with the way various Red Cross actors appealed for funds, which certainly made other private relief organizations more attractive as alternative humanitarians.

For some civilians, the problem was not what they found when they escaped, as in Jordan, but the problem of not being able to escape Baghdad's control at all. In August of 1990, Iraq announced that citizens of "aggressive" states then in Iraq would not be allowed to leave. Further, Saddam Hussein announced that they would be used as human shields to protect strategic sites against attack. In turn, many western states turned to the ICRC for some resolution of this problem. The deployment of human shields was clearly prohibited by IHL. Since the ICRC had representatives in Baghdad, although they were frequently given the cold shoulder by Iraqi authorities, western governments hoped the organization could somehow counteract Iraqi policy on this question.

Responding to this pressure, ICRC President Cornelio Sommaruga flew to Baghdad and carried out fruitless talks with Iraqi officials. Some at the ICRC, like Christophe Girod, suggested this may not have been a wise course of action. There was little prospect for success from such talks, and thus the prestige of the highest level of the organization was committed but probably doomed to failure. Also, in this critical view, the ICRC appeared to be a handmaiden to western governments, jeopardizing its image of independence and neutrality. However, certain ICRC officials in Geneva, along with the head of delegation in Iraq, prepared a draft agreement and pushed ahead. In any event, the organization showed a high-level interest in innocent civilians being victimized by illegal policies, even if the ICRC initiative came to nothing.[10]

From the beginning of the conflict, the ICRC expressed concern about the effect of UN mandatory economic sanctions on the civilian population of Iraq. Not only in the fall of 1990, but also later, particularly from March 1991, the ICRC was one of the first and most insistent voices calling attention to the civilian disaster in Iraq. The ICRC, maintaining its presence in Baghdad, was well positioned to start providing civilian relief, which it did from the early days of fall 1990, and which it expanded even in the midst of intense combat from early 1991. Concern for Iraqi civilians increased particularly in Baghdad after the coalition bombing in January 1991. Electricity was out, the water system did not function, disease was rampant, medicines were in short supply, nutrition was greatly reduced, infant mortality shot up.

ICRC statements and reports were later confirmed by other actors such as the World Health Organization and a special UN emissary, Martti Ahtiasaari, by March 1991. The sum total of all of these critical reports was finally an adjustment in continuing UN sanctions during the 1990s so as to allow more food and medicines to reach the Iraqi population. The ICRC had been a leader in this effort for the civilian population in Iraq, not only by issuing reports and press statements, but also by President Sommaruga's meeting directly with US, British, French, UN, and other officials to press the humanitarian arguments in behalf of Iraqi civilians.

On this and on other subjects, the ICRC persistently manifested an effort to display independence from the United States and other western governments that were the driving forces behind coalition and UN policies. The ICRC stressed a "global approach" to various problems in quest of protecting its neutral image. True, as noted above, Sommaruga's trip to Baghdad in September of 1990 could appear as hasty humanitarian diplomacy occasioned by western pressure. Otherwise, however, the ICRC did not hesitate to raise questions about the policies of the United States and its allies. It did so, as noted, regarding the wisdom of general economic sanctions that greatly harmed the Iraqi population. It objected to the appearance of Iraqi POWs on western television, the public display of POWs being prohibited by the Third GC of 1949. It pressed Saudi Arabia for not promptly registering the Iraqi POWs turned over to it after capture

---

[10] Girod is circumspect on this issue, it is hard to read as to where he finally comes down on this matter. His account was supplemented by interviews in Geneva.

by coalition forces, although after the start of the coalition's land war in January the sheer numbers of these POWs made prompt registration impossible. (Saudi Arabia never did fulfill its obligations in this regard, and since the United States and other coalition partners were indifferent about this matter, the ICRC itself finally registered Iraqi POWs as part of the process of ascertaining their voluntary cooperation for repatriation after the conflict.)

The organization advised states not to use weapons of mass destruction in ways that violated IHL, this advice being directed primarily toward the United States and Israel. The ICRC feared that these states might resort to nuclear weapons in retaliation for some Iraqi policy – perhaps the use of chemical weapons. The organization tried to get the western-based press to show concern for civilians affected by coalition military measures, but that press was more interested in the fate of coalition POWs.

Even though Iraq was never to cooperate with the ICRC to any great extent during the conflict for control of Kuwait, and even though Baghdad repeatedly committed serious violations of IHL, the ICRC sought to maintain an image independent from the United States and its military coalition, and the UN. Even when Iraq refused the ICRC access to captured coalition pilots, or abused those pilots, or abused civilians in occupied Kuwait, the ICRC still strove for independence, neutrality, and impartiality in its operations.[11]

As part of this pursuit, the ICRC was mostly silent about the specifics of Iraqi violations of IHL. Likewise, the ICRC had not publicly protested the Iraqi gassing of ethnic Kurds at Halabja in 1988. Only in the dying days of active combat in 1991, when Iraq was clearly the defeated party, did the ICRC blow the whistle publicly about specific Iraqi actions. This policy certainly raised some questions. Is it that the organization is protecting its reputation for serious attention to humanitarian standards (something it did not do when it remained silent about the Holocaust)? But what is the point of specific public statements if they come very late and are only directed against defeated or weaker parties? But at what point does hope for cooperation from a recalcitrant party yield to an effort at specific public pressure, even if such publicity firmly closes the door on access to victims?

---

[11] It is worth noting in passing that Mikhail Gorbachev in February 1991 took up with Baghdad the question of detained coalition pilots, to no avail. Certainly this was one of the very few occasions in which an official of the Soviet Union lobbied for greater attention to IHL. But then the Soviet Union in 1991 was not the same state that it had been earlier.

Finally allowed into Kuwait after the expulsion of Iraqi forces, the ICRC met halting cooperation from Kuwaiti officials restored to power by the coalition's intervention. The organization's desire to supervise detention conditions met with only slow and partial success, and when ICRC delegates started their detention visits they found alarming situations. This was not the first war where violations of humanitarian standards were committed by those who had just been victimized by their adversaries. The ICRC found not only ample reason for regular detention visits in Kuwait but also the need to follow various judicial proceedings in an effort to monitor those procedures for conformity to IHL. There were also brutal deportations, especially of Palestinians whose leaders had lined up with Saddam Hussein, that the ICRC observed but could not prevent.

Staying on in Iraq beyond the end of combat in the spring of 1991, ICRC delegates, along with the rest of the world, knew of Saddam Hussein's brutal repression of Iraqi Kurds in the north and Iraqi Shi'ites in the south. After a review of the situation by ICRC headquarters in Geneva, the organization decided not to protest publicly over what its delegates had observed. As ever, there was hope for more cooperation from the Saddam regime through quiet diplomacy. Then there was the fact that the situation was arguably one of civil war regulated by the sparse provisions of Common Article Three from 1949, Iraq not having ratified Protocol II from 1977. Despite the failure of its discreet diplomacy with Baghdad to have produced much in the past by way of humanitarian advance, the ICRC remained silent about the massacres. As already noted, it had remained silent about Saddam's suppression of a Kurdish uprising in 1988 through the use of poison gas against civilians. On the other hand, the ICRC had issued public statements about the coalition's bombing of Iraq during the combat of early 1991, even though the violations of humanitarian norms, involving the vague concept of collateral damage, were much less clear.[12]

Not surprisingly, in the north of Iraq in the late spring of 1991, where certain western states had carved out a zone free from Baghdad's control, the American, British, and French Red Cross Societies acted as extensions of their states. There was no pretense of operating under the leadership of the ICRC as called for by Movement guidelines. These National Societies

---

[12] In chapter 2, we noted that in retrospect some ICRC officials thought that, in the Vietnam war, the organization should have raised more questions about US bombing policies. On the one hand, one could not fairly accuse the ICRC of consistently tilting toward the US and coalition forces regarding Iraq in 1990–91. But one could raise questions about inconsistent policies regarding the taking of public positions.

were more quasi-governmental agencies than units of an integrated Red Cross Movement. The ICRC did not contest these facts, but rather left these completely nationalized Red Cross agencies to their own plans, while looking to establish completely separate ICRC programs in areas where the United Nations refugee office (UNHCR) was not active so as to help internally displaced persons.

The Balkans, 1991–1995

The world does not stop turning so the ICRC can prioritize its activities. Such was the case back in the late 1960s when the Nigerian civil war and the third Arab-Israeli war occurred at more or less the same time, along with other entanglements for the ICRC. For that matter, it was "inconvenient" in 1956 for the Hungarian and Suez crises to occur almost simultaneously. After the Cold War, the Persian Gulf was not the only area requiring humanitarian attention. The Balkans was also deteriorating into a humanitarian disaster.

As Slobodan Milosevic stoked the fires of ethnic nationalism through his maneuvers for a dominant Serbia within federal Yugoslavia, this provoked independence movements in Slovenia and Croatia.[13] Milosevic did not really care about Slovenia, since few Serbs lived there, and a semi-comic, two-week war left Slovenia independent. Croatia was a different matter, with a large Serb minority at risk from a Croat government manifesting its own version of chauvinistic nationalism. But the major problem was to be Bosnia and Herzegovina, which initially was not in favor of independence from Yugoslavia, because it was hard to foresee peace and prosperity for its multi-ethnic population in a region being destroyed by ethnic passions. In addition to those who identified as Yugoslav, Bosnia was made up of Serbs, Croats, and Muslims.

As events spiraled downward into a humanitarian catastrophe, the ICRC came to play an important if frustrating role. Its importance can be seen in the fact that various levels of the ICRC were in constant touch with international mediators and others trying to manage the conflict; the ICRC was an important player in many negotiations.[14] In addition to

---

[13] From a voluminous literature see especially Warren Zimmermann, *Origins of a Catastrophe* (New York: Times Books, 1996), and his *War in the Balkans* (New York: Council on Foreign Relations, 1999); see also Misha Glenny, *The Fall of Yugoslavia* (London: Penguin, 3rd edn, 1996).

[14] See, for example, David Owen, *Balkan Odyssey* (New York: Harcourt Brace, 1995).

trying to perform its traditional detention visits, the organization came to manage the second-largest civilian relief operation for that theatre, second in size only to that of the UN refugee office. Particularly with regard to relief, for a considerable time the major states trying to manage the conflict used the ICRC and other humanitarian actors as a substitute for decisive involvement. During most of 1991–95, the United States and its European allies avoided hard decisions that would cost them significant blood and treasure. Instead, they "hid behind" the ICRC and various UN actors, plus the NGOs that worked with UN agencies.

The western states tried to give the impression of doing something about the horrible things happening to the people of the Balkans, in order to satisfy those from the media and broader publics who were demanding that something be done about the atrocities.[15] But in the early 1990s the US Secretary of State, Warren Christopher, articulated the view of many outsiders when he characterized Balkan events as constituting a "problem from hell."[16] Fearing another Vietnam, and after the autumn of 1993 fearing another Somalia, and consistent with the lack of western intervention in Rwanda in 1994, the United States and most other western states did not want to place troops on the ground – given the brutally Machiavellian policies of all the principal parties in this conflict.

With regard to the general civilian population, the ICRC was left with the choice of helping to move people out of harm's way, and thus contributing to the ethnic cleansing desired by some belligerents, or seeing civilians killed. International humanitarian law was not supposed to allow this, but IHL in the Balkans was largely "Potemkin law," divorced from any power to enforce. Faced with this Hobbesian choice, the ICRC could only withdraw or help persons relocate. As a general orientation, it chose the latter, especially since the local population besieged it to do exactly that.[17]

---

[15] This was the same logic that led to the western-dominated UN Security Council creating the International Criminal Tribunal for the former Yugoslavia in 1993.

[16] See Samantha Power, "A Problem from Hell": America and the Age of Genocide (New York: HarperCollins, 2002).

[17] The ICRC obtained all sorts of paper agreements among the fighting parties endorsing humanitarian principles and in particular the protection of civilians, but these proved worthless in effectively regulating humanitarian protection on the ground. The agreements may have had some legal significance for the ICTY. Likewise an extensive ICRC dissemination program fell on deaf ears. See further Erin D. Mooney, "Presence, Ergo Protection? UNPROFOR, UNHCR, and the ICRC in Croatia and Bosnia and Herzegovina," International Journal of Refugee Law, 7 no 3 (summer 1995), 407–35.

From the late 1980s the ICRC had been maintaining a dialogue with various levels of federal Yugoslavia with regard to detention matters, especially pertaining to Kosovo.[18] Eventually the organization received permission to see what Belgrade explicitly called convicted political prisoners. But as had happened so often elsewhere, the ICRC was denied access to political prisoners arrested and undergoing interrogation. Once again the ICRC accepted partial access. This time the organization was able to get authorization within a couple of years to see all political prisoners.

It was against this background that the ICRC successfully mediated various prisoner issues during and after the Yugoslav–Slovene fighting. Avoiding the legal debate about whether this was an international armed conflict with prisoners of war (as seen by Slovenia) or some type of internal armed conflict where one does not have, legally speaking, POWs (as seen by Belgrade), the ICRC concentrated on practical humanitarian progress.

Detention activities, plus the usual contacts with various parts of the Yugoslav Red Cross, left the ICRC well positioned when actual fighting broke out during late summer 1991. Even so, there was a "shocking" lack of ICRC resources devoted to this region during the fall of 1991. The UNHCR was not yet involved, Doctors Without Borders was concentrating on medical affairs, and the ICRC found itself virtually alone in dealing with growing numbers of displaced civilians, particularly as the fighting evolved between Croatia and Serbia. Given the early limited role by the ICRC, when it had only about fifty persons in the field and was also heavily engaged in Iraq and Somalia, the UNHCR and UNICEF began to expand their field operations in the region. The ICRC was well positioned and knowledgeable about Balkan affairs, but it was still a small agency stretched very thin from its global role. The organization was eventually to field almost 1,000 persons to cope with war in the Balkans.

The drift of things was forecast by events at Vukovar in November 1991. The ICRC managed to get one, then two of its delegates into this Croatian city that had fallen to the Serbs. As the ICRC tried to neutralize the main hospital and register as many patients as possible, its delegates met with repeated obstructionism. With the delegates negotiating in the front of the building, patients were being taken out the back, never to be seen alive

---

[18] Unless otherwise noted, this section is based on Michèle Mercier, *Crimes sans châtiment: l'action humanitaire en ex-Yougoslavie 1991–1993* (Brussels: Bruylant, 1994). Mercier was an ICRC official. A later English edition was published.

again.[19] Most women, children, and senior males were allowed to leave the city; in this ethnic cleansing the Serb authorities allowed an ICRC presence. But younger males were detained; the ICRC was not allowed to register them, much less visit them systematically; many went "missing."

From the beginning of this conflict, the ICRC manifested good relations with the UNHCR and other UN agencies. It was with the agreement of the ICRC that in early 1992 the UNHCR became the lead agency for dealing with displaced civilian populations, particularly as the fighting expanded between Croatia and Serbia and then spilled over into Bosnia. The ICRC and UNHCR repeatedly agreed on who was to do what, and where, throughout the early 1990s. Sometimes the ICRC and the UNHCR would give joint press conferences.

The ICRC often had better relations with the UNHCR and UNICEF and the World Food Programme than it did with some units of the Red Cross Movement. The ICRC knew, but was powerless to correct, the fact that some units of the Red Cross Movement were extorting people in distress. The Red Cross Society attached to Bosnian Serbia, headed by the wife of Radovan Karadic, the chauvinistic politician later indicted for various crimes by the ICTY, sometimes helped Croat or Muslim civilians out of harm's way only in return for payment of fees. This Red Cross unit in particular was as corrupt as many other organizations and networks in the Balkans. It was anything but impartial and neutral; it certainly was not a reliable partner in humanitarian protection for the ICRC.[20] But then, much the same could be said for many other Red Cross or Red Crescent Societies or their sub-units in this theatre of conflict.

Some ICRC officials were looking to the Movement Conference in Budapest in 1991 to bring some unity and coherent humanitarian action to the Balkans. When that meeting was cancelled because of disagreement over how to treat a Palestinian delegation, these officials were disappointed. But it was a pipe dream to think that the Red Cross Conference could bring a coherent humanitarian program to the fragmented and brutal Balkans.

---

[19] Jean-François Berger is blunt; they were summarily executed. *The Humanitarian Diplomacy of the ICRC and the Conflict in Croatia 1991–1992)* (Geneva: ICRC, 1995), 23. This work chronicles, among other things, the efforts of the organization to bring the representatives of the Croats and Serbs to Geneva in order to arrive at agreements on detention, relief, tracing, and complaints about IHL. This study notes as well the violation of the signed agreements by both sides.

[20] In the last chapter we noted that the ICRC finally, after the Bosnian war, asked Ms. Karadic to step down as local Red Cross official, under the pretext of problems with donors.

In May 1992 the ICRC head of Delegation for Bosnia, Frédéric Maurice, was killed outside of Sarajevo when his convoy, although clearly marked with the Red Cross emblem and following a route agreed upon in advance by the belligerents, was intentionally fired upon. The organization never aired its views about the source of the attack, only stressing its intentional nature. This incident was similar to the one in Chechnya in 1996 in which six Red Cross workers were intentionally murdered at night in their residence.[21] The incident claiming the life of Maurice, shocking to Geneva, caused the organization to withdraw from Sarajevo for seven months. Some, including several within the ICRC, think that top ICRC leaders overreacted and that the organization withdrew for too long a period. So the argument went, the organization should have seen from the continuing efforts of the UNHCR and other aid agencies that field operations in that area could be continued, even if they remained risky. The ICRC did resume operations in the rest of Bosnia from mid-summer 1992. In certain places its delegates used passive security measures such as flak jackets and armored vehicles. Other aid agencies, like Doctors Without Borders and the UNHCR, were also subjected to intentional attacks and lesser harassment.

From the summer of 1992 the ICRC went public with its concerns in a general way, having seen Maurice intentionally killed, its other delegates harassed and blocked and stalled, and numerous humanitarian agreements effectively shredded by the brutal behavior of the fighting parties. The ICRC did not name names or give details, but there was no doubt about what was occurring in the Balkans.[22] These ICRC statements

---

[21] The attack in Bosnia could have been done by either side. The Bosnian leadership was known to have blocked for a time the resumption of the water supply for Sarajevo, because the situation was producing media coverage in the West that was calculated to increase the chances of a significant western intervention. So Bosnian authorities were not averse to creating hardship for their own citizens if it might bring the western states in on their side. On the Serb side of the siege of Sarajevo, it was clear that snipers were targeting civilians to spread terror and increase Muslim flight. The Serb general in charge of the Sarajevo sector was convicted by the ICTY for ordering, or allowing, these attacks on civilians.

   Likewise in Chechnya, either the Russian or the separatist side could have wanted the ICRC and other western-based groups out of the area. Both sides were known to have used brutal tactics and would not have wanted a western-based organization to see what was occurring. Each side sought to cow the civilian population into denying support to the other side, and neither side regularly observed established human rights or humanitarian standards. Fred Cuny, the well-known American humanitarian consultant, was killed by the Chechnyan side, but the Russian record on humanitarian matters was, and is, hardly better.

[22] The "new" ICRC policy on public statements was not all that different from the old. The organization made more statements, but they remained general, often commenting on the behavior of all belligerents, and omitting the kind of detail published by human

and speeches had no discernible impact on western states – the states with the power to stop ethnic cleansing and other atrocities. What would be decisive was "political" humanitarianism, military force to compel the protagonists to respect the rules of the game. This was the kind of humanitarianism that the independent and neutral ICRC could call for but not participate in. It was left with appealing to law and the honor of the belligerents, but in the Balkans there were mostly warriors without honor.[23]

Special meetings of the UN Human Rights Commission and reports from its special rapporteur on former Yugoslavia did not cause outsiders to intervene decisively to stop either Serb aggression or various atrocities by various actors. The UN special rapporteur, the former Polish Prime Minister Tadeusz Mazowiecki, who had been briefed extensively by the ICRC, resigned in protest over the lack of response to his reports, but this, too, failed to move western states. For most of 1991–95 these states lacked honor too, being more interested in public relations maneuvers than stopping an ethnic cleansing that sometimes constituted genocide.

What seemed to change things briefly was British television coverage of Serb-run concentration camps during the late summer of 1992. This and other media exposure of the horrifying facts of ethnic war in the Balkans, such as by Roy Gutman in *Newsday* during early August, did result in better ICRC access to those detained, as well as increased unease over policies by western governments. The ICRC, in fact, confirmed what Gutman wrote. Also, ICRC officials cooperated quietly with both television and print journalists to spread the word about general detention conditions and other humanitarian problems. "In the former Yugoslavia, the ICRC's public story offered emotionally charged but ethnically neutral descriptions of humanitarian tragedy, whereas the private back-channel story, told by its delegates and high officials, did not hesitate to attribute blame and responsibility and recommend political action."[24]

In the brutal fighting in former Yugoslavia, the ICRC was determined not to be charged again, as it had been after 1942–45, with remaining silent in the face of atrocities. So in addition to making lots of general press statements, it cooperated quietly with journalists. Yet ethnic

---

rights advocacy groups. See Delorenzi, *ICRC Policy*, 51; and Mooney, "Presence, Ergo Protection," 426.

[23] Ignatieff, *The Warrior's Honor*.

[24] Michael Ignatieff, "Television and Humanitarian Aid," in Jonathan Moore, ed., *Hard Choices: Moral Dilemmas in Humanitarian Intervention* (Lanham, MD: Rowman and Littlefield, 1998), 296. This book project was supported by the ICRC. See also Roy Gutman, *Witness to Genocide* (Middletown, WI: Lisa Drew, 1993).

cleansing and other attacks on non-combatants continued by both Serb and Croat parties, while the Muslim authorities in Bosnia compiled their own record of illiberal maneuvers. The Prosecutor's office of the ICTY studied whether to indict President Alija Izetbegovic, who died in 2003, for various violations of international law.

All parties engaged in rape as a weapon of war, including the rape of men. The ICRC persistently refused to confirm the much-used figure of 20,000 women subjected to rape. Some ICRC officials thought that figure had been "politicized" by groups trying to emphasize the issue.

On the other hand, the ICRC persistently stuck to its figure of slightly over 7,000 males missing in connection with the massacre at Srebrenica in July 1995. Events there were bad enough without any controversy over the exact number killed, and the basic facts are now well known at least to those who follow international relations.[25] A UN safe haven, supposedly under UN protection, but sometimes used by Muslim parties to make military raids, was taken over by Bosnian Serbs, who expelled the Dutch peacekeeping detachment, then proceeded to kill a large number of Muslim males while allowing women, children, and senior males to leave. The ICRC was promised access to detainees for its traditional role but was never granted it. Those outside parties who were interested in the use of force to compel Serb moderation fought an uphill and finally futile battle.[26] This situation left the ICRC without powerful support, and left key Serb parties free to stall the organization while proceeding to implement their planned slaughter.

In her widely acclaimed book about genocide, Samantha Power is very critical of the ICRC in the Srebrenica affair.[27] Two ICRC officials, however, on the basis of their information about the massacre, but before the press picked up the story, went to Ratko Mladic, the Bosnian Serb Commander responsible, and confronted him with their findings. They demanded an accounting, but predictably he was not forthcoming.

After the fact the ICRC spent a great deal of time constructing a list of the missing, hence the figure of slightly more than 7,000 killed. If so, this would be the worst massacre in Europe since the Second World War. Thus far forensic examinations have failed to account for 7,000 bodies,

---

[25] See especially David Rohde, *End Game: The Betrayal and Fall of Srebrenica, Europe's Worst Massacre since World War II* (Boulder: Westview, 1997), which won a Pulitzer Prize.

[26] Richard Holbrooke, *To End a War* (New York: Random House, 1998), 70.

[27] *Problem from Hell*, 411.

but it is quite possible that Serb parties tampered with the mass graves.[28] Mladic, indicted by the ICTY, has yet to be arrested. At the time of writing the ICTY has convicted one Bosnian Serb military official for genocide because of his role at Srebrenica.[29] It was clear that the killing derived from premeditated mass murder, and not from combat or mistaken ambushes.

Srebrenica did finally produce some western military pressure on the Serbs through UN-approved NATO air strikes. This, plus western support for a Croat–Muslim coalition to offset Serb power, along with US mediation of the 1995 Dayton Accords, finally brought the worst of the fighting and atrocities in the Balkans to a close.[30] Conflict over Kosovo would produce more NATO air strikes in 1999.

The ICRC was left with an all too keen awareness of the limits of its neutral humanitarianism. One delegate talked about an "inventory of impotence" and how "the deserving efforts of a delegate isolated in a world ruled by anarchy are utterly wasted."[31] Yet according to one journalist who is not a persistent admirer of the ICRC, "The honor of the world was redeemed in Bosnia by those who worked for the NGOs, the nongovernmental aid organizations, the International Committee of the Red Cross, and the Office of the United Nations High Commissioner for Refugees."[32]

Somalia, 1991–1992

An ICRC humanitarian presence was no less complicated in Somalia – a patchwork of former British and Italian territories that has never known much stability since its independence in the summer of 1960.[33] Caught up in the Cold War, with first the Soviets and then the Americans propping up a shaky central government, and damaged by a long war with Ethiopia, Somalia degenerated into chronic clan fighting as the Cold War wound down. From early 1991 there was no effective central government as strongman Siad Barre fled the country. The ICRC, already present in the country to deal with prisoner matters, was doing what it could to

---

[28] See further Rohde, *End Game*, 348.
[29] *Prosecutor v. Krstic* (Case No: IT-98–33-A), Judgment, 19 April 2004.
[30] See further Holbrooke, *To End a War*.   [31] Mercier, *Crimes sans châtiment*.
[32] David Rieff, *Slaughterhouse: Bosnia and the Failure of the West* (New York: Simon & Schuster, 1995), 190.
[33] In addition to the sources indicated, this section is based on interviewing in Geneva and elsewhere.

aid the civilian population, despite the killing of one of its Belgian staff members in late 1991.

In the winter of 1991 to 1992 the scale of clan fighting, with attendant civilian distress, attracted international attention. This was in part because the ICRC, with some reluctance about the ethics involved, paid for journalists to come see the misery at first hand. "[I]n the course of five weeks between August and September . . . 730 journalists were brought from Nairobi into Somalia and transported back to Kenya, briefed and otherwise taken care of by the ICRC."[34] This effort, along with publicity from other groups, finally produced coverage by the *New York Times*, the BBC, *Le Monde*, and other major western media centers. The office of the UN Secretary-General, already concerned that the Balkan wars were getting more attention than African problems, attempted mediation, and the Security Council imposed an arms embargo and called for humanitarian assistance. The Council decreed that to interfere with that assistance was a war crime, but various Somali armed groups paid little attention to such legalistic statements emanating from New York. After all, this was a country in which "virtually no one with a weapon had heard of the Geneva Conventions."[35] The Somali clans and sub-clans fought for territory and status and power, while they and still others fought to seize the relief. Rice became the most important currency in the country.[36]

By early 1992, both governments and the few international agencies that stayed in Somalia were reporting a famine of massive dimensions, worse than the Ethiopian famine of 1984–85. The ICRC, with a few other NGOs, stayed on during the toughest times, as the UN relief agencies first bickered among themselves and then withdrew to neighboring Nairobi. The performance was so poor among most UN agencies that even an ICRC delegate was led to criticize them publicly.[37] The Organization of African Unity was impotent. The new UN field mission (UNOSOM I), authorized by the Security Council, was ineffective both at delivering relief on a large scale, and at providing general security. By mid-summer

---

[34] Claudio Caratsch, "Humanitarian Design and Political Interference," *International Relations*, 11 (April 1993), 308.

[35] Jennifer Leaning, "When the System Doesn't Work: Somalia 1992," in Kevin M. Cahill, *A Framework for Survival: Health, Human Rights, and Humanitarian Assistance in Conflicts and Disasters* (New York: Basic Books, for the Council on Foreign Relations, 1993), 112.

[36] Lori Fisler Damrosch, ed., *Enforcing Restraint: Collective Intervention in Internal Conflicts* (New York: Council on Foreign Relations, 1993); and James Mayall, *The New Interventionism, 1991–1994* (Cambridge: Cambridge University Press, 1996).

[37] *Ibid.*, 238, n. 17.

of 1992, the ICRC reported that 95% of Somalis showed malnutrition, with 70% "enduring severe malnutrition."[38]

During 1992 the ICRC made heroic efforts.

> [B]etween February and June 1992 the ICRC brought in a total of 53,900 MT of food into Somalia through twenty different entry points, by sea, by air, and overland across the Kenya–Somalia border. Multiple delivery points at small locations circumvented the extortion network that was centered on Mogadishu.[39] The ICRC operated 400 kitchens, feeding more than 600,000 people in Mogadishu and six other towns. These small community kitchens, created to avoid the looting of large stockpiles and to protect women and children who did not have to travel long distances, provided up to two cooked meals daily. The ICRC also handled the distribution of food to several hospitals in various cities and sustained daily rotations of airlift delivery from Mombasa, Kenya, to Mogadishu, Belet Uen, and Baidoa. Most of the US food sent to Somalia was handled by the ICRC.[40]

The ICRC was larger, better organized, and with better local contacts than others. It was clear that the ICRC, working with the Somali Red Crescent, had the best network in the country for distribution of food and other relief, especially in rural areas.[41]

It was not as if the ICRC and the Somali Red Crescent had a long and close history. Rather, in the early 1990s the ICRC found that the leaders of the Somali Red Crescent were independent from the major clans vying for control of Mogadishu and the putative central government. So the ICRC built up the local capacity of the National Society as a hasty and expedient measure. The Norwegian Red Cross Society played an especially helpful role, and a few other National Societies also helped. But back in about 1990, the Somali Red Crescent had been as weak and non-operational as many other National Societies in the underdeveloped countries.

Despite impressive efforts, the ICRC itself was too small and too committed elsewhere in the world (e.g., in Iraq and the Balkans) to provide

---

[38] Ibid., 212.

[39] See further John Prendergast, Frontline Diplomacy: Humanitarian Aid and Conflict in Africa (Boulder: Lynne Rienner, 1996), 69.

[40] Mohamed Sahnoun, Somalia: The Missed Opportunities (Washington: US Institute of Peace Press, 1994), 20–1. Sahnoun, an Algerian diplomat, was the Special Representative of the UN Secretary-General in Somalia and first head of UNOSOM I. The number of 400 kitchens may be too low by almost half.

[41] See further Jane Perlez, "Accord Reached, Somalia Airlift Will Start Today," New York Times, 28 August 1992, A3.

the scale of relief needed, despite committing about one third of its field budget and one half of all its relief programs to Somalia during this time. In mid-1992 the ICRC's relief in Somalia, which reached about 1.5 million beneficiaries, was greater than in Cambodia (and Thailand) a decade earlier, although its relief effort in Bosnia was to be even larger. In August 1992, the ICRC reached a paradoxical agreement with a few western military establishments. These latter flew in relief via unarmed planes as demanded by the ICRC, consistent with its neutral and supervising role in other places like the Sudan and Ethiopia. Then the ICRC arranged ground transport as protected by local armed groups. The air bridge would be military but unarmed; the neutral Red Cross convoys would have armed protection – not against the "political" clans but against looters. It was clear over time that this arrangement was not a full solution to starvation in Somalia.

Given the inability of the United Nations to bring stability to Somalia, either through mediation or through military deployment, the George H. G. Bush Administration, with Security Council approval, deployed almost 30,000 troops in late 1992 to guarantee the delivery of humanitarian relief primarily through the Red Cross network.[42] The ICRC, after debate in its Assembly, and with strong support from President Sommaruga, agreed to work in tandem with these military forces. This was a first in ICRC history. (In the Balkans, the ICRC agreed that some liberated prisoners should be protected by UNPROFOR, the UN security mission, as they made their way through dangerous areas where snipers were known to exist.) The US military deployment in Somalia, called Operation Restore Hope in Washington and UNITAF in New York, while officially the backbone of a UN enforcement operation under Chapter VII of the UN Charter, had the quiet approval of the major clans in the country. The military force was therefore initially directed at providing a secure environment for humanitarian relief directed by the ICRC on the ground, and not at coercion against any major clan or clan leader. This is a main reason why ICRC cooperation was forthcoming, as an exceptional matter, for relief under military protection. It was also the case that as a pragmatic matter, ICRC cooperation with the US military, under an international mandate, would be necessary to reduce starvation in Somalia. No other relief agency was positioned to do it.

---

[42] A good overview, with lots of facts and figures, concentrating on UN–US relations, can be found in Thomas G. Weiss, *Military Civilian Interactions: Intervening in Humanitarian Crises* (Lanham, MD: Rowman and Littlefield, 1999), 69–96.

Since even 20,000–30,000 soldiers were insufficient to guarantee security in the country, the ICRC continued to employ local armed units in areas not protected by the western troops. ICRC payment at the rate of about 4 dollars per day to perhaps 500–600 armed guards at any one time made only a small contribution to the war economy. Even considering that the "technicals," modified vehicles with perhaps a mounted machine gun in the back, went for about 40 dollars a day, this ICRC contribution to the local war economy remained slight. Other "security" units were on the ICRC payroll as a type of "insurance" against disruption of relief. But it was hardly the case that ICRC payments to local forces kept the war going or added up to a major economic dimension to the war. ICRC expenditures for security paled against the spending on arms that flooded the country. The ICRC used the Somali Red Crescent as well as its own experience to identify reliable local partners.[43]

Two contradictory trends were evident in Somalia during 1993. First, large-scale relief under military protection – with the ICRC playing a key role – increasingly broke the back of massive starvation, as the complex international military presence brought much of the looting under control. (There was the US-directed large military force: there was the new UNOSOM II including a few Americans serving under Turkish command, and there was a smaller US rapid reaction force directed by Admiral Howe of the US Navy.) Looting, which had disrupted possibly up to 80% of food relief in some areas, was now back down to perhaps 10%. Somewhat later the ICRC abandoned the "soup kitchens" for fear of perpetuating dependency. Once the famine was under control, the organization did not want the feeding centers to lure Somalis away from their usual farming and other commercial ventures.

Secondly, not only was there persistent fighting by various clans and sub-clans for political control of Mogidishu and other areas, but also the international presence was increasingly at odds with the Habar-Gedir sub-clan of the Hawiye clan, led by Mohammed Farah Aideed. It was this latter conflict, comprised of a whole series of incidents and clashes and rumors, that led to the fateful events of October 1993. After the US Delta and Ranger teams of the independent rapid reaction force botched a

---

[43] Even this system of protection was exceedingly complex. To demonstrate which "technicals" were associated with the ICRC rather than some "political" clan, the organization wound up having a daily code. On a given Monday, ICRC "technicals" would display an "A." On Tuesday it might be "M." Thus ICRC officials, and others with a need to know, could discern who was protecting ICRC relief. Otherwise, all 'technicals" would be carrying some sort of Red Cross/Red Crescent emblem.

snatch and seize operation against Aideed's lieutenants, and then suffered eighteen deaths and more casualties, and wound up killing large numbers of Somalis, the US effectively withdrew from Somalia by the spring of 1994. Because of US shifting policies, starting in 1994 Somalia found itself once again an insignificant backwater in western-dominated international relations. The UN Security Council and other outside parties lost interest in the fate of an apparently ungovernable Somalia, and as of the time of writing still no stable, effective, central government existed there. The nutritional situation, however, was not as bad as it was between 1991 and 1993, and there were intermittent negotiations about the composition of a central government.

In 1994, however, the ICRC was forced to remove its expatriate delegates to Nairobi. The organization was trying to operate in the midst of a series of kidnappings for ransom. As it was to do in Chechnya after 1996 and also in Iraq in 2003, it relocated its foreign personnel across the border, from where it supervised relief convoys run by local Somalis. Again the Somali Red Crescent was instrumental in identifying reliable partners. The ICRC paid via cash deposits in a Nairobi bank after each mission, thus creating a secure payment system that could not be looted inside Somalia. It left to the locals the security of the convoys. If one clan or sub-clan interfered, there would be retaliation from the clan or sub-clan that stood to lose goods and money. The system worked, demonstrating yet again the creative pragmatism of the ICRC in the field. This was not exactly a system foreseen by IHL.

Perhaps the one blemish on the ICRC record in Somalia was the behavior of some of its male delegates, who became socially involved with Somali women, thus projecting the organization into clan competition. Others got involved with Somali women or girls in Nairobi, likewise creating problems for the image and operations of the organization. These problems, not as great as the ICRC faced (or itself created) in Angola, and not nearly as great as the UN faced because of the behavior of some of its peacekeeping personnel in the Balkans and other places, nevertheless did complicate the ICRC's field presence. These problems usually led to the quick recall of the delegate in question. All of this reminded one of the ICRC presence in Nigeria at the time of August Lindt, and demonstrated that the ICRC still did not have a perfect policy regarding its delegates socializing with locals in a theatre of sensitive operations.[44]

---

[44] There has been a sizeable problem involving the exploitation of women and girls through an international presence in and after wars, complex emergencies, and failed states. The

Yet overall the ICRC record in Somalia is impressive. One analyst wrote the following:

> At least one chapter in the history of the response to the Somali crisis offers inspiration. When the final saga is written, the profiles in courage that will emerge are those of the staff members of the ICRC and four private relief agencies that stayed in Somalia during the darkest days of the civil war and the subsequent mayhem ... [These NGOs] and the ICRC basically assumed the role the UN relief agencies traditionally played, and in the process saved untold thousands of lives.[45]

Other field work

Of course the ICRC was involved in many other conflicts after the Cold War in addition to Iraq–Kuwait, the Balkans, Somalia, and the "war" on terrorism. These four cases, however, give a good indication of the complicated field work of the ICRC in international armed conflict, internationalized internal wars, and complex emergencies or failed states. The cases do not, of course, capture all the difficulties of ICRC field operations in places

UNHCR and various UN peace operations have drawn most of the attention in places like East Africa, the Balkans, and Southeast Asia. Beyond the topics of sexual trafficking in women and girls, pedophilia, forced prostitution, coerced sexual favors, contribution to various sexually transmitted diseases including HIV/AIDS, etc., there is the more general issue of whether it is appropriate for officially mandated expatriates to socialize in intimate ways with the beneficiaries of their presence.

For the ICRC in Somalia, some delegates socialized with parts of the local population who were not direct beneficiaries of their humanitarian work. There seems to be no case where the women in question were direct beneficiaries of ICRC relief. But even this practice, which sometimes presented no problems in other locales, did complicate the ICRC role when clan competition and resentment resulted. On particular topics of clear sexual misconduct such as pedophilia, in places like Nairobi, the ICRC seems to constitute a very small part of the larger story. On the more general question of intimate socializing with parts of the local population that can complicate the official mission, the ICRC has a very permissive attitude. After all, what is wrong with delegates meeting and falling in love with and eventually marrying someone from the local population?

With regard mostly to UN actors, and the NGOs that subcontract with UN agencies, see for example: Human Rights Watch, *Uncertain Refuge: International Failures to Protect Refugees* (New York: Human Rights Watch, 1997); UNHCR, "Note for Implementing and Operational Partners by UNHCR and Save the Children-UK on Sexual Violence and Exploitation," 26 February 2002, www.relief web; InterAction, "Report of the Task Force on Protection from Sexual Exploitation and Abuse in Humanitarian Crises and Plan of Action," www.interaction.org, 20 August 2002; A Naik, "UN Investigation into Sexual Exploitation by Aid Workers: Justice Has Not Been Done," *Forced Migration Review*, 16 (2003), 46–7; Charlotte Lindsey, *Women Facing War* (Geneva: ICRC, 2001).

[45] Jeffrey Clark, "Somalia," in Damrosch, *Enforcing Restraint*, 228.

like Chechnya, former Zaire, East Timor, Colombia, Liberia, Sudan, and so on.[46] A brief word, however, is in order concerning Rwanda.[47]

In Rwanda in 1994, when militant Hutus unleashed genocidal attacks on Tutsis (as well as attacks on moderate Hutus interested in social accommodation and power sharing), the ICRC stayed in-country and provided what aid and shelter it could. It thus helped about 50,000 Tutsi, at the price of not denouncing the genocide that claimed perhaps 800,000 lives. It certainly tried to make known to the outside world what was transpiring in Rwanda, but without using the term genocide. At this time, important outside actors with the ability to intervene, like the United States, avoided the term genocide. They did so in order to avoid the legal obligation, as a party to the 1948 Genocide Convention, to take action to stop the genocide. Whether ICRC public use of the word genocide would have affected policy makers in the United States is an interesting question. But as with other aid agencies in Rwanda, the ICRC could not have passed legal judgment on the nature of the conflict and remained operative inside the country. Militant Hutus had made that very clear. The ICRC did protest the intentional mass killings, but without using the "G" word. Most ICRC personnel were not harmed by those carrying out genocide, despite operating in strategically valuable locales, with the exception of some Rwandan female nurses working in conjunction with the ICRC.[48]

It was highly ironic, given the history of things, that field operatives of Médecins Sans Frontières had to be incorporated into the ICRC delegation in Rwanda to survive. Far from being able to denounce human rights or

---

[46] To take one example about the fate of individuals and IHL, see Human Rights Watch, "Russia: Abuses in Chechnya Continue to Cause Human Suffering," press release of 29 January 2003, referring to its new report, "Into Harm's Way," available at www. hrw.org.

[47] For background and overviews see especially Michael Barnett, *Eyewitness to a Genocide: The United Nations and Rwanda* (Ithaca: Cornell University Press, 2002), which is very good at explaining why there was no military intervention to stop genocide; Philip Gourevitch, *We wish to inform you . . .* (New York: Picador, for Farrar, Straus and Giroux, 1999), which provides a readable history but is deficient in explaining the position of the UNHCR in providing relief to refugees; and Joint Evaluation of Emergency Assistance to Rwanda, *The International Response to Conflict and Genocide: Lessons from the Rwanda Experience* (Copenhagen: Steering Committee, 1996), 5 vols., which is essential for understanding the refugee relief effort.

[48] See Lise Boudreaux, "The Role of the International Committee of the Red Cross," in John A. Berry and Carol Pott Berry, eds., *Genocide in Rwanda: A Collective Memory* (Washington, DC: Howard University Press, 1999), 161–4.

IHL violations while remaining operative in the field, MSF representatives had to don the ICRC emblem and keep a relatively low profile in order to avoid being attacked. MSF personnel agreed to the ICRC terms of engagement, namely, to exercise public caution in order to be perceived as neutral. The ICRC rotated its personnel several times, not only to relieve delegate stress but also to that its delegates who observed genocide by the militant Hutus did not become biased against them.

After the slaughter, when the minority Tutsis controlled the new government, the ICRC took the unusual decision to pay for the construction of prisons housing those accused of genocide and other crimes, while awaiting trials. Rwanda, never rich, had been decimated by the fighting and mayhem. A number of lawyers and judges had been killed. The penal system was in a shambles. Being concerned for prisoner conditions, the ICRC felt the only way to change the abysmal conditions for prisoners, who were being held in squalid confinement for long periods, was temporarily, as an exceptional matter, to get into the prison construction business.

The Movement

After the Cold War there were also important developments pertaining to the Movement. In a distinct understatement, one author wrote that "competition . . . has occasionally reared its head within the International Red Cross Movement itself."[49] The Federation did not have the status in international law, or connections to leading governments, that the ICRC had. In a telling comment, in 2000 Canadian George Weber, the retiring Secretary-General of the Federation, was asked: "Which moment has given you the greatest satisfaction?" He replied, "Obtaining the status of permanent observer at the United Nations, in as much as the ICRC and certain members of the [UN] Security Council were not in favor."[50] Strangely, his greatest achievement was not saving so many lives in this or that natural disaster or coping with the big problems in situations here and there. His great accomplishment was matching the status of the ICRC, already a permanent observer at the UN since 1990, especially

[49] Delorenzi, *ICRC Policy*, 75.
[50] "Balance Sheet and Perspectives, Interview with George Weber," *Red Cross, Red Crescent*, Magazine of the Red Cross Movement, volume for the year 2000 (no. 1), 20. Translation from the French edition by the author.

when the ICRC supposedly sought to block that status. So much for humanitarian priorities compared to the importance of organizational competition.[51]

Although we have just reviewed continuing fragmentation of the Red Cross presence in the early 1990s in both the Persian Gulf area and the Balkans, in general there was growing awareness by most of the constituent units of the Movement of the need for improved integration.

One might have thought that major donors like the US Agency for International Development and the US Bureau for Population and Migration, both in the US Department of State, and the European Community Humanitarian Office (ECHO) under the European Union, would have compelled the Movement to cease its internal bickering. Such was not the case. Rather, it seems that particularly the ICRC and the Federation saw that it was in their own best interests to improve relations. There was an increasing number of actors involved in relief, and the fragmented Red Cross with some weak units did not always present the most attractive image to donors and publics. In any event this improved cooperation progressively transpired as one moved toward the turn of the twenty-first century. By the mid-1990s pragmatic managers for both agencies were meeting and coordinating on a regular basis in Geneva. Even at higher levels there was less competition and friction, certainly compared to the 1970s and 1980s. At one point the Federation's Secretary-General, Didier Cherpitel, was invited to address the ICRC Assembly, where he received a standing ovation.

It is in this context that one should view the Seville Agreement of 1997.[52] This accord has the potential to become much more important than previous "peace treaties" between the ICRC and the Federation in 1969, 1974, and 1989. At Seville the members of the Movement's Council of Delegates (namely, representatives of the ICRC, the Federation, and certain National Red Cross or Red Crescent Societies) agreed on and

[51] It might also be noted that when the ICRC sought permanent observer status at the UN, it did so in its own name and not in the name of the broader Movement. When the old ILO building in Geneva became available, before it became the WTO headquarters, it was offered to an integrated Red Cross Movement. The ICRC declined the offer, not wanting to be under the same roof as the Federation. It was said by some at the time that ICRC information about detention visits, etc. was too sensitive to be put at risk in a building housing the multinational secretariat of the Federation.

[52] Reprinted in *International Review of the Red Cross*, 322 (March 1998), 159–76. The rest of the current analysis is drawn from David P. Forsythe, "Refugees and the Red Cross: An Underdeveloped Dimension of Protection," *Working Paper No. 76*, New Issues in Refugee Research, UNHCR, Evaluation and Policy Analysis Unit, January 2003.

further clarified the notion of lead agency in field operations. In practical terms this accord has mostly to do with whether it is the ICRC or the Federation (or on occasion even a National Society) that represents the Movement when dealing with refugees and displaced persons. From the view of the UN refugee office or other UN actors, the Seville agreement specifies which Red Cross actor is the responsible partner in the protection of refugees and others in a refugee-like situation. Hence the agreement has practical as well as symbolic significance.

One way of viewing the Seville Agreement is that it reflects a willingness on the part of the ICRC to curtail some of its previous field operations and to recognize the enhanced competence of the Federation and its partners at the national level. It is for this reason that some members of the ICRC's Assembly disliked the Agreement, feeling that it gave away a certain primacy that the ICRC had built up over the years when dealing with civilians affected by conflicts. Going as far back as 1919, the ICRC had acted broadly to help various types of refugees and displaced persons, then endorsed the creation of the refugee office (Nansen office) under the League of Nations. Later, the ICRC had again acted very broadly to help refugees in places like the Middle East in the late 1940s, before the creation of either the UNHCR or the separate UN agency that works with Palestinian refugees (UNRWA). These critical members of the ICRC Assembly still did not trust the Federation (and its various National Societies) to carry out effective, neutral, and impartial humanitarian protection for refugees and displaced persons. But the critics in the Assembly constituted a minority, and in the last analysis the Assembly approved what both President Sommaruga and the Directorate recommended, namely a reduction of ICRC focus.

Under the Seville Agreement, the ICRC remains the lead Red Cross actor when the matter is the protection of persons (including provision of relief, as explained in the next chapter) in armed conflict and internal strife. The ICRC remains the lead agent for the Movement when dealing with the "immediate effects" of these situations, covering the entire territory of the state in question. The ICRC is primary for the Movement when dealing with persons fleeing from one state engulfed in armed conflict into a neighboring state that is also characterized by war. If a natural disaster occurs during the course of an armed conflict, the ICRC remains the lead Red Cross agency.

On the other hand, the Agreement specifies that the Federation becomes the lead coordinator for Red Cross relief when an armed conflict subsides into a situation of "reconstruction and rehabilitation." It is the

Federation that is responsible for the care of refugees in countries not seized by armed conflict. Even a National Society can become the lead Red Cross actor in certain situations, but only with the "concurrence" of the ICRC and the Federation.

Another way to view the Seville Agreement is that the ICRC wanted to concentrate on detention visits (unaffected by any part of the Agreement) and relief measures tightly connected to armed conflict and major internal strife. But with regard to refugees and displaced persons in peace, or what passes for peace in the modern world, the ICRC was ceding leadership in operations to the Federation and its component units. After all, from a legal point of view, refugees from persecution and war, when in a country not characterized by armed conflict, were not covered by IHL, and thus the ICRC had no special connection to them.[53] The Federation retains the lead role in natural and technological disasters unrelated to "man-made" conflicts, the ICRC having no operational interest in such situations.[54]

The wording of the Seville Agreement, while reflecting a renewed effort at a harmonious division of labor among especially the ICRC and the Federation, is not free of ambiguity. When does occupation of a country after armed conflict, falling under the aegis of the ICRC and the Fourth GC, become a situation of reconstruction and rehabilitation? What are the "direct effects" of a conflict, and when do they subside for sure? Who is the lead Red Cross actor when there is a large-scale movement of refugees into a country with some political instability and low level of political strife, where the ICRC is already making detention visits? Nevertheless, in the late 1990s in both Kosovo and also the north Caucasus region, the ICRC and the Federation reached amicable agreement about who was to do what with regard to uprooted civilians. Iraq in 2004, however, was a different matter after major combat had officially been declared over.

There remains the lingering question of whether particularly National Red Cross or Red Crescent Societies can provide impartial and neutral relief beyond natural disasters, since these Societies are quasi-governmental entities. Refugees and displaced persons often constitute

---

[53] See especially Jean-Philippe Lavoyer, "Refugees and Internally Displaced Persons: International Humanitarian Law and the Role of the ICRC," *International Review of the Red Cross*, 304 (March–April 1995), 162–91.

[54] In 2003, however, at the time of an earthquake in Iran, the ICRC turned over some of its stocks of supplies in that country in order to help with the humanitarian response. There was no armed conflict or major internal trouble in Iran at that time. The ICRC did not just turn over relief to the Federation, but for a time managed its contributed goods. The reasons for this ICRC involvement in a natural disaster have never been made clear.

matters of great interest to the strategic calculations of various governments, because such persons can be linked to instability, armed movements, and various pressures on both the home and host governments. Whether the Federation can guarantee relief operations in keeping with Red Cross principles of impartiality and neutrality in such situations of forced displacement, which is a much more sensitive subject than natural disasters, is a question to be carefully tracked in the future. Impartiality and neutrality depend for their exercise on Red Cross independence from governmental concerns. The Federation and its National Societies have not always displayed this independence in the past. At the time of writing, discussions were under way to further specify and make more effective the Seville agreement.

In some ways the increased concern for a more integrated Red Cross Movement has come far too late. Some of the expectations articulated for the "new and improved" integrated Movement seemed idealistic, given how much National Societies had been nationalized into governmental structures, and also militarized in the sense of becoming the handmaiden of national military establishments.[55] It was unlikely that 150 years of decentralized and fragmented Red Cross action in international relations could be completely undone or overcome. After all, most members of and donors to the American Red Cross had no idea who Henry Dunant was, or that the original rationale of "the Red Cross" pertained to neutral action in war. Most National Societies, in the view of their publics, were associated among other programs with support of national military ventures, and not at all with neutral and impartial action – much less independence from government. One can only imagine the national furor in the United States if the American Red Cross had shown an interest in the health of Al Qaeda or Taliban fighters, or other detainees, after 11 September 2001, on grounds of neutral and impartial humanitarianism.

Still, at least the ICRC and the Federation in Geneva were seeking new modes of cooperation and had suspended their more injurious competitions. The Federation seemed less interested in stealing thunder from the ICRC, and the latter seemed more secure and less defensive when dealing with the Federation. It is likely that there would always be some tension between the two Geneva headquarters of the Movement. Both interested

---

[55] Two roles for the National Societies, either as auxiliaries to national governments or as more tightly integrated into the Movement, are well presented in Christophe Lanord, "The Legal Status of National Red Cross and Red Crescent Societies," *International Review of the Red Cross*, 840 (December 2000), 1053–78.

themselves in the development of the National Societies, and as the ICRC more often drew on personnel from these Societies this reduced the pool of experienced personnel available to the Federation.

On the other hand, since some personnel of the National Societies worked with both the ICRC and the Federation, this tended to break down past organizational prejudices and jealousies. There was a Red Cross code of conduct for relief personnel that also cut across traditional Movement divisions.[56] And the Sphere Project, developed by the Federation with ICRC participation, tried to specify standards for civilian relief in all emergencies, whether natural or "man made."[57] There were lots of indications of greater Movement unity in the International Conference held in Geneva in 2003. Resolution 6 even called for National Societies to study a better equilibrium or balance with states, which constituted a muted call for more independence for Red Cross units.[58] But then these sorts of resolutions and statements, supported broadly as measured in Conference votes, had not always meant much in the past. One author argued that "the Red Cross" was good at shams,[59] and one of the great shams of the past was that the Movement was unified and integrated.

Conclusion

The ICRC had a higher profile in international relations in 2004 than fifteen years earlier. This was partly because of its relief work in the Balkans, Somalia, and other bloody conflicts. And it was partly because the Bush Administration, as it waged "war" on its various enemies, engaged in policies that brought it into public conflict with the ICRC. This, and the Islamic extremists' attacks on the ICRC and other western-based humanitarian organizations, is the subject of the next chapter.

---

[56] *Code of Conduct for the International Red Cross and Crescent Movement and Non Governmental Organisations (NGOs) in Disaster Relief* (Geneva: Red Cross, n.d. [1993]). This was sponsored by Caritas Internationalis, Catholic Relief Services, the Federation, the International Save the Children Alliance, the Lutheran World Federation, Oxfam, the World Council of Churches, and the ICRC.

[57] "Humanitarian Charter and Minimum Standards in Disaster Response," http://www.sphereproject.org/.

[58] See *International Review of the Red Cross*, 852 (December 2003), 959.

[59] Morehead, *Dunant's Dream*, 296.

4

The ICRC and the US "war" against terrorism

We're admired – we've won three Nobel Peace Prices – but we're not liked.

Urs Boegli, former head, Washington Office, ICRC, quoted in
New York Times 20 February 2002, A10

The Al Qaeda attacks on New York and Washington of 11 September 2001, which killed almost 3,000 Americans, changed much in the United States and the world – and also changed a great deal for the ICRC.[1] The attacks themselves were a frontal assault on established humanitarian principles, being a form of total war that disdained universally endorsed norms against attacking civilians. The attacks therefore led to another round in the long struggle to get unconventional forces to observe conventional humanitarian limits. The ICRC repeatedly condemned these and related attacks, as in Madrid in 2004 when almost 200 civilians were killed by bombs hidden in trains by Islamic radicals. But the organization was also to find itself engaged in persistent friction with the United States and its allies. Washington and its friends, like Britain, in their fervent zest to wage "war" against terrorism, sometimes also resorted to a type of total war that disdained traditional legal and humanitarian restraints. Even some initial supporters of the George W. Bush Administration's foreign policy recognized the dangers of seeing the American nation as an especially good people whose government, when attacked, should not be bound by complicating rules of law.[2]

---

[1] All statements of fact in this section not attributed to published sources are based on interviews in Geneva and Washington as late as July 2004. As this chapter was being finalized in late October 2004, Amnesty International published a long report (118 pages, 771 reference notes) entitled "The United States of America: Human Dignity Denied; Torture and Accountability in the 'War on Terror.'" The AI report and this independently researched chapter are in agreement on major findings, but no attempt has been made to fine tune the relationship between the two studies, in order not to delay submission of the final book manuscript. Of course this chapter presents an emphasis on ICRC policy making not found in the AI report.

[2] Michael Ignatieff, *International Herald Tribune*, 30 June 2004, 5.

After the attacks of 9/11 the United States, claiming a right of self-defense that was approved by the United Nations Security Council, used military force in Afghanistan starting in late 2001. The immediate goal was to overturn the Taliban government and to dislodge the Al Qaeda network of non-state operatives that was intertwined with it. In the spring of 2003 the United States also attacked Iraq. Arguing that the Saddam Hussein regime not only was evil but also possessed weapons of mass destruction and was linked to Al Qaeda, the Bush Administration undertook force without UNSC approval. Its claim to a unilateral right of preventative war, even in the absence of an agreed clear and present danger, was highly divisive in international relations. Among the many humanitarian issues arising from these armed conflicts was notably the question of treatment of detainees.

Overview of US policy toward detainees

Given the information available at the time of writing, particularly in the western press, there is no reason to question the assertion of prominent journalists and lawyers that highly coercive interrogation of certain prisoners taken in connection with the "war" on terrorism was official US policy.[3] After all, a standard CIA work on the subject, widely studied in US security circles, touts the ability of coercive interrogation, particularly in the form of isolation and sensory deprivation, to produce desired results.[4] At the same time, the US army engages in the training of interrogation methods that are more humane and in keeping with international humanitarian law (IHL).[5]

---

[3] See Seymour Hersch, "The Gray Zone," *The New Yorker*, 24 May 2004, posted at http://www.newyorker.com/printable/?fact/040524fa_ct; and his "Torture at Abu Ghraib," *The New Yorker*, 30 April 2004, posted at http://www.newyorker.com/printable/?fact/040510fa_ct. These short treatments later were folded into his book, *Chain of Command: The Road from 9/11 to Abu Ghraib* (New York: HarperCollins, 2004). See also James Risen, David Johnson, and Neil A. Lewis, "Harsh C.I.A. Methods Cited in Top Qaeda Interrogations," *New York Times*, 13 May 2004, A1. The US policy of abusive interrogation was so clear that many newspapers and journals featured debates about the wisdom and permissibility of torture in the war on terrorism from spring 2004 on. See also Reed Brody, "Prisoners Who Disappear," *International Herald Tribune*, 12 October 2004, 8.
[4] Mark Bowden, "The Dark Art of Interrogation," *Atlantic Monthly*, October 2003, 51–76, referring to the CIA's Kubark manual, later followed by the Agency's Honduras manual. HRW published various quotes from unnamed US officials who said that coercive interrogation was yielding important information for the United States after 9/11.
[5] Michael R. Gordon, "The Army and Torture: What the Rule Book Says," *International Herald Tribune*, 18 June 2004, 2.

The Bush Administration, it is reasonably clear, sought early on to free itself from most legal restraints in dealing with these prisoners. This position was reflected in highly flawed memos written by various lawyers in the White House, the Justice Department, and the civilian branch of the Defense Department.[6] Not only did these lawyers argue that most prisoners in the "war" on terrorism were not covered by IHL, but a key White House lawyer argued that provisions from the 1949 Geneva Conventions were "quaint." These lawyers also constructed flawed arguments suggesting that high US officials were exempt from the Torture Convention, which remains legally in force during armed conflicts. Certain lawyers in the State Department and the Judge Advocate General's (JAG) office in the Pentagon objected to these legal memos, as they used specious reasoning and reflected an arrogant unilateralism that was dangerous to captured US personnel and to US foreign policy in general.[7] The cumulative intent of these permissive memos, in contrast to the dissenting ones, was to encourage US operating agencies to take an unrestricted and tough approach to interrogation of many detainees captured in the "war" on terrorism. The memos, and other policies, sought to create a US commander in chief unlimited by law, domestic or international.[8] They sought to give legal cover to military and CIA interrogators, who, if necessary, could claim that governmental lawyers had advised them that their abusive actions were legal.

The Administration did agree that the Fourth GC from 1949 applied to its occupation of Iraq from April 2003 until at least 28 June 2004, although

[6] A concise review can be found in Neail A. Lewis, "Memos about Legality of US Interrogation," *International Herald Tribune*, 10 June 2004, 10. See also Rosa Ehrenreich Brooks, "Congress Must Pursue Possible US Violations," *Minneapolis Star Tribune*, 2 June 2004, AA6. And HRW, *The Road to Abu Ghraib*, http//-hrw.org/reports/2004/usa0604. Any first-year law student could spot the errors of legal interpretation presented in these memos. For example, despite the Torture Convention's focus on the deliberate infliction of intense pain as a defining feature of torture, certain US memos tried to argue that torture did not exist unless something like "organ failure" resulted.

[7] John Barry, Michael Hirsch and Michael Isikoff, "The Roots of Torture," *Newsweek*, 17 May 2004, http://www.msnbc.msn.com/id/4989422/; Pete Yost (Associated Press), "Abuse Scandal Focuses on Bush Foundation," *Anchorage Daily News*, 16 May 2004, http://www.and.com/24 hour/front/v-printer/story/1371265 p-860295c.html. On the importance of the prisoner scandal, and the view that it merited the impeachment of President Bush, see William Pfaff, "When Laws Get in the Way of Torture," *International Herald Tribune*, 12–13 June 2004, 7.

[8] The point is well made by Anthony Lewis, "Putting the Law above the White House," *New York Times*, reprinted in the *International Herald Tribune*, 30 June 2004, www.iht.com/articles/527174.html.

it subsequently argued that the Fourth GC allowed special detention for some prisoners. The Administration also agreed that the captured Saddam Hussein was a prisoner of war entitled to ICRC visits.[9] The US Attorney General, John Ashcroft, later tried to downplay the importance of certain internal memos in congressional hearings that seemed to permit abuse, and he tried to argue that the Bush administration opposed torture and mistreatment of prisoners.[10] The White House later issued statements and released some memos advocating humane treatment for detainees.[11] Among these was a White House statement, actually meaningless given its vagueness, stating that "enemy" prisoners would be treated humanely within the limits of military necessity. But the statement implied that prisoners might be treated inhumanely if US security so required.[12]

Certain facts undercut these high-level statements purportedly supporting humane treatment of detainees. First, US military lawyers were excluded from certain US-controlled prison facilities for "enemy" detainees after 9/11, unlike during the 1991 Persian Gulf war. The purpose of excluding JAG lawyers was precisely to allow room for treatment of detainees without legal restraint. Thus the JAG lawyers, with an eye on IHL, participated in the selection of bombing targets but not in the treatment of prisoners. Because of Administration policies toward detainees, in 2003 a group of JAG lawyers paid two visits to Scott Horton, then head of the Committee on Human Rights of the New York City Bar Association. The point was to bring pressure on the Bush Administration to take IHL more seriously.[13]

---

[9] The United States, having given POW status to Manuel Noriega when he captured by US military forces in Panama in 1989, could not logically refuse POW status to Hussein. The ICRC continued to visit Noriega in his Miami jail, as he served a forty-year sentence for conviction of various crimes, even as it began visits to Hussein.

[10] Neil A. Lewis, "Ashcroft under Fire for Memos on Torture," *New York Times*, 9 June 2004, A1.

[11] E.g., News Conference with King Abdullah II of Jordan, 46 Weekly Comp. Pres. Doc. 800, 801 (6 May 2004).

[12] The memo is reproduced in Steven Strasser, ed., *The Abu Ghraib Investigations: The Official Reports of the Independent Panel and the Pentagon on the Shocking Prisoner Abuse in Iraq* (New York: Public Affairs Press, 2004), Appendix B, Presidential Memo of 7 February 2002. The wording of the memo is eloquent, suggesting the intention of eventual release to establish a paper trail. After asserting various arguments that minimize US obligations under international law, the memo states that US authorities will hold foreign authorities responsible for proper application of international law regarding any US citizens detained. The double standard could not be more obvious.

[13] Adam Liptak, "Legal Review Could Have Halted Abuse, Lawyer Says," *New York Times*, 19 May 2004, A14.

Second, certain detainees, and apparently one sent first to Guantanamo Bay (Gitmo), were "remanded" to foreign governments friendly to the United States who could be counted on to carry out interrogations in a determined way safely beyond the reach of US law and judges. As of mid-2004, the ICRC was still asking publicly and privately for access to these transferred detainees.[14] The Torture Convention, to which the US is a party, and which remains in force in armed conflict and occupation, prohibits the sending of persons to countries where torture can be expected to occur. The main purpose of such transfer, however, was obviously to allow coercive interrogation.

Third, the US Naval Base at Guantanamo, Cuba was chosen as a major holding and interrogation center in an effort to deal with prisoners beyond the reach of law. The clear purpose of this Bush policy was to permit whatever type of interrogation was deemed necessary, and for whatever length of time. The US Supreme Court, however, ruled in the summer of 2004 that US courts did have jurisdiction over Guantanamo, and that prisoners held there had the legal right to use US courts to challenge their continued detention.

Fourth, the US operated a secret gulag for certain "enemy prisoners," presumably those in the leadership of terrorist organizations, and some of these were held within US jurisdiction. These were the "ghost" or "disappeared" detainees. That is, while some prisoners were "remanded" to foreign territory for interrogation unrestricted by US law and courts, other prisoners were forcibly "disappeared" within US jurisdiction.

According to the journalist Seymour Hersh, "No amount of apologetic testimony or political spin could mask the fact that, since the attacks of September 11th, President Bush and his top aides have seen themselves as engaged in a war against terrorism in which the old rules did not apply. Interrogating prisoners and getting intelligence, including by intimidation and torture, was the priority."[15] No less than *The Army Times*, a journal of the uniformed military, concluded that the responsibility for US prisoner abuse lay with the highest civilian leadership, and that legal accountability was in order.[16] It is difficult to accept at face value the

---

[14] Reuters, "ICRC Concerned for Detainees in Secret US Jails," 21 May 2004: "Le CICR inquiet pour les prisonniers 'fantomes,'" *Tribune de Genève*, 19–20 June 2004, 5; and Naomi Koppel, AP, "Red Cross Fears US Is Hiding Detainees," Yahoo News, 13 July 2004, www.yahoo.com/news?tmpl=story&u=/ap/20040713/ap_on_re_eu/red_cross_us_det . . .

[15] *Chain of Command*, 46.

[16] See Hendrik Hertberg, "Unconventional War," *The New Yorker*, 17 May 2004, www.newyorker.com/printable/?talk/040524ta_talk_hertzberg

comments of former Secretary of Defense James Schlesinger in the fall of 2004 when he said: "Our [investigative] panel found no policy that encouraged or justified [prisoner] abuse . . . we found no indication of a policy encouraging abuse."[17]

Prisoners at Guantanamo

From the winter of 2001–2, the United States detained in Afghanistan (and other places) certain individuals who were then transported to the Guantanamo Bay detention facility. This prison was on land leased in perpetuity from Cuba. Gitmo being technically on Cuban soil, executive officials argued that US law and courts had no writ. But the US Supreme Court rejected this argument in June 2004, also holding that detainees had a right to challenge the government's reasons for detention.[18] The Bush Administration also made a blanket determination that none of the prisoners was protected by IHL.

IHL is very clear that individuals in a zone of armed conflict, whether international or internal, are covered by IHL – whether they are combatants or civilians.[19] Afghanistan for much of late 2001 and early 2002 was characterized as an international armed conflict between the United States and Afghanistan, and simultaneously as an internal armed conflict between the Taliban government and the Northern Alliance and other domestic armed factions under identifiable military command. Thus it cannot be logically sustained that IHL did not apply in one way or another to many, if not most, of the initial Gitmo detainees. The issue was not just who was entitled to prisoner of war status, but who was entitled to the humane treatment mandatory for all those who are detained as a result of armed conflict. Even if one was an irregular combatant, much less a civilian, individuals detained in armed conflict are legally entitled to minimum standards of humane treatment. This point is contained in 1977 Additional Protocol I, Article 75, which the ICRC regards now as part of international

---

[17] "The Truth About Our Soldiers," *Wall Street Journal*, 9 September 2004, A16. He did allow that interrogation had been "aggressive."

[18] 542 US, *Hamdi v. Rumsfeld 124 S. Ct. 2633, 72 USLW 4607 (2004)*; 542 US, *Rasul v. Bush 124 S. Ct. 2686, 72 USLW 4596 (2004)*.

[19] Among many sources see Leila Nadya Sadat, "International Legal Issues Surrounding the Mistreatment of Iraqi Detainees by American Forces," *American Society of International Law Insight*, May/July 2004, 5, 12, 13.

customary law. The ICRC argues that the United States has agreed with this view.[20]

Once the major combat ceased and the Hamid Karzai government was in place, it may be that the law pertaining to international armed conflict ceased to be applicable in Afghanistan, the situation differing from Iraq during 2003 to 2004 in that, in legal terms, there was not a foreign occupation of the country. In so far as Karzai's Afghanistan continued to be characterized by one or more internal armed conflicts, IHL continued to be applicable via Common Article 3 from the 1949 GCs. These legal distinctions can be overblown, because once the ICRC carries out prison visits, its concerns for minimal and fundamental protections of human dignity are the same regardless of the legal label attached to a situation.

Washington, using a concept from its own history that has no status in international law, claimed that Gitmo detainees were "enemy" or "unlawful" combatants. It therefore attempted to place the prisoners beyond the reach of law, whether national or international. It tried to place prisoners at Gimo in a legal black hole.

Some persons, seized by the United States outside of Afghanistan, were simply abducted to Gitmo without regard for any legal provision or due process.

Given that Gitmo existed primarily as an interrogation center for allegedly important enemies, why the Bush Administration permitted traditional ICRC visits there is not at all clear. Bush officials may have planned to disregard whatever the ICRC might discreetly report.[21] This would be similar to Israeli policy about occupied territory in the Middle East: rejecting the formal applicability of IHL, promising to observe humanitarian principles, but having repeated differences of view with the ICRC over proper treatment. It could be that different officials in the Bush Administration had different views about the treatment of prisoners, with no overall coordination of views. It is also conceivable, though not likely, that some officials desired the presence of the ICRC as an external audit to

---

[20] See the ICRC website, response to the Schlesinger report, fall 2004. Adam Roberts agrees that the United States has accepted Protocol I, Article 75, as part of international customary law; *Washington Post*, Outlook Section, 3 February 2002.

[21] A cover argument for this view might be that the ICRC was not really neutral, was really anti-American and anti-Israel, because it went public on violations by these democracies but not on other violations. See the attack by Lee A. Casey and David B. Rivkin Jr. in the *Washington Times*, 17 June 2004. These lawyers, in a Washington law firm, were likely reflecting some views in the Bush Administration.

ensure that coercive interrogation was limited to only certain detainees. Washington officials would have been extremely naïve to think that the ICRC was going to concern itself only with limited issues like the treatment of youthful detainees and facilities for Muslim prayer, and not with abuse of detainees.

Early on in 2002 a US army general, Major General Geoffrey Miller, was given overall command of Gitmo. Highly coercive interrogation was authorized for at least one prisoner who was assumed to have special knowledge about terrorism (after considerable debate within Administration circles).[22] The general prison regime manifested other interrogation techniques that violated both international human rights and humanitarian standards in serious ways, resulting in progressively testy relations between General Miller and ICRC delegates.[23] For example, the use of dogs was authorized to terrify prisoners, at least for a time, to break their will to resist US interrogations. The ICRC suspended visits for a time after discovering that prison authorities were using medical records of individuals to calibrate interrogation techniques.[24] The ICRC was denied access to some prisoners.[25] When General Miller testified in Congress that some US military personnel were reassigned or otherwise reprimanded for improper treatment, this was very far from being a completely truthful statement.[26] Some personnel may have been chastised for violating US guidelines, but many of those guidelines clearly violated norms on proper treatment found in international human rights and humanitarian law. What was proper treatment from General Miller's view might not, and indeed often was not, the same as proper treatment from the ICRC view. Intentional abuse of detainees was apparently widespread and on-going into 2004, not limited to a handful of high-ranking suspects.[27]

---

[22] David Johnston and Thom Shanker, "Pentagon Approved Intense Interrogation Techniques for Sept. 11 Suspect at Guantanamo," *New York Times*, 21 May 2004, A10. AFP, "Some Prisoners Abused at Guantanamo: Military," Yahoo news, http://story.news.yahoo.com/news/tmpl=story&cid=1521&e=5&u=/afp/20040519/pl_afp/ . . .

[23] Scott Higham, "A Look Behind the 'Wire' At Guantanamo," *Washington Post*, 14 June 2004.

[24] Peter Slevin and Joe Stephens, "Guantanamo Interrogators' Access Criticized," *Washington Post*, 10 June 2004.

[25] *Ibid.*   [26] Johnston and Shanker, "Pentagon Approved Intense Interrogation."

[27] Neil A. Lewis, "Broad Use of Harsh Tactics Is Described at Cuba Base," *New York Times*, 17 October 2004, A1. This story is based on interviews with former guards and others who had direct knowledge of events.

Some youthful detainees were given separate accommodations, and progressively into 2003 and 2004 a number of prisoners were released – after much pressure was directed to the Administration on this issue.[28] Some prisoners were finally scheduled to be tried before US military commissions. US investigations about charges of mistreatment at Gitmo were continuing at the time of writing.

As for the ICRC, it stated its view on the applicability of IHL, making note of Article 5 in the Third GC of 1949 which indicated that if a question arose as to POW status, an independent and competent tribunal was supposed to make the determination. As the Bush team continued to resist the applicability of IHL in general, as well as the precise provision on judicial determination of individual status, the ICRC did not engage in repeated public debate about legal points. However, the highest levels of the ICRC continued long discussions with the US diplomatic mission in Geneva about IHL and Gitmo.

On the Gitmo issue of indefinite detention without legal charge, the ICRC did go public. First on its website about half-way through 2003, then in October 2003 through the verbal remarks of Christophe Girod, then head of its Washington office, and later through a press release at the time of President Jacob Kellenberger's visit to DC in January 2004, the ICRC drew attention to the deleterious effect of indefinite detention without legal charge on the mental health of the prisoners. Girod said in the fall of 2003 that in the preceding eighteen months, twenty-one prisoners had made thirty-two suicide attempts. Other prisoners were suffering depression.[29]

On the issue of coercive interrogation and harsh conditions of prisoners, the ICRC decided by May 2003 that the treatment of Gitmo detainees was improper and that US responses to its prison reports were inadequate. It issued a very brief and bland public statement when President Kellenberger visited Washington.[30] This was surely not a serious effort at

---

[28] The ICRC, on the matter of indefinite detention without legal classification or charge, had some important domestic allies, particularly in the person of Republican Senator John McCain. He had been a POW during the Vietnam war and badly treated by Hanoi. He too pressed for a change in the Bush policy of indefinite detention. It is possible, but difficult to prove, that ICRC public statements regarding indefinite detention pushed McCain and others within the United States to press for change.

[29] *New York Times*, A1. There was very little reaction to this public information in Washington and the country. Most media outlets and members of Congress paid little attention.

[30] ICRC press release 03/36, 28 May 2003.

public pressure. At this time Kellenberger had private talks with high US officials to indicate ICRC concerns.

Again in the fall of 2003 President Kellenberger sought another round of meetings with high Bush officials to discuss Gitmo (and Afghanistan), but the Administration only agreed to a visit in January 2004. In meetings with Secretary of State Colin Powell, National Security Advisor Condoleeza Rice, Under Secretary of Defense Paul Wolfowitz, and others, President Kellenberger reminded these officials of ICRC policy about confidentiality and its alternatives: the ICRC might go public with its concerns if there were major violations of IHL that were not ameliorated by discreet diplomacy over time, and if the ICRC thought that a public denunciation would aid the victims. The basic ICRC approach was to bring up possible scenarios while avoiding what might be perceived as overt threats. This ICRC position was overtaken by the public circulation of scandalous pictures confirming US abuse of prisoners in Iraq, which generated – at least briefly – increased citizen, congressional, military, and international attention to all US detainee matters, not only in Iraq but also in Afghanistan and Gitmo.

While ICRC delegations stated their concerns about Gitmo from the very beginnings of visits in early 2002, it was not until January 2004 that President Kellenberger pressed the issue of the unacceptability of detention policies at Gitmo. This pattern of policy signals a change from the ICRC's silence about the Holocaust in October 1942. Unlike in 1942, the ICRC took up the question of detainees repeatedly with various levels of the detaining authority. At Gitmo, moreover, one did not have murder, much less genocide, and the ICRC was allowed to continue its visits. But ICRC tactics about Gitmo raise again the question of whether the organization is too cautious in the face of what it knows about systematic abuse of persons. How many Gitmo prisoners were abused between early 2002 and early 2004, how serious was the abuse, and how insistent was the Geneva headquarters in pressing its concerns on high Washington officials?[31]

Top ICRC officials were careful that the organization not slip into an anti-Americanism then fashionable in certain European circles, leading

---

[31] If the claims of a Swedish national are true, namely that he was abused at Gitmo over a long period of time before being freed, and if his experience was typical for many detainees there, then the question remains: why did the ICRC take its time in pressing its views on Washington? Jan Strupczewski, for Reuters, "Freed Swede Says He Was Tortured in Guantanamo," 14 July 2004, Yahoo News, www.news.yahoo.com/news?tmpl=story&u=nm/20040414/ts_nm/sweden/guantanamo_d . . .

to public criticism of Washington that deviated from discreet policies followed in other comparable situations around the world. This was ironic, given that some Bush officials were leaking scathing views to the *Wall Street Journal*, criticizing the ICRC as a leftist and naïve European organization (see below). Former Secretary of Defense Schlesinger, at the time of his report in early fall 2004, was equally nationalistic, acerbic, and critical of the ICRC. In his view the organization was nothing more than a prisoner auditing agency, and had no business taking a stand on whether the United States was obligated under IHL.

A central problem with the ICRC approach at Gitmo was that many prisoners were apparently being abused between the start of detention and early 2004, while the organization was testing the willingness of the Bush Administration to bring about major corrections. As before in history, and despite its own rhetoric about staying close to victims, the Geneva headquarters seemed to lack passion and a sense of urgency about the situation. Its cautious approach might be interpreted as displaying more concern for an image of perfect neutrality than stopping abuse of prisoners in short order. The Council of the Assembly, the office of the President, the level of the Director-General and Directorate all followed the situation, debated and discussed options, and agonized over policy choices. With one or two individual exceptions, most high ICRC officials agreed that the general line of policy chosen by the organization was correct.

If history shows, however, that considerable and serious abuse of detainees occurred at Gitmo from the beginning of detention at least through early 2004, when prisoner abuse in Iraq drew a spotlight to all detention matters in the US "war" on terrorism, then serious questions will no doubt be raised about ICRC tactical choice.[32] If the ICRC witnessed serious abuse, and if the United States continued this abuse for some two years, then how long should the ICRC wait before sending its President to Washington? Should the organization allow that visit to be postponed? Should the President and the organization do more than issue a bland press release and then wait for journalists to schedule interviews?[33] In

---

[32] For an example of criticism of the ICRC re Gitmo, see Charles Poncet, in *L'Hebdo*, 3 June 2004. This is an open letter to the ICRC by a Swiss lawyer arguing that ICRC discreet access meant little if the organization was not able to stop abuses in Gitmo, Afghanistan, and Iraq.

[33] The ICRC press release of January 2004 generated little attention in Washington and the country. The ICRC statement occurred when the Democrats were conducting presidential primaries, when a number of Americans were being killed in Iraq, and when other major

sum, how much abuse must occur during a two-year period for the ICRC to press its case vigorously at the highest levels of officialdom, and/or to speak out in a dynamic way? Is ICRC publicity undertaken seriously to make an impact, or only pro forma to be in technical compliance with its own doctrine? How much progress can be shown by the detaining authority to avoid ICRC public pressure?

The answers to such questions do not stem from any science on that matter, but from a judgment at the Geneva headquarters that is particular to each situation, even if viewed against the background of other, similar situations. It seems safe to say that many close observers regard the ICRC as having been too cautious regarding Gitmo. Some of these observers believe that the ICRC was reluctant to take on publicly its largest donor. It seems, however, that the driving consideration behind the ICRC's approach to Gitmo was quest of consistent neutrality and reluctance to depart from discretion. Gitmo prisoners were probably not terribly helped in the short run by this general orientation at the Geneva headquarters.

Yet it is sometimes the case that both prisoners and the ICRC are in favor of continuation of discreet visits, even if abusive policies do not change, because ICRC visits give prisoners the will to carry on in the face of abuse. Sometimes it is ICRC visits that, while not causing a change in detention policy, show the prisoner that he has not been forgotten by the outside world, which allows the prisoner to endure the abuse and eventually survive. Of course if the detaining authority understands all this, there is reduced incentive to stop the abuse.

The ICRC was continuing its Gitmo visits at the time of writing. The Bush Administration was allowing journalists to visit the island prison and was trying to repair its image.

Prisoners at Bagram Air Force Base, Afghanistan

Space does not permit an analysis of ICRC relief work in Afghanistan from 2002. US military forces twice bombed an ICRC warehouse near Kabul, apparently by mistake both times. Midway through 2004 one ICRC delegate had been killed in the line of duty. Relief protection was therefore dangerous in the extreme, especially given that personal security outside

stories were being covered by the media. Congressional Democrats were still concerned not to appear too "soft" on foreign policy and national security. The notorious pictures of prisoner abuse in Iraq had not yet surfaced. The ICRC's Washington office did not vigorously lobby the media and Congress re the press release. And so this ICRC public statement had little effect on most officials and citizens.

Kabul remained highly uncertain well into 2004. Five persons from Doctors Without Borders were intentionally killed in Afghanistan in 2004, with Al Qaeda operatives claiming that all western-based aid agencies were enemies of that radicalized Islamic network. This brutal view obviously had relevance for the ICRC.

As for detainees, Washington and its NATO allies held most prisoners at Bagram Air Force Base. It appears that the US Army was directly in charge of most prisoners, with a special unit from the Defense Intelligence Agency (DIA) in charge of most interrogation, and Army Military Police in charge of detention security at Bagram Collection Point. The DIA commanding officer in charge of most interrogation, at least from July 2002 to December 2003, appears to have been Captain Carolyn A. Wood. CIA officials were also involved.[34]

At least three prisoners appeared to have been killed while in US custody, although the United States was obviously in no hurry to make public the results of its investigations. Two were in the custody of the military, and one in the control of the CIA. There were numerous reports of other abuses directed toward prisoners, with advocacy groups such as Human Rights Watch (HRW) and media sources such as the New York Times publishing the results of interviews with released prisoners.[35] The abuses reported were similar to those photographed in Iraq, as explained below. US authorities did not respond promptly or effectively to the charges by HRW and others. Until the public circulation of pictures of prisoner abuse out of Iraq in 2004, neither the American public nor the Congress seemed to focus at all on the details of the US presence in Afghanistan once the major combat was concluded, although a few media outlets ran stories on prisoner abuse there.[36] For all the reasons noted thus far in this chapter, there is every basis for believing that highly coercive interrogation of detainees in Afghanistan, certainly for those who were believed to have

---

[34] Douglas Jehl and David Rohde, "Afghan Deaths Linked to Unit at Iraq Prison," New York Times, 24 May 2004, A1.

[35] Ibid.; and HRW, "Prisoner Abuse: What About the Other Secret US Prisons?" http://hrw.org.english/docs/2004/05/04/usint8542.htm, also published in the International Herald Tribune on 4 May 2004.

[36] Dana Priest and Barton Gellman, "For CIA Suspects Abroad, Brass-Knuckle Treatment," Washington Post, reprinted in the International Herald Tribune, 27 December 2002, www.iht.com/articles/81546.html. "Is Torture Ever Justified?," [cover title], The Economist, 11th–17th January 2003. At the time of the Post exposé, there was more reaction abroad than in Washington and the country itself. Neither the American media nor the Congress reacted strongly to the Post story. One or two members of the Congress, notably Senator Patrick Leahy of Vermont, wrote letters to the executive branch asking follow-up questions.

knowledge of interest to Washington, was *de facto* US policy. It is possible that Afghanistan was like Gitmo, especially after international combat was greatly reduced after early 2002. The more stable situation, although far from completely peaceful, allowed for a highly controlled processing of prisoners. While some US military officials were eventually charged with prisoner abuse in Afghanistan, it remained unclear at the time of writing who had issued what orders to do what, where, and when.

Although the ICRC was given at least some access to prisoners at Bagram, it did not always have immediate access to them. Thus, similar to its policies in Israeli detention facilities, Geneva accepted *de facto* that detaining authorities could keep the prisoner isolated from international inspection for a time. The ICRC asked for notification of detention, and access to the prisoner at a given point in time, hoping that its access after isolation would prove a control on treatment during that time. There were also reports that the ICRC only had partial access to prisoners, meaning that the organization was denied access to certain prisoners altogether who were presumed to have important knowledge.[37] Given that in Iraq certain prisoners were hidden from the ICRC for a time, and occasionally at Gitmo as noted above, it is likely that the same situation prevailed in Afghanistan.

The ICRC did not have access to prisoners held in Afghanistan prisons other than Bagram from 2001 until about halfway into 2004, when most prisoners were transferred to Bagram in the wake of publicity about US and British abuse of prisoners in Iraq. Human rights advocacy groups claimed that conditions were harsh in these regional prisons. In Shiberghan jail, a number of prisoners in detention under the control of the warlord Abdul Rashid Dostrum, an ally of the United States, starved to death during 2002.[38] It was well into 2004 before the ICRC got access to a US prison in Khandahar.

---

[37] Carlotta Gall, "US Military Investigating Death of Afghan in Custody," *New York Times*, 4 March 2003, A14. See further Human Rights Watch, "Afghanistan: Abuses by US Forces," 8 March 2004, internet press release, referring to the longer report, *Enduring Freedom: Abuses by US Forces in Afghanistan*. On the basis of interviews with former detainees, HRW charged the US with beatings and other abuses of prisoners in Afghanistan. HRW also called for the US to account publicly for the deaths of three persons while detained.

[38] Dexter Filins, "Marooned Taliban Count Out Grim Hours in an Afghan Jail," *New York Times*, 14 March 2002, A1. Note also that in a jail in Kandahar, Afghanistan, visited by the ICRC, one man had been kept in leg irons for thirty-five years. Craig Smith, "Red Cross Oversees Afghan 'Place of Aid,' Where a Man Has Been Chained for 35 Years," *New York Times*, 25 February 2002, A12. www.nytimes.com/2002/ 02/02/opinion/ 02LEAN.html?todaysheadlines=&pagewante.

The same agonizing policy debate took place in Geneva regarding Afghanistan that occurred regarding of Gitmo. Did Geneva take into account eventual US claims to conducting seventy-five investigations into abuse in Afghanistan prisons?[39] But some of these cases dated back to 2002, hardly a sign of vigorous pursuit of facts. Since Afghanistan, along with Gitmo, was on President Kellenberger's agenda when he visited Washington in January 2004, it was likely that the treatment of prisoners there merited far more attention than given by the western press for most of the time in question.

Two representatives of Physicians for Human Rights found many prisoner problems when they visited Afghanistan in 2002. Their observations raised serious questions about the timeliness and value of ICRC detention visits, at least from the view of curtailing abuses.[40] The ICRC stresses the role of discretion in securing access to victims, but the question persists as to humanitarian impact after access. Still, as already noted, there is the belief in some circles that ICRC visits provide moral solidarity with detainees, which allows them to survive such abuse. As in Iraq, the ICRC has not gone public regarding detention matters in Afghanistan at the time of writing. Eventually we will know if this discretion was justified, especially because of improvements not known to outsiders, or if the record eventually discredits the organization for being too cautious.

Apparently the ICRC bears some responsibility for the humanitarian disaster at Shiberghan prison in 2002. The ICRC knew about this detention site and had visited it earlier. A fully dynamic agency would have provided the food and water necessary to avoid prisoner starvation.

Prisoners in Iraq from 2003

After some forty days of combat in late spring 2003, the United States and its coalition partners became, in legal terms, occupying powers of Iraq as legally foreseen by the Fourth GC of 1949. In general Washington agreed that the Fourth GC applied, it being hard to avoid the conclusion that its invasion (or intervention or preemptive strike) by regular state military forces was indeed an international armed conflict that resulted in the control of foreign territory.

[39] Margaret Neighbour, "US General Admits Abuse of Prisoners Widespread," *The Scotsman*, 20 May 2004, http://thescotsman.scotsman.com/pring/cfm?id+572682004&referringtemplate+http%3A% . . .

[40] Jennifer Leaning and John Heffernan, "Forgotten Prisoners of War," *New York Times*, 2 February 2002.

During that war, a highly prepared ICRC maintained a delegation in Iraq, doing heroic work with regard particularly to water and sanitation issues. It was also highly active in helping with the situation in Iraqi hospitals. It developed a remarkable communications policy regarding the latter, sending real-time communiqués to the rest of the world about conditions in those hospitals. These reports were read by the highest levels of the US State Department, the information not being available through other channels. The ICRC did, however, shy away from persistent, high-level commentary on the subject of civilian collateral damage from US military attacks. It could have interviewed medical personnel and patients in order to establish the extent of civilian death and damage, but it did not. The agency mostly left this important question to journalists and advocacy groups.[41]

Coalition abuse of Iraqi prisoners became a major scandal in the spring of 2004. This was not only a humanitarian disaster. It was a disaster for the US position in the world. It was difficult, if not impossible, for Washington to picture itself as a civilizing force in the world, fighting against unspeakable evil, hoping to transform Iraq into a stable liberal democracy and a model of change in the rest of the Arab world, when the US engaged in widespread abuse, including sexual humiliation, of individuals. Therefore high levels of the Bush Administration, including the President himself in his May 2004 speech at the US Army War College in Carlisle, Pennsylvania, claimed that the problem stemmed from a few soldiers of low rank who had violated established and humane policy. The actual US record on detainees in Iraq, especially when viewed in relation to Afghanistan and Gitmo, indicates a more complicated picture.[42]

It was very clear that a quick and decisive military victory was not followed by a well-planned and executed occupation.[43] It was also clear

---

[41] See further HRW, "US Investigate Civilian Deaths in Iraq Military Operations," hrw-news@topica.email-publisher.com, 18 June 2004. There were some ICRC or Movement comments about collateral damage. See for example a Movement magazine story about an incident in which Coalition forces damaged an Iraqi mental hospital, then did not secure it. Many patients ran away, some female patients were raped, the facility was looted. Christine Aziz, "Al Rahid Psychiatric Hospital Baghdad," *Red Cross, Red Crescent*, 4 (2003), 20–1.

[42] See the overview of the situation in *Newsweek*, 7 June 2004, comparing the President's remarks with the facts as known at that time.

[43] On the failure of the Pentagon to plan properly for occupation, see James Fallows, "Blind into Baghdad," *Atlantic Monthly*, January–February 2004, 53–74. See also Michael R. Gordon, "How the Postwar Situation in Iraq Went Awry," *International Herald Tribune*, 19 October 2004, www.iht.com/articles/2004/10/18/news/war.html. By all accounts, there

that as part of this general débâcle after the end of major combat, prisoner matters were badly managed by the United States and its coalition
partners.

Even after considerable publicity about prisoner matters in Iraq, including some congressional hearings, through autumn 2004 it still was not
absolutely clear who was in charge of what, who had issued what orders,
and who had read – and had responsibility for responding to – ICRC
reports.[44] In addition to the well-known fog of war, there was a "war
of fog," as various military and civilian officials put out a "vapor trail"
of vague and contradicting statements.[45] At the time of writing, neither
the US military nor the Congress was dealing with Iraqi prisoner abuse
in a candid and forthright way. Further congressional hearings, Pentagon
investigations, and various legal proceedings would likely shed more light.
At the time of writing, the following seems to have been the case.

Major General Miller was moved from Gitmo to Iraq in late summer
2003, obviously for the reason of instituting a rigorous Gitmo-style detention and interrogation system in Iraq. Captain Wood of DIA, who had
served in Afghanistan during the time of prisoner abuse there, was also
transferred to Iraq to employ the same of type of detention-interrogation
system practiced at Bagram.[46] It was apparently a US Army General, sent
from the Pentagon to improve the collection of intelligence from prisoners, who started the practice of terrifying prisoners through use of military
dogs.[47] It was reported that the top US Army General in Iraq, Ricardo
Sanchez, leaned on especially DIA Colonel Thomas Pappas to abuse

was extensive planning for the post-combat phase of the US invasion of Iraq, mainly by the
State Department; but the civilian leadership of the Department of Defense consistently
blocked the State Department from a meaningful role in managing the occupation.

[44] Eric Schmitt, "2 Generals Outline Lag in Notification on Abuse Reports," New York Times,
20 May 2004, A1.

[45] John Tierney, "Hot Seat Grows Lukewarm under Capital's Fog of War," New York
Times, 20 May 2004, A14. His skeptical report is mirrored by Peter Grier and
Faye Bowers, "Military Denies Pattern," Christian Science Monitor, 20 May 2004,
http://www.csmonitor.com/2004/0520/p01s02-usmi.html. In this latter story, retired military officials suggest there is an effort to obscure command responsibility for prisoner
abuse.

[46] Tim Golden and Eric Schmitt, "General Took Guantanamo Rules to Iraq for Handling of
Prisoners," New York Times, 13 May 2004, A1. Douglas Jehl and Eric Schmitt, "Afghan
Policies on Questioning Taken to Iraq: Harsher Interrogation Practices Are Cited," New
York Times, 21 May 2004, A1.

[47] UPI, "Report: General Urged Dogs for Abu Ghraib," 26 May 2004, http://
www.washingtontimes.com/upi-breaking/20040526–071342–5775r.htm. It is possible
that this same tactic has been used by Israel against Palestinian detainees.

prisoners in order to improve intelligence.[48] Brigadier General Janet Karpinski, also with some responsibility for interrogation of prisoners there, told the press she was ordered aside by DIA officials. She further told the press she tried to get General Sanchez to deal publicly with the abuse, once reported, but that he allegedly refused to do so. (In May 2004, General Sanchez was rotated out of the Iraq command by the Pentagon.)

It is clear that much of this coercive interrogation amounted to torture, prohibited not only by IHL, but also by the international torture convention. In so far as US actions amounted to the intentional infliction of severe mental or physical pain on detainees, they constitute torture. The press reported on-going investigations in at least nine cases of death in detention in Afghanistan and Iraq. Some other reports referred to more than thirty deaths in detention in these two countries.

Specifically with regard to the notorious Abu Ghraib prison, the following appears to capture basic facts. Certain military reservists, operating under the eye of army military police, probably encouraged by persons in the DIA, almost certainly in the context of informal pressure from higher-ups in the military chain of command, engaged in widespread abuse. The initial pressure from superiors was no doubt driven by a quest for more actionable intelligence, given that the occupation had turned very bloody and embarrassing. CIA officials and private contract persons seem to have been involved also.[49]

Much detail about this abuse at Abu Ghraib is not in question, having been publicized during the course of 2004.[50] The various pictures of abuse circulated widely within military circles in Iraq before becoming known in the United States. Much of the abuse occurred in open spaces, and in the presence of numerous persons. Some US military personnel were photographed gloating over mistreated or even deceased Iraqis. This was not a matter of a few persons run amok, or of aberrant behavior carried out in a dark and secluded place. The US Army's Taguba Report in the spring of 2004 concluded that the abuse was widespread.[51] This first report was confirmed by a second military report, although the conclusions

---

[48] Douglas Jehl, "Officers Say US Colonel at Abu Ghraib Prison Felt Intense Pressure to Get Inmates to Talk," *New York Times*, 19 May 2004, A11.

[49] This summary paragraph is based on the press reports already cited in this section.

[50] See further Neil A. Lewis, "Red Cross Found Abuses at Abu Ghraib Last Year," *New York Times*, 11 May 2004, A11.

[51] The report can be read on-line at: www.globalsecurity.org/intell/library/reports/2004/800-mp-bde.htm.

of this second report tried to avoid what its own evidence presented – namely that abuse was systematic and widespread.[52] Both of these reports confirmed what the ICRC had reported, namely that abuse was systematic. Widespread abuse cannot occur unless the military and civilian chain of command allows it to occur. Whether by commission or omission, high US officials, both civilian and military, clearly have considerable responsibility for Iraqi prisoner abuse, not just a handful of lower-ranking soldiers. At the time of writing it still was not clear who had issued what orders, verbally or in written form, to do what, where, and when. The book by Seymour Hersch, *Chain of Command*, does not provide clear evidence on this point.

The ICRC gained access to most places of detention in Iraq from the time of combat in March 2003. As at Gitmo and Bagram, it was not clear why the Bush Administration had two contradictory policies in place: intentional abuse of at least certain detainees and agreement to ICRC visits. Some of these visits were unannounced. The organization was therefore reasonably well informed as to detention conditions, although some prisoners were kept from the agency – apparently successfully – by US officials.[53] It can be said, however, that the ICRC was slow to understand the extent of abuse at Abu Gharib, was apparently in the dark until tipped off by a disgruntled US intelligence agent, and might have been visiting the prison more often than every five to six weeks. In other times and places, the ICRC sometimes visits detention facilities weekly.

On the other hand, one delegate was intentionally killed in July, and in October the ICRC headquarters in Baghdad was attacked via a car bomb, leading to the loss of life of several local staff plus bystanders. The UN headquarters in Iraq had previously been attacked, leading to the deaths of more than twenty people, including the head of the UN mission there. The ICRC therefore decided to relocate most of its expatriate delegates to Jordan and do in-and-out visits with reduced staff. This situation impeded

---

[52] For a summary of the 321-page Mikolashek report, see Eric Schmitt, "Report Denies Systemic Failure Led to Iraq Abuse," *New York Times*, reprinted in the *International Herald Tribune*, 23 July 2004, www.iht.com/articles/530753.html.

[53] Douglas Jehl and Eric Schmitt, "C.I.A Bid to Keep Some Detainees Off Abu Ghraib Roll Worries Officials," *New York Times*, 25 May 2004, A1. Apparently at least one prisoner in Iraq was ordered to be kept from the ICRC by Secretary of Defense Rumsfeld, at the request of CIA Director George Tenet. Eric Schmitt and Thom Shanker, "Rumsfeld Ordered Unlisted Detention," *International Herald Tribune*, 18 June 2004, 8.

the type of detention monitoring that otherwise would have occurred. However, an ICRC official was quoted as having said that the organization should have been visiting Abu Ghraib more often.[54]

Geneva decided in the fall of 2003 that there was enough improvement in the overall prisoner situation in Iraq to justify a continuation of its normal discreet approach. While the details of this record are not in the public domain at the time of writing, high ICRC officials were confident that the historical record would present the organization with no embarrassment. It seems true, as reported in the press, that the focus of Kellenberger's visit to Washington in January 2004 was Gitmo and Afghanistan, not Iraq, suggesting that certain improvements in detention matters were underway in Iraq before the notorious photos surfaced in early 2004.

However, some media coverage said that at the time of the November ICRC reports about Abu Ghraib, some US officials responded by trying to curtail unannounced ICRC visits and arguing that the agency could be legally denied access to certain prisoners.[55] This was hardly an encouraging response that merited a continuation of discreet communication because substantial improvements were in process. Moreover, major Pentagon investigations into prisoner abuse in Iraq were apparently not set in motion until photographic evidence was made known in early 2004. Apparently it was not the ICRC preliminary report on Abu Ghraib in November 2003 that triggered those investigations, nor the summary report of all ICRC visits in Iraq that was submitted in February 2004.[56] It appears that US military officials also had reports of prisoner abuse from US military sources, in addition to the ICRC, months before matters escalated in early 2004.[57] All of this again raises the important question of how much high US officials knew in late 2003, and what kinds of improvements were in course at that time. All of this feeds into the

---

[54] Pierre Gassmann, as quoted in the *Wall Street Journal*, 21 May 2004.

[55] Douglas Jehl and Neil A. Lewis, "US Military Disputed Protected Status of Prisoners Held in Iraq," *New York Times*, 23 May 2004, A10. Memos surfaced from various officials in Washington, certainly at the time of the strong ICRC representations about prisoner abuse in November 2003, arguing that certain prisoners could be kept from the ICRC, at least for a time, and that they did not fall under the protections of IHL. Certain high-profile prisoners were kept at Camp Cropper, run by DIA, in darkness for twenty-three out of twenty-four hours, but visited by the ICRC.

[56] Ananova, "Concern over Iraq Detainees," 18 May 2004, http://www.ananova.com/news/ story/sm_960007.html?menu=news.royals. This is a British information service.

[57] Andrea Elliott, "Unit Says It Gave Earlier Warning of Abuse in Iraq," *New York Times*, 14 June 2004, A4.

continuing debate about how assertive and/or public the ICRC should have been about Iraqi prisoner abuse in late 2003.

Several high ICRC officials do not understand why the Bush Administration has not released certain ICRC reports showing corrections of at least some abuses in Iraq. It seems that President Kellenberger and Secretary of State Powell had a number of telephone conversations about this matter. It is likely that Kellenberger pushed Powell to release reports showing improvements, since such a step would have been in the interests of two parties then under vociferous attack (but for different reasons). However, if Washington released ICRC reports on Iraq showing what improvements were in course, it might also feel pressured to release ICRC reports on Gitmo and Afghanistan where presumably humanitarian improvements were not so evident. It also seems to be the case that Powell was not very influential within Washington on a number of matters pertaining to detention in the "war" on terrorism.[58]

At the time of writing the ICRC has not gone public on any aspect of detention in Iraq.[59] When one of its reports about Abu Ghraib was finally leaked to the press, specifically the *Wall Street Journal* (*WSJ*), President Kellenberger quickly, on his own, without consulting with the Council of the Assembly, confirmed publicly the authenticity of the report. This led to a vitriolic attack on the organization in the editorial pages of the *WSJ*, suggesting the ICRC had leaked the report, which was false, and that the organization was naïve and an impediment to US national security.[60] Since this editorial repeated certain views critical of the ICRC that had been circulating in the Administration for some time, the editorial was probably the work of certain Administration officials.[61] The ICRC responded in this emerging war of editorials with a statement by President Kellenberger in

---

[58] On Powell being pushed out of Bush's inner circle by Cheney and others, see James Mann, *Rise of the Vulcans: The History of Bush's War Cabinet* (New York: Penguin, 2004).

[59] It was highly ironic that certain American circles were criticizing the ICRC for going public about democracies, given ICRC caution and concern for a neutral image. See Casey and Rivkin Jr., *Washington Times*, 17 June 2004.

[60] 14 May 2004.

[61] As the Iraqi prison abuse story broke in April and May 2004, certain circles in American society and the Congress took the view that too much attention was being paid to the issue, thus distracting attention from the nature of Saddam Hussein's regime and the nature of those now fighting US forces in Iraq. See for example the views covered in Maureen Dowd, "What Prison Scandal?," *New York Times*, 20 May 2004, A31. So in the United States, the ICRC, the press, human rights advocacy groups, even Republican Senator Warner, chair of the Senate Armed Services Committee, all came under attack for paying too much attention to the fate of prisoners.

the London *Financial Times*, diplomatic in tone, stressing that no state
was above IHL.[62]

A number of ICRC officials, especially delegates on the scene, wanted to
go public in the fall of 2003 when its preliminary reports about Abu Ghraib
did not change the situation there.[63] Supposedly, these ICRC officials
believed that improvements at places like Uum Quasr were marginal and
insignificant in the larger picture. There was, as usual, a debate among
high officials about the course of action to follow, but, as with Gitmo, there
was general agreement among high ICRC officials about the conservative
policy approach chosen.

Events were to show clearly that prisoners in Iraq benefited from the
embarrassing publicity of spring 2004, as many were released and US
interrogation was more carefully monitored. The United States initiated
various administrative and legal proceedings about prisoner abuse in
Iraq, but at the time of writing the targets of these actions were all low-
ranking personnel, with no one charged above the rank of captain. But, for
example, the question of who ordered General Miller to Iraq, with what
precise orders, had not been officially addressed. Particularly the role of the
civilian leadership of the Defense Department, and in particular the role
of Secretary of Defense Rumsfeld, Douglas Feith, and Steven Cambone,
had not been officially addressed. Likewise, the exact relationship among
the Defense Department, the CIA, the FBI, and private contractors was
not at all clear when it came to responsibility for prisoner detention and
interrogation and supervision. Early congressional interest in oversight
of this delicate subject faded away, at least as of the fall of 2004.

Summary of US detention policies

The US "war" on terrorism raises anew the ancient tension between
"military necessity" and humanitarian norms centered on individual
human dignity. US high officials have often enough stated their primary
goal of preventing any more attacks on the homeland. This articulated
goal contributed presumably not only to the controversial invasion of
Iraq, but also more rationally to coercive interrogation of prisoners in

---

[62] 19 May 2004, reproduced on the ICRC web site.
[63] Agathe Dupart and Serge Michel, "CICR et maison-blanche: le torchon brule," *L'Hebdo*,
27 May 2004. This is a Swiss magazine whose reporting often reflects inside contacts at the
ICRC. See also *Wall Street Journal* of 21 May 2004, reporting on debates inside the ICRC
delegation in Iraq. Pierre Gassmann, head of that delegation, confirmed the debate about
going public.

various locales.[64] Some useful information has apparently been obtained from some of these procedures.[65] At least those US officials leaking this view to the western press want outsiders to think that.

The ICRC, on the other hand, represents the moral obligation to try to establish a humanitarian quarantine for prisoners, based on the notion that the battle stops upon detention. In addition to such international and neutral views, there are reinforcing national and self-interested ones – that information extracted under duress may well prove unreliable, and that one cannot claim the high moral ground in global power struggles while abusing detainees. Moreover, abuse of "the other" today may lead to abuse of your forces when captured tomorrow.[66]

The humanitarian imperative to protect the human dignity of prisoners, one of the fundamental rules of IHL, has often been hard to implement. In the Korean war, the North Koreans pressured US POWs to defect to the North, while Washington taught its soldiers how to use code in Red Cross messages to communicate sensitive things to the outside world.[67] The same humanitarian standard was hard to implement in the Israeli–Palestinian conflict, and the conflict over Northern Ireland, when detaining authorities used coercive interrogation to try to maintain power while curtailing attacks on civilians. Protection of individual dignity was also hard to implement in most decolonization struggles, as the forces of the status quo like Britain and France used mistreatment and torture to try to stave off the forces of change who themselves committed atrocities against civilians and colonial officials.

While the ICRC and IHL, along with the Convention Against Torture, endorse a total ban on prisoner mistreatment and torture, a competing view is that, realistically speaking, responsible detaining authorities should follow a policy of selective coercive interrogation but minimal damage to individuals. When entering the gray area (of proper responses to national security threats), authorities should draw a clear red line (about what is absolutely prohibited or definitely limited). They should minimize abuse by directing it only to those likely to yield important information, and to stop short of fatal and otherwise permanent harm. This used to

---

[64] Debate remains about whether US officials really thought Saddam Hussein's regime was linked to Al Qaeda, or whether that argument was made as a smokescreen for other motives.

[65] Riesen, Johnston, Lewis, "Harsh C.I.A. Methods."

[66] When an American was captured by insurgents in Iraq in 2004, the captors reportedly stated that he would be treated like the prisoners in Abu Gharib.

[67] Michael Walzer, "Prisoners of War: Does the Fight Continue after the Battle," *American Political Science Review*, 63 no. 3 (September 1969), 777–86.

be and perhaps still is the *de facto* Israeli policy toward certain Palestinian detainees.[68] The United States adopted *de facto* a similar view, but the policy ran out of control at Abu Ghraib in Iraq through poor training and inadequate supervision.

In a way, the ICRC defers to this policy of coercive interrogation while opposing it. It could have withdrawn in protest in Gitmo, Afghanistan, and Iraq, as it could have in Israel and elsewhere, when encountering systematic coercive interrogation. But it usually stays, seeing the prisoner after isolation and pressure, hoping to limit the damage to persons. It can try public pressure as a last resort, if the organization thinks it will help detainees, but the ICRC seems almost congenitally opposed to this option. The majority of ICRC officials say that most of the time efforts at publicity do little good. When the ICRC does go public, about Israeli policies, US indefinite detention at Gitmo, or the secret transfer of prisoners to third parties, its style is antiseptic; it does not vigorously lobby its view like AI or HRW. When Kellenberger went to Washington in January 2004 to remind US officials about ICRC policy covering possible public denunciation, unless major improvements were made, he made himself available for media interviews. But the ICRC did not forcefully lobby Congress and the media with its views. And the American media, not to mention Congress, paid almost no attention to Kellenberger.

Despite the fact that in the United States from early 2004 US prisoner abuse was public knowledge, as was the existence of the US policy of "ghost detainees" or "forcibly disappeared" prisoners, the subject did not figure at all in the presidential campaign and debates that fall. Nor did members of Congress seriously press the issue after some preliminary and inconclusive hearings. The Bush Administration had obvious reasons for not emphasizing the policy of hiding and coercing prisoners. It did not object to certain proceedings against lower-ranking personnel, especially for abuses at Abu Ghraib, because these proceedings about officially unauthorized mistreatment actually deflected attention away from the policy

---

[68] See the concise and accurate review of coercive interrogation by Israel in Warren Richey, "Making Them Talk: The Moral Debate," *Christian Science Monitor*, 26 May 2004, http:www.csmonitor.com/2004/0526)p0s01-uspo.html. See also the interview with Carmi Gilon, former head of Israel's Shin Beth internal security organization, now called Shabak, endorsing coercive interrogation of certain detainees, in the special section in *Le Monde*, 30 June 2004, VI. While the Israeli Supreme Court has now ruled against physical abuse during interrogation, many complaints of abuse have been filed with Israeli authorities and no Israeli security agents have been prosecuted in recent years. See further Eitan Feiner, "The Painful Lesson Israel Learned about Torture," *International Herald Tribune*, 1 June 2004, www.iht.com/bin/print.php?file=522627.html.

of intentional mistreatment of targeted prisoners. And Democratic candidate for President John Kerry, as well as other Democrats, had reason to sweep the issue under the metaphorical rug. They sought to present themselves to the electorate as tough on security issues. They found electoral reason not to raise question about mistreatment of "enemies."

So once again the ICRC found itself without important support in its effort to protect the human dignity of "enemy" detainees. It was vociferously criticized by the Schlesinger Report of 2004, and by former Secretary of Defense Schlesinger himself, for asserting international standards against US policy which arguably Washington had already rejected. What was really at issue in this dispute, certainly in part, was a highly charged American nationalism, both in the Bush Administration and on the part of outside persons like Schlesinger, who deeply resented a European-based, international view that dared to question policies deemed by official Washington to be necessary for US security.

The ICRC was supported by advocacy groups like HRW and AI. All three, plus other actors like a few journalists, tried to focus on international standards for the protection of prisoners. But in general, in the wake of 9/11, neither American public opinion nor the Congress seemed prepared to direct much attention to prisoner abuse. At the time of writing, US courts were only slowly beginning to address some of the issues raised under US law.

PART TWO

Policy analysis

5

ICRC principles and policies

It is not enough to call upon great humanitarian principles. In a fluid situation it is necessary to lay down rules of behaviour which must be respected by everyone, from the [ICRC] President down to the last delegate.

Freymond, "Humanitarian Policy and Pragmatism," *Government and Opposition*, 11 (Autumn, 1976), 425

From the historical overview presented in the previous chapters one can extract and analyze the basic principles and policies of the ICRC. These principles and policies allow us to situate the organization more clearly in international relations by allowing us to distinguish the ICRC's role, strategy, and tactics from other relevant actors. In the "international community" one finds numerous actors dealing from time to time with humanitarian affairs – states, United Nations organs and agencies, Doctors Without Borders, Amnesty International, the European Union's Humanitarian Office, and so on. The ICRC, while not ruling out the possibility of some type of cooperation with most of these, cooperates (or not) according to a particular set of principles and policies. The ICRC has historically marched to its own drummer.

Two fundamental subjects

To set the stage, we can focus briefly on two fundamental subjects: the ICRC's core role of humanizing war, and the relevance to the organization of the official seven Red Cross principles.

Limiting versus opposing war

From the beginning, the ICRC approach to protecting war victims left itself open to the charge that it was in bed with governments and their bellicose policy makers. A basic and persistent attack "from the left" was that the ICRC was working with governments to make war acceptable by making it less inhumane. If the horrors of war went unmitigated, so the argument runs, society would do away with war – just as society had put other important institutions, from slavery to foot binding to jousting, in the trash heap of history. But the ICRC has always tried to achieve improvements in the human condition in war and other conflicts by way of cooperation with governments (and later would-be governments such as rebel or liberation movements), while staying away from a specific criticism of specific wars – and the frontal challenge to states that such an approach would represent. Thus legal norms for the process of war (*jus in bello*), the domain of the ICRC, were separated from law for the start of war (*jus ad bellum*) in the first place.

However much the ICRC founding fathers thought war was a pronounced evil, and they did,[1] the organization has always left to others a direct challenge to particular wars. Like so many ICRC policies, "the organization's attitude toward war is very Swiss."[2] Switzerland has known centuries of peace, despite Napoleon's occupation for fifteen years, but this peace is based on armed neutrality and preparedness for war. Switzerland is not a pacific culture, but rather believes in an alpine version of realism that anticipates the worst and seeks to deter it by making invasion costly to any contemplating it.[3] Moreover, the Swiss Confederation has long had military conscription for males and an active arms sales program abroad. Switzerland was never Costa Rica (the latter having abandoned its national army in favor of pacific views). The Swiss approach to war, affecting the ICRC, was more pragmatic than idealistic, more a matter of adjusting to the war-prone state system than radically trying to change it.

In the traditional terminology of the Red Cross world, that network "condemned war on moral grounds, [but] it regarded the problem of its prevention as a political matter in which the Red Cross could not intervene."[4] Max Huber when ICRC President made the strained argument that the Geneva Conventions of 1864 and 1906 contributed to the League of Nations Covenant and its effort to outlaw aggressive war.[5] Once in a

---

[1] See especially Durand, *The ICRC*, 56–66. His analysis first appeared as three essays in the *International Review of the Red Cross* during 1981.
[2] Michael Ignatieff, *The Warrior's Honor* (New York: Vintage, for Random House, 1998), p. 121.
[3] "Realism" is used here in the sense of a realist theory of international relations and foreign policy. See further Stanley Michalak, *A Primer in Power Politics* (Wilmington, DE: Scholarly Resources, 2001).
[4] Durand, *From Sarajevo*, 195.
[5] Max Huber, *The Red Cross: Principles and Problems* (Geneva: ICRC, no date given), p. 72.

while an ICRC official when writing in his private capacity might say that the Red Cross approach was really designed to oppose war itself, since if all the humanitarian limitations on war were taken seriously fighting war would be impossible.[6] But this was personal hyperbole. It bears recalling that a Swiss military officer (General Dufour) was one of the founding five. Of these five only Dunant – in his later years after he left the ICRC – became a pacifist.[7] The ICRC has never been a traditional "peace and justice" lobby, even though it has won or shared three Nobel Peace Prizes in its own right.

Especially after the Cold War, and after the efforts by European communists and the Federation to emphasize peace issues in the Red Cross network, the ICRC made clear its activity remained linked to *jus in bello* rather than *jus ad bellum*.[8] Its central role was protection of victims of war, not passing judgment on the issues involved in recourse to war.[9]

As an ICRC official wrote in 2001, the ICRC has never pretended to be a mediator on the big questions of war and peace; the most that can

---

[6] Freymond, *Guerres, révolutions, Croix-Rouge,* x, and later in the same work, 138–42. This personal view by a former Vice President and Acting President of the ICRC, and also a former colonel in the Swiss army, has never been endorsed by the organization.

[7] After World War I, ICRC Vice President Edouard Naville floated the idea of presenting a formal motion to recommend the prohibition of standing armies and compulsory conscription, but the idea did not advance and the motion was not presented. Durand, *From Sarajevo,* 197.

[8] The Federation, whose activities occur more in peacetime than war as a general rule, had long sought to link the Red Cross idea to peace, much more so than the ICRC which focuses on war and domestic troubles and tensions. During the Cold War the European communists launched a peace offensive, part of which was directed to the Red Cross Movement. These two elements, the Federation and the National Societies of communist states, among other things pushed for a special Red Cross meeting on peace, which occurred in Belgrade in 1975. Other meetings, publications, and discussions followed. The ICRC tried to make the best of the situation by participating in these developments and arguing that it was all for peace as an abstract value and even indirectly contributed to peace through its traditional activities. The Red Cross Conference passed various resolutions committing the Movement to directly advancing the spirit of peace, a position to which the ICRC did not object. The Tansley Report, occurring in the midst of these developments, supported the ICRC position that the evolution of things was a danger to neutral humanitarian protection as practiced by the ICRC. See further various issues of the *International Review of the Red Cross,* especially between 1975 and 1980, as per nos. 168, 203, 217, and so on.

[9] For an example of incorrect understanding of the ICRC and issues of peace and war, see Charles O. Berry, *War and the Red Cross: The Unspoken Mission* (New York: St. Martin's Press, 1997). Written in the style of a journalistic scoop, this book "lets out the secret" that the ICRC has worked for a long time to undermine war. Berry relies on a number of quotes by the ICRC official Yves Sandoz. But the ICRC as an organization has always refused to challenge state decisions to go to war. Commentary on such issues was never part of its mandate.

be said is that its humanitarian diplomacy may have contributed to a more general lessening of tensions or a movement away from escalation of violence.[10] Even when it got involved in the Cuban missile crisis of 1962 as an exceptional matter beyond its traditional mandate, it did not mediate the substantive issues. Even when Red Cross actors in El Salvador and Mexico helped organize peace negotiations in either civil war or domestic unrest, Red Cross agencies did not mediate the substantive issues. The ICRC's *raison d'être* has always been the amelioration of threats to human dignity in war and similar conflict. Any contribution to a more general peace among states has been indirect – a by-product of its more narrow humanitarian focus.[11]

There has also been a persistent criticism of the ICRC's role of humanizing war "from the right" – namely that "moderation in war is imbecility."[12] Or as Clausewitz would have it, "To introduce the principle of moderation into the theory of war itself would always lead to logical absurdity."[13] A variation on this view argues that no party will moderate its war fighting if that means losing the war. A modern version of this view is that fighting total war is actually the most humane process, as it presumably shortens the war – thus attenuating suffering. Some justify the atomic bombing of Japanese cities in 1945 under this logic.

Significantly, no state or military establishment now officially endorses unrestricted warfare. Virtually all states are parties to the 1949 Geneva Conventions codifying limits on the waging of war. Whether political leaders and military personnel really believe in these barriers against total war is another matter – especially when it is their country or their elite status that is under attack.

[10] Jean-Luc Blondel, "Rôle du CICR en matière de prévention des conflits armés: possibilités d'action et limites," *International Review of the Red Cross*, 844 (December 2001), 923–46.

[11] As a very minor matter, it can be noted that the ICRC, acting under Red Cross Conference resolutions committing the Movement to advancing the spirit of peace, is not opposed to supporting educational programs showing the damage done via violence, as compared to making judgments about peace and war in particular situations. Early this century the ICRC cooperated with UNESCO and the Swiss Red Cross in preparing and distributing educational material dealing with peace and violence. ICRC, Communication to the press No. 02/32, 6 June 2002.

[12] Attributed to the British Admiral of the Fleet Lord Fisher by Paul Fussell in "Hiroshima: A Soldier's View," *The New Republic*, 22 and 29 August 1981, 30.

[13] Quoted in Ward Thomas, *The Ethics of Destruction: Norms and Force in International Relations* (Ithaca: Cornell University Press, 2001), 1.

The official Red Cross principles

For a long time the ICRC acted to help individuals in conflicts but without any official principles, much less doctrine or general policies. The emphasis was on pragmatic moral accomplishments – even if there was some attention to legal rules and precedent. In the evolution of the Red Cross, for a long time "the appeal to the intellect has taken second place[,] and the philosophy of the Red Cross has been traditionally . . . a matter of rationalizing past actions."[14]

Dunant clearly had a view of the essentials of what became the Red Cross Movement, and Moynier had an eye for systematic practice. Both the ICRC and the Red Cross conference articulated certain principles as they evolved, either for the recognition of National Societies or to summarize forms and styles of action. But for a long time there was no formal or "coherent definition" of Red Cross principles.[15] When the Federation and the Conference tried to enunciate some official principles after the Second World War, the result was "confusion."[16] This indicated, among other things, that the principles were not a very important matter in the Red Cross family, confirming the judgment above that the Red Cross network at that time was more about pragmatic action than careful and systematic reflection. It was at this point that the ICRC, led by Jean Pictet, tried to bring some order out of the chaos, first in 1956 and then in 1965. In the latter year the Red Cross Conference, meeting in Vienna, adopted the currently official version of Red Cross principles, which was explained by Pictet in greater detail in 1979.[17]

Of the official seven Red Cross principles that are supposed to guide activities of the Movement (humanity, impartiality, neutrality, independence, unity, universalism, volunteerism), only the first four really count for the ICRC in the last analysis. Impartiality, neutrality, and independence are essential means to the central goal of ICRC humanitarian protection.

One of the remaining three principles, unity, apparently means only that there should be one National Society in a given state and that it

---

[14] Ian Reid, *The Evolution of the Red Cross*, Background Paper No. 2 to the Tansley Final Report (Geneva: Henry Dunant Institute, 1975), 48. Red Cross principles did not even merit an entry in the index of the 1998 book by Caroline Morehead, or in the 1996 book by John F. Hutchinson.

[15] Bugnion, *La protection*, 424.   [16] *Ibid.*, 426.

[17] See further Jean Pictet, *The Fundamental Principles of the Red Cross: Commentary* (Geneva: Henry Dunant Institute, 1979).

should represent all in the nation. In so far as one might like to transform this principle into the notion of international moral solidarity, in a practical sense any such moral solidarity has always been challenged by the reality of nationalism. Persistent national friction has accompanied some cooperation within the Movement, and this has always been the case. The Movement has long been nationalized into competing components as Swiss, French, Russian, American, Swedish, and other particular factions struggled for influence. Moreover, national competitions were cross-cut by organizational ones, as principally the ICRC and Federation competed intensely as well as cooperated occasionally after 1920. Ideological differences manifested themselves during the Cold War. As the Tansley Report clearly stated in 1975, what is sometimes called the International Red Cross is not really a tight organization but rather a loose, non-unified network. So while there is unity in the matter of one National Society per state, there is much disunity within the Movement.

One principle, volunteerism, has only indirect relevance to the ICRC beyond its regular Assembly members, since ICRC permanent high officials and staff are paid professionals. It is true, however, that some ICRC accomplishments are partially built on the work of National Society volunteers – for example in Cambodia circa 1980. And one principle – universality – simply means that the Movement should pertain to all states that accept IHL, and to all victims of war even in the states that may not.

This leaves independent, impartial, and neutral concern for humanity to be reflected in the core notion of ICRC humanitarian protection. What follows is a new analysis of these and related fundamental factors in the humanitarian protection of the ICRC.

Humanity: the ICRC as a social liberal agency, with a strategy of minimalism

The central purpose of ICRC humanitarian protection is to safeguard the basic worth and welfare of individuals in distress in conflict situations.[18] Philosophically speaking, the ICRC tacitly endorses a type of liberalism emphasizing the equal value and autonomous worth of the human

---

[18] The first half of this chapter borrows heavily from: David P. Forsythe, "Humanitarian Protection: The International Committee of the Red Cross and the United Nations High Commissioner for Refugees," *International Review of the Red Cross*, 843 (September 2001), 675–97; and Forsythe, *UNHCR's Mandate: The Politics of Being Non-political*, Working Paper No. 33, New Issues in Refugee Research, UNHCR, (Geneva: UNHCR, March 2001), pp. 1–34.

being – the individual taking no direct and active part in conflict matters – regardless of national identity or any other distinguishing characteristic other than personhood.[19]

Minimal social liberalism

Humanitarian protection is to be impartial, making no distinction among victims in need. In a telling phrase coined by Jean Pictet, blood always has the same color everywhere.[20] This impartiality does not rule out special attention to the especially vulnerable – the old, the young, the orphaned, the lame, the pregnant, and so on. But one starts humanitarian protection from an impartial baseline – human need for basic dignity.

If one is not an active combatant, and thus not a permissible military target, one is entitled to humanitarian protection. Even if one has once been a combatant, when sick, wounded, or captured, and thus *hors de combat*, one is entitled to humanitarian protection. As noted earlier, these ideas in the European context can be traced at least as far back as to Jean-Jacques Rousseau and his argument that when a national soldier is out of the fight, he (women were not combatants in his time) reverts to being just a universally recognized human being who should be treated humanely.

The ICRC was the first actor to extend this thinking from military to broader security realms. The ICRC came to regard security or political prisoners as also deserving of humanitarian protection even though existing outside situations of armed conflict. For the organization, those viewed as the enemy by public authorities in situations of internal troubles and tensions merit the same basic protections as those detained in war. Technical legal provisions may vary for the prisoner of war or the interned civilian in international war, the detained fighter in a civil war, the security prisoner in internal troubles. But for the ICRC the fundamental

---

[19] Some at the ICRC object to use of the word liberalism, believing it an amorphous term that carries negative baggage. One should not confuse liberalism as a general philosophy, centering on the worth of the individual, with political "liberalism" as practiced in Europe – featuring moderate center-right parties opposed to a large welfare state. It should be emphasized that the ICRC is part of the western liberal philosophical tradition, and that the rhetoric of neutrality cannot obscure that fact. Max Huber actually said much the same thing, albeit in a vague and convoluted way, in *The Red Cross*, 63. Liberalism is used here in the same sense as Nelson Mandela when he wrote, "In later years, the International Red Cross [sic] sent more liberal men who wholeheartedly fought for improvements [in prison conditions]": Mandela, *Long Walk to Freedom* (Boston: Little, Brown, 1995), 411.

[20] Jean Pictet, *Le droit humanitaire et la protection des victimes de la guerre* (Leiden: Sijthoff, 1973), 55.

protections are the same. Any enemy under the control of an adversary is in need of an impartial and neutral intermediary in order to guarantee protection of human dignity. Here again, the legal technicalities in IHL about different categories of detainees, imposed by states via diplomatic conferences, can obscure the moral consistency of ICRC diplomacy.

These fundamental protections sought by the ICRC are minimal[21] and center on humane detention conditions, basic nutrition and health, and essential news about family connections. One reason why the ICRC is so often accepted by warring protagonists, and why treaties on IHL are widely endorsed – and even occasionally and partially implemented – is because the organization does not push for the maximum in humanitarian protection. The ICRC asks not for the release of the unjustly or arbitrarily detained person (except occasionally on grounds of age or health) but that the person be treated with minimal humanity while detained.[22] The organization asks not for luxurious levels of food, clothing, shelter, and health care, but for the minimal acceptable in a hostile context. It does not seek to transmit a full account of a person's conditions but only gives relatives basic information.[23] As one ICRC delegate said, the humanitarian effort was "an effort to bring a measure of humanity, always insufficient, into situations that should not exist."[24]

Some ICRC officials like to contrast the organization's focus on "humanitarian mimima"[25] with modern human rights standards. To these officials, the modern human rights movement strives for a perfect world but is able to achieve very little of it because governments – while endorsing human rights norms – fail to follow through with implementation. By

---

[21] See further Ignatieff, *The Warrior's Honor*, 147.

[22] In 2002, the ICRC requested – and partially got – the release of certain aged detainees held for more than two decades in the conflict over territory in North Africa. No other outside entities, and certainly not western governments and journalists, were interested in the plight of these individuals. See ICRC press release 02/38, 7 July 2002, "Morocco/Western Sahara: 101 Moroccan Prisoners Released and Repatriated." Later there were other, similar releases from this same conflict.

[23] When well-meaning citizens of the United States sought to send messages to prisoners detained by the US at Guantanamo because of the US "war on terrorism," the ICRC refused to transmit those messages, even though they would have boosted the morale of prisoners. Only family members were said to have the right to communicate with prisoners. US authorities opposed the citizen messages, wanting to hold the prisoners in isolated conditions.

[24] Philippe Gaillard, quoted in Rieff, *A Bed for the Night*, 178.

[25] Hans-Peter Gasser, "The International Committee of the Red Cross," in Jurg Martin Gabriel and Thomas Fischer, eds., *Swiss Foreign Policy: 1945–2002* (London: Palgrave Macmillan, 2003), 3 in prepublication copy.

contrast, they say, humanitarian norms can achieve practical protections precisely because of their modest objectives. According to Jean Pictet: "Humanitarian law will be received and will triumph to the extent that one would be able to place it on the universal level and to the extent that it will conform to the reciprocal and well understood interest of diverse nations, because that which is useful to the majority always ends by triumphing."[26]

As ever, views diverge, and what is minimal for the ICRC may seem excessively generous to a military commander or prison director. Certainly over time the ICRC has sought to expand on the definition of minimal. But the organization has believed as a matter of principle that when public authorities resort to force, or otherwise feel threatened and thus do things like implement a policy of exceptional detention on security grounds, one should strive for minimal standards of decency.

Social liberalism is not the same as political liberalism. On the one hand the ICRC takes no position on voting and elections, or the value, status, and power of liberal democratic states and their inter-state organizations. This, despite the fact that liberal democratic states are the philosophical allies of the ICRC, as shown by funding patterns for the organization (covered in the next chapter). But the ICRC does not intentionally favor them in comparison to other states. On the other hand, if one recognizes the reality that the ICRC reflects social liberalism, centering on individual welfare, one can better understand the organization's persistent difficulties in dealing with various illiberal authorities such as communist states during the Cold War.

One can overstate the extent to which political liberals like Britain, France, or the United States remain liberal when engaged in war or other security conflicts. Britain and France engaged in brutal torture when trying to hold on to their colonies in places like Aden, Cyprus, and Algeria.[27] As shown at some length in the previous chapter, the United States abused many prisoners during its "war" or terrorism after 11 September 2001, not just by human frailty but by intentional policy. There seems ample reason for the ICRC to treat all detaining authorities, whether liberal or illiberal in form of government, as presenting a danger to "enemy" detainees. A

---

[26] Pictet, *Le droit*, 148.

[27] On the British in Aden, see for example Kirsten Sellars, *The Rise and Rise of Human Rights* (Phoenix Mill, UK: Sutton Publishers, 2002), chapter 5. For a good review of the French in Algeria, and the broad significance of French torture, see James Le Sueur, *Uncivil War: Intellectuals and Identity Politics during the Decolonization of Algeria*, (Philadelphia: University of Pennsylvania Press, 2001).

broad cultural predisposition to favor humanitarian norms, based on a form of international liberalism and supported by a legal culture, can be negated by perceived short-term security interests.

The ICRC tries to advance its minimalist social liberalism at least as part of the military code of honor, even if a military establishment represents dictatorship or other forms of illiberal states. Sometimes this works. The Argentine military junta followed many of the norms of IHL in the Falklands/Malvinas armed conflict of 1982.[28] But many times the rejection of humanitarian protection stems from the fact that military authorities from illiberal states – and other armed factions – do not in reality accept the miminalist liberalism found in the military code that underlies IHL and the work of the ICRC. This was true, as detailed in chapter 3, in the nasty Balkan wars of the 1990s in which one saw "warriors without honor."[29]

The ICRC has certainly shied away from presenting itself as a liberal agency – for understandable reasons given its desire to be accepted by fighting parties from various cultures and regions. A controversial Swiss author believes that many Swiss organizations strive to present themselves as a strictly service organization that reflects no philosophy.[30] He believes the Swiss innkeeper is the unspoken model for these organizations – the innkeeper making guests comfortable in food and lodging but retiring to the backroom when the philosophical debate starts. Many ICRC officials genuinely believe they are part of a strictly service agency that reflects no philosophy. They certainly have a doctrine, demonstrated below, but for them the emphasis is on pragmatic humanitarian service, not trying to turn principles and doctrine into a Red Cross philosophy.

---

[28] Sylvie-Stoyanka Junod, *Protection of the Victims of Armed Conflict: Falkland–Malvinas Islands* (Geneva: ICRC, 1985). At the same time, the Argentine military junta was engaging in systematic gross violations of internationally recognized human rights in its domestic policies.

[29] Ignatieff, *The Warrior's Honor.*

[30] Ziegler, *The Swiss, the Gold, and the Dead,* 176–7. Because Ziegler, a well known if controversial public figure, is prone to point an accusing finger at many of his fellow Swiss citizens, he is not popular in many Swiss circles. Of the Swiss ruling class of the 1940s he has said that they were "Arrogant, over-weening, self-righteous, and ever ready to dispense moral advice to others [but] regard Switzerland as a special case," 264. He was not one to skip over the fact that ICRC President Max Huber was chairman of Alusuisse that "employed several hundred Ukrainian slave laborers bought from the SS," 62. Supposedly Ziegler wanted to be coopted into the ICRC Assembly but never was. This would not be surprising; see chapter 6 concerning the type of person asked to join the Assembly.

But the fact remains that humanitarian protection as practiced by the ICRC is a type of minimalist social liberalism in action. The starting point is the equal and autonomous value of the individual qua individual. This is the core of classic philosophical liberalism. It was not incongruous for the ICRC to have arisen in the Christian West, sustained at first by the Genevan charitable impulse.

Assistance and protection

We should be clear that assistance is a type of protection. Many ICRC statements and publications confuse an understanding of this point. Often ICRC officials speak of "assistance and protection" as if they were two different things. ICRC publications, such as annual reports, present protection as if it pertained mainly to detention visits, and then present separate entries covering various types of "relief." Charts about expenditure do likewise, presenting the costs of protection, meaning detention visits, as separate from the costs of "health and relief."

One ICRC official takes care to specify two meanings of "protection": a general meaning including assistance, and a particular meaning referring to something different from assistance.[31] Recall, however, that ICRC protection started with medical relief to the war wounded. Henry Dunant sought to protect the war wounded at Solferino from additional misery and agonizing death. Past ICRC officials like Max Huber, even after the First World War and the development of more extensive prison visits, said that providing assistance was the primary mission of Red Cross actors.[32] It is for this reason that some ICRC officials have been very clear that medical and nutritional assistance, among other types, is a form of protection.[33] Yet overall the organization has not consistently followed this approach. It is not an adequate defense to say that the ICRC Annual Reports, other publications, and the ICRC website on the Internet are confusing on this matter because certain donors do not want to fund detention visits but rather only relief, and therefore relief has to be presented as something apart from protection.

---

[31] François Bugnion, *Le Comité International de la Croix-Rouge et la protection des victimes de la guerre* (Genève: CICR, 1994), xvi.

[32] Huber, *The Red Cross*, 71

[33] Yves Sandoz, "La notion de protection dans le droit international humanitaire et au sein du Mouvement de la Croix-Rouge," in Christophe Swinarski, ed., *Etudes et essais sur le droit international humanitaire et sur les principes de la Croix-Rouge* (Geneva: CICR, 1984), especially at 983.

Although customary usage of the English language makes this subject awkward to present, in reality the ICRC's humanitarian protection in the field encompasses primarily traditional protection and relief protection.[34] In traditional protection, the ICRC observes the behavior of public authorities according to international humanitarian norms, either legal or moral, and then makes representations to the authorities for the benefit of persons of concern to it – namely victims of war and of other conflict situations. The objective is to see that victims are not abused or otherwise treated inappropriately. In relief protection, there can be an element of supervision and representation, along with the central effort to provide the goods and services necessary for minimal human dignity in conflict situations. When the ICRC makes detention visits and also provides goods and services to those detained, it can clearly be seen that assistance is part of protection. The detainee is to be neither beaten nor starved.

Protecting a person from death by starvation is just as important as protecting a person from death by torture. Protecting a person from hypothermia is just as important as protecting a person from confinement in painful positions. Some threats to human dignity call for diplomatic or legal representation, and some threats to human dignity call for that process plus the provision of socioeconomic goods and services. In both cases one is engaged in protecting the individual from unacceptable harm. And sometimes, if the ICRC did not provide relief protection, there would be no one to watch over in traditional protection. The victim would be dead.

Just as the Universal Declaration of Human Rights and related documents endorse socioeconomic rights as well as civil-political rights in general, so ICRC traditions and IHL endorse relief protection as well as traditional protection. In IHL as well as ICRC traditions, there is a right to assistance, although the law does not specify who is entitled to provide such relief in armed conflicts. But, for example, starvation is no longer legally permitted as an act of war, and the ICRC acts in keeping with this standard in its diplomacy.[35]

A broad notion of humanitarian protection counters the notion that other actors might take over relief in conflicts, as if ICRC strategy and

---

[34] Humanitarian protection also includes legal development efforts and family reunification activities, but here I emphasize only provision of relief and detention visits for reasons of space.

[35] Jelena Pelic, "The Right to Food in Situations of Armed Conflict: The Legal Framework," *International Review of the Red Cross*, 844 (December 2001), 1097–1110.

tactics were only necessary for detention visits but not for provision of assistance. ICRC humanitarian protection requires mostly the same image and basic policy calculations in relief action for the civilian population as in detention visits. Of course large-scale relief to the civilian population requires certain managerial and logistical skills not necessary in traditional detention visits. Still, in relief the ICRC has to secure access to those in need, maintain an image of neutrality in the context of power politics, and fend off efforts to manipulate the organization, all the while maintaining an eye for the rules of IHL.[36]

Liberal ends but conservative means: ICRC tactics

While the ICRC exists to protect human dignity in conflicts, which is a liberal *raison d'être,* it tries to do so through means that are essentially conservative. By conservative I mean cautious, time tested, and respectful of public authority and public law.

From the start the lawyerly Gustav Moynier, who personally was cautious and prudent,[37] sought the approval of states for Henry Dunant's idea of private, voluntary aid associations to help the war wounded. According to one ICRC delegate turned historian, "On 26 October 1863, the representatives of sixteen *States* [my emphasis] met in Geneva and on 29 October adopted after four days of discussion, ten resolutions which constituted the founding charter of the Red Cross."[38] Even though the October conference was not a diplomatic conference, and many who attended such as military doctors were not sitting as state representatives, from the very beginning the ICRC sought the approval of the Confederation and other states for launching its endeavors, even before the 1864 diplomatic conference. In contemporary human rights circles one sometimes speaks of GONGOs: governmentally organized non-governmental organizations. Despite all the emphasis on private initiative, the ICRC was, in its origins, very close to being a GONGO. This is one reason why the ICRC became the establishment humanitarian organization. Its initial and core role was approved by states.

---

[36] See further David P. Forsythe, "Humanitarian Assistance: A Policy Analysis," *International Review of the Red Cross,* 314 (September–October 1996), 512–31.

[37] Morehead, *Dunant's Dream,* 119; Coursier, *La Croix-Rouge Internationale,* 19; Jean de Senarclens, *Gustave Moynier: le batisseur* (Geneva: Editions Slatkine, 2000).

[38] Durand, *The ICRC,* 7.

As stressed in chapter 1, from its earliest days the ICRC tried not to exceed the bounds of state goodwill.[39] As one historian has noted more critically, in the history of the Red Cross Movement there was "tension between Dunant's vaulting universalism and his colleagues' unquestioning acceptance of the limitations imposed by the existence of nation-states."[40] When the ICRC arranged the dispatch of two observers to the war in Schleswig-Holstein in 1864, they carried a letter of recommendation from the Swiss Confederation in Berne.[41]

So, unlike Amnesty International or Doctors Without Borders, the ICRC has long preferred a cooperative rather than an adversarial role *vis-à-vis* public authorities. Its basic *modus operandi* is a discreet search for cooperation in humanitarian matters, preferably in keeping with IHL. It engages in public criticism only as a last resort, and it places little systematic reliance on public naming and shaming in order to protect human dignity. It can be recalled that conservative tactics ultimately distinguished the ICRC in the Nigerian civil war from Joint Church Aid (the more radical faith-based coalition not tied to the Geneva Conventions).

The ICRC manifests conservative tactics in yet another sense. The ICRC likes to be able to present itself to authorities as a known commodity with a limited mandate. It strives for predictability in pursuing minimal individual protections, figuring that this will enhance its acceptability to parties in a conflict. Its officials who exceed agency guidelines or who are not evaluated as sufficiently predictable do not last very long or advance very far in the organization.

Reference to IHL as a tactical matter is a complex subject. In that the law contains some liberal substance, codifying protections of human dignity in armed conflict in the space left over from codification of military necessity, reference to the law can be liberal. But reference to that law can also be conservative, in the sense of providing a legal rationale for *not doing something that benefits individuals.*

One sees this conservative use of law in certain efforts to defend the ICRC's record with regard to the German concentration camps in the 1930s. As an ICRC author stated, "Thus, the ICRC was singularly devoid of means with which to ensure the protection of civilians," because its legal drafting efforts resulting in the Tokyo draft legal instrument for civilians

---

[39] Boissier, *De Solferino*, 23.

[40] John Hutchinson, *Champions of Charity: War and the Rise of the Red Cross* (Boulder: Westview, 1996), 24.

[41] Knitel, *Les Délégations*, 17.

had been rejected before the war.[42] Rather than acknowledging the defects of ICRC *humanitarian diplomacy*, the writer uses *law to justify inaction*. This was the conclusion of Arieh Ben-Tov, namely, that the ICRC had been legalistic about the possibilities for protecting European Jews during the Nazi era, seeing legal impediments rather than political/diplomatic possibilities.[43] The ICRC's shortcomings in this regard were all the more evident in that the ICRC's Edmond Boissier had warned at the time, with regard to political prisoners, that the organization's "authority is damaged by inaction and excessive caution."[44] A problem in the 1930s was the organization's tendency to say that since IHL did not cover political prisoners, its hands were tied. In any event, the fundamental point is that the ICRC's approach to helping person's in distress was sometimes exceedingly cautious when the situation was not clearly covered by IHL.

Whether reference to IHL reflects liberal ends or conservative means, there is such a thing in ICRC diplomacy as creative conservatism. There is ample room for dynamism within ICRC conservative tactics. Delegates are expected to be creative, resourceful, and industrious within legal norms and agency guidelines. Frédéric Maurice was such a recent delegate before he was killed in the Balkan wars of the 1990s, just as Marcel Junod was such a delegate in the 1930s and 1940s. But as will become clear by the end of this chapter, delegates are expected to follow organizational guidelines on a whole series of issues designed to promote discreet co-operation with public authorities.

ICRC conservative tactics are also evident as part of its understanding of neutral humanitarianism.

Neutrality: humanitarian protection as political and non-political

Humanitarian protection as practiced by the ICRC necessarily entails a type of politics that the rhetoric of neutrality cannot erase.[45] Analytically speaking, the ICRC confronts three types of politics. It participates in the first, tries to minimize the second, and occasionally may be guilty of

---

[42] Jacques Meurant, "The International Committee of the Red Cross: Nazi Persecutions and the Concentration Camps," *International Review of the Red Cross*, 271 (July–August 1989), 378.

[43] *Facing the Holocaust in Budapest: The International Committee of the Red Cross and the Jews in Hungary 1943–1945* (Geneva: Henry Dunant Institute, 1988).

[44] Quoted in Meurant, "Nazi Persecutions," 379, quoting both Fevez and Ben-Tov.

[45] David P. Forsythe, *Humanitarian Politics: The International Committee of the Red Cross* (Baltimore: Johns Hopkins University Press, 1977).

the third. The same is true for other actors that practice international humanitarian protection like the UN Refugee Office (UNHCR).

Humanitarian politics: lobbying for others

The ICRC consistently and persistently struggles to have endorsed and then implemented the (minimalist) liberal values found in its mandate. So it participates in the political struggle to have one policy predominate over others. Politics broadly defined is about who gets what, when, and how.[46] The ICRC struggles to see that victims of war and security politics get the minimal protection necessary for human dignity, even in the midst of militarized and other conflict. "Humanitarian politics" equates to what Michael Ignatieff calls "moral politics."[47] Other authors still prefer "humanitarian politics."[48] As David Rieff has written, it is an "unarguable point that all actions in the public sphere are in some sense political."[49]

When it helps develop IHL, the ICRC participates in the international legislative process. The legislative process is always a political process, entailing a struggle to have accepted in law one set of values rather than another. Traditional lawyers, some of whom were found often enough within the ICRC of the past, do not always fully appreciate that law is not just a technical language and set of rules but is also codified policy preferences. To some traditional lawyers, what is legal cannot be political. But a more insightful characterization is that IHL reflects at least some preference for humanitarian policy, even if state interest in military necessity is also codified. When the ICRC tries to get states formally to accept IHL, it is lobbying for a set of liberal rules to limit the exercise of military force in order to benefit victims. When it "offers its services" outside of armed conflict, it is trying to persuade states to accept a liberal set of values that limit security policies. Its approach may be low key, but it is still engaged in advocating a policy preference – for humane as compared to brutal policies.

The sum total of ICRC activity in behalf of the treaty banning weapons that cause unnecessary suffering like anti-personnel landmines, or the

---

[46] Harold D. Lasswell, *Politics: Who Gets What, When and How* (No place indicated: Peter Smith Publisher, 1990).

[47] Ignatieff, *The Warrior's Honor*, 119.

[48] Larry Minear and Thomas G. Weiss, *Humanitarian Politics* (New York: Foreign Policy Association, 1995).

[49] Rieff, *A Bed for the Night*, 151.

treaty creating the International Criminal Court, is to lobby for a liberal international legal framework emphasizing the dignity of individuals. This liberal framework is intended to regulate and reduce realist foreign policies in which states might do whatever power allows in their pursuit of what they see as their national interest.[50]

The ICRC, therefore, is highly political in the broad sense that the organization is a public interest lobby (albeit with service duties in the field) pressing public authorities to accept and implement public policy for the good of victims of conflicts. This policy may be codified in IHL, or uncodified but pursued via ICRC diplomacy. Some ICRC officials have a closed mind on the subject, refusing to recognize the reality of the type of politics entailed in humanitarian protection. Other ICRC key players understand fully, but most of these believe the organization can never address publicly this reality of humanitarian politics because of the importance of maintaining the semantics of neutrality.

Power politics: neutrality in context

As least initially, it is easy enough to distinguish ICRC advocacy for others from the self-interested politics of public authorities that involves national and factional advantage. Even while being a public interest lobby (and service agency), the ICRC tries to remain as detached as possible from the type of politics that revolves around the exercise of power for either national or partisan advantage. The ICRC is motivated primarily by concern for others – the victims of war and other major conflicts. This can be compared to traditional state officials who are primarily motivated by national or partisan advantage. As state officials, they are primarily responsible for advancing national interests, not for advancing the good of all – foreigners as well as national. As Michael Walzer has noted, national leaders "have to" come down on the side of national advantage; that is what they are there for, what they are expected to do.[51] As holders of national office, they may also be strongly motivated by considerations of political party competition or other factional advantage.

The ICRC (like the UN refugee office) tries to avoid national and partisan power struggles as much as possible. The ICRC is especially concerned *to be perceived as* neutral. The ICRC tries to avoid, or minimize, or balance

---

[50] See further David P. Forsythe, "The US and Human Rights: Two Levels, Two Worlds," in David Beetham, ed., *Politics and Human Rights* (London: Blackwells, 1996), 111–30.
[51] Walzer, *Just and Unjust Wars*, 325–6.

if possible whatever impact its humanitarian protection may have on the power and status of states and the various factions engaged in power struggles. Now the fact is that even its most basic activities may give some advantage to one public authority as compared to another. This we saw especially clearly with regard to the organization's efforts for political prisoners in Greece in the late 1960s, where its presence in that country provided some legitimacy to the military authorities that had overthrown the democratic government. The realm of humanitarian politics and the realm of power and partisan politics always overlap. There is no such thing as absolute neutrality.

On occasion the ICRC has retreated to the sidelines rather than stay engaged on terms that, to Geneva, violated the principle of neutrality. In 1972 the organization withdrew from visiting political detainees in South Vietnam, believing that the good it was able to do for prisoners was not commensurate with the contribution it was inadvertently making to the reputation of the authorities in Saigon. At one point the ICRC withdrew from visiting *convicted* prisoners in South Africa, since after a considerable period of trying it was not allowed to see administrative detainees and those undergoing interrogation. In Ethiopia in the 1980s, the organization felt it could not provide relief as part of a governmental relocation scheme for the civilian population, because of its impact on the power struggle between the government and rebel sides. The ICRC felt that the terms insisted on by the government meant that the organization was being used to help remove civilian cover for the rebels, without corresponding humanitarian advantage to relocated civilians.

In the more than 140 years of the ICRC's existence, and even with the opening of the organization's archives, there is little evidence of the ICRC *intentionally* trying to favor one state or political party – aside from deferring to the priorities of the Swiss state during the Second World War.

Inadvertent departure from neutrality?

Being made up of Swiss from the governing classes, the ICRC Assembly may have occasionally strayed from a reasonable standard of neutrality. The historian John F. Hutchinson has shown how the members of the Assembly displayed attitudes toward females that were characteristic of Swiss biases of their time.[52] Caroline Morehead has shown how Assembly members displayed demeaning attitudes toward non-white

[52] Hutchinson, *Champions of Charity*.

non-westerners that were also characteristic of Swiss biases of their time.[53] It would be surprising if Assembly members, being human after all, had not occasionally shown a bias in strategic politics as well.

(Neutrality in strategic politics is not the same as impartiality in treatment of victims. For the ICRC, neutrality implies negative limitations – such as a reluctance to engage in specific public denunciation except as a last resort. Impartiality, by comparison, implies a positive duty to take equal action. We noted that in its early history, the ICRC concentrated its activities more in the West than in other parts of the world. But it did not act to privilege one western state or coalition over another. Whatever imbalances existed were related more to impartiality than to neutrality: related more to unequal treatment for victims than to bias in favor of one power center compared to another. We noted that the ICRC in the First World War did not show as much effort on the southern and eastern fronts as on the western one, and that the organization in the 1930s did not show the same concern for non-European victims of war as European ones. All of this has to do with the record of impartiality in historical perspective.)

The question of an informal bias within the organization is a complicated matter. In previous chapters we have cited new research suggesting that a number of high ICRC officials, some of whom also held office in Berne, were part of a Swiss governing class that was strongly anti-communist after 1917.[54] Given the strength of anti-communism in Switzerland in the inter-war years, it would have been remarkable for the ICRC to be totally unaffected by that orientation. ICRC leaders like Presidents Ador and Huber came from the same social milieu that dominated Swiss public life. In that regard it can be noted that the ICRC sought dialogue with the Bolsheviks in Moscow and an in-country presence, whereas the Swiss Confederation pursued a policy of non-recognition and exclusion. Still, we noted at least the possibility that the ICRC did not condemn Italian use of poison gas in Ethiopia during the 1930s in part because it saw the fascists as a barrier to the communists. Caroline Morehead believes that Carl J. Burckhardt manifested those views.[55]

---

[53] Morehead, *Dunant's Dream*, 122.

[54] Jean-François Fayet and Peter Huber, "La mission Wehrlin du CICR en Union soviétique (1920–1930)," *International Review of the Red Cross*, 849 (March 2003), 95–118. See also Morehead, *Dunant's Dream*, 176, arguing that President Ador was strongly anti-communist.

[55] Morehead, *Dunant's Dream*, 311. There is no evidence to date that ICRC personnel intentionally assisted Nazi fugitives in their flight from criminal justice after World War II.

We have already noted (in chapter 2) that the organization may have unintentionally tilted toward the United States in both the Korean and the Vietnam wars, and toward France in Southeast Asia from 1947 to 1954.

It is possible that on rare occasions the organization may have deferred to power, not simply to western powers, but to any powerful state. When China took over Tibet in 1954, the ICRC was silent about whether Tibet became occupied territory subject to the Fourth GC.

In the Nigerian civil war the organization did contribute, through lack of carefully considered policies, to the interests of the rebel side. In defying the Federal blockade on Biafra in order to provide relief, the organization played into the hands of the rebels and their calculations about obtaining arms and getting publicity for their cause.

Neutral motivation does not automatically guarantee a neutral impact. Part of humanitarian politics lies in calculating how to promote a reputation for neutrality in the context of power politics.

Over time, it is clear that the ICRC improved its record of neutrality in East–West power struggles. As already noted, the organization tried to provide impartial protection to communist detainees, among others, in places like Greece in the 1960s. Also relevant here is the ICRC's record in Latin American during much of the 1970s and 1980s. In that region the organization also sought to protect detainees, said to be left wing, from the policies of ultra-nationalists who implemented highly brutal policies to defend the "national security state" in places like Chile, Argentina, Uruguay, Paraguay, Brazil, and El Salvador. The supposedly "left wing political" orientation of the detainees made no difference. Likewise in Cambodia from July 1979, the ICRC convinced the Hun Sen government and its communist Vietnamese backers of the good-faith intentions of the ICRC (and UNICEF) that allowed a relief program to go forward worth more than $100 million.

One way to minimize this potential dilemma is for the ICRC to be accepted as a neutral humanitarian intermediary on both sides of a given conflict. If the ICRC engages in the same type of protective activity on

But it appears to be the case that ICRC offices, especially in Italy, were not careful in controlling the distribution of Red Cross travel documents, which allowed other parties, including Catholic officials, to use them for the benefit of German Nazis on the run like Adolf Eichmann. See Uki Goñi, *The Real Odessa: How Peron Brought the Nazi War Criminals to Argentina* (London: Granta Books, 2002), especially 123, 247–9, 298. There was a Swiss connection to the traffic in war criminals, as several officials in Berne cooperated with both Germany and Argentina in this matter. But ICRC knowledge of the involvement has not been shown. Other states, including the United States, were involved in this traffic which allowed certain Nazi officials to flee criminal justice.

both sides of the struggle, presumably its neutrality of impact will be recognized. But this situation does not always play out as the organization desires. In the First Persian Gulf war between Iran and Iraq during 1980 to 1989, the ICRC carried out detention visits to prisoners of war on both sides. This fact did not prevent Iran's claim that the ICRC was biased against it, a controversy that led to the suspension of ICRC visits on that side for a time (not to mention the physical abuse of an ICRC delegate). In general, however, if the ICRC can function on both or all sides of a conflict, the probabilities are that it will be regarded as having a neutral impact on the protagonists. As mentioned, when the ICRC was able to monitor the return of Israeli military personnel from Lebanon, many on the Israeli side saw better that the organization did not work just for Palestinian detainees but also for Israeli detainees.

Neutrality and discretion

Another way to minimize difficulties over impact while promoting an image of neutrality is to be discreet, which for the ICRC justifies one of its primary conservative tactics. A comparison of the ICRC with the United Nations High Commissioner for Human Rights is illustrative. The second High Commissioner, Mary Robinson, was outspoken in her advocacy of human rights as defined by the 1948 Universal Declaration of Human Rights and other international documents. Robinson claimed that she was being neutral in that her loyalty was to the Universal Declaration and other international legal instruments, not to any particular state or coalition of states.

But various states, particularly the United States, became unhappy about Robinson's public statements and worked actively for her tenure not to be extended, because they regarded her voice as inconveniencing their national policies. When Robinson spoke out about human rights violations in China, for example, Washington found her a nuisance since US policy at that time was one of constructive engagement with China – namely to avoid public controversy over human rights while pursuing economic and security agreements, and perhaps human rights improvements over time. Likewise, when Robinson spoke out in favor of an international investigation of possible Israeli excessive use of force at Jenin in 2002, the United States and Israel regarded her statements as inconvenient, regardless of whether her motivation stemmed purely from a concern for human rights and/or humanitarian law.

Mary Robinson's experience was similar to that of a previous Secretary General of the UN, Dag Hammarskjöld, who also claimed that he was neutral in state power struggles because his loyalty was to the UN Charter. Important states still found his statements and policies inconvenient and unacceptable.[56]

Those who speak out about violations of international human rights and humanitarian norms, like the UN High Commissioner for Human Rights (which has only a small field presence around the world), or Amnesty International (which most of the time does not run programs on the ground), or Doctors Without Borders (which has had great difficulty both "blowing the whistle" and operating in the field), are frequently charged with being political, partisan, or – in a word – not neutral. Their loyalty to international standards, even if a demonstrable fact over time, does not save them from charges of bias and departure from neutrality. States may charge a human rights or humanitarian agency with partisanship if public comments prove irritating enough. The Reagan Administration so charged Amnesty International during the controversies over Central America in the 1980s.[57]

The ICRC believes that one way to avoid some of this controversy is to be discreet. If one makes representations to state officials in a quiet process, one is not going to be charged – at least not rationally – with playing to the grandstand, or seeking media exposure, or trying to raise funds with donors by way of a higher profile, or doing the bidding of adversaries. Other actors like AI who believe in the efficacy of public pressure learn to live with state criticism. The ICRC has tried to minimize public controversy with the goal of being accepted as a neutral intermediary. A former member of the ICRC Assembly wrote that Red Cross actors should "avoid any stand which might jeopardize the success of their work."[58] The organization wants not just to assert its view of neutrality but to be widely *perceived* as being neutral.

---

[56] Hammarskjöld's claims to neutrality based on allegiance to the UN Charter did not save him from the wrath of the Soviet Union and France when he directed UN military forces in the old Belgian Congo. No doubt the Secretary-General, especially given his messianic complex, thought he was being neutral in state struggles. But he was still perceived by Moscow as acting against Soviet interests in Central Africa, and by Paris as encouraging the UN to infringe too much on state sovereignty. See further Thomas G. Weiss, David P. Forsythe, and Roger A. Coate, *The United Nations and Changing World Politics* (Boulder: Westview, 2004, 4th edn,) Part I. On United Nations neutrality see also Theo van Boven, "Some Reflections on the Principle of Neutrality," in Swinarski, ed., *IHL*, especially at 651.

[57] See, for example, Sellars, *Human Rights*, chapter 7.

[58] Max Petitpierre, *A Contemporary Look at the International Committee of the Red Cross* (Geneva: ICRC, 1971), 64.

For many contemporary ICRC officials, however, discretion in pursuit of a neutral image is a tactic to be calculated. Unlike Max Huber, who regarded discretion as an immutable component of Red Cross neutrality, these modern ICRC leaders have a different view. While discretion is the normal operating tactic of the organization, they do believe in going public in defense of principle when the context warrants. But in that case, they run the risks that Mary Robinson encountered.[59]

There can be negative aspects to ICRC discreet neutrality. The organization may be seen as an accomplice to evil, if it is aware of gross violations of humanitarian norms but does not publicly protest. The Nazi Holocaust demonstrates this.[60] In the past the ICRC has forfeited support, since potential supporters could not help the organization because they did not know what its views were or exactly what it was doing. The Tansley Report showed this. It is difficult for the ICRC to be a fully fledged guardian for humanitarian standards if it rarely speaks out in their favor. That is, the ICRC cannot be the conscience of the Red Cross Movement and the champion of IHL if it only engages in quiet diplomacy. More will be said about discreet neutrality below.

Clearly, the organization often faces tough choices about how to maintain the image of neutrality in conflict situations when other parties seek to use the ICRC for their expedient purposes. To be effective one must engage in humanitarian politics. But to maintain the image of neutrality, one has to be aware of perceptions of taking sides in power politics.

Bureaucratic politics: protecting the organization

According to the historian John F. Hutchinson, the ICRC can also be affected by bureaucratic or organizational politics stemming from competition among units of the Red Cross Movement or other humanitarian actors.[61] For him, the ICRC's petty bureaucratic politics was in evidence, for example, when it maneuvered to oppose, behind the scenes, the development of an International Relief Union linked to the Federation in the

---

[59] As early as the First World War, in the context of a British–German dispute over a ship called the *Ophelia*, the ICRC asserted a right to give its public view about humanitarian controversies: Bugnion, *La protection*, 124. But as Bugnion notes in further discussion of the ICRC and public statements, the claims and practices of the organization can seem contradictory. See also 1067–8.

[60] There is the view that the real ICRC error in the matter of the Holocaust was the lack of discreet but dynamic diplomacy with high Nazi leaders, not the lack of public protest.

[61] I refer here to his articles, cited in chapter 2, about ICRC suspicions regarding the proposed international Relief Union.

inter-war years. In public the ICRC could hardly oppose something that might benefit civilians in distress, but in private it was worried about being put out of business. In the Nigerian civil war, one of the reasons why it tilted toward the Biafran side was that it did not want to be preempted by a coalition of faith-based aid agencies (Joint Church Aid) that was getting relief into Biafra.

In its response to the situation in British Palestine, evidence shows that when the ICRC adopted this or that policy it had an eye on maintaining the position of the organization. This evidence shows much discussion within the ICRC about what is good for victims of conflicts. But much focus was also on maintaining the traditional status of the organization and fending off demands for dissolution or change.

Logic would suggest that as the ICRC picked its way through the recommendations in the 1975 Tansley Report, it eventually agreed to develop better relations with National Societies in part to undercut the appeal of the Federation. It eventually agreed to develop more consultations with outsiders in part to stave off demands for internationalizing the ICRC's Assembly.

It can sometimes be difficult to say what position is required within the Red Cross Movement in the name of a well-considered humanitarian policy, and what is a result of organizational pride and bureaucratic self-interest. Some at the ICRC are inclined to say that it contested the creation and expansion of the Federation's roles because only the all-Swiss ICRC, linked to the permanent neutrality of the Swiss state, could provide reliable humanitarian protection. Likewise, in Palestine after World War II, what was at issue, in the view of Geneva, was the continued existence of an ICRC that could do enormous good for conflict victims. In this view, the ICRC did not manifest self-serving bureaucratic interests but only well-considered humanitarian calculations; the ICRC had the interests of the victims at heart, not the status of the organization.

There is considerable truth to this argument. But it is also the case that the ICRC sometimes drifted rather than exercising dynamic leadership, and still it opposed changes within the Movement that threatened its preeminent position as guardian of IHL and leader of humanitarian diplomacy. French-speaking ICRC officials acknowledged in private that there had been periods of "flottement" and indecision and lethargy.[62] And yet ICRC leaders, under the influence of organizational pride and also Swiss nationalism, could not bring themselves to accept more dynamic

[62] Interviews, Geneva.

arrangements that would alter a Swiss-inspired and Swiss-led organization that had carefully nurtured a heroic image. It did not help that Swiss authorities in Berne sometimes urged the status quo on the ICRC. All of this will become clearer when we discuss the independence of the ICRC below.

The ICRC has an admirable history of being primarily motivated to aid victims of war and other conflicts. It has shown remarkable determination in this vocation. But organizational pride and Swiss nationalism have not been absent, and from time to time they have contributed to petty bureaucratic politics. Of course the leaders of the Federation, or the Swedish Red Cross, or the American Red Cross, and so on, have not been angels above the fray in these matters, but that is a subject for detailed analysis elsewhere.

Summarizing humanitarian protection and politics

In its efforts at humanitarian protection, the ICRC is both a political and a non-political actor. One must specify what type of politics one means. Unfortunately the word "political" means many things to many people, regardless of what language is being used. All too often there is a tendency to refer to humanitarianism or humanitarian protection as if a struggle over public policy was not involved. This is pronounced in some lawyers interested in IHL. There is a semantic tradition of referring to humanitarian affairs without definition or sharp analysis, and then arguing that unspecified "politics" should not intrude.[63] This is not helpful to policy making or understanding. When an ICRC Assembly member writes that the organization's "neutrality forbids its interference in politics,"[64] this is so vague as to be meaningless, but it is also partially misleading.

There is such a thing as the politics of being non-political. This the ICRC, like the UNHCR, practices as part of humanitarian protection. At its better moments the ICRC carefully calculates its policies about how to better the lives of victims of conflicts, taking into account the power politics of other relevant actors. Neutral humanitarianism is not an automatic thing; it has to be carefully constructed. Most of the time the organization now carefully calculates its own objectives that benefit victims, while trying to ensure that the organization is not inappropriately

---

[63] Neil McFarland, *Politics and Humanitarian Action*, Occasional Paper #41, Watson Institute for International Studies, Brown University, 2000.
[64] Petitpierre, "A Contemporary Look," 65.

used in the self-interested strategic and partisan struggles conducted by public authorities. It thus resists being drawn into power politics. Lurking in the background is the danger that the ICRC will fall victim to bureaucratic or organizational politics, particularly when its traditional position is challenged by another humanitarian actor.

ICRC independence

One cannot practice neutral and impartial humanitarian protection, whether pertaining to detention visits, relief to the civilian population, or the development of the law that seeks to advance both of those actions, unless one is independent from states and other power centers.

General overview

Certainly in terms of formal decisions and clear evidence, despite failing to achieve a perfect record, which no group of humans can achieve, ICRC independence from the western liberal democracies that provide most of its budget is well demonstrated over more than a century. As noted, the ICRC filed a very strong report with French authorities during the Algerian war clearly documenting French torture and other abuse of Algerian detainees. Below is a discussion of a very candid ICRC report about harsh detention policies by the Dutch in Indonesia during the Second World War. In the previous chapter there was a discussion of ICRC differences with the United States regarding treatment of prisoners in Washington's "war" on terrorism. The dominant pattern, links to the Swiss Confederation aside, is that the ICRC has taken its own decisions on the basis of its view of social liberalism and has not taken instructions from states or clearly deferred to state pressures. To expect ICRC personnel, part of the Swiss middle and upper classes, to be totally free from all social bias, and thus to manifest perfect impartiality and neutrality, is to raise an impossibly high standard of expectation. The fundamental issue is whether, when the ICRC strayed from impartial and neutral action, that action resulted from misperception or from deference to the western states that provided its budget and diplomatic support.

In historical perspective, ICRC independence compares well to most of its peers. The International Commission of Jurists, for example, was first under the thumb of the US Central Intelligence Agency and employed former Nazis before evolving into an independent and fully private organization.[65] Based in Geneva, this legally oriented, human rights, non-governmental organization was headed for a brief time in the early twenty-first century by a former ICRC official, Louise Doswald-Beck.

Amnesty International in its early years had a very cozy relationship with the British government. On several occasions AI officials who were British nationals sought a discreet relationship with British governments in which AI's independence was tainted.[66] Because of these early experiences, AI came to reject all governmental funding and its later overall record became one of fierce independence.

The UN refugee office (UNHCR) is part of the UN system and must answer to an Executive Committee made up of states – and ultimately to the UN General Assembly, also composed of states. The UNHCR displays considerable independence in its protection work for refugees, despite the fact that its budget is provided primarily by western liberal democracies, but in the last analysis it is not as independent as the ICRC.[67]

ICRC relations with the Swiss Confederation

The persistent situation that sometimes has constituted an exception to this pattern of general ICRC independence pertains to relations with the Swiss state. The definitive history of this relationship has yet to be written. It can be recalled, however, that the origins of the ICRC were intertwined with the Confederation; for example, ICRC officials were part of Berne's delegation to the 1864 Diplomatic Conference that approved the first Geneva Convention for Victims of War. The two actors were closely intertwined much of the time during that early period, and the line demarcating the organization from the Confederation was often blurred. In

---

[65] Howard B. Tolley, Jr., *The International Commission of Jurists: Global Advocates for Human Rights* (Philadelphia: University of Pennsylvania Press, 1994).

[66] See especially Sellars, *Human Rights*, chapter 5; and Jonathan Powers, *Like Water on Stone: The Story of Amnesty International* (Boston: Northeastern University Press, 2001), chapter 4. There are parallels between Peter Benenson, the founder of Amnesty International, and Henry Dunant. Both were perceived to be tainted by scandals, both had profound conflict with colleagues, both became outcasts in the eventually prestigious organizations they started, and both were "rehabilitated."

[67] See further especially Gil Loescher, *The UNHCR and World Politics* (Oxford: Oxford University Press, 2001). One who follows the UNHCR can easily observe that while that agency is funded by essentially the same states that fund the ICRC, the UNHCR often publicly criticizes those same states for their refugee, asylum, and immigration policies. The UNHCR engages in public criticism while claiming to be neutral, and in general states accept that state of affairs. Even more to the point, the UNHCR publicly criticizes states while running programs within many of them.

general Berne took a lively interest in the ICRC, seeing it and its work as a projection of the best values of Switzerland. Berne saw the status and success of the ICRC as reflecting well on the nation and state. In general Berne saw the ICRC as helpful to the state as it tried to project a positive national image. Marcel Pilez-Golaz, the head of the Swiss Foreign Office (Department of Political Affairs), said in 1941, "For Berne in principle what is good for the Red Cross is good for Switzerland."[68]

Without trying to be historically comprehensive about this relationship, one can note that during the First World War the independence of the ICRC was not put into serious question.[69] And we have already covered the subject of the ICRC, the Confederation, and the Soviet Union during the inter-war years.

World War II

The ICRC agreed to being generally supervised by Berne during the Second World War, which was a huge and systematic compromise of its independence. If one uses ICRC archives to look at the organization's relations with the Confederation during the Second World War, at least three types of relationships emerge: Berne's periodic control of an agency inclined to chart its own course, conflict between two obviously

---

[68] Quoted by Isabelle Voneche Cardia, "Les relations entre le Comité International de la Croix-Rouge et la Confédération Helvétique durant la Second Guerre Mondiale," unpublished paper, February 2000, read by permission. Financial matters were not decisive; Berne paid about 20% of the ICRC's expenditures during the Second World War.

[69] See further Yves Collart, "l'affaire Grimm–Hoffmann et l'entrée de Gustave Ador au Conseil fédéral," in Roger Durand, ed., *Gustave Ador: 58 ans d'engagement politique et humanitaire* (Geneva: Fondation Gustave Ador, 1996), 27–94. The president of the organization was Gustave Ador, a nationally prominent French speaker from Geneva. The officially neutral Federal Authorities in Berne were exposed as tilting toward Germany to the detriment of France. Some Swiss-German officials in Berne were caught trying to advance a German–Russian peace, which would have left Germany free to concentrate its military might on France. Berne then turned to the Genevan Ador to reestablish Swiss neutrality. True, Ador then became a Federal Councillor and later even President of the Swiss Executive Council while still being a member of the ICRC's Assembly. But he took the status of ICRC honorary member while serving the Confederation and effectively cut off communication with the organization. It was clear that Ador as a French-speaking Genevan was not going to compromise the independence of the ICRC by pressuring it to act in Berne's interests. Rather, Ador was so important to Berne in restoring Swiss neutrality in the eyes of France that there was no question about Berne pressuring the ICRC. Berne wanted Ador's help, but on the basis of his personal reputation as a leader of the French-Swiss, and as ICRC President, rather than someone who would bring the ICRC into line with Swiss policy. Besides, there was little the Confederation wanted from the ICRC *qua* ICRC.

independent actors, and cooperation to the point of obscuring the separate status of the two actors.

Swiss oversight and periodic control

At the start of World War II Berne decided it needed to keep an eye on all humanitarian organizations based in Switzerland, particularly the ICRC and the Swiss Red Cross.[70] Berne put Edouard de Haller in charge of monitoring the Red Cross actors, partly because he was a member of the ICRC's Assembly and partly because he was the brother-in-law of Pierre Bonna who was a high official in the Swiss Foreign Ministry. The ICRC at this time paid more attention to the legalistic appearance of independence than to the reality. Edouard de Haller became an honorary member of the Assembly but retained his voice and vote in meetings. Unlike Gustav Ador during World War I, de Haller, while an honorary member, did not sever all connections with the organization. Indeed, he stayed deeply involved in ICRC affairs. The ICRC under President Max Huber agreed to these supervisory arrangements which contradicted the precedents from the First World War.[71]

It became clear enough over time that de Haller's primary loyalty was to Berne. When de Haller, a member of the ICRC Assembly, would write to Carl Jacob Burckhardt or others at the ICRC, he used Confederation stationery.[72] (Swiss President Etter, also a member of that Assembly, did the same in October 1942.) In autumn 1942 it was de Haller who alerted Bonna and the Swiss foreign ministry that the ICRC might issue a public appeal regarding the Holocaust (treated in some detail at the end of chapter 1). As noted, Philippe Etter, then President of the Swiss Federal Council, and also a member of the Assembly (but he did not take honorary status, and remained a voting member of the Assembly), made one of his extremely rare appearances in the Assembly when the draft appeal was discussed on 14 October.[73] We already observed that de Haller and Etter (along with Burckhardt and others) spoke out strongly in the successful

---

[70] ICRC Archives, CR 224, 13 May 1938, "Active Neutrality of Switzerland." It is clear from this date that the Confederation wants to know what the ICRC is doing and will do. Also, the Swiss Red Cross is unhappy about not knowing about ICRC plans and activities.

[71] ICRC Archives, Procès-verbal of Assembly Meetings, 1942–1947, vol. 18, PV 1, 19 January 1942.

[72] ICRC Archives, "General Correspondence with the Swiss Foreign Ministry," 1939–1941, Box G. 4, at 256.

[73] Previously the ICRC's President Huber had lobbied his colleagues in the Assembly to get Etter admitted to membership, there being doubts about the wisdom of adding him, given precisely his prominence in Swiss partisan politics. Voneche, "Les relations."

effort to block the draft public appeal. (At this time it apparently made no difference whether one was a regular member or an honorary member of the Assembly, since one could participate and vote in Assembly meetings regardless of status.)

Clearly for de Haller and Etter, their primary concern lay in not irritating Nazi Germany even though their arguments were mostly couched in euphemisms. They did not mention Swiss nationalism and national interests *per se*, but rather spoke about ICRC neutrality and effectiveness and action based on international law. For them, their covering argument was that to speak out about the Holocaust was a violation of neutrality. After the Assembly meeting on 14 October, de Haller told his superiors in the Swiss Foreign Ministry that the meeting had gone well and the draft statement had been buried.[74]

Events from October 1942 were but part of a broader pattern in which Confederation officials did not hesitate to try to keep the ICRC under control on issues of major importance to Berne. It is a matter of record that Swiss Federal authorities had decided early on that they would not be reluctant to apply pressure at different levels of the ICRC if it proved necessary to protect Swiss national interests.[75] The ICRC was often not independent but rather under the thumb of Berne. For example, at the request of the United Kingdom, the ICRC wanted to visit Jewish refugees held in camps in Switzerland, but Berne was unhappy about the ICRC request and would not allow it for fear of negative publicity.[76]

On another occasion, de Haller gave his opinion of how the ICRC should handle matters. In early 1945 France had sought the aid of the ICRC regarding some French nationals who wanted to cross Switzerland from Germany. De Haller told the ICRC what kind of reply to make – namely that simple transport was one thing, but the Confederation did not want to wind up having to provide medical assistance.[77]

Unresolved is whether the ICRC's limited but successful effort to establish a presence in the German concentration camps late in the war (from March 1945) came only after the organization was given an explicit green light from Berne. Given other material in the ICRC archives, Berne's authorization was likely, that being the normal relationship between the ICRC and Berne at that time. On German issues judged sensitive to Berne, the organization did not usually proceed

---

[74] Draft Bergier Report, 1999, 254, www.uek.ch.   [75] Voneche, "Les relations."
[76] Draft Bergier Report, 254–5.   [77] ICRC Archives, Box G.23, 20 February 1945.

without Confederation approval. Such a green light could have been given orally.[78]

Swiss Federal authorities through de Haller also pressured, even controlled, the Swiss Red Cross.[79] When that National Society was prepared to offer sanctuary to certain Jewish children being victimized in France, de Haller intervened on behalf of Berne to oppose the plan. He had no objection to the Swiss Red Cross trying to help Jewish children abroad, but on behalf of Berne he did not want that National Society to serve as a magnet drawing Jewish children into Switzerland. Finally Pilet-Golaz in the Swiss Foreign Ministry vetoed the efforts by the Swiss Red Cross on behalf of foreign Jewish children via the program "Aid to Children." Likewise, the Confederation blocked a plan by the Swiss Red Cross to accept clothing from the United States for Jewish refugees in Switzerland. Once again the issue for de Haller and Berne was Berlin: Switzerland should not be seen as doing too much for Jews affected by German persecution.[80] It seems that whereas Berne's control of the Swiss Red Cross was clear and heavy-handed, with the ICRC the Swiss authorities proceeded with more delicacy and euphemisms – and thus sensitivity to ICRC independence while violating it.

The central point for present purposes is that ICRC officials like de Haller were fully part of the effort to treat certain matters as part of Swiss national interests rather than as part of ICRC humanitarian concern. There was neutral and independent humanitarian protection, and then there was Swiss nationalism – fueled by fears of a German invasion, especially after the Nazis took over Vichy France. It was clear that de Haller and his allies at the ICRC were more narrow nationalists than universal humanitarians. When some Jewish children finally were liberated from the camp at Buchenwald, de Haller wanted to make sure they did not wind up staying in Switzerland.[81] President Huber and his alter ego Carl J. Burckhardt, who became ICRC President in 1944, were deeply implicated in all of this, not only by agreeing to supervision by the Confederation

---

[78] See further Monty Noam Penkower, *The Jews Were Expendable: Free World Diplomacy and the Holocaust* (Urbana: University of Illinois Press, 1983, chapter 8, and especially around 236. And see the Draft Bergier Report, 264.

[79] Draft Bergier Report, 264.

[80] In that the Confederation's policy toward Jewish refugees changed dramatically during 1944–45 once it became clear that the Nazis were going to lose and the Allies were going to win, the issue was not so much Swiss anti-Semitism but whether Berne was going to tilt toward the Axis or the Allies. In other words, I have found no statements indicating that persons like de Haller were anti-Semitic.

[81] Draft Bergier Report, 271.

but also by not contesting vigorously the views of those like de Haller. Dispassionate historians like Favez have suggested that Huber is a much overrated President of the ICRC, and they have their doubts about the integrity of Burckhardt.[82]

Morehead quotes Burckhardt as saying in 1944, regarding an improvement in the prospects for Hungarian Jews, that it would be a "very good thing for Switzerland that at least something positive could be done for the Jews. This would produce a good impression abroad and at the same time dispel the resentment that could spread against our country from the stories of the refugees and the internees."[83] In this view, the ultimate concern is the reputation of Switzerland; the fate of the Hungarian Jews was a means to that nationalistic end.

Continuing ICRC independence

It bears repeating that the ICRC Assembly meeting on 14 October 1942 does not capture the whole story about ICRC relations with Berne during the Second World War. Paradoxically, under Confederation supervision, the ICRC sometimes retained its independence and used the system devised by Berne for its own interests and objectives – and with some success. From time to time de Haller served as a conduit from the ICRC to the Swiss Federal Authorities, as the ICRC would use him to try to lobby Berne. This occurred, for example, on the issue of the ICRC obtaining some naval vessels to transport humanitarian relief; the organization got what it wanted, with the Confederation providing key support. Burckhardt thanked de Haller for helping the organization in Berne.[84]

This sort of ICRC initiative, seeking help from an obviously separate Confederation, happened numerous times during the war. This key back channel was employed by a member of the ICRC Assembly (Suzanne Ferrière) to help in the protection of Jews in Hungary in 1944. It was used by another Assembly member (A. Cramer) to enlist Confederation support for the French and Belgian National Societies in that same year.

Occasionally the ICRC did not follow Confederation suggestions. Early in the war Berne obviously wanted the ICRC to recognize the newly created Slovak Red Cross. Berne officials suggested that Germany would be unhappy if the organization did not recognize that appendage of the fascist

---

[82] Jean-Claude Favez, *The Red Cross and the Holocaust* (Cambridge: Cambridge University Press, 1988, 1999).

[83] Quoted in Morehead, *Dunant's Dream*, 453.

[84] ICRC Archives, procès-verbal of Assembly meetings, 1942–1947, Vol. 18, PV/2, 14 April 1942.

Slovak government, and any German unhappiness might have negative repercussions on the Swiss state. In this case, while Confederation officials expressed their views, they also clearly indicated the final decision was up to the ICRC. Given this signal, Huber told the Confederation that the ICRC was going to maintain its tradition of not recognizing new National Societies during an armed conflict.[85]

Also early in the war, the Confederation presumed to tell the ICRC how to present its report covering Dutch detention policies in Indonesia. Dutch detention had led to harsh conditions for a number of German nationals, including women and children. The ICRC had compiled a truthful report detailing the hardships for the German nationals, a report which the organization shared with Berne. The Nazis were already retaliating by deporting a number of Dutch nationals from the occupied Netherlands for even harsher treatment in Germany. So Berne, with an eye on moderating reprisals in Europe, advised the ICRC to rewrite and tone down its report about Dutch-controlled Indonesia before giving it to Berlin. The ICRC decided to maintain its candid detention report as written, while asking for the release of the detained German women and children (but not the German males) held by the Dutch in the Far East.[86]

Moreover, sometimes it was very clear that the ICRC not only tried to establish its independence from the Confederation but also was not very happy about decisions made in Berne. There was repeated friction between Federal officials and the ICRC over their respective roles as Protecting Power and humanitarian intermediary.[87] To give a concrete example, at one point the ICRC sought approval for a special flight to Lisbon, Portugal. Berne thought that an existing Swiss commercial flight could serve ICRC purposes, but the organization persisted. There was a testy meeting in Geneva involving de Haller, who finally suggested that the Confederation would do what the ICRC wanted if the organization could get Germany to agree to the special flight. (Again and again we see Berne's fear of antagonizing Berlin.) At this point on this issue it is clear that the ICRC sees the world through humanitarian rather than Swiss nationalistic eyes; there are two actors arguing, with different interests and different priorities.[88]

It is fair to conclude that at many times during the Second World War the ICRC acted as an independent organization, even to the point of engaging in friction with the Confederation. Even so, when Berne

---

[85] ICRC Archives, Box G.3/12, G.3/13, No. 76 bis, 12 April 1940.
[86] ICRC Archives, Box G.85/43-127, 23 August 1940.
[87] Voneche, "Les relations."   [88] ICRC Archives, notes de dossier, 21 and 25 June 1943.

decided that an issue was truly important to Swiss national interests, the
ICRC yielded.

Humanitarian bureau of the Confederation?

In addition to Berne dominating the ICRC, and the independent organization jousting with Berne, at times the two actors seemed to become
one. Sometimes the ICRC and the Confederation would consult, discuss,
cooperate, and mutually decide on a course of action. There was constant
telephone traffic between Max Huber and Swiss foreign ministry officials
about ICRC delegates, ICRC reports, ICRC money.[89]

Geneva and Berne would discuss what Swiss national was in what part
of the world, and whether such a person had the qualities to represent
either Berne or Geneva. Should the person under consideration be a representative of the Confederation, which was serving as a Protecting Power
for many belligerents, or a representative of the ICRC. ICRC archives
make it seem as if Berne and Geneva were just flipping a coin to see if Mr.
X would represent Switzerland or the ICRC in places like Brazil. At such
times it was difficult to say whether one was dealing with two different
actors or just two branches of the Swiss state. The ICRC certainly seemed
to have few secrets, if any, from the Confederation.

ICRC archives repeatedly show mutual decision making by the Confederation and the ICRC. Berne sometimes seconded personnel to serve
under the aegis of the ICRC. They shared resources such as trucks. Huber
met with Swiss President Etter to discuss various matters, and various
ICRC officials met with various Confederation officials on numerous
subjects – such as how to handle released detainees who did not wish to
be repatriated. When the United Kingdom wanted the ICRC to stockpile
military uniforms for British prisoners of war, Huber made sure to get
Berne's approval before proceeding. Berne took up the question of ICRC
access to detainees with Japan (the Confederation did not do this with
Nazi Germany).

There was a common perception by numerous outsiders, both during
this era and otherwise, that the ICRC was the humanitarian office of the
Swiss foreign ministry. Most of the time the perception was wrong, or
at least not completely correct, although for a long time ICRC delegates
used Swiss diplomatic passports and had easy access to Swiss embassies,
with their telecommunication networks and diplomatic pouches. (The

---

[89] ICRC Archives, General Correspondence, 1939–1941, G.4, at 255.

ICRC now instructs its Swiss delegates to maintain their distance from Swiss diplomatic posts.) When ICRC delegates were taken hostage in Lebanon in the 1970s, the Confederation got deeply involved in efforts for their safety and release. Such delegates, after all, were Swiss nationals as well as ICRC representatives. But such action by Berne clouded the issue of ICRC independence, and a number of ICRC officials were unhappy about Berne playing such a large role in the fate of the organization's personnel.[90]

The basic problem revisited

How could the ICRC yield so much of its independence to the Swiss Confederation when the organization had such a distinguished record of independence and neutrality? Historically the ICRC has been a very Swiss organization. Its leaders like Max Huber and Carl J. Burckhardt assumed that Swiss nationalism was fully compatible with Red Cross humanitarianism. The Second World War showed that this was a false and damaging assumption. Between 1939 and 1945 Swiss national interests were defined by Berne in such as way as to require severe if inconsistent inroads on ICRC independence. Swiss neutrality was different from ICRC neutrality. Loyalty to the Confederation was not the same as loyalty to the ICRC. The ICRC frequently deferred to the Confederation because the former accepted that its humanitarian work depended on the permanent neutrality of the Confederation. If the Confederation's neutrality required handling Germany with the utmost delicacy, the ICRC – led by Swiss-Germans Huber and Burckhardt – accepted that "adjustment" as a fact of life.

Early in the war, on 6 March 1940, the ICRC hosted a private dinner for some Swiss Federal authorities. Marcel Pilet-Golaz from the foreign ministry made a speech saying in part: "Two things always go together, Mr. President [referring to Max Huber], you have already covered this in detail, neutrality and loyalty, in order to assure the functioning of this [Red Cross] humanitarian work . . . The Red Cross has always shared the name of Switzerland, it [the Red Cross] has made Switzerland esteemed everywhere, has made Switzerland respected everywhere."

In his response, skipping the reference to loyalty, Huber acknowledged the diplomatic and financial support of the Confederation for the ICRC.

---

[90] Interviews, Geneva.

He then went on to say that ICRC work "makes up part of the charitable and constructive mission which corresponds to the perpetual neutrality of our country. This national role [of Swiss neutrality] is at the same time a humanitarian role."[91]

It was this sort of thinking, easily assuming that Swiss nationalism and Red Cross humanitarianism were one and the same, that opened the ICRC to debilitating and pernicious Swiss influence during the Second World War. It was this type of naïvety on the part of Huber and others that was to damage the ICRC's reputation for independence and neutrality. Swiss neutrality as defined in Berne required a departure from Red Cross neutrality as practiced by a normally independent ICRC.

It took the ICRC about four decades to correct more fully what had gone wrong in the Second World War. As the result of a process started in the 1940s, accelerated in the 1970s, and finally culminating in the 1990s, the organization stipulated that one could not sit in the ICRC Assembly and hold most public offices in Switzerland. The ICRC also initiated the 1993 signing of a headquarters agreement with the Confederation making its premises and personnel off-limits to Swiss authorities. Some Assembly members, especially those who had held Confederation positions, had resisted the notion that Swiss nationalism and Red Cross humanitarianism were two different things.

In 2002 the ICRC claimed, as it had already stated in 1986 at the time of an earlier vote, that the organization was so independent from the Confederation that the question of the Confederation's membership in the United Nations would have no effect on ICRC humanitarian protection.[92] Presidents Sommaruga and Kellenberger asserted a fierce independence for the ICRC, and it appears to be the case that there was a surprising absence of telephone traffic and social networking between the ICRC in Geneva and Swiss Federal leaders in Berne in contemporary times. Of course when the ICRC needed Berne's donation to its budget, Geneva assiduously courted Berne.

As we will see in the following chapter, while the ICRC is not what it was during the Second World War, it remains very Swiss at the top, with close relations to the Confederation.

[91] ICRC Archives, Box G. 23, at 606.

[92] ICRC press release no. 02/01, 11 January 2002, "Grave Misuse of the ICRC in Campaign on Swiss Membership of United Nations." Compare ICRC press release 1516 of 23 January 1986.

ICRC general policies

Since the ICRC claims to be the guardian of IHL, some think of the organization as a highly legal if not legalistic actor, full of lawyers fixated on IHL and rigidly looking to that law to determine what to do in the field. In fact, for most of its history the ICRC has been a highly pragmatic organization greatly characterized by *ad hoc* reaction to various conflicts.[93] We noted that despite the Geneva Conventions of 1864 and 1906 it had no general plan of action in the First World War. We also noted that Geneva had a tradition of deferring to the delegate in the field on the assumption that the person closest to the problem knew the problem best. By the Second World War, in addition to collating its experiences for the development of IHL, it was beginning to establish certain general policies – for example, refusing to recognize newly created National Societies during armed conflict, but rather waiting until afterwards to see which entity survived and which did not. We noted the Slovak case in 1940.

By about 1975, stimulated by the Director of Principles and Law Jacques Moreillon, a protégé of Jacques Freymond, the ICRC began systematically recording what it called its doctrine, or what can be more accurately called general statements of policy. These take various forms: clear statements of policy with guidelines for field delegations; long studies with policy guidelines interspersed here and there; and sometimes historical surveys concluding that there is no set policy on the question involved. Most were approved by the Assembly, but a few only by the Assembly's sub-group, now the Council of the Assembly (explained in the next chapter). Space does not allow, nor the reader's patience, a detailed discussion of the almost sixty statements. One can give a sense of the process, and some of the content, by presenting a few examples. The ICRC has put in the public domain, usually through publication in the *International Review of the Red Cross*, the main thrust of most of these statements. So, when on 4 November 1998 the Assembly approved a general statement about the importance of the humanitarian dimension of economic sanctions applied by states (in situations such as Iraq after the Persian Gulf war of 1991), a version of the statement was published in the *Review* in December 1999.

Publicizing these statements has both a positive and a negative dimension. On the positive side, when the ICRC approaches a detaining authority, officials can point to general policy and say that the issue is not really

---

[93] See especially Freymond, "Humanitarian Policy," 413, stressing pragmatic action.

country X or government Y or allegation Z, but rather the usual implementation of general policy. This approach the organization has repeatedly taken on the subject of political or security prisoners. On the negative
side, doctrine may lock the ICRC into a policy that may not be totally
appropriate for a given situation.

Discretion

If we take the general subject of discretion and confidentiality, for example,
we find that ICRC personnel around the world try to adhere to common
policies. There is a principle of cooperation with other human rights and
humanitarian actors, but the ICRC will not share sensitive particulars with
them. If the ICRC is dealing with public authorities that systematically
violate important parts of IHL over time and in major ways, and fail
to make ameliorative changes as discreetly requested by the ICRC, the
organization may issue a public denunciation if it feels such action will
aid victims. It will be more inclined to do so regarding violations of IHL
than violations of general human rights or someone's view of morality.
Most public denunciations require the approval of headquarters.

As a general rule, ICRC delegates adhere to these and other guidelines regarding discretion (and the other side of the coin, publicity) with
more consistency than one finds at the UNHCR. By comparison with the
ICRC, the UN refugee office shows great variation in discretion/publicity,
depending on such things as the field representative involved. The ICRC
has settled policy, the UNHCR does not. It is worth noting in passing
that the UNHCR has found that it can publicly criticize governments, at
least sometimes, and also run programs in-country.[94] The ICRC believes
strongly that discretion contributes greatly to obtaining detention visits.

Not all ICRC policy statements on discretion and confidentiality, however, fit nicely together. At one point the Assembly approved a statement
saying that an obsession with discretion could be counter-productive,
and that discretion ought to be the exception while the sharing of information ought to be the norm. Much like the Tansley Report of 1975,
this Assembly-approved statement argued that ICRC discretion could be
counter-productive to building support for the organization in German-
speaking Switzerland and among the National Societies around the world.

---

[94] On the other hand, some believe the UNHCR has become so desirous of achieving state
cooperation for relief that it has not been appropriately assertive regarding legal and
diplomatic representation for the rights of refugees. See further Loescher, *UNHCR*.

Just because the Assembly formally approved this statement, however, does not mean that it became an important document for the organization. Many in the ICRC really do not believe in the efficacy of public pressure most of the time. Many are timid about activating guidelines that call for public denunciation under certain conditions, although some officials claim that the list of denunciations is rather long. Other agencies, especially in the human rights field, can cite some success sometimes for public pressure,[95] but the ICRC tends to say most of the time that public pressure is for others and that its discretionary approach has been proven over time.[96]

Judicial testimony

The ICRC has evolved the policy over time that it will not allow its representatives to testify in criminal proceedings, despite the fact that some of its delegates did so when subpoenaed after the Second World War. This relatively new policy was endorsed by the International Criminal Tribunal for Yugoslavia (ICTY). The ICTY prosecutor sought to make use of the testimony of an ICRC local employee who had volunteered to testify and who had been on the ground in Bosnia. ICRC officials in Geneva intervened against such testimony, citing the needs of discreet field operations. The court upheld the ICRC's position.[97] This policy is now written into the rules of procedure of the International Criminal Court, which came

---

[95] In 2002 Human Rights Watch claimed that public pressure on Israel about its military using Palestinian human shields led to Israel agreeing to change its policy. Amnesty International has long claimed that its public pressure had led to the release of certain "prisoners of conscience."

[96] There are some clear cases of developments stemming from publicity linked to the ICRC. Perhaps the clearest is when the leaking of ICRC reports on torture by France in Algeria led to major changes in French policy both at home and abroad. In chapter 4 we noted that after the ICRC generated public comment in 2003 about US treatment of detainees at its Guantanamo holding facility, not very long thereafter Washington arranged the release or transfer of many prisoners. It may be impossible to say, scientifically, whether these examples are typical or atypical of the effectiveness of publicity in humanitarian affairs.

[97] This was the case of *Prosecutor v. Simic et al.* (Case No. IT-95-9-PT), Decision on the Prosecution Motion under Rule 73 for a Ruling Concerning the Testimony of a Witness, 27 July 1999. See further Stephane Jeannet, "Recognition of the ICRC's Long-Standing Rule of Confidentiality," *International Review of the Red Cross*, 838 (June 2000), 403–25. On a number of occasions the ICRC, while refusing to allow its personnel to testify in criminal proceedings, has provided certain written material to authorities. This process allows the organization to control what information enters the public domain.

into existence in July 2002.[98] According to Jean Pictet: "One cannot at the same time serve justice and charity. It is necessary to choose. The Red Cross, for a long time, has chosen charity."[99]

This is a complicated question with broad reach.[100] Should the same rule of non-testimony be applied to the representatives of other aid agencies? After all, the representatives of the UNHCR and other relief agencies are also on the ground in conflict situations and complex emergencies. But if the representatives of all aid agencies have immunity from testimony, would this undermine criminal justice?

Should the same rule of non-testimony be applied to journalists? In 2002 the Office of the Prosecutor of the ICTY sought to compel the testimony of Jonathan Randal, former journalist from the *Washington Post*. He had quoted a Serbian official from Bosnia as advocating ethnic cleansing of non-Serbs from northwest Bosnia. Randal refused to testify, arguing that journalistic coverage of events was needed for knowledge about violations of human rights. Furthermore, he argued, if journalists were required to testify they would become targets of repression by tyrannical rulers and lose their freedom to report.[101] The ICTY eventually deferred to Randal's position in general.[102]

But if the ICRC, all aid agencies, and all journalists have immunity from testimony in criminal proceedings, what happens to the prosecution of those committing atrocities? Although the question is anathema to many ICRC officials, would it be possible to come up with some balancing test, weighing the needs of criminal prosecution with the needs of humanitarian action and journalistic reporting?

---

[98] Rules 73(4) to 73(6). See further William Schabas, *Introduction to the International Criminal Court* (Cambridge: Cambridge University Press, 2nd edn, 2004).

[99] Pictet, *Le droit*, 81.

[100] The US Supreme Court reached a contrary conclusion regarding whether members of the Secret Service should be compelled to testify in a judicial matter involving the President of the US. The lawyers for President Clinton argued that members of the Secret Service should be immune from testimony, since such testimony would break the essential bond of confidence between the President and those who guarded him. The argument was that testimony would interfere with the provision of presidential protection. The Court did not accept this logic. See further *In re Sealed* (148 F.3d 1073, D.C. Cir., 1998).

[101] William Safire, "Enter the Globocourt," *New York Times*, 20 June 2002, downloaded into hard copy from the Internet, no page number.

[102] Prosecutor v. Radoslav Brdjanin and Momir Talic, Case No. IT-99-36-AR73.9, Decision on Interlocutory Appeal of Appeals Chamber on "Motion to Appeal the Trial Chamber's Decision on Motion on Behalf of Jonathan Randal to Set Aside Confidential Subpoena to Give Evidence," 11 December 2002.

Unauthorized publicity

On another subject, the ICRC has tried to systematize its action regarding unauthorized release of sensitive information. If an authority releases a partial or inaccurate version of ICRC confidential information, such as a detention report, the organization will demand full and accurate publication. In the event of non-compliance with this demand, Geneva itself will publish the report. This policy has come into play in such situations as Greece in the 1960s, the Middle East in the late 1960s, and Iran in the 1970s.

But different situations require different responses. In one case from South America, where a film made reference to sensitive ICRC diplomacy, the organization itself paid for the editing of the film.[103] In the Balmer case,[104] where a young ICRC delegate in El Salvador wrote a book on the basis of his experiences, expressing his frustrations with his work and casting aspersions on US governmental officials and others, the ICRC first sought to block circulation of the book through Swiss legal proceedings. The organization wanted to be able to tell Salvadoran authorities that it was serious about enforcing the rules of discretion. Public opinion in German-speaking Switzerland, however, turned against the ICRC and in favor of Balmer, so Geneva quietly shifted course and tried simply to ignore the book. Publication caused little furor outside the Confederation, although the book did complicate ICRC work in El Salvador. Other unauthorized release of sensitive information has been met by the ICRC in a variety of ways, depending on the facts of the situation.

Judicial observation

Interestingly enough for an organization with lots of lawyers who pride themselves on being the guardians of IHL, the Assembly approved a

---

[103] Interviews, Geneva.
[104] Dres Balmer, *L'heure de cuivre* (Lausanne: Editions d'En Bas, 1984). The book, like the Laurent Marti novel cited earlier, lacks great literary merit. It shows the anti-Americanism of some young Swiss, while also showing the frustrations of an ICRC representative who can do nothing about the most fundamental issues of the conflict but can only deal with the more superficial humanitarian aspects. Like Marti, Balmer shows the tension between the representative in the field and ICRC headquarters in Geneva.

In El Salvador, after a Red Cross Federation official made a public statement praising President Napolean Duarte, the ICRC ran into difficulty maintaining the confidence of the rebel prisoners it was interviewing. Like others, these prisoners were not clear about the difference between the ICRC and Federation and various National Societies. Interviews, Geneva.

statement saying it would be ICRC policy to follow more closely the judicial proceedings of prisoners falling within the ICRC's mandate.[105] The report on which this policy statement was based noted that, whereas the ICRC had concentrated on detention conditions, it had not raised enough questions about whether there was a proper legal basis for detention. In other words, despite all its lawyers, the ICRC had not always paid enough attention to judicial proceedings and legal guarantees. In some cases in the past the ICRC had been able to secure the release of prisoners by pointing out to authorities the violation of proper legal proceedings.[106] In one case ICRC questions led to a presidential pardon for a prisoner whose incarceration violated the judicial guarantees of the Third GC of 1949. In another case, ICRC overtures led an authority to change the death sentence for three prisoners to a sentence of life imprisonment.

Types of conflicts

There is no pope of IHL, and it is primarily up to states to legally label a situation as international or internal armed conflict, or some kind of conflict short of that threshold – such as riot, rebellion, banditry, domestic trouble, and so on. Not surprisingly, states and other actors such as rebel armies may differ in their characterizations, motivated as they are by self-interested concerns about power and status. The ICRC has adopted a policy on this question that says, in effect, "well, it depends." With a view to advancing its field work, the organization may or may not put forward its view as to the legal nature of the conflict. The ICRC asserts that it has the competence to make such a pronouncement, but knowing that certain statements may offend a protagonist and thus endanger humanitarian protection *sur place*, its general policy is to decide each case on its merits. Whatever the legal label that might be applied to a conflict, the ICRC seeks initially the same basic protections for individuals based on moral reasoning and its own traditions.

Relations with National Societies

A similar policy statement, devoid of precise content, concerns whether the ICRC will involve a National Red Cross Society as Geneva deals with

---

[105] Interviews, Geneva.

[106] See further Hans-Peter Gasser, "Respect for Fundamental Judicial Guarantees in Time of Armed Conflict – The Part played by ICRC Delegates," *International Review of the Red Cross*, 287 (March–April 1992), 121–42.

the government in question. After a historical review, the policy statement indicates that the particulars of a situation will determine what the organization does. In general the ICRC will involve the National Society, unless there is sound reason not to. In some cases in the past the National Society did not want to be involved in an ICRC démarche. But in other cases the National Society was of considerable help to the ICRC and was in a good position to follow up on an ICRC initiative. In some cases the National Society was included in a pro forma or diplomatic way, but was left out of more detailed and delicate proceedings. Sometimes the government in question may want to exclude its National Society. As on the question of legally labelling a conflict, relations with National Societies were judged by what would prove advantageous to practical protection.

Action beyond traditional mandate

The ICRC has reflected on its experience in the Cuban missile crisis of 1962 and other situations, and has decided that as an exceptional matter, and when requested by others, it may act as a neutral intermediary beyond the bounds of its traditional activities. The Assembly has decided that it would, if asked, repeat its role in El Salvador in 1984 in helping to arrange for the National Society and the Catholic Church to escort rebel representatives to a negotiating session with the government side. In that case, the ICRC agreed that the Red Cross emblem could be used to advance peace talks, rather than just traditional humanitarian activity. The ICRC played a somewhat similar role in the internal conflict in Mexico involving the province of Chiapas.[107] The ICRC has decided it will not seek out these roles, but if asked, and if no other party seems able to advance worthwhile causes, it will consider such a request on its merits.[108]

In most of these policy guidelines, one sees easily enough the organization's focus on practical protection. While manifesting a concern for consistency, it seems the ICRC has avoided the peril of becoming rigidly or legalistically doctrinaire.

---

[107] See Beatrice Megevand, "Between Insurrection and Government – ICRC Action in Mexico (January–August 1994)," *International Review of the Red Cross*, 304 (January–February 1995), 94–108.

[108] This policy statement does not clearly come through in the article noted in chapter 2 summarizing the ICRC's role in the Cuban missile crisis published in the Red Cross *Review*. Or, there is a disconnect between the statement and the article. This raises question as to how important are the general policy statements within the ICRC. It is possible that the author of the article was not totally familiar with the general policy guideline.

Conclusion

It is somewhat surprising that after 140 years the ICRC should still be addressing questions about the meaning of its impartial and neutral humanitarian protection. It may be that the organization is better at doing it than explaining it. Effective communication has not always been the strength of the ICRC. One rather doubts that ICRC protection is like pornography: known when seen but not subject to general definition. Rather, more careful and systematic thought should be able to make analytical distinctions that aid both understanding and policy. This chapter has suggested one line of analysis.

The organization has, for several decades, tried to act consistently according to a certain doctrine or set of general policies, and in general it has led the way in this regard among other human rights and humanitarian actors. Most of its policy guidelines are well considered, based as they are on historical experience. Some, like that on non-testimony in criminal proceedings, may merit further reflection, although most ICRC officials strongly support the current policy.

Acting President Freymond was right; the ICRC does need detailed principles and systematic policy, both of which go far beyond the seven official Red Cross principles. And the fears of Tony Waters are mostly unfounded; it is usually advantageous to bureaucratize the Good Samaritan.[109] One does need precise policy guidelines and predictable behavior.

It is also possible, given UNHCR experience in particular, that the ICRC could be less discreet without jeopardizing its in-country operations.[110] This particular issue is addressed further in the final chapter.

ICRC humanitarian protection, through striving for impartiality and a certain type of neutrality, and proceeding from a hopefully independent base, can be effective only when applied by capable personnel, acting within proper organizational structures, and supported by adequate resources. It is to the ICRC's personnel, policy-making structures, and resources that we now turn.

[109] Compare Freymond, "Humanitarian Policy," the quote that starts this chapter, with Tony Waters, *Bureaucratizing the Good Samaritan: The Limitations of Humanitarian Relief Operations* (Boulder: Westview, 2000).

[110] See, for example, Konstantin Obradovic, "Que faire face aux violations du droit humanitaire? – Quelques réflexions sur le rôle possible du CICR," in Swinarski, ed., *IHL*, especially at 493.

6

ICRC structure and management: personnel, policy making, resources

> In reality, the ICRC is in permanent reorganization
>
> Freymond, *Guerres, révolutions, Croix-Rouge*, 15

As already demonstrated, what the ICRC did around the world was determined for a long time by a group of volunteer humanitarians now collectively called the Assembly. As noted in chapter 1, it was Gustave Moynier, not Henry Dunant, who interacted with the Assembly to lay the foundations for the modern ICRC during his long Presidency (1864–1910).

While the Assembly has presided over a remarkable history of expanding accomplishments, it was surely the case that particularly Max Huber and his colleagues in the Assembly did not distinguish themselves against Hitler and the Swiss governing class that had tried to accommodate the Nazis (as noted in chapters 1 and 5). This type of failure to develop a well-considered humanitarian diplomacy in the face of brutal power politics was painfully exposed again in the Nigerian affair (1967–70, covered in chapter 2). Media coverage of ICRC difficulties in the Nigerian war and competition from other relief agencies pushed the ICRC into significantly altering its process of decision making.

Progressively from about 1970, considerable influence shifted inside the organization from the Assembly to the Directorate. The top professional humanitarians, the leadership of the professional staff, came to manage the ICRC on a daily basis. The Assembly still established general policy. It and its Council, explained below, still could be a significant factor in ICRC policy making. But many Assembly decisions reflected propositions posed by the Directorate, or more specifically by the Director-General working with the President. (Recall Annexe E, the organizational chart of the ICRC.)

The ICRC President remained the chief spokesman for the organization to the rest of the world, and he still conducted important diplomatic missions. But after the tenure of President Alexander Hay (1976–87), he became relatively less involved in all the daily affairs of the agency. He had reduced influence on ICRC policy historically speaking, that is, compared to Moynier and Ador, but he was still very influential. By 2002 the "CEO duties" of the ICRC were shared by the President and the Director-General. So the ICRC policy-making process came to resemble French politics: each had two executives – a President and a Prime Minister for France, a President and a Director-General for the ICRC. Just as the French Prime Minister had the Cabinet, the ICRC Director-General had the Directorate. As in France, it was sometimes difficult to pinpoint where the influence of the President stopped and that of the other half of the double executive started.

The Directorate, with the Assembly in the background, managed greatly expanded resources – which, however, were still too slight given the humanitarian challenges faced. The nature of human resources, namely the staff, comprised a changing subject with broad significance.

As a cautious organization with a high opinion of itself, and as a historically very Swiss organization that believed in ample collective discussion and decision making, the ICRC was clearly slow to change. But fundamental change in structure and management did indeed occur.

The leadership

The ICRC Assembly, today as for some time, is composed of not more than twenty-five Swiss citizens who are invited to join. Neither the International Red Cross Conference, nor the Federation, nor any of the more than 180 National Red Cross Societies has anything to say about Committee membership. From 1863 until the 1970s the Assembly, led by the President, made general and specific policy in the name of the ICRC, although as a general rule considerable freedom was given to delegates in the field.

Gradually but persistently the Assembly diluted the principle of voluntary service, although voluntarism remains one of the cardinal Red Cross principles. A paid staff was developed as the ICRC's geographical scope and functional tasks expanded. The staff, however, remained rudimentary even after the Second World War. It was not until the late 1960s that the ICRC paid staff was really professionalized in the form of more rigorous recruitment and training, which is when other aspects of a systematic personnel policy were commenced.

The Committee/Assembly

The original five were gradually replaced by cooptation from among their social peers – that is, from the Protestant, French-speaking governing class of Geneva.[1] Most of the early members of the group were from the upper-middle or aristocratic classes. They not only knew each other but also were often related to each other – President Ador, for example, was the nephew of President Moynier. Very much like the lawyer Moynier, they were uniformly conservative in the broad sense of preferring gradual rather than revolutionary change, within rather than outside of legal frameworks. They were also conservative in pursuing strategic minimalism in their humanitarian endeavors, as explained in chapter 5. Furthermore, they were cautious – and very Swiss – in their tactics, preferring a discreet version of neutrality that tried to minimize friction with public authorities. The Committee's social makeup and cautious approach to humanitarian affairs made it acceptable to most governments (most communist governments excepted, most of the time they existed).

Under Moynier's leadership the Assembly developed a reputation for attention to legal and logistical detail. This is also very Swiss. In general the Swiss are very good at counting things, at management details, at making the trains run on time. Whether they are as good at creative and timely grand strategy is an interesting question. Swiss bankers may know a lot about banking details, for example, but whether Swiss bankers know how to keep up with changing climates of world opinion in order to maintain broad confidence is not the same thing. (Conventional wisdom holds that Swiss bankers badly mismanaged the issue of unclaimed bank deposits from the Second World War era.)

The Committee was entirely Genevan, Protestant, white, and male until 1918 when the first woman, Renée-Marguerite Cramer, was coopted. Gender aside, she fitted the mold of a Committee member: she was from the Genevan upper-middle class, was related to seven other Committee members, and preferred working through legal means (as compared to some females in the Swiss Red Cross at a later time who opted for alegal methods in humanitarian efforts in Vichy France).[2] Following the role model of Ms. Cramer, who was active for the International Prisoners of War Agency

[1] Diego Fiscalini, "Des élites au service d'une cause humanitaire: le Comité International de la Croix-Rouge," Mémoire de license, Université de Genève, Faculté des Lettres, Département d'Histoire, 1985.
[2] Monique Pavillon, *Les immobilisées: les femmes suisses durant la Second Guerre Mondiale* (Lausanne: Editions d'En Bas, 1989). The author suggests that the female members of the

during the First World War before she was coopted onto the Committee, women have often played a distinctive role in the Assembly since 1918 and particularly during the Second World War. From 1939 to 1945 the four female members of the Assembly frequently led the effort to provide aid to Jews caught up in the German Holocaust. Suzanne Ferrière became head of a working group charged with that portfolio, and Ms. Frick-Cramer, as she had become by then, was sometimes particularly concerned with Jews in Hungary. In October 1942 all of the four women were initially in favor of the famous (or infamous) draft public appeal to belligerents concerning violations of humanitarian standards.

Some female members of the Assembly have displayed clearly forceful personalities – in particular, Denise Bindschedler-Robert in the 1970s and 1980s.[3] Her determined role was in favor of a legally oriented and conservative approach to humanitarian affairs. She was a law professor and spouse of a prominent Swiss lawyer and diplomat, and she was not much interested in any kind of significant departure from what had been in the past. She was clearly not a shrinking violet, but her gender brought few new policy perspectives to the Committee.

After the Cold War the average female proportion of the Committee was about 15%. Two females, Ms. Bindschedler-Robert and Anne Petitpierre, became regular Vice Presidents of the ICRC, but this is normally not a very important position. No female has become a Permanent Vice President, which is a paid and more influential position. Sometimes a female was a member of the Council of the Assembly, which is a sub-group given varied tasks and exercising shifting influence. Liselotte Kraus-Gurny was such a member, but she was not usually seen as a strong and independent member of the Committee. Presidents have always been male.

In 1923 the Committee admitted its first non-Genevans: Giuseppe Motta (a Catholic from the canton of Ticino and speaking Italian as his first language), Max Huber (a Protestant from Zurich and German-speaking), and Alois de Meuron (a Protestant from Vaud and French-speaking). This broadening of Committee membership was not just a detail of internal Swiss distinctions but was to prove important particularly during the Second World War (as shown in chapters 1 and 5). With the introduction of non-Genevans, and moreover because some of the newcomers also held positions in the Swiss Confederation, Swiss national interests rather than

---

Assembly were discriminated against, in that they were not assigned to certain projects despite their interest and expertise in such matters.

[3] Throughout this chapter, statements of fact not part of general knowledge are based on interviews in Geneva, unless attribution is otherwise.

Red Cross humanitarian interests came to play a larger role in Assembly decisions.

It is probable that Motta, when also in the Swiss Federal Council and head of the Swiss Foreign Ministry, exercised more restraint on the ICRC than Philippe Etter (we have covered Etter's role in the 1942 debate about the agency issuing a public appeal that pertained to the Holocaust, among other issues). Motta was one of the Committee members during the Second World War whose loyalty was more to the Confederation than to the ICRC, more to Swiss national interests than to ICRC independent humanitarianism. We have already discussed the role of Presidents Huber and C. J. Burckhardt (Swiss-Germans) who agreed to Confederation supervision of, and sometimes dominance over, the ICRC during 1939–45. (However Eduoard de Haller, another of those Assembly members giving clear priority to Confederation interests during World War II, was a Genevan.)

In other words, as the Committee became more broadly Swiss and not just Genevan, it became more susceptible to strictly Swiss interests. Before 1923 the Assembly, being dominated by Genevans and led by the likes of Moynier and Ador, reflected a certain Genevan cosmopolitanism in which many Genevans saw themselves as citizens of the world as much as they saw themselves as Swiss.[4] But this Genevan cosmopolitanism at the ICRC was diluted after 1923.[5]

After the Second World War, ICRC Presidents like Paul Ruegger maintained extremely close relations with the Confederation, and the latter made its views known to the ICRC on several occasions. The Confederation tried to push the ICRC into a broader role in the Cuban missile crisis of 1962 (covered in chapter 2), as Berne was pleased with the idea of Swiss personnel helping to resolve the crisis. One source says this Confederation pressure was firmly rebuffed by the Assembly,[6] but in that crisis the organization moved in the direction desired by Berne. Also, the Confederation pressured the ICRC in the 1970s not to advance proposals about a new emblem for the Red Cross Movement that would reduce the centrality of the traditional Red Cross on a white background, the reverse of the Swiss national flag. Berne saw the traditional Red Cross emblem as good for the

[4] See further Irene Herrmann, "Le lien entre Genève et la Confédération," in Durand, ed., *Gustave Ador*, 263–76.
[5] Voting in the city and canton of Geneva still shows marked differences with most cities and cantons in the German-speaking regions, as on questions like membership in the United Nations. Geneva is normally more liberal on social issues, more internationally oriented, than other areas.
[6] Freymond, *Guerre, Revolution, Croix-Rouge*, 24.

Swiss image in the world, and therefore, it is reliably said, a Swiss official wrote a letter endorsing the status quo.[7] The Assembly, in fact, did not seek a change in the emblem at that time, but it is impossible to specify the exact influence of the Confederation in that decision because a number of considerations came into play.

Of course other states lobby or try to pressure the ICRC on various policy issues. The question is whether Berne exercises undue or inappropriate influence on the ICRC because of Swiss connections.

For much of the Cold War period there was a fairly even pattern of cooptation between Genevans and non-Genevans.[8] Most Committee members remain male and Protestant. There has been one Jewish member. No members of racial minorities have ever been elected to the Assembly. (In the history of the country, racial minorities had made up a minute portion of Swiss society.) Prevalent professions represented were and are: law, medicine, banking, diplomacy, education, with a few Committee members from journalism and trade union organizations. The typical age at entry has been around fifty. Most of these facts make for a generally conservative group. The first socialist, E. Gloor, was not coopted onto the Committee until 1945.

The earlier trend was for Committee memberships of long duration, classically represented by the long presidencies of Moynier (forty-six years) and Ador (total of fifteen years with a break in the middle), but after Huber (sixteen years, with a break) the trend was toward shorter Committee tenure. Original appointment is for four years, subject to renewal. There is an Assembly committee on membership, whose primary duty is proposing new members. To enter the Assembly one must obtain a simple majority vote by that body. But for a second term one needs a two-thirds vote, and three-quarters for a third. There is thus some built-in pressure on Assembly members to be diligent and active. There is an age limit of seventy, and discussion of term limits as well. As is always the case with any group, it is still the case that some members are more attentive and involved than others. Some German-speaking members of the Committee think that Genevans still exercise great influence in that body, since they are close to headquarters and can interact more easily with the rest of the organization in between Assembly meetings.

Clearly the Assembly has now reduced its role. It selects top officials, determines the formal policy-making process, and approves general policy as well as the core budget. These latter matters normally originate

[7] Interviews, Geneva.   [8] Fiscalini, "Des élites."

as proposals from the Directorate. The Assembly, presided over by the President, now meets only five times per year. However, it receives the reports of an independent audit commission and so has its own sources of financial data. And while it rarely initiates important policy, since it has become mostly a reactive and supervisory body, similar to parliaments in modern democracies, in general it takes its role seriously. It has been known to debate budget proposals for hours. It sometimes raises questions about the details of field operations. Once it asked whether certain ICRC medical treatment of combatants was really necessary, since they were not in enemy hands, and thus whether decisions in the field at the sub-delegation level exceeded the mandate of the organization.[9] At the end of the day the Assembly may only make changes in perhaps 10% of the reports and proposals that come before it. But it does indeed supervise and play the role of ultimate policy maker for the organization. On occasion it sends proposals back to the Directorate for further fine tuning.

Almost from the beginning there has been discussion about the wisdom of the ICRC having a mono-national and coopted Committee when the rest of the Red Cross Movement is multinational and where the Federation, National Societies, and Red Cross Conferences manifest certain democratic tendencies. We have already seen that as far back as 1867 Moynier was in favor of some type of a broader group at the top of the ICRC as elected from National Societies. But by the late nineteenth century, with the defeat of various proposals for change at Red Cross Conferences (1887, 1897) the agency became wedded to Committee membership and manner of selection as we now know it.[10] Later efforts within the modern Red Cross Movement to internationalize the Assembly, for example after the Second World War, came to naught as we noted in chapter 2.

In contemporary international relations there is no important actor calling for the internationalization of the ICRC Assembly, and this question has become moot for the time being.[11] Some keep the issue alive by pointing out that Committee members do not emerge from a broad democratic vote (there is a democratic vote in the Assembly regarding membership, but no democratic vote in the larger Red Cross Movement). Critics also allege that the Committee is not really responsible or accountable to

---

[9] Interviews, Geneva.

[10] A proposal for a special Red Cross relief bureau in time of war was defeated at the 1889 Hague Diplomatic Conference.

[11] But see James Ingram, "The Future Architecture for International Humanitarian Assistance," in Thomas G. Weiss and Larry Minear, eds., *Humanitarianism across Borders: Sustaining Civilians in Times of War* (Boulder: Lynne Rienner, 1993), 190.

anyone – at least not in a formal or institutional sense. In this view, there ought to be change.

The Committee believes that mono-nationality, when linked to permanent Swiss neutrality, still provides conflicting parties with the guarantee that someone from "the enemy" will not be on the supreme policy-making body of the ICRC. In this view, the handwriting has been on the wall since the Franco-Prussian war of 1870–71, when the two National Societies in question were unable to rise above nationalism in order to implement neutral humanitarianism.[12] Thus the Committee still believes that mono-nationality guarantees the independence, impartiality, and neutrality of the organization. The defenders of the status quo like to argue that the mono-nationality of the ICRC just happens to be Swiss rather than, say, Irish, Tunisian, or Costa Rican.

The current widespread satisfaction with the nature of Committee membership as it now exists stems, in addition to the logic above, from: the mostly impressive record of the field operations of the ICRC from about 1970; the evident truth that during the Cold War multinational decision making in United Nations organs like the Security Council was largely paralyzed by national disagreements; and evident efforts by the ICRC, covered below, to try to ensure that its structures for policy making are attuned to the needs of the times. The fact that the ICRC Assembly is less important than it once was has certainly played a role in reducing demands for change in its composition – at least for those few who are well informed about such things.

It is also the case that even in democratic polities there are non-elected bodies. Democratic states have appointed judges and other appointed officials – in the United States one has the officials of the Federal Reserve System for monetary and banking affairs – who are intentionally shielded from democratic pressures in the name of fair judgments and effective policies. True, these officials are appointed by persons who are elected. The closest parallel for the ICRC is that votes in the International Red Cross Conference, for example in approving the Statutes of the Movement, have endorsed the ICRC in present form. Thus there is some broad democratic legitimacy for current arrangements.

Furthermore, informally the ICRC is accountable both to the victims its serves and to the states that fund its budgets. When Nelson Mandela eventually went to ICRC headquarters in Geneva, after his release from detention by the white government of South Africa in 1990, and paid

[12] See further Bugnion, *La protection*, 1138–41.

his prominent respects to the organization, his visit was not just a media event but a high-profile vote of confidence in the ICRC by one who had benefited from its efforts. Likewise, in 2002 Daw Aung San Suu Kyi of Burma (Myanmar), the Nobel Laureate and head of the most important democracy movement there, went to the ICRC delegation in Rangoon after her release from house arrest and thanked the ICRC for all of its work in that country. It was another high-profile vote of confidence in the organization.

When, upon the recommendation of the Executive Branch, the US Congress regularly renews the appropriation for the ICRC without much controversy, as is normally the case, there is a type of review and account-ability at work – especially when one understands that historically the Congress is not fond of making payments to international or foreign organizations.[13] Were the ICRC to be widely criticized by former victims of war or by former political prisoners, or were the ICRC to lose the confidence of the western liberal democracies that are highly influential in much of international relations, the Assembly could well come under renewed criticism.

Ironically, it is possible that the Committee itself has approved arrange-ments that could lead to renewed debate about the internationalization of the Assembly in the future. Owing to the need for more and specialized human resources, the Assembly agreed to internationalize the ICRC pro-fessional staff in 1992. Eventually some of these Canadians, Belgians, and others who are bilingual in English and French will rise to the top staff positions and enter the Directorate that manages daily affairs. Non-Swiss are now eligible for any post on the professional side of the House. When one or more of the non-Swiss enter the Directorate, and especially when the Director-General, the ICRC *de facto* CEO, is non-Swiss, it may be more difficult to maintain an all-Swiss Committee.

In July 1999, an ICRC internal report contained the following sentence: "An ICRC [as] defender of these universal [Red Cross or humanitarian] values is better represented by an international staff."[14] This same logic could be applied to the Committee.

If the ICRC retains its record of effectiveness and integrity when the pro-fessional leadership has become multinational, then the question might be raised as to why the Committee should not be multinational also. If

---

[13] In chapter 7 I note a bogus or cosmetic effort in the US Congress to restrict funding to the ICRC.

[14] Document in the possession of the author. Translation from the French by the author.

Belgians and Canadians can be discreet and effective staff, as fully committed to Red Cross humanitarianism as the Swiss delegates, and then members of the Directorate, why not members of the Committee? If a Canadian were elected to the Committee, why would anyone presume that his or her loyalty would be to the Canadian government rather than to the ICRC? After all, the Executive Committee of Amnesty International is multinational. That body has not been paralyzed by that fact, nor have votes in that body by the various national members been attributed to governmental pressures. By 2025, by which time non-Swiss should be in the Directorate, the ICRC Assembly could be under more pressure to internationalize. In addition to ICRC personnel policy, other factors contribute to this possibility: the decline of totalitarian states, freeing the individual of any nationality to be a universal humanitarian; the rise of a dynamic international civil society, in which individuals of various nationalities have become champions of human rights and humanitarian values; and the Confederation's joining the United Nations, making its position not very different from other states claiming a tradition of neutrality.[15]

Even when the ICRC head of delegation in some country may be Pakistani and the ICRC Director-General Belgian, however, the Assembly is likely to resist changing from its all-Swiss nature. ICRC tradition has been very strong over its long history. As noted already, the Assembly likes to stress the benefits of mono-nationality and play down the Swiss composition of the Assembly. No doubt the Assembly will continue to argue that its mono-nationality has served the victims of conflicts well across time. But that tradition has been damaged by the facts of intrusion of Swiss national interests into Assembly decisions. Confederation pressures, contemporary ICRC personnel policy, as well as the changing nature of international relations, all undermine at least some of the logic for an all-Swiss Assembly.

Then again, if the organization functions well, why undergo the risks of change?

---

[15] Should the Confederation join the European Union, there would be even less reason to think that the ICRC Assembly has to be tightly tied to a distinctive Swiss state. The more the Confederation appears essentially like Ireland or Sweden or any other European state with a tradition of neutrality, the less reason there is to think that the ICRC Assembly *must be* all Swiss. What is called Swiss permanent neutrality appears less and less distinctive in contemporary International Relations. Most of the European neutral states, not just the Confederation, show a very low probability of war in the classical sense.

The President

One of the important things that the ICRC Assembly still does is to select the top personnel of the agency, starting with the President. As one would expect in any group of two dozen or so members, there are always different views about the Presidency – although the Assembly has not been stymied by intense and debilitating factionalism in general during the past decades. There is a strong faction that always wants to go outside the House for its President, usually to the Swiss Confederation but sometimes to Swiss banking or medical circles. The last three Presidents (Hay, Sommaruga, Kellenberger) were all previously officials of the Swiss Confederation. This is striking, especially given the debate about improper pressures on the ICRC from Berne, mainly during World War II but on occasion since then.

When Kellenberger was proposed as President, there was a long debate in the Assembly about whether the body should look in other circles. But there is the view that tiny Switzerland only has so many persons experienced in international relations, and thus the Confederation is a logical place to find the leadership that the ICRC requires. While it would be naïve to think that there is no informal networking between Berne and Geneva about the ICRC Presidency, it appears that Berne has never formally intervened in Assembly proceedings regarding the selection of the ICRC President. One assumes that in present times Berne understands that such intrusion would greatly damage the organization – and not be good for the reputation of the Confederation either.[16]

The Assembly has been willing since 1945 to elect to its membership a few insiders from the professional side of the House: Pierre Boissier, Jean Pictet, Roger Gallopin, Jacques Moreillon, Jean de Courten, Yves Sandoz. But regular membership is not the same as the Presidency.

Even after the era of the Second World War, when the intrusion of Swiss national interests had undermined some of the ICRC's independence, and when the organization had been charged with insufficient attention to the Holocaust, the Assembly selected former Swiss Ambassador Paul Ruegger as President. Ruegger, when representing the Confederation in Italy, apparently supported the idea that the way for Berne to control German

[16] Morehead, in *Dunant's Dream*, 678, makes a grave error when she asserts that Berne pushed Cornelio Sommaruga on the ICRC as President. It was on the initiative of certain Assembly members that Sommaruga was approached to become President. Berne had no role in the process at that stage. One of Sommaruga's superiors in the Swiss foreign ministry may have engaged in some petty maneuvers to hasten Sommaruga's departure from that department. But Swiss officials were not responsible in any significant way for Sommaruga's becoming ICRC President.

(and Austrian) Jewish refugees who had obtained an Italian passport, and who were trying to move from Italy to Switzerland, was to have some special mark, such as "N.A." for Non Aryan, stamped in their passports. This would allow Swiss border authorities to identify Jewish refugees (whether German, Austrian, or Italian) and turn them back, since they might become wards of the Confederation and since Swiss acceptance of them might irritate Berlin. This Swiss suggestion was passed along to Berlin and finally adopted by the Nazis in the infamous "J" for Juden stamped into passports of German Jewish nationals.[17]

Recent ICRC Presidents have been much more independent from Berne than Ruegger. Cornelio Sommaruga was the top civil servant in Berne dealing with foreign economic policy, and Jacob Kellenberger was the top civil servant in the Foreign Ministry as a whole.[18]

When Sommaruga was selected in 1987, there was a strong inside candidate in Jacques Moreillon. Moreillon had risen through the ranks over the years to become ICRC Director-General and was widely regarded as very capable. He had dealt ably with some wily governments and various other actors in places like southern Africa, the Middle East, and Latin America, and by so doing he – along with the Director of Operations, Jean-Pierre Hocke, with President Alexander Hay quietly in the background – had been crucial in restoring the reputation of the organization after the difficulties in the Nigerian episode.[19]

Moreillon knew the broad work of the ICRC as well or better than anyone and had an excellent track record as a professional humanitarian.

---

[17] For a translation of Ruegger's cable of 1938 to Bonna, head of the Swiss Foreign Ministry, see www.dsca.it/Svizzera/Ruegger.html. Conventional wisdom holds that it was Heinrich Rothmund, head of the Swiss Department of Justice, who was the author of the passport stamp idea. And Ruegger was eventually declared *persona non grata* by Mussolini's government.

[18] Comparisons with Amnesty International are striking. At the time of writing, the last two AI leaders have been a man from Senegal and a woman from Bangladesh. Thus, London-based AI has been more sensitive about shedding its western image and reaching out to the Global South than has the ICRC. But then the ICRC is an establishment organization, closely tied to the Confederation, and historically slow to change, whereas AI spends much of its time overtly criticizing various establishments.

[19] See further Morehead, *Dunant's Dream*. Morehead says incorrectly that Moreillon was a lawyer. He had an undergraduate degree in law at the University of Geneva, which is a general, non-specialized, non-technical degree. His advanced degrees were in political science. Sometimes at the ICRC the director of the Division of Principles and Law is not a lawyer. This was true in the careers of Moreillon and François Bugnion, for example. And this shows that the organization's emphasis is on soft law, or law in the policy process, rather than technical law in court cases.

He had post-graduate degrees, was fluent in numerous languages, and manifested such excellent relations within the Red Cross Movement that he had been approached by the Federation to be its Secretary-General.[20] His talents were appreciated in certain factions of the Assembly. So why was he not selected?

His first problem was that he was from inside the House, which caused him to be downgraded by that sizeable Assembly faction that always wanted to look outside. In addition to whatever social bias may be at work, some Assembly members may lack confidence in their own judgment; by selecting as ICRC President someone who has held high position in the Confederation, they are selecting someone who has already been given high office by others. This pattern reflects a deep caution or conservatism by the Assembly. Second, his knowledge and reputation meant that some Assembly members feared domination by him. There were some Assembly members who feared a strong President. This is a very Swiss attitude, as seen in the preference for a collective executive (Federal Council) of the Confederation. In Swiss domestic politics, the emphasis is on collective effort and not on charismatic or strong personalities. And third, Moreillon, in the view of some, had a tendency sometimes to come across as talking down to others, conveying the impression that he thought he was superior.

In fact, after Sommaruga was chosen as President, and after Moreillon resigned from the Directorate and was elected to the Assembly, Moreillon was sometimes perceived as behaving as some members had feared. He made verbal interventions at some length, referring to his many decades of experience, and thus contributed to the impression in some quarters that he saw himself as knowing more than others. In Sommaruga's second term Moreillon gave up on his hope of becoming ICRC President and made valuable contributions to the Assembly on selected issues, based on his extensive knowledge of the organization and its work. Though disappointed, he remained loyal to the institution.

---

[20] Had Moreillon accepted to lead the Federation, he would have emulated William E. Rappard, a well-known Swiss academic who had been a member of the ICRC Assembly and also the first Secretary-General of the Red Cross Federation. Rappard developed frictions with many of his Assembly colleagues for supporting the new Federation and eventually resigned his Assembly membership. Moreillon could have done much to bridge the differences between the ICRC and the Federation, but he never seriously considered making that intriguing move. His loyalty was to the ICRC. For more on Rappard see Victor Monnier, "Les relations avec William E. Rappard," in Durand, The ICRC, 411–37. Rappard, like Huber, was one of those ICRC Assembly members who advised the Confederation while a member of the Committee.

It is not easy to determine the influence of the ICRC President. The internal policy-making process of the organization is definitely not transparent, so it is extremely difficult for an outsider to know exactly when and where power is exercised. Early on the organization was genuinely led by Presidents like Moynier and Ador. They were strong both inside and outside the House. They spoke for the ICRC in its external relations, and they influenced a great deal of policy inside the House. They had more dedication and perseverance than most of their colleagues in the Assembly, and they did not have to contend with a strong professional side of the House. It could be said that someone like Moynier spent so much time on ICRC affairs that he really became a professional humanitarian. He and Ador were not dictators, for the Assembly has always been democratic in its deliberations. This, too, is a very Swiss trait, as the Swiss manifest much democracy through many referenda and other frequent voting.

Max Huber, by comparison with Moynier and Ador, was not in reality a strong ICRC President although he had the third longest tenure (1928–44, and acting President in 1946). While being highly regarded in European legal circles, having been a judge at the Permanent Court of International Justice (and its President), and while he dealt with a weak Assembly, his indecision, ambivalence, and poor health meant that he dominated neither the Assembly nor the professional staff as it was evolving. In the crucial Assembly meeting on 14 October 1942, Huber was ill, not present, and did not try to affect its outcome. Some believe that just as the pragmatic Moynier supplemented the visionary Dunant, so the more pragmatic Burckhardt supplemented the more intellectual Huber. Some think Burckhardt was the operational leader of the ICRC during the Second World War.[21] Huber, when he returned briefly as acting President after World War II, instituted a set of internal reforms designed to place the President at the head of a sub-group of the Assembly that would run

---

[21] Burckhardt was named Swiss ambassador to Paris after World War II, so again we find a Committee member who seemed perfectly acceptable to the political class in Berne. Despite the fact that he had moved easily in Nazi circles during the war, he was acceptable to Charles de Gaulle's provisional government. His appointment as ambassador came after two other nominees had been turned down because they, or their superiors in Berne like Foreign Minister Marcel Pilet-Golaz, were perceived as having been more sympathetic to Vichy France than to the Free French in London headed by de Gaulle. So apparently Paris viewed Burckhardt as not among those Swiss who were known for appeasing the Nazis and/or generally tilting toward various European fascists. Caroline Morehead believes otherwise, as noted. And it is possible that Paris accepted Burckhardt, whatever his past record, in order to move beyond the friction with the Confederation, after the controversy over the first two designated ambassadors.

the organization under the loose guidance of the Committee.[22] Little did he realize that his changes would, some three decades later, weaken the position of the presidency. Huber sometimes called his group the Directorate, and sometimes the President's Council. Eventually the Directorate came to manage the organization on a daily basis, but the modern directorate would be made up of professional staff, not Assembly members, and would formally exclude the President.

Many ICRC Presidents since 1945 have not made a lasting mark on the organization or on humanitarian affairs. Probably the two weakest were Marcel Naville (1969–73) and Eric Martin (1973–76).

When the Assembly decided not to renew Naville, the most capable person in the leadership of the organization was Roger Gallopin. But Gallopin had been professional staff. Rather than elevate Gallopin to the presidency, the Assembly named Martin as President, but made Gallopin the President of the Assembly's Executive Council. Martin was the figurehead while Gallopin made the decisions that mattered. In this context a remarkable public statement by Martin indicated much: "The three-year period and the conditions attached to my function imposed a limit on what I could do and on any ambitions I might have nourished."[23] When Gallopin retired and the Assembly selected Alexander Hay as President, the ICRC of the two presidencies was ended. The Assembly Executive Council, so important under Gallopin, became for a time a pale shadow of its former collective self.

Gallopin and Moreillon faced the same hurdles. A strong argument can be made that both confronted a type of social discrimination inside the Assembly. They had proven themselves as high officials of the ICRC. Thus the argument is weakened that Assembly members had to look to a Confederation official to get a reliable leader. It was not as if Gallopin and Moreillon were totally unknown quantities as policy makers in a complex international relations. It is not entirely rational, but the Assembly prefers to bring in a President from the outside, even though at the start of his term he is an amateur in humanitarian diplomacy, rather than elevate to the presidency someone like Gallopin or Moreillon who is a proven professional humanitarian. Both Sommaruga and Kellenberger basically knew nothing about the Geneva Conventions or the details of Red Cross

[22] Georges Willemin and Roger Heacock, *The International Committee of the Red Cross* (Boston: Martinus Nijhoff, 1984), 120.
[23] Eric Martin, "An Enlightening Three-Year Episode," *International Review of the Red Cross*, 199 (October 1977), 434. Clearly Martin was not a happy camper, but then, why would he take the presidency under those conditions?

neutral humanitarianism. Both had to take a crash course, largely self-taught, on these subjects. Both experienced some rough sledding in the first years as ICRC President. Even though experienced in foreign affairs, these outsiders did not fully understand the ICRC and IHL; consequently difficulties arose.

Although his name is barely known today in most circles, Alexander Hay can make a claim to having been a strong ICRC President (1976–87). Whether first as Director-General of the Swiss National Bank or as ICRC President, he was not a high-profile person, as he did not crave the limelight. But he not only dealt effectively with the Assembly of his time; more importantly he also effectively managed the Directorate. He met with them on a regular basis and approved all important strategic decisions taken during his tenure. He was the last ICRC President to be in direct touch with daily affairs on a broad basis. Moreillon and Hocke were the key players in the Directorate for much of the time in question, but they did not proceed very far or very long without Hay's approval.

Ironically, a recent President like Sommaruga had a relatively high profile outside the House, certainly compared to Hay, but he did not by himself determine much policy inside the organization. Sometimes the Assembly rejected both his candidates for high appointments and some of his policy proposals. In the view of one Assembly member, Sommaruga was a great salesman, but he was not always careful about the rules and details of policy making within the house. Moreover, Sommaruga had less control over the Directorate than Hay. It is true that Sommaruga was briefed regularly about the details of the organization's work by the Director-General. But the Assembly, perhaps jealous of its dwindling authority, had determined that the ICRC President should restrict his role to that of general strategy and avoid micro-managing the Directorate regarding daily affairs.

The restrictions on the ICRC Presidency, determined by the general policy of the Assembly from the late 1980s, may have been one contributing factor as to why several well-informed Swiss have turned down the position when it was informally offered. The Assembly does not formally offer the Presidency to someone until it has been agreed that the person will definitely accept. But several times in the recent past, when the Assembly has made an informal démarche to its first choice, it has had to turn to its second choice. Thus was true, for example, with regard to Ambassador François Pictet.

Some of those who accepted, like Sommaruga, who knew little of the organization at the outset, came to be somewhat frustrated by the lack of independent power in the office.[24] Sommaruga was to complain of what he thought was excessive discussion, consultation, and slowness in ICRC policy making.[25] Certainly in his first term he wanted to be the real CEO of the organization. However, he only made important policy by himself on one issue: in 1994 he committed the ICRC to supporting a full ban on anti-personnel landmines. He did so through a press conference held against an approaching deadline in inter-state negotiations, when the Assembly did not have time to meet, and when the Legal Department and the Directorate had not yet taken a final position on the question.[26] He tried to involve himself directly in other policy-making processes concerning specific issues, but he was generally rebuffed by the Directorate acting under Assembly guidelines.[27] It was probably the case that Sommaruga tried to engage on a wide range of specific issues, without much systematic thought, and that he dissipated some of his influence through that style of engagement. He was by all accounts, however, a clever and strategic thinker.

Sommaruga was an active spokesman for ICRC positions. He did not cave in to governmental pressures, whether by the United States over the landmine issue or otherwise. When he discovered in the early 1990s that the Confederation had contacted some ICRC officials involved in Bosnia with a view to advancing a relief plan involving Russia and Greece, well-known supporters of Serbia, he found the plan neither impartial nor neutral and he successfully worked to block it. He certainly changed the external image of the organization to some degree. He was not aloof or secretive or stuffy, and he was critical of his colleagues who were. He was impatient with those ICRC officials who were arrogant and who thought they had a monopoly on humanitarian good will, as mentioned earlier. So in general Sommaruga contributed to more openness at the organization. A President can change some of the nature of ICRC relations with outside parties – with the Federation and other relief agencies, for example.

One of the things that Sommaruga was able to accomplish, partly because of his own dynamism, was to raise the visibility of the ICRC and its causes in global diplomatic circles. Sommaruga met regularly with the

---

[24] It is worth noting in passing that someone like Sommaruga, who dealt with Confederation foreign economic affairs, initially could be badly informed about the ICRC in the late 1980s.

[25] Massimo Lorenzi, *Le CICR, le cœur et la raison: entretiens avec Cornelio Sommaruga* (Lausanne: Favre, 1998), 90.

[26] He gives a brief account in *ibid.*, 96.

[27] With something less than full admiration, some staff members recall the time Sommaruga tried to address some parking issues at the Geneva headquarters.

UN Secretary-General, and other important figures including the rotating President of the UN Security Council. He also presided over a great expansion of ICRC budgets and staff. Furthermore he tried to get some diplomatic movement on the thorny issue of Israel, its official aid society, and neutral emblems in armed conflict (treated further in the next chapter).

At the same time, while he certainly had strong supporters in the Assembly as well as outside the House, he could manifest on occasion a personality so strong that some saw him as overbearing.[28] One high official, Director-General Guy Deluz, resigned and left the organization in part because he could not work with Sommaruga. Some ICRC delegates in the field dreaded his visits; he could be quite the "high-maintenance" visitor. Some officials in the Federation and also in important National Societies found it necessary to deal with him in small doses. They and some others thought he craved the limelight too much and had an irritating self-assuredness about him. While castigating other parts of the House for being too proud and arrogant, he himself was known not to be hesitant about advancing his own personal credentials. After leaving the ICRC Presidency he became active, among other things, in a Christian organization that had been ultra-conservative during the Cold War.[29]

Sommaruga was certainly an important figure in ICRC policy making during his presidency. But given his high profile in ICRC external relations,

---

[28] See Morehead, *Dunant's Dream*, 679.

[29] Interestingly enough, Sommaruga, having stressed ICRC discreet neutrality for twelve years, later accepted to serve in several positions requiring broad policy statements. He served on a panel appointed by the Canadian government to evaluate the status of "humanitarian intervention." He was credited by some with getting that panel to stress state "responsibility to protect" persons rather than the notion of "humanitarian intervention" – thus preserving the concept of "humanitarian" for agencies like the ICRC. See further: *The Responsibility to Protect: Report of the International Commission on Intervention and State Sovereignty* (Ottawa: International Development Research Centre, 2001).

He was also appointed to a United Nations panel to investigate Israeli military operations in Jenin in the occupied territories during 2002. With regard to the latter, Israel objected to the composition of the panel, and false rumors were circulated that Sommaruga was anti-Semitic. The panel was disbanded by the UN Secretary-General in the face of Israeli opposition. Some ICRC officials were relieved that the panel never became operational, because they thought that Sommaruga's presence on the panel made great difficulties for the ICRC. In fact, some ICRC officials were incensed that Sommaruga would complicate ICRC relations in the Middle East by agreeing to serve on this UN panel which was designed to pass public judgment on Israeli policy. Sommaruga, however, saw no problem since he would have been on the panel in his individual capacity after having left the ICRC. In the controversy over his alleged anti-Semitism, ICRC officials did not come to his defense, primarily because they did not want him to serve on the UN panel.

he was often viewed as being more influential than he was inside the House. His style, as well as the policy-making process decreed by the Assembly, caused him to be resisted from time to time both by the Assembly and by the Directorate.

As for the ICRC President at the time of writing, Jacob Kellenberger, who was widely respected for successfully negotiating the Confederation's relationship to the European Union, it is – as always – difficult for outside observers to know exactly what is going on inside the organization. It seems that Kellenberger does not like publicity and public events, even relative to a self-effacing President like Alexander Hay. He apparently does not like, or think useful, personal diplomacy at diplomatic cocktail parties. In this regard he is the polar opposite of Sommaruga. His strong point is perhaps personal negotiation or discussion, where he comes across to many as a man of warmth and integrity. He is comfortable to meet, easy to converse with. This may explain why he appears to get on well with most of his colleagues in the Assembly. Historians may eventually show that his personnel and policy preferences were accepted by the Assembly at a greater rate than for Sommaruga. In the view of some insiders, Kellenberger understands how to marshal his influence, engaging on selected issues but leaving other issues to the Directorate. He has struck some Assembly members as adhering carefully to the policy-making process they designed, whereas Sommaruga sometimes gave a different impression.

Kellenberger got off to a good start in 2000, but then he stumbled. In the past, as the leading civil servant in Berne dealing with Swiss foreign policy, he was generally perceived as thoughtful and tenacious. He seemed to have a thoughtful agenda for the ICRC.[30] In face to face negotiations in Moscow, he secured ICRC access to Chechnyan fighters detained by the Russian side. He was widely praised for this achievement. But then there was a brouhaha stemming from the Middle East.

The head of the ICRC delegation for Israel and the Occupied Territories, Rene Kosirnik, said publicly as part of a wide-ranging press conference in the spring of 2001 that the introduction of Israeli settlements into the territories was a war crime.[31] The ICRC's own publications had often stated

[30] Jean-François Berger, "Etat des lieux: interview avec Jakob Kellenberger, président du CICR," *Croix-Rouge, Croissant-Rouge*, 2 (2001), 20–1.

[31] *International Herald Tribune*, 18 May 2001, 4. For a follow-up interview with President Kellenberger about this incident, see Béatrice Schaad and Anne-Frédérique Widmann, "A Week of Tension," *L'Hebdo* (14 June 2001). This is a Swiss news magazine with inside information about the ICRC. The Kosirnik affair is another example of tension between ICRC staff and leadership.

that such settlements contravened the Fourth GC from 1949. Whether the settlements constituted grave breaches of IHL under both the 1949 and 1977 law was a matter that lawyers could debate, because Israel had never ratified Protocol I from 1977.

Kellenberger, as advised by the Directorate, immediately and publicly disavowed Kosirnik's statement – which seemed to many in the professional staff to be a matter of headquarters not supporting the delegate in the field. Further, Kellenberger issued a later statement which appeared to say that since so many in Israel had suffered through the German Holocaust, one should be careful about using the phrase "war crimes" in the Israeli context. To some, this statement appeared to say that Israel did not have to observe IHL as found in the Fourth GC of 1949 because of earlier atrocities against the Jews between 1933 and 1945, an untenable position from a legal point of view. And finally, Kellenberger responded quickly to a letter from a single US Member of Congress, Representative Eliot Engel of New York, who represented a congressional district with a large Jewish population and who had threatened reduction of the US financial contribution to the ICRC because of Kosirnik's public statement. The content of Kellenberger's letter plus the rapidity of reply made it seem to some that Kellenberger was being exceedingly attentive to inappropriate Jewish-American threats.[32]

Kellenberger defended his actions vigorously. The Directorate of that time agreed with the general outlines of what the ICRC President had done, even if individual members of the Directorate did not approve of all aspects of how Kellenberger handled things. Part of the problem was that under ICRC general guidelines, public denunciations of parties for violating IHL were supposed to be approved in advance by headquarters, as we noted in chapter 5. Public criticism was to be coordinated with overall ICRC diplomacy, based on the larger context of affairs existing at that time. Kosirnik's statement was one part of an ex cathedra press conference. It was not as carefully phrased as it should have been. And it was insensitive to the inflamed context of the Israeli–Palestinian struggle.

---

[32] At this time, as explained in the next chapter, Kellenberger was trying to advance a new protocol to the 1949 law that would have created a new neutral emblem for humanitarian agencies in armed conflict. This would have allowed Israel's Magen David Adom to be recognized by the ICRC as part of the Red Cross Movement. So, however unfairly, some may have thought that Kellenberger's handling of the Kosirnik affair was further proof of a pro-Israel bias on the part of the ICRC President.

Perhaps more important than the reaction of some members of the staff and the Directorate was the fact that certain circles in Switzerland were so critical of the ICRC President in this episode that they contacted some members of the Assembly and tried to advance the view that Kellenberger should be faced with a vote of no confidence in the Assembly.[33] This did not transpire, and the Kosirnik affair was, while not forgotten, submerged in the rush of other matters. It proved a continuing irritant, however, and when interviewers later tried to bring up the matter with Kellenberger, the President brusquely told the questioner he did not want to discuss ancient matters.[34]

The Kosirnik affair demonstrated that, while the ICRC President did not make policy in the Middle East or elsewhere by himself, in his role as spokesman to the outside world for the organization he could certainly complicate the situation. Kellenberger's penchant for writing his own letters and speeches could also generate problems on occasion. Kellenberger had not been careful enough about giving the impression of embarrassing and undercutting delegates in the field with difficult assignments. His style of communication, or even lack thereof, continued to contribute to frictions with staff even years after the Kosirnik affair. Kellenberger had also overreacted to one US legislator who was currying favor with his constituents. In this case Kellenberger seems to have been badly advised by those around him. It is noteworthy that the Assembly as a collective was not a player in any of this episode, even if several individual Committee members followed matters closely.[35]

The debate continues as to whether it is possible for Kellenberger to be as strong as Moynier or Ador, or stronger than Sommaruga, in policy making inside the house. Kellenberger was successful in placing his choices in the

---

[33] Geneva could have said, for example, that Kosirnik was just responding to a question in a press conference, that what he said was nothing new in essence, and that his statement was not cleared with headquarters and did not represent any new departure in ICRC positions. Such an approach would have played down, rather than played up, the situation. Publicly rebuking Kosirnik, but leaving him in place in the Middle East, and then engaging in other public diplomacy had the effect of magnifying events without resolving them to widespread satisfaction.

[34] Alex Plaut, interview with Kellenberger, *Coopération* [a Swiss publication], 3 April 2002, downloaded from the Internet, no page number. Kellenberger: "I would prefer not to have to revisit an event which occurred almost a year ago."

[35] After a broad round of interviewing in 2003, I concluded that the top levels of the ICRC were not very good at communicating their views to the rest of the house, and that at those top levels there was a certain arrogance involved. The view there seemed to be that the staff had made serious mistakes and needed to get in line behind the leadership. The leadership had nothing to reconsider.

key positions in the Directorate – Angelo Gnädinger as Director-General and Pierre Kraehenbuel as Director of Operations. He met with Gnädinger weekly in one-on-one sessions. This process made it difficult to determine if a proposal or report sent to the Assembly was the work primarily of the President or of the Director-General and his Directorate. At the time of writing, virtually all such documents reflected the synergy of both the President and the Director-General. They had not disagreed openly about any major policy decision. Kellenberger directly contacted individuals on the professional side of the house to get information; the President did not just rely on the Director-General in this regard. Kellenberger did not hesitate to seek information about the specifics of daily operations – but only on selected issues. When the President, the Director-General, and the Director of Operations were in agreement, they controlled a great deal of ICRC policy – probably in the range of 90%.

There are times, however, when Kellenberger lost on votes in the Assembly and its Council. The Council of the Assembly met about once a month (summers excepted), plus special sessions, and could have varying influence depending on who were its three elected Assembly members (who are joined by the President and Permanent Vice President). History will eventually give us the answer as to the pattern of Kellenberger's influence – how often did he get his way, and on what issues; and how Kellenberger's record of winning and losing votes at the top compared with Sommaruga. However, the Assembly strives for consensus, and during a given year there were not that many "roll call" votes.[36]

Especially when assertive, informed, and independent members were elected by the Assembly to its Council, the latter could be a serious check on the President and an influential factor in ICRC policy making. Council members like Ernst A. Brugger, Moreillon, de Courten, and so on were not shrinking violets in acting as representatives of the Assembly. There is every indication that the Council of the Assembly is a more influential body than foreseen when the current policy-making system was instituted.

It may turn out to be the case that the somewhat reclusive Kellenberger, while not always beloved by the professional side of the House, was better at personal relations with Assembly members than Sommaruga. History will tell us if Kellenberger was quietly more collegial, and thus a very strong

[36] Assembly votes on personnel matters are entirely confidential. The minutes of these "huis clos" sessions are not distributed. On other policy matters, in both the Assembly and the Council of the Assembly, the minutes are distributed fairly widely within the House but not outside. These minutes may be "cleaned up" or "sanitized" a bit, but the basics of governance decisions are circulated to about 150 persons.

player in the making of ICRC policy – while being decidedly less visible in public relations. It was clear that he periodically "took the temperature" of the Assembly to make sure that a certain initiative would be supported or that a line of decisions would be endorsed. It also seemed to be the case that Kellenberger would identify certain issues with broad significance for the organization – like the question of the emblem. On these issues he would be determined and tenacious and attentive to details. And on other issues of smaller importance, he gave much leeway to the Directorate. At the end of 2003 Kellenberger was re-elected without controversy. The ICRC tradition is that the President can have a second term if he wishes. The only President to be eased out after one term when he wanted a second was Naville, after Nigeria, when he was quietly advised not to put himself forward for another term.

What was clear in general was that the Assembly had designed a policy-making process that presented the President with a series of checks and balances: the Assembly itself; the Council of the Assembly; a Director-General with personal responsibility for the Directorate; a Directorate chosen on the basis of competence and effectiveness and which was backed by the professional side of the house. It was a complicated and involved system for a President to manage and influence, although Kellenberger seemed perhaps to be the master of it. The Assembly, in true Swiss fashion, wanted a policy-making system leading to careful consideration and pre-dictability of outcome, rather than making ample room for charismatic personalities and unchecked ambition. The Assembly, its Council, and the President constituted the official level of governance, and the Directorate was supposed to manage.[37]

The Directorate

When it became clear after the Nigerian war that the Assembly was too amateurish – namely too large, inattentive, and badly informed as a group – to conduct a sophisticated humanitarian diplomacy, there followed in reality some three decades of experimentation with trying to find the right structure for policy making. While it was widely agreed within the Assembly that its role as a policy-making body for operations should be reduced, even as it continued to establish overall doctrine and basic

---

[37] Like the difference between strategy and tactics, the difference between governance and management was not always clear. President Kellenberger would involve himself with selected details of daily operations.

strategy, agreement proved elusive regarding what alternative structure
of policy making should be substituted. Many Assembly members knew
that they had to arrive at a policy process for operations that met the
challenges of the day, or demands would resurface to internationalize the
Committee.

Two changes were tried simultaneously during the Presidencies of Hay
and Sommaruga. First, building on what Huber had started in the 1940s,
an Executive Council was created that in its first manifestation was a sub-
group of the Assembly. Hence, during the Hay period, the Council was
made up of the President, one of his Vice Presidents, and a few members
of the Assembly. This was an attempt to keep a small part of the Assembly
involved in specific matters, while the rest of the Assembly continued to
meet no more than once a month in dealing with grand strategy and
general policies.

This arrangement did not prove satisfactory to most concerned at that
time, so in its second manifestation from 1991 the Executive Council
was composed of the President and three members of the Assembly, plus
several members of the top professional staff. This version reflected an
attempt to integrate at least part of the Assembly with the professional side
of the House who knew the situation on the ground. But this version of
the Council likewise fell by the wayside. The Assembly members did not
know as much as the staff members, and in the case of the staff members
they were reviewing themselves – they had set the daily policies that were
reviewed by the Council, and naturally they were inclined to endorse what
they had already decided. In 1989 a former staff member, Guy Deluz, was
brought in from the business community to improve management on the
professional side. But this, too, did not work out, in part because Deluz
and Sommaruga did not have the right chemistry. Deluz resigned in early
1992.[38]

To cut a long story short, by 2002 the Council existed, now again in
its original form as a sub-group of the Assembly with Assembly members
only. It was symbolically important that the word "Executive" dropped
out of its title, because it was no longer really an executive or administrative organ. Typically it was made up of the President, the Permanent
Vice President, and three elected Assembly members. It was primarily an
effort to see that the Assembly did not become completely distanced from
specific events, or in other words to protect the Assembly in the face of
the growing power of the professional side of the House. The Council

[38] ICRC press release No. 1613, 24 August 1989, and No. 1699, 20 February 1992.

met regularly about ten times a year, but special sessions brought the total number of meetings to fourteen in 2003. It sometimes served as a screening committee or permanent general working group to further review proposals from the Directorate before action by the Assembly. Sometimes ideas were generated here that led to later decisions by either the Assembly or the Directorate. On occasion it set important policies, with the President sometimes outvoted by his colleagues on the Council. The Council was central, for example, in decisions about whether to stay in occupied Iraq in 2003 or leave. To give another example, the Council decided that the then Director of Law and Cooperation with the Movement should remain in the Directorate in 2004, even though he was not the nominee of the President and Director-General.

More importantly, from the mid-1970s it was generally agreed that the professional humanitarians should have a greater say in ICRC operational decisions. Especially after 1981 it was agreed that a Directorate, a kind of cabinet, should exist on the professional side of the House. But which of the top permanent staff should be in the Directorate, what authority should they have, and how should they take their decisions? From the mid-1970s through 1991 and then again from 1998 (the interim period was the time of the hybrid Executive Council, part Assembly and part staff) one could find a Directorate of eight, five, three, two, or six members. After 1981 decisions were taken in the Directorate by majority vote, which meant that there was collective responsibility. Sometimes when there were eight or six members, the Director-General was awarded two votes in order to break any ties. Hence the Directorate evolved to be very Swiss, as a collective executive without a prime minister or real CEO, even if the Director-General might be *primus inter pares*. It was not an altogether clear and efficient arrangement. As of 1983 it could be said accurately that "the ICRC has thus never had a strong Secretary General [*sic*]."[39]

By the late 1970s, the so-called "Hay system" was in place. Even though there might be a third or fourth or even fifth member of the Directorate, the most important players were Director-General Moreillon, Director of Operations Jean-Pierre Hocke, and President Hay.[40] The President was involved, and not as figure head or rubber stamp but as a superior policy maker. The two professionals might know the facts on the ground, but the President knew what might prove acceptable to the Assembly. By the

---

[39] Willemin and Heacock, *Red Cross*, 121.

[40] In 1982, for example, the Directorate was made up of Hocke, Moreillon, and E. Regenass as Director of Administrative and Financial Affairs. But Regenass was not a major player regarding general ICRC policy.

mid-1980s there were only two in the Directorate, Moreillon and Hocke's replacement for Operations, André Pasquier.[41] And even though in fact Moreillon was the dominant figure, he and Pasquier officially were collectively responsible for what they recommended to Hay and the Assembly.

To make a long and complicated story short, by 1 July 2002 the Assembly had decided, with some members quite opposed, to create a real CEO to head the Directorate. Given the request by the existing Director-General, Paul Grossrieder, to step down, and the request by the Director of Operations, Jean-Daniel Tauxe, to be reassigned, the opportunity was taken to appoint Angelo Gnädinger as the first Director-General who would be individually responsible to the Assembly for the daily operation of the organization. He would manage a reformed Directorate as the clearly superior person. Thus, after Sommaruga, the Assembly did what Sommaruga had wanted (and what Jacques Freymond had wanted long before), at least on the professional side, which was to reduce collective responsibility and deliberation, and emphasize personal responsibility and streamlined decision making.[42]

---

[41] Hocke left to become the UN High Commissioner for Refugees. He had built a reputation for effectiveness as ICRC Director of Operations, and several ICRC colleagues praised his dynamism and negotiating skill. By some accounts, in the Cambodian operation of 1979–80 he out-performed his UNICEF counterparts. But he was something of a lone wolf and a loose canon. He often proceeded on his own, with little coordination with the rest of the House, and at one point the Assembly was on the verge of sacking him. His colleagues sometimes referred to his era as operations by terror, for by all accounts sensitivity to personal relations was not his strong point. Although he accomplished a great deal at the ICRC and helped rebuild the organization's reputation after Nigeria, he was not a polished diplomat known for collegial relations. That he should have been named to the top UNHCR post indicated that those making that decision, especially those in Washington, did not have full knowledge about what was really going on inside the ICRC. At the UNHCR he was not a success, making a number of internal enemies and losing the support of a number of important governments. For an accurate portrait of Hocke as UN policy maker see Gil Loescher, *The UNHCR and World Politics: A Perilous Path* (Oxford: Oxford University Press, 2001), 247–64.

When Moreillon left the Directorate to become Secretary-General of the World Organization of Scout Movements, it was said in some circles that Hocke had accepted something at the UNHCR far above his abilities, and Moreillon had accepted something with the Scouts far below his.

In the 1990s the ICRC had difficulty in replacing the Moreillon–Hocke team, a team that reminded some of Dunant–Moynier and Huber–Burckhardt in terms of combining ideas with action.

[42] It is interesting to recall that former Acting President Jacques Freymond resigned when he failed to get the Assembly to transform itself into a small body of professional humanitarians. In creating the Directorate and finally a Director-General as real CEO, the Assembly took a big step toward doing what the now deceased Freymond had wanted – which was to have much ICRC policy made by a small number of professional humanitarians. Not for the first time did ideas move slowly at the ICRC.

The new Directorate contained the first-ever female Director, Doris Pfister. (Several females had previously served as Assistant Directors – e.g., M. Harroff-Tavel, F. Krill.) Virtually all operational policy of direct significance to victims was made by the Director-General and the Directorate. The ICRC President was frequently informed but not really in the official chain of command regarding most daily policies. For a time the Permanent Vice President, Jacques Forrester, met with the Directorate. His role was to convey information to the Assembly and the Council of the Assembly, not to participate in Directorate decisions. As in the Kosirnik affair, the President was sometimes brought into the loop by the Directorate to handle public diplomacy.

The first Director-General with personal responsibility for the Directorate, Gnädinger, was soon sidelined by a serious illness, so as of 2004 the Director of Operations, Kraehenbuehl, despite his youth, doubled as Director-General. The new system of policy making, although it is not radically different from what preceded it, has yet to be fully tested at the time of writing. In particular, we do not know what would happen if the President and the Director-General had a disagreement over major issues.

The staff

Since originally the ICRC did not intend to interject itself directly into conflicts as compared to providing rearguard coordination for national aid societies, the question of staff, and certainly of sizeable staff, did not immediately arise. Indeed, when members of the original five, including Henry Dunant after he had resigned from the ICRC, interjected themselves into conflicts, they were disavowed by Geneva.[43] When ICRC field operations expanded more systematically during the First World War, the Assembly relied heavily on volunteers. In August 1914 the ICRC had only twelve persons working for it.[44] The ICRC manifested few paid delegates in the field during the inter-war years. Dr. Marcel Junod, mentioned in chapter 2, was the best known of these. As observed earlier, he and his colleagues recognized that the few professional humanitarians in the field were completely inadequate to make much of a dent in the brutal power politics of the 1930s and 1940s. During the Second World War the ICRC assembled 1,900 paid staff and 1,800 volunteers.[45]

---

[43] Willemin and Heathcock, *Red Cross*, 23.
[44] Philippe Ryfman, *La question humanitaire* (Paris: Elllipses, 1999), 38.   [45] *Ibid.*, 129.

Immediately after World War II the ICRC largely disbanded its paid staff, those numbers dropping to fifty by 1950. Even that number was reduced by another 50% by the early 1960s under the pressure of meager financing.[46] The organization felt a moral obligation not to give a long-term contract to paid staff, fearing the inability to pay the person in the future, especially when the number and size of conflicts could not be predicted. The organization did devise a system in which a number of Swiss citizens were identified and earmarked for emergency and short-term call-up as temporary delegates, much like a military reserve system.[47] It was the 1967 war in the Middle East and its resulting prolonged occupation that propelled the organization's paid staff toward an apparently permanent increase in numbers. Until then, the organization was reluctant to hire and train professional delegates for fear of facing no emergency in which to use them, and no funds with which to pay them. By 1995 the ICRC had over 1,000 expatriate delegates in the field for the first time.[48]

For a long time the ICRC delegate was dispatched to the field with virtually no training and often with no precise guidelines. In 1973, for example, to deal with the war between India and Pakistan, and involving tens of thousands of prisoners of war, the ICRC appointed as head of delegation a former businessman with minimal ICRC experience. The assumption seemed to be that if he were a proper Swiss, well chosen by headquarters, he would make the right decisions on the ground. Delegates were always male, although tracing activities were carried out in Geneva mostly by females, perhaps because much of the work seemed quasi-secretarial – viz., the tedious checking of names in card files. (Occasionally a Dutch or Swedish national, etc., might be appointed as an ICRC delegate.) In any event the amateurish Assembly was hesitant to try to control its (amateurish) delegates in the field.

Despite the evident weaknesses of this system, some of those delegates who served abroad for long periods of time became very good at what they did – for example Georg Hoffmann in Africa and Melchior Borsinger in Europe. Many delegates learned somehow to balance skepticism about human nature and public authorities with dedication and commitment to the cause.[49] But others were less impressive when crises erupted – in Greece in the late 1960s, for example. Of all the ICRC delegates hastily recruited during the Second World War, only one turned out to be a bad

---

[46] *Ibid.* During the Second World War the ICRC had levied a "tax" on relief shipments, paid by the major belligerents. This funding, of course, ceased after the war.
[47] *Ibid.*, 131–2.   [48] Internal document in the possession of the author.
[49] See also Ignatieff, *The Warrior's Honor*, 143.

apple and was immediately sacked when headquarters became aware of his engaging in black market trading. (The ICRC delegation in Frankfurt after the war, however, was not stellar.[50]) Of all the delegates over the years, there have been precious few like Dres Balmer in El Salvador, as noted in chapter 2, who blatantly violated their contractual arrangement to remain discreet about the details of their work.

It was only from about 1970 that the ICRC realized it needed to be more systematic about training and guidelines and consistency of policy.[51] Up until then it had developed some Red Cross principles, as we saw in the preceding chapter, but the search for real policy consistency only began in the 1970s. Most statements of ICRC "doctrine" started in the 1970s. The ICRC Department of Human Resources, by whatever name, also dates from this era. Again, prolonged occupation in the Middle East contributed to recognition of the need for doctrine. ICRC delegates would come and go, while Israeli officials stayed put. New delegates would have to find out from state officials what had been done in the past. This obviously was not satisfactory in Geneva.

It was also during that time (from 1970) that the ICRC began to provide systematic training for its newly recruited delegates. First at Cartigny, just outside of Geneva, now at Versoix, also a suburb of the city of Geneva, it began to have its experienced personnel oversee simulation and other forms of training to prepare new staff for negotiations with national officials such as prison superintendents, Ministers of Justice, and the like. Handbooks were provided to staff in the field covering their responsibilities, duties, objectives, and techniques. In fact, tremendous demands were placed on field delegations: to promote IHL, develop relations with the various units of the National Society, build good relations with various governmental agencies, carry out detention visits, provide relief, trace missing persons, develop teaching materials, stay in touch with local representatives of NGOs and inter-governmental organizations, and provide an accounting of what had been done. Eventually, great attention was given to the security of staff in the field, given the murderous attacks on ICRC delegations in places like Burundi (June) and Chechnya (December) 1996 – three intentionally killed in the former and six in the latter.

Again to cut a long story short, from about 1970 the staff was more and more composed of truly professional humanitarians. Many outsiders commented positively on the professionalism and consistency of ICRC delegates found in conflict situations around the world. Some worried

---

[50] Morehead, *Dunant's Dream*, 535.   [51] Willemin and Heacock, *Red Cross*.

that in the 1970s the ICRC became more of a traditional bureaucracy. They were worried about the élan of the organization. On the one hand the ICRC continued to want to give some leeway to creative persons in the field. On the other hand the organization wanted everyone to follow consistent general policy with a great deal of consistency in tactics. Some critics thought this was like trying to herd cats. There was persistent tension between headquarters and the field,[52] a problem perhaps present to some degree in all sizeable organizations whether the ICRC or, say, the US Federal Bureau of Investigation (FBI). Occasionally this friction at the ICRC would surface in public acrimony, as occurred in the late 1980s.[53]

At the time of writing, those who saw headquarters as too slow and stodgy and who saw field operations as creative, flexible, and in tune with developments were numerous. One result was the decision in 2002 to create a strong Director-General who would be superior to the collective Directorate. In general, despite various tensions, morale of staff remained high. When there was first the prospect of vastly expanded repatriation of prisoners between Iran and Iraq in 1990, and then many Iraqi prisoners of war captured during the liberation of Kuwait who were held in Saudi Arabia in 1991, virtually all of the ICRC professional staff then stationed in Geneva volunteered to go into the field if needed.

Through the mid-1980s the ICRC seemed to have sufficient numbers of Swiss nationals who wanted to work for the organization – at least for a while. Finishing university in Switzerland and then working for the ICRC seemed a desirable career path. According to a survey in 2000,[54] the ICRC remained an attractive career option for Swiss (and non-Swiss) university graduates. The exact ranking of the ICRC, compared to other organizations, varied according to which faculty (or school or college in

[52] Recall the books by Marti and Balmer, where delegates in the field question the wisdom of headquarters. It is impossible to provide better documentation on this issue, because most insiders do not publish on this question, and most outsiders do not have access to "the facts."

[53] Morehead, *Dunant's Dream*, 680. She does not say so, because she has her dates wrong, but some of this staff unrest was because of the perceived ambivalence and caution when Andre Pasquier was Director of Operations. Also, there were others who wanted to be Director of Operations. Morehead says that Moreillon and Pasquier were at war. This is not quite right. Director-General Moreillon became concerned about operational effectiveness and wanted a personnel change, but Moreillon had recommended Pasquier to start with and thought highly of his intellectual abilities. Jean de Courten eventually replaced Pasquier. At times the ICRC can comprise its own little political system, with various manifestations of factional politics, frequently linked to personal ambitions. On staff unrest, also recall the Kosirnik affair, treated above.

[54] "Le CICR manqué de bras," *LM*, 20 July 2002, 15. This is a Swiss newspaper.

American English) the students were enrolled in. But at the end of the day the ICRC was the most attractive humanitarian option, and almost as attractive as working for UBS, the banking giant, or the SwissAirGroup (before it tanked). One could always change tack later and move into Swiss business circles or public affairs.

Then it became evident that the ICRC began to lack sufficient numbers of both general delegates and particularly specialized personnel. In the mid-1980s the ICRC averaged about 500 staff in the field per year. Fifteen years later field personnel were almost three times that number. How many specialists in tropical medicine do Swiss medical schools produce? And Swiss university graduates seemed to be finding that it they stayed with the ICRC very long, career options in business tended to be closed off. While an ICRC delegate might be on the ground doing humanitarian work in Kenya, other Swiss were getting MBAs at the Harvard Business School and taking the best jobs at Nestlé and PriceWaterhouse Cooper. Sizeable relief operations in places like Cambodia accentuated the problem, as did short-term contracts that were not renewed. Then there was the evident danger and stress from working in conflict areas characterized by extreme brutality. A number of field staff required psychological counselling after witnessing atrocities.

By the year 2000 the ICRC was in need of about 300 new staff each year, as about 15% of the staff left each year,[55] a relatively large number for an organization with an average of about 2,000 staff. In fact, on average, for each 100 new staff recruited, 75% had left at the end of three years. As the ICRC came to emulate in some ways working for a national security organization or foreign ministry, with obligations at all hours of the day and night, dealing with pressing emergencies around the world, some staff decided to emphasize family rather than career. Some women, in particular, decided not to try to become a member of the Directorate, or to get out of the organization altogether, as did some men. For top staff, the demands of being a professional humanitarian became all-consuming. Moreover, in 1992 Switzerland was voting on whether to draw closer to the European Union, with its transnational labor laws. Had Switzerland entered what was called the European Economic Space, perhaps a step toward EU membership, the ICRC would have had either to abandon the all-Swiss nature of its staff, or to ask for a special exemption. All of these factors led to a review of mono-nationality applied to staff.

[55] *Ibid.*

It was in this context that the ICRC put more emphasis on systematic recruitment and opened up its staff to all nationalities in 1992, provided of course that new personnel were fluent in both French (the internal language of the House), and English (the external language most useful). The language requirement greatly limited the personnel pool. In any event the organization moved in two directions at once: to make more use of non-Swiss seconded from National Societies; and to recruit more non-Swiss from beyond the Red Cross Movement. A decade after the 1991–92 decisions to make the professional staff multinational, about 30–35% of the professional staff, which numbered about 2,000, were non-Swiss.[56] By 2004, 50% of ICRC staff were non-Swiss.[57] Of total ICRC staff, about 10% came from National Societies, and about 20–25% from outside the Movement. The total number seconded to the ICRC from National Societies remained stable throughout the 1990s. Of the non-Swiss, only about 4–5% came from countries of the Global South. Not quite half of the new staff were women. The organization had found that while female delegates were unacceptable in a few Islamic countries, elsewhere they had worked out very well. Sometimes detainees seemed to confide more in a female delegate than a male.

Given this remarkable historical change in the composition of staff, the organization made a concerted effort during training to stress what it called an ICRC "nationality." There was even discussion of trying to develop and have accepted an ICRC "passport." In any event the Directorate certainly paid attention to whether non-Swiss identified as much with the organization as Swiss delegates had in the past. The early judgment was that the non-Swiss were just as devoted to the organization and its humanitarian causes as the Swiss. The Directorate still preferred to recruit from the Swiss labor market.[58]

There were problems that came with a multinational staff, but some were not entirely new. As before, one had to match a person to his or her context. One could not put an American into certain situations where anti-Americanism was strong, or a British national into certain former British colonies. In 1999, at the start of NATO's bombing in Serbia, some 60% of ICRC personnel in that area were from NATO countries. They

---

[56] These figures do not include locally recruited logistical and support staff. If these figures are added, then the ICRC was annually employing about 12,000 persons, 10,000 of them locally recruited non-Swiss.

[57] Vincent Bourquin, interview with Jakob Kellenberger, *Tribune de Genève*, 14 February 2004, downloaded from the Internet, no page number.

[58] Internal document in the possession of the author.

had to be replaced. Serb authorities also demanded that Swiss nationals be withdrawn. Adjustments were made and the humanitarian work went forward. In Afghanistan in 1998, when the United States carried out cruise missile attacks on suspected terrorist training facilities, some sixty ICRC staff from NATO countries had to be rapidly withdrawn and others inserted. In the past matters were not entirely different. For example, the ICRC had had to be careful about not putting a tall, blond Swiss male into Afghanistan; he might be mistaken for a Russian with fatal consequences. Already the Directorate had had to be careful about where to assign Swiss female delegates.

One still had the problem of high turnover, as those seconded from National Societies operated mostly on short-term contracts. Certain visa and tax matters had to be taken up with authorities from the Confederation, to try to ensure that non-Swiss delegates were not discriminated against in terms of taxation and other technicalities. But the agency was committed to a multinational staff and was trying to manage differences to maintain a common and strong identity with the organization. There were no official limits on how high non-Swiss could rise in the ICRC's professional management system.

One could only speculate about how much the Confederation or the Swiss public would support the ICRC when heads of delegations, heads of departments, and even a Director-General were non-Swiss. A very few French or French-Swiss had already been in the Directorate, but this fact went mostly unnoticed by those outside the House. The Directorate originally thought that a multinational staff did not raise any question about a mono-national Assembly, but perceptive members of the Assembly knew better. The Assembly requested a broad review of multinational staffing, which showed the role of the Assembly in supervising and fine-tuning ideas originating from the Directorate.

Funding

The modern ICRC has always been funded primarily by voluntary contributions from the wealthy liberal democracies that fund most extant international programs. For some time the largest contributors to the organization have been the United States and the Swiss Confederation, with the other European states and the European Union close behind. A few other states like Australia, Canada, Japan, and New Zealand are also important contributors. These states normally provide about 80–85% of what the ICRC spends. Most of the rest comes from the National Societies of these same states. Private gifts make up the remaining 3%, on average. In any given year around 2000, 50% of what the ICRC spent came from the United States, Switzerland, the UK, and the EU.

There is no assessed payment system associated with IHL. States can be parties to the 1949 Geneva Conventions and 1977 Additional Protocols and pay nothing, or a pittance, for the ICRC's humanitarian work that is undertaken against the background of those treaties. States can pretend to endorse IHL and gain whatever benefit in prestige and legitimacy that such ratification brings, while avoiding the costs of applying the law through ICRC diplomacy.[59]

Despite considerable efforts from Geneva, the wealthy Arab states have never been major contributors to the ICRC. Some of these states were quite outspoken in pressing for the Fourth GC to be applied by Israel for the benefit of the Palestinians, but these same states were never much interested in helping to pay the bill for ICRC work in the occupied territories. Experience with armed conflict by states such as Iran and Iraq, leading to the belligerents' close knowledge of ICRC humanitarian efforts, has not led to their increasing their contributions to the organization. The case of Kuwait was slightly different (the details being easily tracked in ICRC annual reports).

The ICRC runs on two budgets: a headquarters budget (basic and predictable costs), and an operations budget (corresponding to conflicts around the world). In recent years the HQ budget has been about 20% of the total. About 7.5% of the HQ budget goes for administrative expenses in the field. The field budget is obviously not fully predictable, in which case crises and emergencies result in special appeals and sometimes deficit spending until matters can be sorted out.[60] The organization, with the concurrence of major donors, maintains a reserve fund to help cover the costs of responding to unexpected conflicts. The ICRC participates in the consolidated appeals system organized by the United Nations, in which all "aid agencies" or "humanitarian actors" make their fund-raising

---

[59] In reality, the assessed payment system associated with the regular or administrative budget of the United Nations rests on voluntary compliance. If the United States chooses to violate its treaty obligations regarding such payments, it cannot be taken to court or coerced into paying its assessed dues. But treaty obligations create pressure on the United States, and others, to pay, if only to avoid the embarrassment of losing one's vote in the UN General Assembly when arrears amount to two years of obligated payments. So if IHL did have an assessed payment schedule, payment would still rest – to a very great extent – on voluntary compliance or contribution, at least for the Great Powers.

[60] From roughly 1945 to 1967, the ICRC would first "quite passively" await financial donations before engaging in extensive field actions: Willemin and Heacock, *Red Cross*, 159.

appeals to states at the same time. The ICRC does so in an independent way, not putting itself under UN aegis, but the organization acts in consultation and coordination with the UNHCR, UNICEF, the UN Office for the Coordination of Humanitarian Affairs (OCHA), and so on.

After the Cold War the ICRC underwent a major budgetary expansion. By the time of writing, total spending was averaging $600 million per annum, an increase of roughly 300% from a decade earlier. This annual figure was about half of what the United States spent for the 2003 occupation of Iraq *per week*. In 2003 the United States was spending about $900 million per annum for its military presence in Bosnia. ICRC annual expenditure was less than that of the UNHCR, which around the year 2000 spent slightly more or less $1 billion. This latter annual figure of $1 billion was approximately 1/60th ($60 billion) of what the United States spent for the Persian Gulf war against Iraq in 1991, the actual fighting of which took only a few days. It can easily be seen, therefore, that even with the expansion of the budgets of "aid agencies" in the 1990s, including the ICRC, various measures showed that state spending for military purposes still dwarfed humanitarian spending by the ICRC.

ICRC expanded funding was based on several lines of reasoning, some of them by no means charitable to victims. In many of these conflicts large numbers of civilians were endangered, sometimes because of being intentionally targeted by the fighting parties. There was, especially given western media coverage, some expanded concern with the fate of these individuals in conflict situations, as in Somalia, the Balkans, the Great Lakes Region of Africa, and so on. But major military powers, above all the United States, were mostly unwilling to commit their military forces to decisively ending most of these conflicts. Therefore the willingness of Washington and other western capitals to support humanitarian efforts occurred in lieu of enforcement action. So, the strange logic went, if the conflicts seemed to endanger western military forces, then why not send in unarmed relief workers? At least outsiders would appear to be doing something.

Finally, there was the desire of the major funding sources, above all the United States and the EU, not to put all their resources into one humanitarian basket, but to fund the ICRC along with shifting UN agencies (e.g., UNHCR or UNICEF or the World Food Programme) and a network of NGO aid agencies (e.g., Oxfam, Caritas, World Vision). There was much talk about improved coordination of international humanitarian work, but in fact some logic argued for a multiplicity of actors. In Somalia in the early 1990s, the ICRC was better positioned to deliver and supervise food relief, compared to other possible intermediaries. But in other situations UNHCR or UNICEF might rationally be chosen as the lead agency for international relief.

Was the ICRC more expensive than other relief agencies? Did the ICRC make up the "gold plated humanitarians?" Certainly to many staff members of some of the smaller private relief agencies, ICRC delegates seemed to be very well paid and very well supported. Strangely enough, no one seemed to know whether it was more expensive to provide relief via the ICRC compared to UN relief agencies. At the time of writing no studies existed comparing, say, the cost of ICRC relief and UNHCR relief in the Balkans from 1992 to 1995. Both agencies were active in that region, and theoretically it should be possible to separate out non-detention relief costs from the costs of detention visits. Both agencies brought in relief primarily through ground transport, and not by airlift – the most expensive means of delivery. But neither the funding agencies in North America and Europe nor the humanitarian agencies themselves had carried out any such comparison. One view within the ICRC is that such studies cannot be done, because, for example, sometimes the ICRC stayed while the UNHCR pulled out for security reasons, or vice versa. Moreover, its delegates might engage in some detention visits or tracing activities while delivering relief. Another view, held by some outside the ICRC, has it that such comparative studies can indeed be done, but that the ICRC in particular resists doing them, fearing they will show the "gold plated" nature of it work.

It was widely thought that the ICRC was a relatively expensive actor, if only because it tended to support its delegates in the field well, believing that field staff had to be well rested and cared for in order to do their job properly. ICRC staff frequently had state of the art vehicles and communication equipment, at least until thefts and assaults caused the organization to lower its profile abroad in this regard. Certainly its work is labor intensive. And on occasion it provided financial support to other relief agencies. But again, no precise comparative studies existed to prove that the ICRC was or was not a "gold plated" humanitarian actor.

The principal donor agencies – for example, the US Bureau for Population and Migration in the State Department – seemed intuitively satisfied with ICRC cost-effectiveness. The ICRC obtained an external technical audit of its operations in Kosovo during 1999, and donor agencies seemed satisfied with what they knew of the cost-effectiveness of that operation. There was also an outside evaluation of various private "relief agencies" active in the Rwanda crisis of 1994, a study that did not single out the

ICRC for being "gold plated." The organization exercises two internal audits itself, plus a commissioned outside audit by a private accounting firm.

Conclusion

In retrospect, ICRC internal changes after 1967 regarding policy making, budgets, and personnel were historic. Because of these changes in management and resources, the ICRC by 2004 was a vastly different agency compared to 1965. It was an agency less strictly Swiss in both composition and culture, at least below the level of the Assembly. Its basic mandate was still the same, as were it specific tasks. But the ICRC pursued its goals and adjusted its tactics through a different policy-making process, with expanded resources including a multinational staff. Whether all of this would lead to fundamental change in the composition and/or thinking of the all-Swiss Assembly was an interesting question whose answer would be provided, like so much else in ICRC history, slowly. As the first Swiss Permanent Representative to the UN said of his country, so it can be said of the Swiss at the top of the ICRC: "The Swiss are cautious. They do not change their views easily. It takes a long time. They are risk-averse."[61]

Postscript: Swiss society, political culture, and the ICRC

In the rarefied air of general impressions, it is logical to think that an organization like the ICRC that has manifested mono-national general policy making since 1863 would reflect certain national traits. Not to be too academic about it, the ICRC has been thoroughly Swiss from top to bottom from 1863 to at least 1992. Even after its professional staff was internationalized, all of its key policy makers remained Swiss (and white males for that matter, but here I am only interested in the Swiss element). Surely the ICRC has been affected by being Swiss. But being Swiss is difficult to translate into definite and precise characteristics.

Is it really true, by comparison, that American policy makers, whether in the public or private realm, are persistently characterized by "Yankee ingenuity," or the British by an aversion to strategic thinking and a preference for "muddling through," or the French by "hauteur," and so on?

---

[61] Chris Hedges, "Point Man at the U.N. as Switzerland Takes Sides," *New York Times*, 5 April 2002, A21. Interview with Jeno C.A. Staehelin.

When put in bold terms this way, those who rely on national traits to explain a good bit about policy and policy making may be on thin ice.

There is, however, a respected school of thought that links national traits to policy making. In the view of the esteemed diplomat-scholar George Kennan, buttressed by the scholar John Spanier, for example, among other traits the Americans supposedly have a fondness for moral and legal discourse.[62] The theorist Henry Shue writes of the American tendency to "overmoralize international affairs."[63] Still, this school of thought falls considerably short of relying on absolutely clear evidence to prove its assertions.

All of which is prefatory to my argument that Swiss society has greatly affected the ICRC over time. But I readily admit I cannot prove my view with scientific certainty. In part, the problem stems from the complexity of Swiss society. If language is the basis of culture, then there is not a rigorously defined Swiss culture. But there remains a Swiss society, made up of three primary language groups and two primary religious traditions, and there does seem to be a Swiss political culture, comprised of persistent views toward public life and public policy.

I suggest the following counter-factual to begin to make my point. Had the ICRC been linked to, say, Swedish rather than Swiss neutrality, and had the ICRC been dominated by Swedish rather than Swiss personalities, its tactics would surely not have been so discreet. In general Swiss neutrality in both the governmental and the humanitarian realms is not given to high-profile statements, whereas relatively speaking Swedish neutrality is much more given to public judgments. For example, the neutral Swedish government was much more public in its criticisms of the United States in Vietnam than was the neutral Swiss government. In a phrase, Swedish neutrality as a broad phenomenon is less cautious, less "buttoned down," than Swiss neutrality similarly defined. The Swedish Red Cross has been less cautious, less discreet than the ICRC on numerous issues arising within the Red Cross Movement over the years – for example in the Nigerian war.[64]

---

[62] George Kennan, *American Diplomacy 1900–1950* (Chicago: Mentor, for the University of Chicago, 1951); Steven W. Hook and John Spanier, *American Foreign Policy since World War II* (Washington, DC: CQ Press, 15th edn, 2000). This latter work holds that there is a distinct American style to foreign policy making, characterized by an American sense of destiny, depreciation of power, penchant for crusading, and intensive introspection.

[63] *Basic Rights: Subsistence, Affluence, and US Foreign Policy* (Princeton: Princeton University Press, 1980, 2nd edn 1996), 179.

[64] Most of this large subject I leave to the sociologists and social historians. Swiss political culture is an especially complicated thing, given that views of public authority and public policy in the Canton of Geneva may be very different in some ways from the Canton

It can be argued that it is responsibility, not nationality, that imposes discretion, and that if the Swedes controlled ICRC governance they would have to be discreet also. Perhaps, but I continue to believe Swiss political culture has influenced the ICRC to a considerable degree.

The controversial Swiss author Jean Ziegler argues that Switzerland manifests an "ideology of secrecy," inherited from its Huguenot Protestant heritage, which is clearly evident especially in the banking industry. This led, he says, to Swiss bankers saying that they had no political opinions; they just offered their services.[65] The parallels with ICRC thinking are very clear.

If we look at conventional wisdom about Swiss society, which of course is not science, the Swiss are well known for, in general, a lack of fondness for public displays of emotion.[66] As one journalist noted, reflecting a widespread assumption, "Outrage is not a common trait in the Swiss character."[67] Another journalist suggested that the Swiss nation "prides itself on icy reserve."[68] A documentary film presented by the British Broadcasting Corporation (BBC) characterized the ICRC as lacking passion.[69] An ICRC delegate himself commented on the dominant ethos in the organization to the effect that its officials were supposed to manifest icy calm and a reserved demeanor: "ICRC delegates are not famous for their unbridled emotions."[70]

I know of only one source that has dealt with the subject of a generalized Swiss influence on the ICRC, even in a cursory way. Hans-Peter

---

of Appenzell or St. Gallen. Moreover, despite differences in political culture between the Swedes and the Swiss, their neutrality during the Second World War was similar in that both nation-states sought to accommodate the Nazis when German power was predominant. But my central point remains. ICRC discretion is informed not only by rational calculation of effective humanitarian protection, but also by Swiss political culture in all its complexity.

[65] Ziegler, *The Swiss, the Gold, and the Dead*, 241 and *passim*.

[66] See, for example, Elizabeth Olson, "Broken Plates and Flying Chalets Celebrate Swiss Foibles," *International Herald Tribune*, 24 June 2002, 5. This story covers a Swiss national fair in Biel, in which, among other things, Swiss visitors are encouraged to have fun and be publicly expressive. Ms. Olson writes, "And, in a bit of fun aimed at the Swiss reputation for repressed emotions, another Biel pavilion offers white china plates and marker pens for writing a message or a name on the plates, which the visitor is then invited to smash. 'This isn't very Swiss,' said an elderly lady." This reference, of course, is anecdotal journalism, not scientific sociology. I do believe that ICRC discretion, for example, is partly the result of Swiss society and not just rational calculation of what makes for effective humanitarian protection.

[67] Mark Landler, "Clockwork Switzerland Sees Safety Winding Down," *International Herald Tribune*, 15 July 2002, 5. Again, this is anecdotal observation.

[68] Hedges, "Point Man at the U.N."

[69] "Crossing the Lines," Fulcrum TV Productions West.

[70] Mercier, *Crimes sans châtiment*, 198.

Gasser wrote the following: "The ICRC's present governing elite are of Swiss nationality, have received their education in Swiss schools and universities, and live in a Swiss environment. Is there any reason to believe that the Swiss perception of international problems and Swiss approaches to solving them should be absent in Geneva? That Swiss affinity probably creates links that are much stronger than any outside attempt to influence individual decisions."[71] While his point is well taken that similar views prevail in Berne and Geneva, this brief passage of course fails to specify what are the "Swiss approaches" that prevail in both institutions.

One common approach to public policy by Berne and Geneva has been indirectly documented at some length. In a study of diplomatic good offices practiced by the Swiss Confederation, the terms neutrality, impartiality, and consent appear time and time again.[72] In fact, in reading this work, one can easily forget whether it is the Confederation or the ICRC that is being analyzed. Moreover, the ICRC's Assembly often coopts those with experience in Berne. It is not very surprising then that the top level of the ICRC has been persistently conservative and risk averse in humanitarian diplomacy, as has the Confederation in offering its "good offices" in international relations.

One recent study is extremely helpful for present purposes. In effect, it comprises an argument about Swiss political culture, as least as pertaining to international relations. In an essay on Swiss foreign policy and its domestic roots, Jurg Martin Gabriel discusses the following central notions: collegiality, smallness, neutrality, a cautious version of good offices that shies away from mediation, a combination of sovereignty–autonomy–unilateralism, preference for quiet diplomacy, reluctance to change until the external environment requires it, and effort to avoid moral judgments about others especially on human rights.[73] The parallels to ICRC thinking are obvious.

Building on the above, in my judgment the following traits are prevalent within Swiss society. Some of them affect public life and public policy and thus are also part of Swiss political culture. In my view, whether

---

[71] "The International Committee of the Red Cross as a Humanitarian Actor in Conflict Situations: Development since 1945," in Jurg Martin Gabriel and Thomas Fischer, eds., *Swiss Foreign Policy in a Changing World* (New York and London: Palgrave Macmillan, 2003), 105–26, with attention to the ICRC and Switzerland at 120–3, quote from 122.

[72] Raymond R. Probst, *"Good Offices" in the Light of Swiss International Practice and Experience* (Dordrecht: Martinus Nijhoff, 1989).

[73] Jurg Martin Gabriel, "The Price of Political Uniqueness: Swiss Foreign Policy in a Changing World," in Gabriel and Fischer, eds., *Swiss Foreign Policy*, 1–22. Another author in this collection mentions the emphasis in Switzerland on "sober" public demeanor.

these factors can be viewed as social or "political," they have affected the ICRC: liberalism and democracy, collective policy making, emphasis on personal integrity/honesty, managerial expertise, attention to detail, careful financial accounting, slowness to regard women as fully equal, unilateralism/aloofness, discretion/secrecy, conservatism and risk aversion, aversion to public moral judgments, and stolid public demeanor.

For example, just as the Swiss Confederation has failed to join the European Union and was very slow to join the United Nations, so the ICRC was slow to see the need for and benefits of a truly integrated Red Cross Movement. Unilateralism runs deep in Swiss society and political culture. In the prize-winning and best-selling novel *Bel Canto*, author Ann Patchett has the fictitious Red Cross representative, Messner, say about the hostage situation: "The Swiss never take sides . . . We are only on the side of the Swiss."[74]

Hopefully some other authors will take up this subject in the future. Over time it may be possible to specify whether the internationalization of staff from 1992 has changed the organizational culture of the ICRC.

[74] Ann Patchett, *Bel Canto* (New York: Perennial, for HarperCollins, 2001), 88.

7

The ICRC and international humanitarian law

War is so awful that it makes us cynical about the possibility of restraint, and then it is so much worse that it makes us indignant at the absence of restraint. Our cynicism testifies to the defectiveness of the war convention, and our indignation to its reality and strength.

Walzer, *Just and Unjust Wars,* 46

No century [compared to the twentieth century] has had better norms and worse realities.

Rieff: *A Bed for the Night,* 70

Apparently the phrase "international humanitarian law" (IHL) was first used by the ICRC in 1953.[1] In this chapter I will first show that there remains a lack of clarity about the precise scope of IHL. Then I will show that there is often confusion about its relation to international human rights law (HRL). Finally I will show that in relation to IHL the ICRC exercises three roles by whatever name: helping to develop the law, helping to disseminate the principles and rules of the law, and helping to apply the law. The central point of this chapter is not to provide a legal commentary on the specifics of IHL, but rather to discuss its practical relevance to victims of conflicts through the efforts of the ICRC.

A theme running throughout this chapter is that one can overemphasize IHL as a technical legal subject compared to humanitarian diplomacy. Just as some authors, including some law professors, believe that much

---

[1] Dietrich Schindler, "Significance of the Geneva Conventions for the Contemporary World," *International Review of the Red Cross,* 836 (December 1999), 715–29, note 4. There is some debate about the exact content and boundaries of the terms IHL, law of war, law of armed conflict, and neutrality laws. There is also some debate about how to describe IHL: the law to protect human dignity in armed conflict, versus the balancing of military necessity with concern for humanitarian values in war. The UN *ad hoc* criminal court for former Yugoslavia tried to sort all of this out. See *Prosecutor v. Tadic* (Case no. IT-94-1-AR72), Decision on the Defence Motion for Interlocutory Appeal on Jurisdiction, 2 October 1995 (1997) 105 I.L.R. 453, 35 I.L.M. 32, para. 87.

attention to human rights has become legalistic, with too much attention to legal technicalities, this chapter suggests that much attention to humanitarian affairs has become legalistic.[2] There is too much attention to the abstract logic of precise legal wording, and not enough accurate attention to the realities of humanitarian protection in the field. Up until about 1993, there were very few important international or national court cases judicially specifying the details of IHL. That law was applied, to the extent that it was applied, mostly through the soft law process of diplomacy and military training rather than through the hard law process of court adjudication. When ICRC representatives in Sierra Leone or Liberia faced child soldiers on drugs armed with automatic weapons, the details of IHL were about as relevant as theoretical physics. It is well to recall that in Somalia in the early 1990s "virtually no one with a weapon had heard of the Geneva Conventions."[3]

Without doubt IHL is important to the ICRC. It is often useful for the ICRC to be able to point to IHL and say to a belligerent that the international community has approved this or that norm to regulate the process of war. Thus IHL gives the ICRC a legal basis from which to make requests to protagonists in armed conflicts. In some cases a legal argument may be helpful. But in some cases IHL is no more than a vague background factor that, while contributing to the legitimacy of ICRC humanitarian endeavors in certain circles, does not come remotely close to guaranteeing success to ICRC efforts in the field.

For the most part, even without IHL the ICRC would continue to do most of what it is doing, and in the same way. One sees this especially clearly in detention visits to security or political prisoners. Such detainees are not covered by IHL. But the ICRC carries out the visits in almost exactly the same way as if the Geneva Conventions and/or Protocols were applicable. For all of the legal profession's emphasis on IHL, the ICRC

---

[2] On legalistic approaches to human rights, see Abdullahi A. An-Na'im, "The Legal Protection of Human Rights in Africa: How To Do More with Less," in Austin Sarat and Thomas R. Kearns, eds., *Human Rights: Concepts, Contests, Contingencies* (Ann Arbor: University of Michigan Press, 2001). See also Rieff, *A Bed for the Night* 282: the western human rights movement relies on an "essentially legalistic framework."

[3] Jennifer Leaning, "When the System Doesn't Work: Somalia 1992," in Kevin M. Cahill, ed., *A Framework for Survival: Health, Human Rights, and Humanitarian Assistance in Conflicts and Disasters* (New York: Basic Books, 1993), 112. After the Second World War, a number of national war crimes trials were held, particularly in Germany. Perhaps because many of these trials were seen as embodying a type of victors' justice, these trials had little effect on the development of IHL or on ICRC practice. See further UN War Crimes Commission, *Law Reports of Trials of War Criminals: United Nations War Crimes Commission* (Buffalo, NY: William S. Hein and Co., 1997).

remains a pragmatic humanitarian actor relying mostly on morality and pragmatism, to protect those victimized by conflicts. The organization emphasizes exactly what one author had called for, an emphasis on consequences for individuals, rather than rigid emphasis on law.[4] It is ironic that the ICRC helps develop IHL primarily for others. In its own field work it often stresses pragmatic and relative accomplishments, not legal justice. As a former Acting President of the ICRC wrote: "[ICRC policy is] carried out by using the only practicable method, the pragmatic approach. The Red Cross expresses itself first of all in action. Jean Pictet has constantly stressed this [when] he wrote [that the Red Cross] 'is above all made of practical actions, which are very varied and often improvised . . . the Red Cross from the first modelled itself upon human nature and it is in the rude school of life that its dogmas were forged.'"[5]

Nevertheless, a recent study conducted by the ICRC found that legal rules, not appeals to moral standards, were more likely to bring about improved conditions for victims of war.[6] It remains to be seen if more independent studies can replicate these findings. The study emphasized the importance of the presence of a reliable system of criminal justice, in order for the rules of IHL to decisively affect behaviour in conflicts. Unfortunately in many situations the prospects for punishing those who violate IHL are highly uncertain, to put it mildly. So questions can still be raised about the influence of IHL in many conflicts.

Moreover, reference to IHL sometimes actually defeats what the organization is trying to accomplish, since state officials may deny the ICRC access to victims in order to prioritize claims to state sovereignty. Often the ICRC will avoid reference to IHL in order to gain access to victims.

Furthermore, much ICRC activity occurs in situations said to fall short of internal armed conflict or what the United Nations sometimes calls complex emergencies. These situations are not covered, or not clearly covered, by IHL. The term "complex emergencies" came into use at the UN precisely to allow international action to go forward while bypassing discussion of whether IHL applied. Some governments, faced with instability perhaps combined with natural disaster, agreed to cooperation

---

[4] David Kennedy, *The Dark Sides of Virtue: Reassessing International Humanitarianism* (Princeton: Princeton University Press, 2004).

[5] Jacques Freymond, "Humanitarian policy and pragmatism," *Government and Opposition*, 11 (Autumn 1976), 413. Footnotes omitted.

[6] Daniel Munoz-Rojas and Jean-Jacques Fresard, "The Roots of Behaviour in War: Understanding and Preventing IHL Violations," *International Review of the Red Cross*, 853 (March 2004), 189–206.

with international action as long as no reference was made to unpleasant things – such as a possible armed conflict. Admission of internal armed conflict indicated loss of control of part of the country's territory, and/or recognition of a certain success by violent opponents. States, having negotiated IHL, found wisdom in bypassing its formal application. A rigorously legal approach to international relations is not always a good thing. Flexible diplomacy can sometimes be progressive.

In short, IHL is important, but not as important as many law professors suggest. We should retain a healthy scepticism about the power of legal rules to shape behavior in the face of brutal ideologies and persistent if sometimes mindless nationalism.[7] We would do well at the outset of this chapter to remember the famous commentary by the distinguished British legal expert Hersch Lauterpacht: "If international law is, in some ways, at the vanishing point of law, the law of war is, perhaps even more conspicuously, at the vanishing point of international law."[8] While there has been some progress in holding some individuals legally responsible for war crimes since 1993, IHL – comprising the bulk of the law of war – constitutes a weak reed on which to lean in many situations.

IHL: boundaries

Some history

More distant history records instances of rules for the limitation of war in the name of humanity. These trace back thousands of years and derive from various cultures.[9] Without doubt more recent western history gave a push to the laws of war. Winston Churchill, for example, held that Joan of Arc when captured in 1430 benefited for a time from European traditions for "warring aristocrats" that made her a prisoner of war.[10] To the argument that all such limitations in the West were nothing more

[7] See especially Adam Roberts, "Land Warfare: From Hague to Nuremberg," in Michael Howard, George J. Andreopoulos, and Mark R. Shulman, eds., *The Laws of War: Constraints on Warfare in the Western World* (New Haven: Yale University Press, 1994), 116–39.

[8] "The Problem of the Revision of the Law of War," *The British Year Book of International Law*, 24 (1952), 360–82, at 381–2. See further Antonio Cassese, *International Law* (Oxford: Oxford University Press, 2001), 325.

[9] See, for example, James T. Johnson, *Ideology, Reason, and the Limitation of War: Religious and Secular Concepts, 1200–1740* (Princeton: Princeton University Press, 1975). And Geoffrey Best, *Humanity in Warfare: The Modern History of the International Law of Armed Conflicts* (London: Methuen, 1983).

[10] *Churchill's History of the English-Speaking Peoples*, arranged for one volume by Henry Steele Commanger (New York: Barnes and Noble, 1955, 1957), 98.

than a *passé* European chivalry, Michael Walzer has a thoughtful answer: "In any case, the death of chivalry is not the end of moral judgment . . . war is still, somehow, a rule-governed activity, a world of permissions and prohibitions – a moral world, therefore, in the midst of hell."[11] The oxymoron not withstanding, there is an "ethics of destruction"[12] that results in legal limits on the process of war. We can agree that in war, "normative factors are important even if not all-important."[13]

Such rules received renewed attention in the middle of the nineteenth century, as we noted in chapter 1, through such events as the 1864 Geneva Convention in Europe and the promulgation of the Lieber Code in the American civil war of 1861 to 1865. Since this era the international community has recognized the ICRC as the non-governmental guardian of the core of these legal developments designed to reduce the realm of military permissiveness and to increase humanitarian space in the midst of war.[14]

It might be argued that for a time the Swiss Confederation was the closest thing to being a guardian in the public domain, as it calls diplomatic conferences related to IHL and serves as the depository for at least the core of this body of law. According to the 1949 Geneva Conventions, states that are parties to IHL have the obligation to "respect and ensure respect" for that law. This wording is now understood to mean that virtually all modern states have become guardians of IHL, since almost all states have formally accepted the 1949 law, although this is clearly a legalistic argument. Rare is the state that out of genuine humanitarian concern is willing to inconvenience its own narrow interests in order to push for the proper implementation of IHL. There is also reason to argue that now the United Nations Security Council and various international courts have ultimate responsibility to ensure the enforcement of the law. We discuss various enforcement matters below.

Core conception of IHL

Strangely enough, beyond a general definition of IHL no one is perfectly sure what is precisely the body of law contained under this label.

---

[11] Michael Walzer, *Just and Unjust Wars: A Moral Argument with Historical Illustrations* (New York: Basic Books, 1977), 35–6. A third edition has now been published.

[12] Ward Thomas, *The Ethics of Destruction: Norms and Force in International Relations* (Ithaca: Cornell University Press, 2001).

[13] Richard Falk, "Human Rights, Humanitarian Assistance, and the Sovereignty of States," in Cahill, ed., *A Framework for Survival*, 35.

[14] See Yves Sandoz, *The International Committee of the Red Cross as Guardian of International Humanitarian Law* (Geneva: ICRC, 1998).

Certainly its core consists of the ten treaties developed under the aegis of the ICRC (and the Swiss Confederation) intended to benefit victims of war: the Geneva Conventions for the Protection of Victims of War of 1864, 1906, 1929 (two treaties), 1949 (four treaties), and 1977 (two protocols to the 1949 law). Up through 1949 the humanitarian subject matter of these legal instruments pertained primarily to victims: first sick and wounded combatants, then prisoners of war and other types of detained combatants, and eventually civilians under the effects or control of an adversary. A central idea in this modern law is to denote the neutrality of medical personnel and facilities to treat the sick and wounded, the neutrality of such persons *hors de combat* themselves, and equally so to denote the neutrality of the ICRC and other humanitarian actors for several tasks. These include visits to various types of detainees, provision of humanitarian relief, and tracing of missing persons. A second central idea pertains to the distinction between active combatants (permissible targets of military attack) and civilians and their essential goods (impermissible targets).[15] A third central idea is that even combatants are entitled to a humanitarian quarantine when they are *hors de combat.*

Clearly there is some customary IHL to go with this treaty or conventional law applicable to the same subject matter jurisdiction – victims of war. But no one is absolutely sure of the full dimensions and contents of international customary law for victims of war. This is not the place for a long discourse on international customary law and its ambiguities. At the time of writing the ICRC, at the request of state parties to the GCs, was completing a study on customary IHL. This study will surely lead to debate, especially among states, as to which relevant practices and non-treaty principles and rules have passed into binding legal status.[16]

---

[15] Among the modern threats to this fundamental distinction are "corporate warriors," presumably civilians who are in the area of combat and are essential to military efficiency. Modern military establishments, as in the United States, sub-contract or "out-source" some traditional military tasks to for-profit agencies and their unarmed, non-uniformed personnel. See P. W. Singer, *Corporate Warriors: The Rise of the Privatized Military Industry* (Ithaca: Cornell University Press, 2003). There are other problems, conceptual and practical, concerning the key distinction between combatant and civilian. Israel allows presumably civilians to be armed to protect Jewish settlements in the disputed territories in the Middle East. These persons are not part of the regular Israeli military establishment, but are armed with the knowledge of the Israeli government.

[16] See especially Louise Doswald-Beck *et al., Customary International Humanitarian Law: Rules* (Cambridge: Cambridge University Press, 2004). This is an early version of part of the ICRC study, but published under personal names so as to avoid ICRC responsibility. See also Théodore Meron, *Human Rights and Humanitarian Norms as Customary Law*

Geneva and Hague traditions

The ICRC itself has tried to broaden the scope of IHL by including under that label various treaties dealing with the means and methods of combat. Thus in addition to "Red Cross Law" or "Geneva Law" made up at least of the ten aforementioned treaties focusing on victims, the organization has in effect said that the "Hague Law" dealing with means and methods is now part of IHL. Thus the ICRC considers such documents as the 1925 treaty against poisonous and asphyxiating gases and the 1997 Ottawa treaty banning anti-personnel land mines, *inter alia*, to be part of IHL. In this accounting, then, IHL is made up of at least twenty-one treaties – and related if ambiguous international customary law.[17]

If the Geneva tradition of law, focusing on victims, which was developed through treaties between 1864 and 1977, is the core of IHL, then the Hague tradition, focusing on means and methods, which was developed through treaties between 1899 and 1997, is an important addition. Given that the Hague tradition has no modern guardian, or lost its guardian with the demise of the Russian Tzars, then it was logical for the ICRC to take over sponsorship of the Hague Law. After all, when limiting means and methods of combat, victims benefit, just as if new rules had been written into Geneva Law.[18] This is why, from 1918, the ICRC at least episodically spoke out against the use of poison gas in war. The organization played a large role in promoting the 1925 poison gas treaty.[19] The merger of the Geneva and Hague traditions can be seen in the 1977 Additional Protocols to the 1949 GCs. The Protocols contain provisions on means

---

(Oxford: Oxford University Press, 1972). The International Court of Justice declared in *Nicaragua v. the United States* (1986) that GC Common Article 3 was also a statement of customary international law, once again showing that the distinction between treaty and customary law is a complex matter.

[17] ICRC, "What Treaties Make Up International Humanitarian Law?," 1999, ICRC home-page, the internet, humanitarian law, humanitarian law in brief: www.icrc.org. Note that certain parts of the Convention on the Rights of the Child, for example Article 40 or the protocol pertaining to a minimum age for combatants in armed conflict, could be logically considered part of IHL.

[18] See further, François Bugnion, "Droit de Genève et droit de La Haye," *International Review of the Red Cross*, 844 (December 2001), 901–22. The distinction between the Geneva and Hague traditions of law was never clearly delineated. Some of the Hague Conventions dealt with prisoners of war, and were thus victim focused.

[19] While the ICRC played almost no role in the 1898 and 1907 Hague conferences (one Com-mittee member attended the first as part of the Confederation delegation), it did help to mobilize support for the 1925 treaty against gas warfare: François Bugnion, "The Interna-tional Committee of the Red Cross and the Development of International Humanitarian Law," *Chicago Journal of International Law*, 5 no. 1 (Summer 2004), 2000.

and methods of combat as well as on direct protection of victims through norms pertaining to medical aid, detention visits, and civilian nutrition, *inter alia*. The 1998 Statute of the International Criminal Court codifies individual criminal responsibility for violations of certain norms in both the Geneva and the Hague traditions of law.

Nuremberg tradition of individual responsibility

In the 1990s, building on the Nuremberg and Tokyo war crimes trials of the 1940s, the UN Security Council created two *ad hoc* international criminal tribunals to prosecute individuals for war crimes, crimes against humanity, and genocide arising out of events in the former Yugoslavia from 1991 and in Rwanda during 1994. In 1998 a Diplomatic Conference meeting in Rome adopted the Statute of the International Criminal Court (ICC), which came into legal existence on 1 July 2002. The ICC also hears the same three types of cases against individuals as the two UN *ad hoc* tribunals.[20] Some commentators, including some legal experts, refer to this evolution regarding individual responsibility for international crimes as part of IHL. This is not quite correct.

In so far as crimes against humanity and genocide can occur outside of situations of armed conflict, then norms prohibiting such behavior are not part of IHL. It should be reasonably clear by now that IHL, in either its narrow (Geneva) or broad (Geneva plus Hague) conceptions, refers to that part of the laws of war (armed conflict) with a humanitarian orientation – that is, designed to limit military necessity in war for the benefit of human dignity.

To the extent that, for example, a crime against humanity consisting of systematic torture against a major part of the civilian population could take place apart from a situation of international or internal war, then one would be faced with a crime against humanity not regulated by IHL. One can perhaps think of Chile under the dictatorship of Augusto Pinochet to see an example of an alleged crime against humanity apart from armed conflict. There appeared to be a systematic attack by the government on a substantial part of the Chilean population, through pervasive torture and forced disappearances, *inter alia*, but most states and other authoritative voices in international relations did not regard the situation as one of armed conflict.

---

[20] The ICC will hear cases dealing with individual responsibility for aggression when that concept is properly specified in international law.

Not to get lost in legal hair splitting, it remains central that IHL pertains to legal norms designed to protect humanity in armed conflict (war). On the other hand, there may be gross violations of human rights in "peace," including some forms of crimes against humanity and perhaps some situations of genocide.[21] This should become clearer below.

IHL and human rights law

Some history

According to Geoffrey Best, "what human rights, strictly understood, had to do with the law of war was a question upon which clever men might disagree."[22] IHL is distinct from, and much older than, international human rights law. Whereas modern IHL dates from the mid-1860s, most of HRL dates from the 1940s and thereafter. The international bill of human rights, which is a diplomatic and not a legal term, consists of the Universal Declaration of Human Rights (1948), and the two core International Covenants (1966) – one covering civil and political rights, and the other covering economic, social, and cultural rights. Parts of HRL, broadly defined, encompass a few legal documents dating from before 1945 – for example, certain treaties on labor rights developed by the International Labor Organization (ILO) which came into existence after World War I, and certain provisions pertaining to legal aliens and minorities. The fact remains that international legal efforts to protect the dignity of persons are manifested primarily in two different legislative histories and two different bodies of law – IHL and HRL. They are both concerned with protecting human dignity, but mostly in different contexts and by different rules.

IHL did not originally – and still does not to any great extent – use the language of human rights.[23] IHL mostly employs the language of state

---

[21] There is a tendency for genocide and crimes against humanity to occur in situations of armed conflict. This was true, for example, of the Nazi Holocaust, many of the atrocities visited upon Turkish Armenians, and the 1994 attacks by Hutu on Tutsi and moderate Hutu in Rwanda. See further Martin Shaw, *War and Genocide* (Cambridge: Polity Press, 2003).

[22] Best, *Humanity in Warfare*, 319. See further René Probst, *International Human Rights and Humanitarian Law* (Cambridge: Cambridge University Press, 2002). The latter work emphasizes the differences between the two bodies of law. The International Court of Justice has addressed the relationship in *Legality of the Threat or Use of Nuclear Weapons*, Advisory Opinion, 8 July 1996, para. 25.

[23] The treaty language presents a mixed picture. In Protocol I, Article 32, for example, it is clearly stated that families have the "right . . . to know the fate of their relatives." In

obligations and duties regarding victims and medical matters. This was partly because of the social and philosophical origins of the ICRC. This foundation was rooted in Christian charity and the Swiss bourgeois variation of *noblesse oblige* – however much such notions originating with the European upper classes may suggest (at least to some) paternalism, racism, and class thinking. Moreover, the traditional discourse of international relations and international law was based on the assumption that only states were legal subjects of the law; only states were said to have full legal personality or legal subjectivity. Individuals and groups of individuals were considered passive objects that might be affected by public actors and public law; individuals had no *rights* in the international public domain. Clearly, while international relations was characterized by various moral concerns and movements, the language of human rights was mostly absent until 1945.[24] IHL reflected these assumptions in 1864, 1906, and 1929.

It may be that with the establishment of the United Nations in 1945, and its subsequent attention to human rights especially in the remainder of the 1940s, IHL began to take on more connotations of human rights in armed conflict rather than just state duties to observe certain restraints for the benefit of passive victims.[25] If so, this was despite the explicit decision by states in 1949 at the diplomatic conference on IHL *not* to situate the 1949 GCs in the human rights discourse. If so, the linkage between IHL and HRL remained very weak until at least 1968. Until then, the dominant pattern was that the UN, especially through the Security Council, but also through other bodies such as the International Law Commission and the

the 1949 GCs, articles 5/5/5/6 and 6/6/6/7 prohibit the renunciation of personal rights conferred. See further René-Jean Willhelm, "Le caractère des droit accordés à individu dans le Conventions de Genève," *International Review of the Red Cross*, 380 (August 1950), 561–90. But, on the contrary, for example with regard to visits to detained persons under 1949 GC 3 and 4, the treaty language in III/126 does not speak of individual rights to interviews, but rather of the right of the representatives of Protecting Powers and of the ICRC to conduct visits. The emphasis remains on the rights of states, Protecting Powers (also states), and the ICRC.

[24] Jan Herman Burgers, "The Road to San Francisco: The Revival of the Human Rights Idea in the Twentieth Century," *Human Rights Quarterly*, 14 no. 4 (November 1992), 447–77. Western liberal democracies like the United States and France used the language of human rights in their domestic affairs from the late eighteenth century, at least in the form of "the rights of man." But they did not institutionalize that thinking and discourse in international relations until the 1940s.

[25] See further Théodore Meron, "The Humanization of Humanitarian Law," *American Journal of International Law*, 94 no. 2 (April 2000), 239–78. See also Schindler, "Significance of the GCs," 716; and Cassese, *International Law*, 330.

Human Rights Commission, paid scant attention to IHL. The development, dissemination, and application of the law were largely left outside the UN for the first twenty-five years of the organization's existence. This meant that the ICRC, the Red Cross Movement, and the Swiss Confederation retained their traditional centrality re IHL. And the semantics of IHL remained focused more on state duties to other states than on the personal rights of victims.[26]

Things changed somewhat in 1968 when the UN Conference on Human Rights, meeting in Teheran, Iran, and then the UN General Assembly called for further attention to "human rights in armed conflict." We pursue this historical evolution below. Here it is well to outline further the key relationships between IHL and HRL as they exist at the time of writing.

IHL and HRL in armed conflicts

The existence of two legislative histories and two bodies of law concerned with human dignity in global context has contributed to full employment for law professors and ample studies by their students. The relationship between the two bodies of law does have some practical significance for the ICRC, as well as for courts on occasion. To what international legal norms may the ICRC properly appeal when acting in international war, internal war, or other conflicts such as various forms of domestic unrest or instability or trouble? To what extent do human rights advocates need to be familiar with IHL? What international norms should inform courts in these same situations?

To begin, one can say that HRL creates norms to protect human dignity in general. These norms pertain both to situations of normality and to exceptional situations called national emergencies. However, if we take several of the major treaties on international human rights,[27] they are written so that states may derogate from their obligations to protect most

---

[26] For an example of changing usage by the ICRC, see its press release No. 03/113, 19 September 2003, "Ascertaining the Fate of the Srebrenica Missing." After giving statistical information, the ICRC says that it "is committed to ensuring that the families' *right to know* is respected," emphasis added. As noted, these semantics are in keeping with Protocol I, Article 32. Even more striking is the ICRC press release 03/31, "Southern Caucasus: Eliminating Tuberculosis in Prisons," 24 March 2003. This broad ICRC program is justified not by reference to IHL but because "investment in health promotes human rights and reduces inequality." We note in the final chapter that the ICRC now sometimes blurs the distinction between human rights and humanitarian affairs.

[27] See especially International Covenant on Civil and Political Rights, Article 4.

human rights in national emergencies threatening the life of the nation, at least to the extent required by the situation. This means that states are not free to derogate automatically from applicable HRL rules, but if the "life of the nation" requires derogation it is legally permissible, subject to a hard core of HRL rules that is non-derogable. If, as often stated, the first casualty of war is truth, the violation of many human rights cannot be far behind. HRL reflects this ugly fact by allowing states to derogate from their commitments to protect most human rights in exceptional conflict situations.

War (armed conflict) falls within the concept of national emergency. Under the HRL of national emergencies, only a few human rights remain non-derogable: the right to life, the right to freedom from torture and other degrading or humiliating treatment, freedom from slavery, the right to a nationality, freedom from forced disappearance or the positive right to be a legal person, freedom from discrimination, freedom from imprisonment for debt, freedom of thought and religion, and the right to freedom from *ex post facto* legal charges.[28]

For those national emergencies comprising armed conflict, IHL sometimes supplements and specifies these general human rights norms that are non-derogable. But we will eventually have to deal with the legal fact that IHL delineates four types of armed conflict.

The non-derogable principles from HRL remain valid in war, since war is a type of national emergency, providing a foundation for more detailed provisions in IHL. For example, HRL prohibits torture and mistreatment always, and IHL specifies the meaning of this for different types of detainees in war. Thus the Third GC of 1949, and relevant parts of Protocol I from 1977, supplement and specify the right to life and freedom from torture and mistreatment for prisoners of war and other fighters detained in international armed conflict. In other words, IHL overlaps with and builds upon HRL. There is no real conflict between the two bodies of law in this case.

---

[28] As with much of international law, which remains underdeveloped in many respects, there is debate about exactly which rights comprise the hard core of non-derogable rights. See further General Comment No. 29 by the UN Human Rights Committee, especially paragraph 7, adopted in 2001. See also paragraph 9, which stipulates that states cannot use the notion of national emergency to breach IHL in armed conflicts. See further Louise Doswald-Beck and Sylvain Vite, "International Humanitarian Law and Human Rights Law," *International Review of the Red Cross*, 293 (April 1993), 94–119. See also Office of the UN High Commissioner for Human Rights, *Training Manual on Human Rights Monitoring* (Geneva: United Nations, no date), especially chapter 3.

In national emergencies comprising armed conflict, sometimes IHL clarifies what might be vague to some observers of HRL. Take the example of the HRL norm (International Covenant on Economic, Social, and Cultural Rights, Article 11) mandating that states provide adequate nutrition for citizens. This norm might not be seen at first glance as part of the inviolable and hard core of HRL,[29] but in armed conflict IHL clearly prohibits starvation as an act of war and requires that nutritional relief be provided to the civilian population.[30] Goods essential to the civilian population must also be protected. (IHL does not stipulate exactly who is to provide such relief, only that states have a duty to see that it is provided.) Thus the vagueness or complexity of HRL about some rules in national emergencies is explicitly clarified by IHL.

National emergency short of war

To national emergencies not comprising armed conflict, but rather constituting unrest, riots, rebellions, uprisings, and other domestic troubles and tensions falling short of war, IHL does not legally apply. In so far as a given state declares such instability to be a national emergency, the bulk of HRL may not apply either, if the security situation requires reasonable derogation. This leaves only the inviolable core of HRL as legally applicable. The ICRC may indeed make reference to this part of HRL in its various overtures to controlling authorities.[31] In addition, the ICRC can appeal

---

[29] See again General Comment No. 29, cited above, by the UN Human Rights Committee. It is only in this General Comment that one finds the idea that the non-derogable norm of right to life includes prohibition of policies contributing to starvation. On the need for further codification of "famine crimes," see David Marcus, "Famine Crimes in International Law," *American Journal of International Law*, 97 no. 2 (April 2003), 245–81.

   The International Covenant on Economic, Social, and Cultural Rights is not structured the same way as its companion Convention on Civil and Political Rights. There is no Article 4 in the former pertaining to derogation. The economic, social, and cultural rights contained in the socioeconomic treaty are presented in a conditional way, being made subject to the ability of the state to implement them, and thus these treaty rights are, on their surface, not considered part of the hard core of non-derogable rights. No derogation clause is logically necessary, given the way the treaty is worded.

[30] See the exceptionally clear analysis in Jelena Pelic, "The Right to Food in Situations of Armed Conflict: The Legal Framework," *International Review of the Red Cross*, 844 (December 2001), 1097–1110.

[31] There are other human rights documents to which the ICRC makes occasional reference. For example, there are international documents pertaining to treatment of detainees. These documents do not specify whether they apply in peace or war, national emergency or otherwise. Particularly in "domestic troubles" not covered by IHL, the ICRC may find these documents useful. See further Djamchid Momtaz, "The Minimum Humanitarian Rules Applicable in Periods of Internal Tension and Strife," *International Review of the Red Cross*, 324 (September 1998), 455–62.

to the basic principles of IHL, perhaps calling them moral humanitarian principles, even though states are not legally obligated to follow them in non-war situations. The ICRC can also appeal to its own traditions – namely, its basic humanitarian concerns regardless of the legal label an authority may attach to a situation.[32]

ICRC traditional activity in conflicts of various types has been endorsed both by the resolutions of Red Cross Conferences and by the Statutes of the Movement, for which states as well as other delegations have voted. In theory, then, these decisions by the Red Cross Movement give the ICRC a normative, or permissive, base for its activities even where states argue that no armed conflict exists. Whether this reference to Movement decisions is used by the ICRC in its field work, or makes any difference to parties in conflict, is another matter.

There is thus a type of conflict – all too prevalent – that is covered neither by IHL nor by the bulk of HRL. In these situations of national troubles, unrest, or instability falling short of war, the history of ICRC operations is especially important. That history, reflecting fundamental moral concern for the fate of victims of conflict, allows a humanitarian initiative that skirts legal complexity and debate. Simply put, the ICRC can – and often does – approach an authority by saying that it does not care about legal labels or rules; it just wants to carry out its traditional activities. IHL is not always relevant – or even helpful – in efforts to protect human dignity. Reference to IHL can impede humanitarian efforts by causing governments to elevate considerations of status and power over humanitarianism. It remains true, however, that the values reflected in ICRC diplomacy are the same as the fundamental principles of IHL.

It is a fact that protagonists in conflict often see IHL (and also HRL) as an impediment to their struggles for power. In 1954, in dealing with Algeria, France initially said that Paris was not involved in an armed conflict, and thus that IHL did not apply. Later it agreed that it faced an internal armed conflict or Common Article 3 situation. While under this 1949 article common to the four GCs ICRC detention visits are not mandated, those visits occurred. Britain, in dealing with Northern Ireland throughout those persistent "troubles," said that London was not faced with an internal armed conflict, and thus neither Common Article 3 from 1949 nor Protocol II from 1977 applied. Both of these states, however, allowed the ICRC to carry out detention visits on the

---

[32] Some national emergencies could spring from natural or technological causes having nothing to do with political unrest.

basis of its traditional concerns, as long as the organization did not insist on legally characterizing the conflict in a way disliked by London or Paris.

Complexity about types of conflicts

We should not underestimate how much state self-interest, rather than humanitarian concern, has driven the form and controlling interpretation of IHL. States have historically insisted on a complicated IHL involving an unclear distinction between international and internal armed conflict, and an equally unclear distinction between internal armed conflict and domestic unrest.[33] What is even worse, in IHL we now have, since 1977, at least two types of international war and two types of internal war. As for international war, we have a traditional international armed conflict (not defined in the treaty law despite an amorphous GC Article 2, but only by amorphous state practice) and a war of national liberation. As for internal war, we have a Common Article 3 situation, and a Protocol II situation.[34]

---

[33] To make matters worse, the Tadic case of the ICTY speaks of a protracted armed conflict, as does the 1998 Statute of the ICC in Article 8(2)(f).

It is not correct to say that IHL was clear and logical until 1977, and only after that date did IHL become horribly complex. Even in the Spanish civil war, the participation of outside states like Germany, Italy, and the Soviet Union raised question as to whether this was an international or an internal war. All armed conflict over decolonization raised the same question. In Vietnam after 1954, the same question arose, for which there was no clear answer. Richard J. Goldstone, the first prosecutor for the International Criminal Tribunal for former Yugoslavia, regarded the structure of modern IHL, with its various distinctions, as unworkable. He was pleased when that Tribunal blurred the difference between international and internal armed conflict, but unhappy when the Rome statute of the International Criminal Court reinforced those distinctions. Richard Goldstone, *For Humanity: Reflections of a War Crimes Investigator* (New Haven: Yale University Press, 2000), especially at 124. For a further argument that distinguishing between international and internal war is increasingly a bad idea, see James G. Stewart, "Towards a Single Definition of Armed Conflict in International Humanitarian Law: A Critique of Internationalized Armed Conflict," *International Review of the Red Cross*, 850 (June 2003), 313–50.

[34] A Common Article 3 conflict is not precisely the same as a Protocol II conflict. In other words, some states might be obligated to apply both Common Article 3 and Protocol II when dealing with an internal war, whereas another state might only have to apply Common Article 3 – which is shorter and more vague than Protocol II. The difference has to do with the material field of application of Protocol II, which sets various conditions that presumably trigger the application of that instrument, and which are different and more demanding than found in Common Article 3. All of this results from the priority that states in a diplomatic conference give to strategic considerations rather than to an overriding concern for a simplified and more effective IHL benefiting victims. Note that

All of this indicates that, in IHL, states have often elevated their various non-humanitarian interests over concern for victims of conflicts. They have emphasized national freedom of decision making, avoidance of bothersome rules that might apply to them, and advocacy of rules that would limit adversaries.[35]

If we look at the 1949 GCs, we find that most of the norms are for traditional international war, with only Common Article 3 applicable in internal wars. By 1977, Protocol I supplements and develops IHL for international war, adding wars of national liberation to that category. And although Protocol II supplements and develops Common Article 3, it has a different, more restricted, material field of application than Common Article 3.

Much of this complexity does not have to exist. In the best of all worlds, any time a state had to use its military forces to deal with a conflict, the full corpus of a revised and simplified IHL would be applicable. Such an approach would eliminate debate about the difference between international and internal war, or between internal war and other forms of domestic violence. But states try not to permit such simplicity. It would aid victims but might interfere with desired security policies. In particular, those states fearing internal war do not want an extensive IHL to apply to that type of situation. Most states want a vague demarcation between domestic troubles and internal war; they want to be able to claim that the former exists rather than the latter, so as to minimize their obligations under IHL.

Consistent with the above, states have historically opposed a centralized and authoritative determination of when and where the various types of armed conflict exist.[36] They have historically preferred a decentralized process of determination, based on extensive state sovereignty, which

the Rome Statute of the International Criminal Court, in Article 8(2)[f] mentions an undifferentiated "internal armed conflict." It seems to me this wording implicitly refers to the two types of internal war found in IHL.

[35] Like Kennedy in *The Dark Sides of Virtue*, we should beware of glorifying IHL when it codifies nationalistic values that impede protection of the human dignity of individuals. For example, 1949 GC III, article 126 provides that ICRC visits to detainees can be blocked "for reasons of imperative military necessity," but "only as an exceptional and temporary measure." Under this wording, some states have sought to deny ICRC access to detainees for considerable periods of time, in order, *inter alia*, to allow for coercive interrogation.

[36] David P. Forsythe, "Who Guards the Guardians: Third Parties and the Law of Armed Conflict," *American Journal of International Law*, 70 no. 1 (January 1976), 41–61.

maximizes the opportunity for self-serving interpretations.[37] As noted in chapter 3, the ICRC reserves the right to give its view on when a particular type of armed conflict may exist. But often it does not articulate that view, fearing that disagreement with a party to the conflict may jeopardize its field operations. The ICRC has given priority to helping persons at the expense of legal opinion.

Summing up

Especially since 1977, a very complicated IHL, organized according to two types of international war and two types of internal war, supplements a few basic principles from HRL in providing a core legal framework for the protection of human dignity in armed conflict.[38] Walzer is correct: war remains a rule-governed activity. As *Le Monde* put it in 2004, "Whoever says war says law of war."[39] All modern military establishments accept this notion in principle. It is only uninformed civilians who still try to argue that in war law is silent. On the other hand, while law in war may not be silent at least legally speaking, it may only be a whisper in actual combat. We have clear if complicated legal theory regulating war, and then we have the reality of much unchecked violence. We have the extensive and complicated law on the books, and we have the weak law in action.

The fundamental point of the moment remains that IHL and HRL are distinct but related. In some ways they are complementary and not particularly troublesome. Sometimes IHL specifies for armed conflict the

---

[37] What states have created through diplomatic conferences, the UN *ad hoc* tribunal for the former Yugoslavia (ICTY) has partially altered. In several cases the ICTY has applied norms for international armed conflict, bypassing claims that the situation – for example in Bosnia during 1992–95 – was an internal rather than an international armed conflict. The court referred to an agreement among the parties, mediated by the ICRC, from 25 May 1992, in which they agreed to try to apply large parts of the IHL to the fighting then occurring. Notably, the ICTY decreed that grave breaches of the 1949 GCs, involving individual responsibility and thus prosecution, can occur in internal as well as international war. This is not what the 1949 and 1977 laws indicate. This particular development about individual responsibility in internal war has been codified in the 1998 Rome Statute of the ICC. Certain UN resolutions have also referred to IHL without distinction between international and internal war. See further Schindler, "The Significance of the GCs."

[38] See further Cornelio Sommaruga, "Humanitarian Law and Human Rights in the Legal Arsenal of the ICRC," ICRC homepage, www.icrc.org, 16 March 1995; and ICRC, "Human Rights and the ICRC: International Humanitarian Law," ICRC homepage, www.icrc.org, 1 December 1993. For a clear overview see Frits Kalshoven, *Constraints on the Waging of War* (Geneva: ICRC, simultaneously with Martinus Nijhoff, 1987).

[39] "Au cœur de l'argumentaire américain," special section on the law of war, 30 June 2004, IV.

meaning of the inviolable principles of HRL – for example, pertaining to treatment of detainees. Sometimes IHL provides in armed conflict for what might otherwise not be clearly required by HRL – for example, pertaining to nutrition for civilians. And not sometimes but always, domestic unrest manifests minimal international legal regulation. It is a situation to which only the few hard-core principles of HRL legally apply. But ICRC traditions of action help provide a humanitarian supplement to the thin legal framework of this latter situation.

It cannot be stressed too much that for the ICRC humanitarian wisdom frequently lies in not emphasizing the IHL that it has helped develop. This policy choice stems from dominant state influence on IHL, in both its development and its application, regardless of ICRC desires. States often make and interpret IHL with a view to their power and prestige, not the well-being of victims. IHL is not the panacea that some law professors suggest. For many victims, especially in situations not fully agreed upon as constituting armed conflict, ICRC alegal diplomacy can be more important than the law on the books, at least while the fight rages. No doubt all levels of the ICRC prefer to have a universally approved legal rule to anchor their work, when such a rule actually facilitates their humanitarian efforts.

The ICRC and development of IHL

A book was published in the year 2000 making much of the fact that Amnesty International not only tried to help individual "prisoners of conscience" in various ways but also tried to help develop HRL so that AI's concern for detainees would be systematic and broad reaching.[40] The founders of the ICRC came to a similar conclusion between 1863 and 1864 concerning humanitarian affairs. It sought to build on what Henry Dunant had done at Solferino by lobbying for – and providing an initial draft of – what became the 1864 GC for sick and wounded combatants.[41] The ICRC has been trying to promote the development of IHL from its very beginnings. The reasons are obvious. If one can get approved a legal framework for humanitarian protection, then such protection will presumably be more systematic and broad reaching than otherwise. The

---

[40] Anne Marie Clark, *Diplomacy of Conscience: Amnesty International and Changing Human Rights Norms* (Princeton: Princeton University Press, 2001).
[41] Bugnion, "The International Committee of the Red Cross and the Development of International Humanitarian Law."

central logic is to transfer the basic humanitarian obligation from private parties to public authorities. The logic is impeccable, if one assumes that IHL indeed reflects humanitarian values more than *raisons d'état*, and if the law manifests effective means of enforcement.

Historically the ICRC was at the center of IHL development. A legislative system was established over time. Based on its experiences and observations, the organization drafted legal texts that were submitted first to Red Cross bodies for comment, then to governmental experts. Finally in modern times it participated as an observer in diplomatic conferences called by the Swiss Confederation that made final decisions about the revised draft texts.

The ICRC maintains a stable of international lawyers whose job it is, in part, constantly to produce reports and other documents, including draft treaties about every quarter-century, with a view to the further progressive development of IHL. IHL is always one war late, in that states can only bring themselves to develop the law when they reflect on the horrors of the last war. As George Aldrich, head of the US delegation to the 1974–77 Diplomatic Conference on IHL, wrote, "After each major war, the survivors negotiate rules for the next war that they would, in retrospect, like to have seen in force during the last war."[42]

There frequently remains at the Geneva headquarters some tension between the legal side of the house and the operations side. This split also occurs at the UNHCR. The "operations culture" is, relatively speaking, more interested in pragmatic action to aid victims than in whether such action can be rationalized in terms of legal rules. In 1999 the ICRC Director of Operations, Jean-Daniel Tauxe, wrote that he doubted whether a legal approach could benefit the organization very much in prevalent internal wars, since various fighting parties in such situations were undisciplined, and either were motivated by economic interests or intentionally targeted civilians. In these situations, he stressed a pragmatic and ethical approach, not a legal approach.[43] At the time of writing, the ICRC Director-General Angelo Gnädiger, head of the Directorate, was a lawyer with considerable field experience, thus bridging somewhat the legal–operations divide.

[42] "Some Reflections on the Origins of the 1977 Geneva Protocols," in Christophe Swinarski, ed., *Studies and Essays on International Humanitarian Law and Red Cross Principles* (Dordrect: Martinus Nijhoff, 1984), 129.

[43] Jean-Daniel Tauxe, "Faire mieux accepter le Comité International de la Croix-Rouge sur le terrain," *International Review of the Red Cross*, 833 (March 1999), 55–61.

States and the ICRC in diplomatic conferences

In the Geneva diplomatic conferences for IHL, the ICRC has not played the role of an outspoken lobbyist or a hard-driving pressure group. By the time of the diplomatic conference, the organization traditionally has held the view that its work in trying to advance humanitarian norms for war has been mostly finished. The ICRC has been more the expert drafting secretariat than the vociferous advocate prepared to duel publicly with states to the final day of a diplomatic conference. By the time of the diplomatic conference the ICRC has had a pretty good idea of what is and is not acceptable to states. Moreover, as ever, the ICRC has not relished public disagreements with states.[44]

For example, in the 1930s the ICRC, having seen the effects of warfare on civilians particularly in Ethiopia and Spain, tried to advance a new convention for the protection of civilians. Governmental opposition to this project, particularly as indicated in Red Cross meetings, caused the organization to shelve the project until 1949 – to the great misfortune of civilians during the Second World War. The ICRC was clearly ahead of the curve regarding the need for civilian protection, but states controlled the codification of IHL. Again in 1957 the ICRC tried to advance some new legal rules for the benefit of the civilian population in war, but after the meeting of the International Red Cross Conference in New Delhi it was clear that governments were not prepared to endorse additional restrictions on their security policies. So ICRC efforts further to develop IHL had to await the diplomatic conference of 1974–77.

Neither the ICRC nor the Swiss Confederation really wanted that conference. Developing states of the Global South, many of which had not been legally independent in 1949, had long resented being bound by an IHL they had not influenced. Furthermore, they saw an opportunity in the mid-1970s, after an accelerating decolonization in the 1960s had increased their numbers, to advance their strategic concerns of the moment. These had to do mostly with their perceptions of continuing imperialism, neo-colonialism, and racism. Along with the Soviet Union and the communist camp, these latter being interested in creating difficulties for their western protagonists, they pushed for further attention to what they called "human rights in armed conflict." Although unsure that the 1970s was

---

[44] See Georges Willemin and Roger Heacock, *The International Committee of the Red Cross* (Boston: Martinus Nijhoff, 1984), 112. "The Committee is convinced by experience that there is no point in publicly challenging States."

the right moment to revisit the 1949 GCs, the ICRC could hardly stand aside and refuse to play its historical role for the development of IHL.

According to the head of the US delegation to that conference, the United States agreed to participate because of a "pervading sense of defensiveness, if not guilt, about the suffering caused by the [Vietnam] war and by aerial warfare in particular."[45] For some, US bombing policies in Southeast Asia, particularly during the 1960s, contributed to the progressive development of IHL through Protocol I adopted in 1977.

At that diplomatic conference, for present purposes one can say that there were two categories of issues. There were the issues of broad "political significance" in which states took great interest. In this category fell debates about wars of national liberation, whether or not there would be a second protocol for internal war, the status of mercenaries, and so on. In a second category fell the more precise and technical issues, mostly dealing with the details and refinements of the law. The ICRC was not very influential regarding the first, but was more influential in a quiet way – particularly through its drafting role – regarding the second.[46] In general, the ICRC exerted less influence in the mid-1970s than in 1949, owing to the fact that IHL was no longer so heavily influenced by a western club.

For example, Pakistan's acceptance of Protocol II covering some forms of internal armed conflict, and its outspoken endorsement of that document at the final stage, was far more important than the ICRC's desire for further regulation of internal war. It was Pakistan's leadership on this issue that brought along a number of states from the lesser developed ranks, and thus made possible the adoption of that Protocol.[47] But the ICRC had made its quiet contributions at earlier stages of drafting. In fact, much of Protocol II, as it progressed through the Diplomatic Conference, was revised by Canadian and ICRC officials, working together extremely closely.

---

[45] Aldrich, "Some Reflections," 132.

[46] Even if states had their priorities set on the big, strategic issues, there were many more minor issues, frequently of humanitarian import, on which the ICRC was strangely quiet in the diplomatic conference. The organization certainly did not risk offending governments by being brazenly brash in stating its preferences. The 1975 Tansley Report characterized the ICRC approach as one of "conservative legalism" (22). Some ICRC "lobbying" did occur, at least in the form of speeches on the conference floor: see Aldrich, "Some Reflections," 135. The key point is that the ICRC preferred quiet drafting to more traditional and vocal lobbying. Its role was indeed one of conservative legalism.

[47] See further David P. Forsythe, "Legal Management of Internal War: The 1977 Protocol on Non-International Armed Conflict," American Journal of International Law, 72 no. 2 (April 1978), 272–95.

To take another example, the Third World's determination, supported by the Soviet bloc, to word Protocol I so as to encumber primarily Israel and South Africa, and to give additional status to "national liberation movements" made up of black South Africans and Palestinians, was far more important to parts of that Protocol, particularly Article 1, than anything the ICRC said or did. Many states saw Protocol I as a weapon in the strategic struggle against racism and imperialism, rather than as a strictly humanitarian document for the benefit of war victims. To them, Protocol I was a means to require Israel and South Africa to apply all of IHL for international armed conflicts, and to recognize opposing combatants as prisoners of war when captured. For these states, the legislative game was primarily about power and status, not humanitarianism – certainly not humanitarianism traditionally defined.[48] On the other side of the debate, Israel and the United States saw Protocol I as a charter for terrorism, and thus refused to ratify it. The ICRC could do nothing about all this.

Yet on many other articles in Protocol II, such as in Part IV pertaining to non-combatants, the fingerprints of the ICRC were all over various articles negotiated before and during the conference.

Declining ICRC influence?

We noted above in passing that IHL broadly defined seems to be made as much in contemporary times by court cases and UN resolutions as by formal diplomatic conferences. This may be a very good thing, in that progressive development of IHL can occur without states having to give their explicit consent to treaty wording. We noted that the ICTY decreed that individual responsibility for war crimes existed in internal war, not just international war. Had this proposition been put to states in a diplomatic conference in the 1970s, there is no guarantee they would have approved such wording (although after ICTY rulings, states wrote the principle into the ICC Statute as noted above).

---

[48] The result of the policies of the Third World and the Soviet bloc was that the definition of international armed conflict was expanded, through Article 1 of Protocol I, to include wars of national liberation. One could argue that this was good from a humanitarian point of view. More conflicts were fully legally regulated than otherwise. Unfortunately this expansion was achieved at the price of non-ratification by the United States and Israel, inter alia, who charged that IHL had become "politicized." So particularly Protocol I joined the list of treaties that went unratified in Washington, even as the latter argued that the parts of Protocol I approved by the United States had entered into customary law.

Certainly when we consider customary IHL rather than just treaties, the making of the law depends on a broad array of factors making up state practice, not just ICRC drafting of treaty texts. This has always been the case.

There is another process at work as well that challenges the centrality of the ICRC in legislating IHL. Since about 1968 the ICRC has seen other actors display much interest in the development of IHL through treaty law. UN bodies, a wide range of states, private human rights groups, and associations of lawyers have all paid more attention to humanitarian treaties. The ICRC was much more important in the development of the 1929 GC on prisoners of war than it was in the development of the 1977 Protocols. Indeed, the way the game is played now, coalitions, networks, or movements – made up of states and other actors – push for various developments in international law.[49] No private agency determines IHL legal developments by itself anymore – not even in the early stages.

Example: the landmine treaty

If we accept that IHL covers the Hague tradition pertaining to regulation of means and methods of combat, the ICRC has no special historical claim to overseeing the drafting of this part of the law. The 1997 Ottawa treaty on landmines, for example, saw leadership by the Canadian government and a broad coalition of "like minded states" and private groups, including the ICRC, not just the ICRC acting alone. The organization did, however, play a very important role in the development of the Ottawa treaty. In this regard, reports of its demise in legislating IHL may be quite premature.

The organization had certainly been concerned and active regarding anti-personnel landmines.[50] It was one of the first voices to call attention

---

[49] In general, and with particular reference to implementing rights of personal integrity, see Thomas Risse, Stephen C. Ropp, and Kathryn Sikkink, *The Power of Human Rights: International Norms and Domestic Change* (Cambridge: Cambridge University Press, 1999). This book is not about developing IHL, but what it says about coalitions in support of human rights fits with trends in the development of IHL. In the same vein see Margret Keck and Kathryn Sikkink, *Activists beyond Borders: Transnational Advocacy Networks in International Politics* (Ithaca: Cornell University Press, 1988).

[50] On the important role of the ICRC in the effort to ban landmines, see: Louis Maresca and Stuart Maslen, eds., *The Banning of Anti-personnel Landmines: The Legal Contribution of the International Committee of the Red Cross* (Cambridge: Cambridge University Press, 2000); Cameron A. Maxwell, Robert J. Lawson, and Brian W. Tomlin, eds., *To Walk without Fear: The Global Movement to Ban Landmines* (Oxford: Oxford University Press, 1998);

to the human costs from landmines, especially since many civilians suffered from these indiscriminate weapons long after they were deployed
by fighting parties. The ICRC had much experience with the number
of persons in places like Cambodia, Angola, and Afghanistan, *inter alia*,
needing prostheses because of the pernicious effects of landmines. All too
often the victims were farmers trying to grow crops, women gathering
firewood and water, or children at play. The ICRC, with its usual keen eye
for details, compiled numbers and publicized statistics. It initially pushed
the Canadian government to take up the issue.

In the broad campaign to develop the Ottawa treaty, the ICRC was
active and effective in conveying to others its own experience in coping
with the victims of landmines. The organization undertook an unprecedented publicity campaign in behalf of the projected treaty. Along the
way it manifested excellent contacts in various military circles, and uti-
lized retired military personnel in its communications and presentations.
While it contributed a certain status and expertise to the landmine campaign, it left to other partners in that coalition the explicit and public criticism of particular governments and other fighting parties. It coordinated
effectively with numerous National Red Cross Societies, who themselves
were sometimes effective in lobbying their governments, and it consulted
often with other states and NGOs that supported the emerging treaty. The
United States, opposed to the treaty as drafted, lobbied the ICRC directly
to back off from its commitment to a total ban on anti-personnel mines,
but the organization, with President Sommaruga playing a key role, stood
firm.[51]

The general result was that the ICRC was a very important member of
the coalition against landmines, finding a role for itself that did not compromise its traditional views on neutrality and cooperation with public
authorities, but certainly showing that it should not be excluded from
broad legislative efforts. The Ottawa treaty was the result of a broad public and private concern that transcended the ICRC and the Red Cross
Movement, but Red Cross actors – especially the ICRC – were centrally
involved.

Ramesh Thakur and William Maley, "The Ottawa Convention on Landmines: A Landmark
Humanitarian Treaty in Arms Control?," *Global Governance*, 5 no. 3 (July–September
1999), 273–302; Don Hubert, *The Landmine Ban: A Case Study in Humanitarian Advocacy*,
Watson Institute, Occasional Paper #42 (Providence, RI: Brown University, 2000).

[51] See the previous chapter regarding Sommaruga and ICRC endorsement of a total ban on
anti-personnel landmines.

Example: Israel and "the emblem"

It was clear in other ways too that the ICRC still had a special role in legal development. At the start of the twenty-first century, the ICRC, with President Kellenberger pushing for rapid action, drafted a third protocol to be added to the 1949 GCs dealing with the issue of "the emblem."[52] It was a protocol designed, in part, to satisfy Israel, Eritrea, Kazakhstan, and in fact the Red Cross Federation. It would have reduced conflict broadly speaking, and it would have permitted more unity and integration within the often dysfunctional family known as the Red Cross Movement.

The parties mentioned above either used the double emblem of both the Red Cross and the Red Crescent, which had no neutral or protective status in public international law, or refused to use either the Red Cross or the Red Crescent alone. Thus, either the three states mentioned refused to accede to the 1949 GCs and 1977 Additional Protocols altogether (e.g., Eritrea), or they failed to have their designated humanitarian society recognized by the ICRC as part of the Movement and to be admitted to membership in the Federation (e.g., Kazahkstan and Israel). Eritrea and Kazahkstan eventually changed policy, leaving Israel as the state that was "odd man out."

To join the Red Cross network of actors, the official national humanitarian society has to use a symbol approved by IHL as made by states.[53] This is a very good example of the negative effect of tying the Red Cross Movement so tightly to states, although it must also be admitted that state acceptance of neutral emblems is crucial for their effectiveness in conflicts. So the ICRC, in particular to resolve the issue of whether there was discrimination against Israel and MDA,[54] drafted new law that would allow states to approve some symbol in addition to the Red Cross and the Red Crescent. Obviously MDA in Israel was not going to use either the Red Cross or the Red Crescent, but rather chose the Red Shield of David or the six-pointed star.

The ICRC, keenly interested in resolving this controversy that had led to accusations of bias against it, consulted with various key governments

---

[52] François Bugnion, "Vers une solution globale de la question d'emblème," *International Review of the Red Cross*, 838 (June 2000), 427–65. Bugnion was at the center of legal and diplomatic developments on this question. He published an updated version in 2003.

[53] For a statement of the ten conditions required since 1948 for the ICRC to recognize a National Society, see *Handbook of the Red Cross* (Geneva: ICRC, 1994).

[54] Recall that Iran's symbol of the Red Lion and Sun had been accepted by states and the Red Cross Movement. This acceptance has not been formally rescinded at the time of writing. On its own, Iran changed over to the Red Crescent after 1979.

and various Red Cross partners, as well as with the Swiss Confederation, with a view to calling a diplomatic conference that would approve its draft protocol.[55] The draft protocol accepts the emblems now in use (the Red Cross, the Red Crescent, the double emblem of Red Cross and Red Crescent together, and the Red Shield of David). The protocol also establishes a new emblem consisting of an open red square turned on one of its points to make a diamond. States and officially recognized humanitarian agencies could use any of these emblems, or combine emblems – for example placing the Red Cross within the Red Diamond. The supporting logic is that the Red Cross and the Red Crescent have too much protective value to be abandoned entirely; other existing emblems such as the Red Shield of David should also be accepted, but a new symbol devoid of political or religious connotation should also be added to give states and their National Societies the choice of avoiding one of the existing emblems if they so desire.

But the second intifada, or Palestinian uprising against Israeli control of Palestinian territory, interrupted developments. Especially given the renewed controversy in the Middle East, most Arab and other

---

[55] At the turn of this century the American Red Cross (ARC), under the dubious leadership of Dr. Bernadine Healey, withheld membership payments to the Red Cross Federation (amounting to about 25% of the Federation's budget) over the MDA/emblem controversy. The fact that the Federation could not admit to its membership an aid society not already recognized by the ICRC seems not to have fazed Dr. Healey and her associates in the ARC at all in their policies toward the hapless and helpless Federation. And the fact that the ICRC could not recognize an aid society that did not use a neutral emblem as codified in IHL, as fashioned by states, seems not to have entered the collective mind of the ARC either. Dr. Healy was eventually forced out because of this and other controversies pertaining to fund raising and the purity of the blood supply. See Katharine Q. Seelye, "Red Cross President Quits," *New York Times*, 27 October 2001, B9. For highly subjective analysis see further Deborah Sontag, "Who Brought Bernadine Healy Down?," *New York Times Magazine*, 23 December 2001.

In the early twenty-first century, the US Congress in several years passed a law (the Fitzgerald–Clinton–Dole amendment to the omnibus spending bill) authorizing the withholding of 25% of the US contribution to the regular/headquarters budget of the ICRC, unless the Secretary of State determined that Magen David Adom was allowed to participate in activities of the Red Cross Movement. At the time of writing the Secretary of State had always made that determination, because MDA personnel did indeed participate in various Movement relief activities, did meet with ICRC and Federation officials, etc. The ICRC developed a very active program of field cooperation with MDA, and with the Palestinian Red Crescent, for that matter. In fact, this US law was designed to satisfy certain domestic constituencies, mainly Jewish, and to preempt a more draconian law that might in reality impede the work of the ICRC. That is to say, the law was cosmetic from the start, drafted to make a general statement for domestic consumption without in fact hurting the ICRC. Interviews, Washington.

Islamic governments were not prepared to allow Israel to have MDA so recognized. These states saw IHL through the lens of strategic calculation about power politics rather than humanitarianism. A new definition of neutral emblems in war was seen by certain states as a concession to Israel, enhancing its legitimacy, not something that would enhance neutral humanitarianism in conflicts.[56] Still, up to a point, the ICRC had been central to efforts at legislative change.

To conference or not

As per above, the ICRC in consultation with the Swiss government has to make a decision from time to time about the wisdom of NOT calling a diplomatic conference. Given that IHL reflects a dialectic between *raisons d'état* and humanitarianism, one has to be shrewd about the timing of such conferences. It could be that states, driven by strategic and military calculations, would actually approve so-called IHL that would *reduce* the level of humanitarian protection supposedly guaranteed by treaties. Or, as feared in the imbroglio over neutral emblems, states might kill a progressive draft, and thus set back useful codification efforts for some years.

In the mid-1970s the ICRC was not at all sure that the 1974–77 diplomatic conference would result in the *progressive* development of IHL. But, given the push for such a conference through the UN, not always for

---

[56] Back in 1975 the Tansley Report (125–7) had recommended new steps regarding neutral emblems in IHL. What the ICRC drafted in the late 1990s was very similar to what Tansley had recommended long before – namely, continue to recognize the Red Cross in honor of the origins of the Movement but allow each state and National Society to use also the emblem of its choice – whether it be the Red Crescent, the Red Shield of David, or whatever. Privately Tansley said it could be a Red Snowflake for all he cared; the point was to resolve the controversy that showed how fragmented the Red Cross family was. A problem with this proposal was that a National Society might adopt an emblem offensive to some others. In some Asian societies, for example, the swastika does not have the same connotation as it does in modern, mainstream western thought.

It would be interesting for historians to try to sort out whether the drift in the intervening twenty-five years was primarily due to ICRC lack of dynamism on the issue, or whether the ICRC accurately saw that a large number of states were just not open to a new initiative on this subject. Some ICRC officials believed that Israel was rather content with the status quo before Dr. Healey and the ARC rocked the boat so vigorously. In their eyes, the Israeli view was that it would be bad to have a new proposal shot down by states, thus demonstrating the continuing ostracism of Israel and maybe leading to military attacks on MDA property and personnel. In the field, MDA symbols were rarely if ever attacked. This logic explains why Israel did not press for change in the status quo at the 1974–77 diplomatic conference, a status quo that had obtained since 1949 when Israel narrowly lost several votes about recognizing the Red Shield of David in IHL

humanitarian reasons, the organization had to do the best that it could to see that new codification efforts did not lead to back sliding in humanitarian protection. The ICRC did eventually regard the 1977 Protocols as, on balance, a progressive development,[57] but to many at the ICRC it had been a close call.

After the terrorist attacks in the United States on 11 September 2001, and given subsequent controversies about the 1949 GCs and 1977 Protocols especially as applied to combatants *hors de combat* seized in Afghanistan and Pakistan, some voices were raised for a new diplomatic conference to revise existing IHL. But given the climate of opinion then in international relations, featuring principally state concern for national security and a concomitant desire to reduce rights pertaining to detainees, any diplomatic conference at that time would have probably reduced legal protections for various categories of detainees in armed conflict. That being so, the ICRC was not in favor of a new diplomatic conference, but rather argued that the existing legal framework was adequate for dealing with various issues arising out of primarily Afghanistan.[58] The 1906, 1929, and 1949 Geneva Conventions had been negotiated *after* major wars. ICRC leaders doubted that IHL could be wisely updated *while* wars supposedly related to terrorism were underway.

Certain experts in international relations and international law, like Adam Roberts of Oxford University, agreed that much of IHL was still relevant to situations like Afghanistan in 2002–3. But for those like Professor Roberts who thought some slight tinkering with IHL was in order, one wondered how to ensure, once a diplomatic conference was called, that states did not open Pandora's box by making radical changes to the detriment of victims of war.

Summing up legal development

In IHL as in other parts of international law, states frequently respond to the weakness of law by writing new law that falls short of definitive correction. We see this all the time in HRL. States recognize that the

---

[57] Jacob Kellenberger, "Protocols – More Effective 25 Years Later," *International Herald Tribune*, reproduced on www.icrc.org. And "Special Issue: 20th Anniversary of the 1977 Additional Protocols," *The International Review of the Red Cross*, 320 (October 1997).

[58] Jacob Kellenberger, Statement to the UN Human Rights Commission," 28 March 2002, reproduced at www.icrc.org. The ICRC did participate in meetings, including one at Harvard University in early 2003, that explored possible further development of IHL. But the ICRC was clearly unenthusiastic about most of these meetings, by striking comparison to the Swiss Confederation.

existing core of HRL, or the International Bill of Rights, is ineffective much of the time in the short run, so they write a new treaty on torture or on the rights of the child, inter alia. But the new law, like the old, does not contain rigorous enforcement provisions. Some parties, both states and NGOs, try to improve the law through additional semantics and further diplomatic attention, but the changes fall short of decisive enforcement. The existing climate of opinion in international relations allows some progressive codification, but progress falls short of what is required for fully effective law.

So it has been with IHL historically. To take a concrete example, after the Second World War states moved to approve the Fourth GC dealing with protection of civilians in international armed conflict. But neither the 1949 law nor the relevant parts of Protocol I in 1977 provided for centralized and authoritative enforcement of the new provisions for civilian protection. Again Walzer is right, as indicated in the quotation that begins this chapter. We start out being cynical about law in war, but then the atrocities and destruction are so appalling that we resolve to improve what he calls the war convention, meaning IHL. But states, controlling the legislative process as they do, have historically not been able to bring themselves to make the law really effective, because that would significantly reduce state sovereignty and freedom of national policy making. In many ways, states are today using their sovereignty to reduce their sovereignty. They are using their treaty-making authority to reduce their independent freedom of action, in the quest for improved collective action. But states have not been able to bring themselves to do this decisively in the field of IHL, such are the fears about insecurity and hostile opponents.

Still, the awfulness of war has perpetually, if belatedly, driven the legal development of IHL. As Professor Schindler wrote in 1999, "the remarkable developments of the past ten years [in favor of IHL via creation of courts and their judgments pertaining to war crimes] would not have been possible without the gross violations which occurred in the same period."[59] The ICRC remains one important part of this broad and complex legislative process.

Dissemination of IHL

Dissemination is an antiseptic word for spreading the message about humanitarian principles and law. In a sense, everything the ICRC does is

[59] Schindler, "Significance of the GCs," 719.

a type of dissemination,[60] because all efforts at humanitarian protection are intended to spread the message as widely as possible. For most people it is not a very glamorous process, but it is fundamentally important. If one waits until the passions of conflict are unleashed in order to preach the fundamental point about humanitarian limits on the exercise of power, it is too late to have much of an impact. In the absence of prior teaching and training in IHL and its underlying moral principles, one winds up with situations as seen in the My Lai massacre in Vietnam in 1968. Lieutenant Calley was responsible for leading the killing of numerous Vietnamese civilians because, so he claimed, he was taught that all communists were the sub-human enemy whether armed or not, whether actively resisting or not. His was the excuse of having been taught total war during the Cold War. He and the men under his command were poorly trained in general, and especially poorly trained in the laws of war.[61]

Certainly a major objective of ICRC dissemination efforts is to teach the warrior's code of honor – that an honorable soldier does not attack or otherwise mistreat civilians, does not abuse an enemy combatant who is *hors de combat*, does not attack medical personnel and installations.[62] For a long time the organization has manifested a broad dissemination effort tailored to the different needs of developed and less developed states around the world. Since 1995 it has had a specialized advisory service to help National Societies and states bring their national law into compliance with IHL.

In the best of all possible worlds, states would not lie about steps they were taking to instil the values of IHL in their armed forces. But in the world as it is, many states – like most of the European communist states during the Cold War – ratify the treaties of IHL but then ignore those legal instruments. The ICRC has published something that confirms the experience of Donald Tansley. According to the ICRC:

> In one of the States that became independent after the collapse of the Soviet Union, two young colonels encountered in an empty office of the future Ministry of Defence told an ICRC representative one day that in their

---

[60] See further Ignatieff, *The Warrior's Honor*, 147.

[61] But even Calley's excuse fails to provide a rationale for the rape of women and the abuse of infants. Most of what he and his men did represented wanton cruelty born out of the frustration of trying to fight an elusive and unprincipled enemy. Proper training is supposed to reign in such passions by keeping the exercise of military power focused on proper military objectives. It is in this sense that IHL can be seen as compatible with military efficiency.

[62] Ignatieff, *The Warrior's Honor*.

military careers they had never even heard of the Geneva Conventions. Yet according to official reports that regularly reached the ICRC before 1991, international humanitarian law formed part of the program of military instruction.[63]

As one ICRC delegate said when dealing with the situation in the Balkans in the early 1990s, given that IHL had not been treated seriously by the communist regimes of that region, he was now faced with "Potemkin-style humanitarian law."[64] It is not always different in other parts of the world featuring other types of ruling elites.

The ICRC, along with a few other agencies, tries to do what it can to fill the dangerous void left by the current state of affairs. In the world of liberal democracies there are indeed some reliable partners. The organization works with the Institute for Humanitarian Law in San Remo, Italy; the Asser Institute for Public Law in Leiden, the Netherlands (publisher of the *Yearbook of International Humanitarian Law*); the European Institute for Human Rights in Strasburg, France; the Center of Human Rights and Humanitarian Law at American University in Washington, DC; the Irish Centre for Human Rights in Galway, and so on. Beyond this world, the well-established and even moderately financed partners are not so numerous.

IHL has become horribly complex because of state strategic calculations. Indeed, some of the law's distinctions are unworkable much of the time. How many times since 1977 has it been possible by consensus to identify a Protocol I type of conflict? How many times since 1949 has there been international agreement on when the legal threshold is crossed between domestic troubles and internal war meriting the application of Common Article 3? But the basic moral principles contained in IHL can be made comprehensive even to an undereducated teenager with an automatic weapon. In numerous places around the world, the ICRC engages in this simplified approach to IHL.

But the organization's dissemination efforts go far beyond this.[65] For the ICRC and its specialists in this area, dissemination means bringing

---

[63] Editor, *International Review of the Red Cross*, 319 (July–August 1997), 354. Tansley came back from a fact-finding trip in the Soviet Union and other European communist states in the mid-1970s and remarked how, when he explained his "Big Study" on the Re-appraisal of the Red Cross, he was asked by his Red Cross interlocutors, "What are the Geneva Conventions? We never heard of them."

[64] Quoted in Mercier, *Crimes sans châtiment*, 202.

[65] See the special issue, "Dissemination: Spreading Knowledge of Humanitarian Rules," *International Review of the Red Cross*, 319 (July–August 1997). In that year the Agency had about fifty persons concentrating on dissemination, spending about $20–25 million; *ibid.*, 375.

the message of humanitarian limits on power struggles to a wide range of recipients: school children, university students, the general public, the communications media. For the organization, dissemination means comic books, puppet shows, radio and TV talk shows – all in the local dialect and linked with local traditions. For maximum impact in military circles the ICRC often employs former military officers. Sometimes the line between education and direct humanitarian protection can be blurred, as in the ICRC's extensive landmine awareness program in Bosnia. Teaching about the danger of landmines, and their locations, is crucial for saving lives and limbs. For a time the organization had not only an extensive mine awareness program in that country but the only program, which it eventually transferred to the various National Society units.

Trying to gauge the effects of ICRC dissemination efforts is not a subject that lends itself to scientific precision. One can certainly observe the attention that humanitarian norms receive in the midst of conflict. But the state of learning in various locales regarding humanitarian values is normally quite amorphous before and after conflict. One author, for example, found that the activity of the ICRC, including conscious dissemination efforts, indeed had a positive effect in the Horn of Africa, a region characterized by persistent low-intensity violence.[66] Whether this observation was true, and whether it held for other conflict-prone regions, was difficult to say.

Enforcement of IHL

It is arguably the case that thus far ICRC success in protecting victims is due more to the wisdom of its policies than to the existence of IHL. No doubt those parts of IHL giving the ICRC a mandate to visit combatant and civilian detainees are important for the organization. Still, various parties – North Korea in the Korean war, North Vietnam in the Indochina war, Iraq during the 1991 and 2003 wars – violate these IHL rules. It is up to ICRC creativity and ingenuity to see if the organization can gain access anyway. A court order is not going to resolve the issue for the benefit of detainees. The balance between judicial and diplomatic approaches could change – especially with the creation of international courts with authority to adjudicate war crimes, crimes against humanity, and genocide. Given developments in international criminal law, IHL might become more

---

[66] John Prendergast, *Frontline Diplomacy: Humanitarian Aid and Conflict in Africa* (Boulder: Lynne Rienner, 1996), 47.

hard law through court cases, and thus presumably more effective. To date, IHL has been mostly soft law whose effect is more or less manifest, to the extent that it is manifest at all, in extra-judicial ways such as foreign policy decisions, military training, and ICRC field operations.

The ICRC has been very consistent through the years in seeking a positive relationship with public authorities, which minimizes conflict for, and judgment by, the organization. To the extent that the ICRC helps with the enforcement of IHL, it does so mostly through cooperation in application of services and programs, and not through – most of the time – public denunciation and shaming. We noted in chapter 5 the ICRC's conditions for going public about violations of IHL. We know that the organization only engages in public denunciation as a last resort. We have seen already that the ICRC objects to its personnel testifying in modern war crimes trials, for fear of impeding its field work.

Another clear example of the organization's orientation comes from the 1974–77 diplomatic conference leading to the two additional protocols. At one point in the diplomatic conference some states wanted to improve the means of supervision of particularly the first protocol on international armed conflict. If a protecting power, as a neutral state intended to help implement the provisions of IHL, was not appointed by a fighting party, the proposing states wanted the ICRC to become an automatic substitute. To the proposing states, the language they offered would increase pressure on a belligerent to appoint a protecting power. Or, failing such appointment, their language would guarantee a substitute in the form of the ICRC. Either way, the protecting power or its substitute would function to direct more attention to IHL.

The ICRC opposed this initiative. It did not want to assume a conflictual position *vis-à-vis* states. It did not want to have its presence forced on states. It did not want to appear authoritative over states. The organization believed that it could function in armed conflict only on the basis of real state consent. It was reluctant to find itself in a position in which it might have to pass public judgment on state policies. Its views in the 1970s were not that different from the 1890s when it opposed a Russian initiative, mentioned earlier, to have the ICRC assume an authoritative position *vis-à-vis* states during war.

The result of the ICRC position in the 1970s was to guarantee the failure of this legislative initiative at the diplomatic conference. The failure of this initiative meant that after 1977, at least until two UN *ad hoc* international criminal tribunals were created in 1993 and 1994, the means for enforcing or otherwise applying IHL would remain weak.

In most modern international armed conflicts, protecting powers are not appointed any more. It is a dying tradition. True, protecting powers were never the equivalent of a policeman or judge. Rather, protecting powers like Switzerland or Sweden during the Second World War functioned more as friendly legal advisor or perhaps as management consultant. Still, it was more advantageous to IHL to have them than not. And the ICRC could serve as a substitute for a protecting power, but nothing in IHL guaranteed that this eventuality would transpire. The belligerent state was free to accept or reject the organization as a substitute.

Broad and systematic enforcement of IHL was not to improve in any significant measure until, in the wake of the two *ad hoc* tribunals, the International Criminal Court was created in 2002. Then, the ICRC was in favor of the ICC, but refused to testify about war crimes in it. The ICRC was consistently in favor of strong enforcement of IHL, as long as the organization itself was not placed in an adversarial position *vis-à-vis* belligerents. The ICRC has always been hesitant about openly challenging public authorities. The priority is to try repeatedly for discreet cooperation with states.

In practice, one can count on the ICRC in armed conflict "to offer its services" to the fighting parties. This will happen regardless of the wording of IHL. Given not only that the ICRC has a recognized "right of initiative" in international law but also its own traditions, ICRC diplomacy will occur with or without IHL. There is no denying that without the cooperation of the fighting parties, not much humanitarian good can be achieved. Still, it disappointed a number of parties that the ICRC opposed wording intended for Protocol I that would have increased pressure on fighting parties to pay more serious attention to IHL.

True, states approved via Protocol I a fact-finding commission that might be activated by belligerents to help resolve disputes over IHL issues. But this was a weak measure, and as might have been predicted by the non-use of arbitration agreements negotiated around the turn of the previous century, the voluntary and non-automatic fact-finding commission of Protocol I has yet to be activated in a single armed conflict since 1977.

The point remains that the ICRC in the 1970s refused to be drawn into a substitute role that might have caused the organization to position itself in open conflict with a belligerent state that opposed its presence. Of course this open conflict often transpires anyway. Given that the ICRC has the legal right under IHL to check on the detention conditions of combatants (1949 GC no. 3) and civilians (1949 GC no. 4), when a North Korea or a

North Vietnam or an Iraq refuses to allow these visits to occur, the ICRC finds itself in open conflict with belligerents because of their policies. Why the ICRC accepts the role of automatic supervisor of detention, but declines the role of automatic substitute for a protecting power, is not clear to this writer. Of course the role of substitute for a protecting power is broader than that of detention supervisor. But that distinction should not logically lead to any great difference of principle.

Whether the climate of opinion in international relations has definitively changed after the Cold War in favor of a strong enforcement regime for IHL remains to be seen. As noted, the UN Security Council created two *ad hoc* criminal courts, and then the 1998 Rome diplomatic conference approved the new International Criminal Court. It may be that states are now resolved to be more serious about the importance of IHL. It seems there is some progressive change, but decisive change on this point is still elusive. US policy toward "enemy" detainees, however, suggests movement in the opposite direction (as noted in chapter 4).

The two UN *ad hoc* tribunals were initially created as a result of humanitarian negligence, not because of a change in international morality. The United States took the lead in the establishment of the two courts precisely to avoid having to take direct and costly action in response to atrocities in the Balkans and Rwanda. Faced with extensive criticism for not stopping these atrocities, the United States wanted to *appear* to be doing something, and so the courts were created through US leadership in the UN Security Council. But this step was precisely to avoid a more bothersome military intervention in defence of IHL and other international norms.[67]

Once created, however, the courts took on a momentum of their own, led by the international prosecutor's office (initially common to both courts) and supported by a coalition of like-minded states and private groups. Although created because of *ad hoc* and primarily non-humanitarian reasoning, the two courts contributed to a growing movement toward stronger enforcement of both IHL and HRL.

Still, it remained all too evident that the United States and some other militarily important states (Russia, China, Israel, Iraq, Iran, Libya) were opposed to any scheme for strong enforcement of IHL that might apply to them. The United States, for example, was a strong supporter of the two

---

[67] David P. Forsythe, "The Politics of the Yugoslav War Crimes Court," in Roger S. Clark and Madeleine Sann, eds., *The Prosecution of International Crimes* (New Brunswick: Transaction Books, 1995), 185–206.

ad hoc courts, but remained a strong opponent of the new International Criminal Court and any exercise of ICC jurisdiction and authority over US citizens. Our case study in chapter 4 of US policies toward prisoners detained in its "war" on terrorism also indicated that many high US officials sought to escape the restrictions of IHL and HRL designed to protect prisoner rights. The issue of a strong, broad, and even-handed enforcement of IHL remained very much in doubt.[68] This was especially so when the one Superpower was periodically suspicious of muscular international law and organization, and when it was consistently inclined to see itself as an exceptional nation not bound by law that might be needed for lesser "others," as we saw in chapter 4.[69]

There was another development that indicated some slight change in possible enforcement of IHL. From time to time the state parties to the Geneva Conventions and Protocols would assemble in response to a call from the Swiss Confederation, acting in consultation with the ICRC. Thus there would transpire a humanitarian review conference, focusing on humanitarian problems in such situations as the first Persian Gulf war of 1980 to 1988 between Iran and Iraq or the long-standing conflict between Israel and the Palestinians.[70] But these review conferences, historically an innovation in diplomacy, had not led at the time of writing to bold enforcement action. At best, they indicated to fighting parties some international concern with humanitarian issues arising out of conflict. But this concern had so far proven too amorphous and dispersed to make a concentrated impact on the situation on the ground. It still remained true that non-belligerents were reluctant to risk blood and treasure, or other important self-interests, for the sake of the human dignity of foreigners who had the misfortunate to be victimized by armed conflict.[71]

---

[68] David P. Forsythe, "The United States and International Criminal Justice," *Human Rights Quarterly*, 24 no. 4 (November 2002), 974–91.

[69] Among much literature dissecting American nationalism, exceptionalism, and unilateralism, see Anatol Lieven, *America Right or Wrong: An Anatomy of American Nationalism* (Oxford: Oxford University Press, 2004) and Clyde Prestowitz, *Rogue Nation: American Unilateralism and the Failure of Good Intentions* (New York: Basic Books, 2003).

[70] Re the latter conflict and IHL review conferences, see Pierre-Yves Fux and Mirko Zambelli, "Mise en œuvre de la Quatrième Convention de Genève dans les territoires palestiniens occupés: historique d'un processus multilateral (1977–2001)," *International Review of the Red Cross*, 847 (September 2002), 661–97.

[71] A conference of GC signatories in 1999 was brief and pro forma, but its resolution was later cited by the International Court of Justice in its advisory opinion on the Israeli security wall.

Conclusion

And so, as of the present time, the enforcement of IHL has remained weak, while not quite as weak as before the 1990s. The tasks of the ICRC remained largely unchanged despite the two UN courts, the ICC, and several innovations by some states – for example, a Belgian law encouraging suits in its courts for international crimes.[72] What the ICRC did, and how, remained largely unchanged despite these developments. In any event, even with more judicial attention to IHL, this juridical action came *after* the violations. If one wanted to prevent them, or mitigate them while occurring, one would still need to look – as one major option – to ICRC diplomacy on the ground.

---

[72] For a brief review of this Belgian law, see Daphne Eviatar, "Debating Belgium's War-Crime Jurisdiction," *New York Times*, 25 January 2003, B19. Under US pressure, including threats to move NATO headquarters out of Brussels, Belgium progressively watered down and narrowed the scope of its law on universal jurisdiction.

PART THREE

Conclusion

8

Conclusion: the ICRC and the future

There are human and inhuman warriors, just and unjust wars, forms of killing that are necessary and forms that dishonor us all. The Red Cross has become the keeper of these distinctions; they are the sentinels between the human and the inhuman.

Ignatieff, *The Warrior's Honor*, 1999, p. 161

The International Committee of the Red Cross and its multifaceted activity since 1863 present a complex picture, full of paradoxes. To reiterate points made in the introduction, it is an organization that is primarily private but with public dimensions. It manifests liberal ends but conservative means, championing the worth of the individual but proceeding cautiously on the basis of state consent – which can be slow in manifesting itself. It professes to be non-political but is inherently part of humanitarian politics. It promotes international humanitarian law (IHL) but resorts to public legal judgments mostly as a last resort, preferring to emphasize pragmatic – if principled – service. It is a product of, and is generally sustained by, western (Judeo-Christian) values, but presents itself as a secular and global Good Samaritan. It is part of an international network officially devoted to universal humanitarianism, but one characterized historically by strong nationalism, including in the past Swiss nationalism. It emphasizes a limited mandate, but over time has expanded its activities broadly. Understandably, Caroline Morehead wrote that "the International Committee itself remained a curious animal."[1]

As for summary judgments, two views compete. The first of these presents the ICRC as a heroic leader with impressive accomplishments; the second sees the organization as a marginal social worker on the periphery of the big issues of world affairs. This debate entails a discussion as to whether the ICRC, with its limited mandate, and tied as it is to states and the state system of international relations, can really do

---

[1] Morehead, *Dunant's Dream*, 175.

very much to protect human dignity. It is a discussion centered on the dilemmas of, and alternatives to, Red Cross neutral humanitarianism in conflicts.

Finally there are competing views about the organizational culture of the ICRC. The more positive view sees the organization as constantly striving to make the changes necessary to adjust to new realities, so as to ensure minimal standards of humanitarian protection. The more critical view sees the ICRC as ultra-slow to change, still controlled at the top by excessively cautious traditionalists who are much affected by Swiss society and political culture including some of its negative manifestations – like being risk averse, unilateralist, and slow to recognize gender equality.

Heroic leader versus marginal social worker

On an impressive range of issues related to conflict the ICRC was one of the first to see humanitarian need; and then, through both field action and more general activity, to engage with public authorities to do something about the problem. This pattern was evident from the very beginning with regard to medical assistance to the wounded in international war. Henry Dunant showed the shocking neglect that greeted those wounded in military service. Belligerents callously neglected not only wounded opponents but even their own. Between 1859 and today the situation is decidedly different – at least in legal theory and certainly in the practice of the more affluent and better-organized belligerents. All modern military establishments recognize a moral and legal obligation to protect the war wounded from unnecessary suffering. The ICRC's leadership on this question made a broad and lasting impact.[2]

The fact that certain contemporary rag-tag fighting forces do not provide medical services to their members does not detract from what the ICRC has helped accomplish over time. There is no rethinking of fundamental principles – namely, adequate medical services in war provided on a neutral basis. True, the ICRC itself for a considerable time got out of the business of systematic planning for medical care in conflicts. But this only shows that states and National Red Cross Societies accepted the obligation to provide that assistance to such an extent that the ICRC

---

[2] We noted in chapter 1, relying on the research of John Hutchinson, that while the ICRC motivation was strictly humanitarian, states had mixed motives – humanitarian but also expediential in the sense of shoring up war as a viable policy option that was acceptable on the home front.

mistakenly thought its extensive and persistent role was not needed.[3] After the Nigerian civil war, the ICRC made major changes, featuring the 1975 appointment of Dr. R. Kaeser as Chief Medical Officer. Since then, not just medical planning but medical operations have been one of the leading activities of the ICRC. So in this sense the ICRC has come full circle with its origins.

Were Dunant and his successors naïve, used by states to keep war going, when the human horrors of war, if left untreated, would have ended a brutal method of conflict resolution? Is war on the way out anyway, like foot binding, cock fighting, jousting, and slavery, and the ICRC guilty of prolonging war's inevitable demise?[4]

Major states know that peace is much preferable to war, and has been since at least 1914.[5] In so far as major military powers have gone through this learning process about wars among themselves, certain factors have made traditional war among the major states horribly destructive and not worth the game: military technology, national bureaucratic development and control, and mass democracy plus conscription. These factors, making traditional Great Power war too destructive for rational choice, have been much more important than any ICRC and broader Red Cross impact to keep war viable by making it tolerable.

Beyond what Robert Gilpin called hegemonic war,[6] however, war remains an all too evident choice for conflict resolution at lower levels of destruction. This is obvious in contemporary times both in civil wars and when one state seeks to exploit its putative power advantage over others – for example, the United States versus the Talibans' Afghanistan, the United States versus Saddam's Iraq, Iraq versus Kuwait, Israel versus

---

[3] Henry Dunant would have been shocked, no doubt, to learn that the ICRC left the planning of medical relief to governments and the National Societies, and to various *ad hoc* arrangements, to such an extent that the organization only established a medical division at its Geneva headquarters for systematic planning and policy in this domain during the latter stages of the Cold War. Even in the 1960s the ICRC still had a chief medical officer who showed up at headquarters "every Thursday afternoon" (internal document in the possession of the author). Its medical planning remained "dérisoires": Philippe Ryfman, *La question humanitaire* (Paris: Ellipses, 1999), 79.

[4] For an argument about the declining utility of war, at least among the Great Powers, see John Mueller, *Quiet Cataclysm: Reflections on the Recent Transformation of World Politics* (New York: HarperCollins, 1995).

[5] For the argument that the idea of peace is now accepted as a dominant value among major states, see Michael Mandelbaum, *The Ideas That Conquered the World: Peace, Democracy, and Free Markets in the Twenty-First Century* (New York: Public Affairs, 2003).

[6] Robert Gilpin, *War and Change in World Politics* (Cambridge: Cambridge University Press, 1981).

Palestinian radical groups. In the war calculation for these types of situations, the initiator obviously believes military objectives can be achieved at tolerable cost – including cost measured in terms of persons killed, wounded, and otherwise harmed. In democracies at least, there is usually attention to how much humanitarian cost the public will tolerate. But the role of Red Cross medical relief and other types of Red Cross activity has never been documented to be a very important part of the decision to go to war.

Second in the list of ICRC accomplishments, beyond enhancing medical relief in war, from the 1860s and 1870s, and then especially in the 1930s, the ICRC was one of the first, and no doubt the most persistent, in trying to expand humanitarian protection from international to internal wars. While the early efforts were decidedly limited in impact, in particular the work of Marcel Junod in the Spanish civil war did much to lead official thinking into more attention to the humanitarian horrors of brutal civil wars. Common Article 3 from the four 1949 Geneva Conventions, and Protocol II from 1977, the first treaty on non-international armed conflict, exist to considerable degree because of earlier ICRC field work, followed by its drafting and other efforts concerning the legislation of modern international humanitarian law (IHL) for civil wars.

These parts of IHL are important not so much because of legal technicalities but because IHL is codified public policy universally accepted as the authoritative statement of what norms should prevail in war. True, in reality – compared to legal theory – there is often not a clear distinction between international and internal war. As noted in the previous chapter, a number of authorities have recognized that this current bifurcation of IHL is often unworkable.[7] The central point remains that a quest for humanitarian limitation on the process of war has been extended very broadly, even when what is being fought over is most fundamentally control of national government and/or national resources. The ICRC has made major contributions to this trend of broadening the scope of humanitarian concern.

On this matter the legal technicalities have had some importance. After the Cold War, we saw courts like the ICTY holding individuals responsible for war crimes in internal war in part because much earlier the ICRC refused to limit its activity to international war. Rather, the organization

[7] See especially James G. Stewart, "Towards a Single Definition of Armed Conflict in International Humanitarian Law: A Critique of Internationalized Armed Conflict," *International Review of the Red Cross*, 850 (June 2003), 313–50.

took on the plight of individuals in a disintegrating Ottoman Empire, in the Tzars' collapsing empire, and within Spain in the inter-war years. As in medical assistance to wounded combatants, so in broad concern for the plight of those victimized by internal wars, the ICRC led the way with practical action on the ground and then legal drafting.[8]

Third, particularly from the First World War the ICRC took the lead in trying to see that in international war all fighters *hors de combat*, not just sick and wounded ones, were afforded humane treatment. Being in the POW camps to stop reprisals and provide medical relief, and seeing other issues that affronted the basic humanity of fighters *hors de combat*, the ICRC showed first its moral creativity and then its customary legal follow-up. Drawing vaguely on the Hague Conventions, which the ICRC had not affected in any important way, and which gave the organization no specific rights of supervision or visitation, the organization nevertheless broadened and systematized its concern for fighters *hors de combat*. Like the organization's initial efforts for other victims, states did not tell the ICRC to do this, even if states approved ICRC practice after the fact. Once again, as for those victimized in internal war in this era, the ICRC took the practical lead in responding to human need in conflicts even in the absence of authorization in the 1906 Geneva Convention. The 1929 Geneva Convention for Prisoners of War was based largely on ICRC pragmatic, moral, and alegal action during the Great War.

In contemporary times, at least in many parts of the world, humane treatment of POWs as verified by ICRC visits has become a major issue in conflicts, a benchmark for minimal civilized behavior. In fact, in many modern conflicts it is much safer to be an official combatant rather than a civilian, not only given the way many wars are fought (with intentional attacks on unarmed civilians) but also given treatment while under enemy control. Given reciprocity and military honor, POWs often fare better than civilians. POWs drew extensive legal attention in 1907 and again in 1929, whereas, despite considerable ICRC efforts, civilians obtained broad legal protection only from 1949.

Fourth, the ICRC's attention to "those detained by reason of events" outside armed conflict, or to "political" or security prisoners, comprises

---

[8] We noted the role of others, like Francis Lieber concerning humanizing civil war, or Florence Nightingale and Clara Barton concerning medical assistance, as covered in chapter 1. It seems that Clara Barton was closer to Dunant's vision than Florence Nightingale. The latter was interested only in co-nationals, while the former wanted a more neutral concern for all victims. Over time, however, the American Red Cross, like the British, has adopted the Nightingale nationalistic approach rather than the Barton–Dunant neutral approach.

another considerable achievement. While public international law has never recognized the notion of political or security prisoners, this has not stopped the ICRC, starting in Hungary and Russia after the First World War, from trying to provide humanitarian protection to this category of detainee. While Amnesty International from 1961 did more than the ICRC to publicize what AI came to call prisoners of conscience, the ICRC has been the organization to actually visit security prisoners on a systematic basis.[9] The ICRC in 1935 created a special commission to deal systematically with the problem of political prisoners.[10] This was almost thirty years before the creation of AI.[11]

The deviance in the usual pattern is that thus far the ICRC has not tried to push for recognition and protection in international law for this category of detainee. The organization believes that definitional problems are great and that state political will to legally confront the problem in a positive way is not so great. The principle of reciprocity, which undergirds much of IHL, for example with regard to legal protection of POWs, does not come into play in the same way for "political" prisoners. When a state agrees to ICRC visits to security prisoners, it often sees itself as making a unilateral concession, without any connection to the protection of its citizens abroad. Nevertheless, the fact that ICRC visits to detainees in internal troubles and tensions have become quite systematic indicates that humanitarian progress can be achieved. In many instances the organization and public authorities both know who "enemy" detainees are. Even without legal parameters, the ICRC and public authorities often come to agreement about the focus of ICRC concern.

---

[9] The concerns of AI and the ICRC were not, and are not, identical. While AI officially "adopted" and sought the release of only those persons who had renounced violence, the ICRC did not rule out the need for humanitarian protection for those who had undertaken violence in domestic unrest. AI would not adopt Nelson Mandela since he refused to renounce violence to achieve "regime change" in South Africa under apartheid. The ICRC had no such qualms in visiting Mandela. In fact, the more a detainee in a situation short of war approximated a combatant in war, the more the ICRC paid attention. The issue is complex, and AI had nuanced its position over time in various ways, for example by opposing torture of any political detainees regardless of their stand regarding violence, but the details of AI's evolution need not concern us here.

[10] Jacques Moreillon, *Le Comité International de la Croix-Rouge et la protection des detenus politiques* (Geneva: Henry Dunant Institute, 1973). It is strange that this authoritative work has never been translated into English.

[11] The ICRC and AI in contemporary times have a mostly close and cooperative relationship. The latter organization has become more active with regard to IHL, but without challenging the ICRC's role and emphasis on discretion. The ICRC mostly perceives AI's publicity campaigns as complementary to its own more discreet activities.

Fifth, and overlapping with some of the categories above, we have the ICRC concern with the civilian population in armed conflict and domestic unrest. If the ICRC started with a concern for the wounded fighter, and then emerged from the First World War better known because of its attention to detained fighters, it is certainly true that the ICRC did not ignore civilians – particularly from the Great War on. The organization was clearly ahead of the curve in the 1930s in trying to get public authorities to provide better legal and practical protection for civilians caught up in war situations. One of the bedrock principles of modern humanitarian thinking is that belligerents must make a distinction between combatant and civilian, protecting the latter from suffering not required by military necessity. If one is not an active combatant, one should not be made the object of military attack. The ICRC progressively played a large role in developing this central principle.[12]

This is not to say that the ICRC was always well prepared to act in the light of this principle. In chapter 3, for example, we noted the organization's controversial performance in the Nigerian war of 1967–70, when it vacillated and departed from the principles of IHL in trying to deal especially with the civilian population in secessionist Biafra. We saw that the ICRC did not handle well the complexity it faced: the Biafran leader Ojukwu was prepared to sacrifice the welfare of "his" people by opposing international relief supervised by Lagos (an opposition which symbolized his independence and sovereignty); but the Geneva Conventions provided for a right of supervision over relief leaving a belligerent's territory. The solution Geneva chose, to proceed with relief at its own risk, because of its concern for civilians in need but also because of competition with other relief agencies, led to a débâcle for the organization. The ICRC was widely seen as unfaithful to the principles of IHL and to Red Cross neutrality. Even in the Balkans in the 1990s, we noted in chapter 4 that the organization was slow to mobilize the necessary resources for civilian relief. Nevertheless, the ICRC has remained a leader in focusing on civilians in conflicts, whether in modern times one speaks of the Balkans, Somalia, Cambodia, former Zaire, the Sudan, or other places. Its efforts for civilians in these places was praiseworthy,

[12] In chapter 7 we noted that the line between combatant and civilian had been blurred by several modern practices such as "corporate warriors" and civilian guards armed by governments. But then in the past, as in the Vietnam war, one sometimes found farmers by day who became warriors at night. So the blurring of the line between combatant and civilian is not entirely new.

especially as demonstrated by our case studies on the Balkans and Somalia.

Sixth, and still further in this list of major accomplishments, the ICRC has led the way in what was first called tracing activity and is now more accurately characterized as family linkage efforts. No other organization over time has accomplished so much in linking families divided by conflict. Reflecting this status as well as its expertise, the International Tracing Service at Arolsen, Germany, with a mandate to establish personal facts about civilians from the Second World War, is headed by an ICRC official (since 1955).

The ICRC has shown creativity beyond the now well-known personal information cards that prisoners of war are legally authorized to send to loved ones. For various categories of detainees, whether civilians falling under the Fourth Geneva Convention of 1949 or security prisoners in domestic unrest, the ICRC has often arranged family visits to detention centers or financial payments to distressed families whose chief provider was detained. The number of family members so affected is quite large in places like Israeli-controlled territory since 1967. In the early twenty-first century the ICRC made a major effort to reunite a large number of African children with their relatives in conflicts plaguing such places as former Zaire, Angola, and so on. Some of these activities are not tracing *per se*, but comprise part of the larger realm of protecting family connections which in turn protects sound mental health for those adversely affected by conflict. Trying to reintegrate former child soldiers into society has become a modern preoccupation in this area of endeavor.

The question of tracing or family reunification has not diminished in importance across time. In 2004, given that US and allied forces then occupying Iraq were not systematically notifying loved ones of detained Iraqis, this traditional ICRC activity took on renewed significance.[13] While the ICRC motivation was humanitarian, as usual there were "political" ramifications. The lack of systematic notification and family visits tarnished the occupying powers, as well as fueling Iraqi resentment against the occupiers.

Seventh, there is the ICRC's role in general of assuming guardianship over the Hague tradition of trying to limit the means and methods of warfare, and in particular of helping build opposition to anti-personnel landmines. Perhaps the organization could have limited its focus to

---

[13] Ian Fisher, "Searing Uncertainty for Iraqis Missing Loved Ones," *New York Times*, 1 June 2004, A1.

victims, declaring that means and methods were beyond its mandate. But the ICRC had taken a stand on poison gas in World War I, then helped promote the 1925 treaty prohibiting poisonous and asphyxiating gases. Perhaps the distinction between the Hague and Geneva legal traditions, between a focus on victims and on means/methods of warfare, was always somewhat artificial. (We noted that the Hague regulations covered prisoners of war, for example, and that the ICRC expanded its work with POWs during the First World War partially in order to implement provisions of those Hague rules regarding reprisals.) In any event, in modern times the ICRC clearly agreed to address various weapons issues, then did not shy away from opposing some major states, including its major financial donor the United States, on the issue of a total ban on anti-personnel landmines.

While chapter 7 showed that action against these landmines was shared with many other organizations and personalities, it was ICRC experience in the field, combined with its penchant for maintaining exact statistics, further combined with its official contacts and adept lobbying tactics, that helped produce widespread revulsion against anti-personnel landmines as indiscriminate weapons. Having been the leader in developing prosthesis services because of landmines in places like Afghanistan, Cambodia, and Angola, the ICRC knew very well the misery heaped on farmers, women gathering wood and water, and children at play, long after the conflict had subsided.[14] Finally devising appropriate publicity and lobbying measures, not at all the strong point of the organization historically, the ICRC made a major effort in the largely successful anti-landmine campaign.

Beyond these core accomplishments, others – perhaps of different dimensions – can be cited. The organization has constructed an excellent reputation for integrity. If the ICRC says its delegates have observed a certain situation, one can have confidence in that report. Remarkably, there does not seem to be a single major case of false or mistaken reporting by the organization. Other agencies with a reputation for integrity cannot compare with the ICRC in this regard. Amnesty International from time to time has to admit that some of its reports or testimonies are mistaken. AI, for example, got caught up in Kuwaiti propaganda and falsely said that invading Iraqi forces had taken premature babies from incubators

[14] The International Society for Prosthetics and Orthotics awarded the Brian Blatchford Prize to the ICRC at its World Congress in Hong Kong in 2004. The prize recognized the ICRC's "innovative achievements, particularly in the design and development of . . . prosthetic services in developing countries." ICRC press release 04/91, 6 August 2004.

in 1991.[15] There were a few other examples of AI statements not proving accurate.[16] Over the years the ICRC has been extremely careful about facts, even if this means it did not join western networks reporting very high numbers of rapes in the Balkan wars. Its delegates could not verify those numbers, so the organization marched to its own drummer on that issue. The ICRC's care with facts has contributed to an excellent reputation for integrity and veracity.

Furthermore, among agencies with field operations in conflict situations, the ICRC was the first to establish clear doctrine – or general policy – on a wide range of issues. And ICRC staff were expected to adhere to these guidelines. If we compare the organization to the UN refugee office (UNHCR) and/or Doctors Without Borders (MSF), for example, the ICRC alone has established clear policy guidelines on such matters as publicity versus discretion, or what situation triggers interest in political detainees. Likewise, after the Cold War, it was the ICRC that developed clear policies on how to make its field delegations as secure as possible in the face of possible attacks; other agencies with field operations came to the ICRC for guidance on this perplexing issue. It was the organization from the early 1990s that developed systematic training, including simulation, on security matters.

Still further, as noted briefly in chapter 4, by 2003 the ICRC had developed a most remarkable reporting system in the midst of conflict. In the war over Iraq in that year, the ICRC sent electronic reports to the rest of the world concerning such matters as the state of Iraqi hospitals visited by its delegates, thus providing an instantaneous and independent view of certain humanitarian issues not controlled by any belligerent. For an organization with a woeful record on public information historically speaking, that represented an important shift – although incomplete.

When the ICRC did make its public reports about Iraqi hospitals, it carefully avoided any reference to the extent of civilian casualties and the general subject of collateral damage. It made no attempt to ascertain how many hospital patients were civilians as compared to combatants, and whether the extent of civilian harm might exceed the bounds of permissible collateral damage. So while the ICRC broke new ground in eye-witness, "real time" reporting, it avoided any commentary that might prove embarrassing to the US-led coalition forces. Thus the notion of

---

[15] Sellars, *The Rise and Rise of Human Rights*, 153–6.

[16] See David Gonzalez, "Police Doubts about Attack Cast Cloud on Rights Group," *New York Times*, 6 May 2002, A3, regarding a staged attack on a Guatemalan rights activist on the US west coast, about which AI-USA sent out an alert.

unacceptable collateral damage remained as vague as before the Iraqi invasion, and the public counting of civilian dead and wounded was left to other, less authoritative voices.[17]

Still the ICRC communications department, led by Yves Daccord, continued to provide vivid factual reporting in Haiti, the Dafur region of Somalia, the Democratic Republic of the Congo, and other places. Even if carefully constrained, this public reporting made it impossible for states and inter-governmental organizations to deny certain facts. ICRC public reporting thus generated certain pressures on public authorities to respond to humanitarian need.

It is true that in all these areas of accomplishment, the early ICRC record was more impressive for its creativity and commitment than for its practical impact. ICRC delegates early on were often more witnesses and bystanders, recording things for posterity, rather than managing impressive programs to alleviate the abuses in any significant way. Initial field operations were usually modest. This was true in 1864 when it arranged observers for the war in Schleswig-Holstein, in 1918 in dealing with the movement of civilians after World War I, in the Far East during World War II, and so on.[18] Yet as stressed in previous chapters, the *long-term* significance of ICRC efforts was impressive. Given time, a meager *ad hoc* initiative could become systematic practice with substantive impact, with or without legal codification.

In sum, if one wants a model of leadership for progressive and incremental change in behalf of humane values in conflict situations, over considerable time, the ICRC is a wonderful example. Persistent, dogged, able to reconstitute itself at the top and down the line so as to keep the cause going, overcoming setbacks and mistakes not to mention the callousness and brutality of many belligerents in conflicts, the ICRC has gradually expanded the specific coverage of its consistent focus with impressive results.[19] Naturally it has acted in tandem with others, including various

---

[17] See for example Institute for Policy Studies, and Foreign Policy in Focus, "Paying the Price: The Mounting Costs of the Iraq War," 25 June 2004, communications@irc-online.org. This source estimated Iraqis killed at about 9,000, but did not distinguish between combatants and civilians. Other estimates of Iraqi civilians killed were in the neighborhood of 5,000–15,000. In the fall of 2004, a team of researchers from the Johns Hopkins school of medicine did interviewing in Iraq and reported 100,000 Iraqi deaths during 2003–4. This figure included some combatants. If this figure proved accurate, it would mean that ten Iraqis died for each US military person killed in Iraq during this time frame.

[18] Caroline Morehead makes this point well, *Dunant's Dream*, 297, 298, 304 and *passim*.

[19] While the ICRC has always focused on victims of conflicts, it does so in expanded ways. For example, it now pays more attention to the transition from active conflict to what might

states with their own versions of humanitarianism, to compile the existing record. There are sound reasons for the ICRC to be so widely respected, and the view of the ICRC as heroic leader with impressive accomplishments is not wrong. But it is incomplete.

A more critical basic view of the ICRC is that in international relations it is a marginal social worker, the agency of "the modest morality of small deeds."[20] A similar view is that "the International Red Cross" is in reality not much more than "Europe's pharmacy" or "perpetual first aid station."[21] A candid ICRC delegate remarked about "the inventory of impotence" and the "useless heroism" that characterized the organization in the Balkans in the early 1990s.[22]

The bitter phrase "the well-fed dead" captures certain experiences during World War II, in which the ICRC gained access to a number of detention camps in France. The organization carried out its traditional activities, after which many of the camp inmates were shipped east to the gas chambers. (It is also true that some of the inmates in France survived the German Holocaust; the ICRC contributed to that outcome as well.)[23] The basic problem has not gone away. With regard to Bosnia in the 1990s, one ICRC delegate remarked of non-combatants intentionally targeted for abuse, "the only thing you can do for them is to make sure they are fed before they are shot."[24]

The same "modest morality" that avoids confrontation with many of the major affronts to human dignity in conflict situations is also demonstrated by events from South Africa. True, the ICRC was able to improve the diet of Nelson Mandela, obtain for him more reading and recreational material, and get the South African white penal authorities to

---

pass for stability or normality, thus overlapping with what is often called "development." In so doing, it has also blurred the distinction between humanitarian norms and human rights. The organization, for example, pays more attention now to the long-term mental health of women who have been adversely affected by conflict, sometimes by rape. See especially the article by Marion Harroff-Tavel, "La guerre a-t-elle jamais une fin? L'action du Comité International de la Croix-Rouge lorsque les armes se taisent," *International Review of the Red Cross*, 851 (September 2003), 465–96.

[20] Ignatieff, *The Warrior's Honor*, 144.

[21] Amos Elon, "Switzerland's Lasting Demon," *New York Times Magazine*, 12 April 1998, 40.

[22] Mercier, *Crimes sans châtiment*.

[23] See further Mary B. Anderson, "'You Save My Life Today, But for What Tomorrow?', Some Moral Dilemmas of Humanitarian Aid," in Jonathan Moore, ed., *Hard Choices: Moral Dilemmas in Humanitarian Intervention* (Geneva: Rowman and Littlefield, for the ICRC, 1998), 137–56.

[24] Urs Boegli, quoted by Elizabeth Becker in "Red Cross Man in Guantanamo: A 'Busybody,' but Not Unwelcome," *New York Times*, 20 February 2002, A10.

better respect their own rules concerning prisoner complaints.[25] But on the issue of the racist repression that led to his arrest, and kept him detained for twenty-seven years, the neutral ICRC had nothing to say – beyond operating on its principles of humanity and impartiality. The Red Cross Movement did take a stand against apartheid, but the ICRC did not.

It is true that Mandela emerged from detention with positive feelings for the ICRC, once one got past the point that the first ICRC representative sent to visit him was a white, conservative resident of Rhodesia who did not impress Mandela with his commitment to the black prisoners.[26] But it is also true that if one wanted to do something important to broadly oppose brutal apartheid in old South Africa, the ICRC was not the agency of choice.[27] The all-white and neutral ICRC was not going to boldly confront the major moral evil of racism in any direct and public way. The best it could do was to carry out its traditional activities in conflict in a way that showed impartial concern for all detainees regardless of race. This is something, to be sure, but ICRC activity stood no chance of undermining apartheid.

Of course the organization has a limited mandate, related to armed conflict and domestic unrest. Moreover, some of the limitations on ICRC mandate and tactics, such as not challenging the reasons for war or detention, and certainly not in public, are said to be the price – the downside – of ICRC positive accomplishments. It has been widely accepted that limited mandate and discreet tactics are the price paid for the organization's access to victims. The organization believes that whatever influence it has stems from its "non-political" and limited focus.

One of the reasons that the young ICRC delegate in El Salvador Dres Balmer violated his contractual obligation to maintain discretion, and published some of the details of his experiences there, was that he became frustrated at being unable to do anything about the basic causes of human misery in that internationalized civil war. Successful long-term delegates, like Urs Boegli, accept the fact that often the delegate has to be content with providing not much more than a relaxed conversation in the prisoner's native language, and thus a brief social respite from the monotony or

---

[25] Nelson Mandela, *Long Walk to Freedom* (Boston: Little, Brown, 1995).   [26] *Ibid.*, 410.

[27] Some in Geneva believe that in getting more newspapers and other reading material to Mandela and other detainees in old South Africa, the ICRC helped ensure that he and his colleagues were better prepared to exercise the leadership they did upon release. So the argument runs, Mandela was prepared for the 1990s and not the 1960s because of the ICRC. While an intriguing interpretation, if true, it is strange that Mandela does not mention it in his lengthy memoirs.

tension of confinement.[28] The successful ICRC delegate knows that often he is just a minor social worker, marginal to the big issues of world affairs. Many ICRC delegates are content being able to do the social good they can, while others – like Balmer – are deeply frustrated at this often marginal role in terrible conflicts.

Mandela wrote that authorities feared the ICRC.[29] This view is mostly hyperbole, most of the time. Authorities often cooperate with the ICRC because they know that the organization will not interfere with, or have an important impact on, the major issues comprising the conflict then ongoing.

In South Africa in May 1975, the ICRC did in fact consider suspending its visits. It was advised to continue by Mandela, who is reliably reported to have said: "Always remember that what matters is not only the good you bring but just as much the bad you prevent." This statement has entered the folklore of the ICRC, comprising part of its organizational culture. Mandela is often cited to confirm the wisdom of not denouncing and withdrawing. There is no empirical proof of the bad that might be prevented by a continuation of visits, so there is no way to really test the wisdom of the "Mandela axiom." The cautious tactics of the organization are endorsed by no less than Mandela, and there is almost no way under this axiom to reliably criticize a continuation of discreet visits by the ICRC.

Whether the ICRC is more heroic leader than marginal social worker is difficult to say. The answer often varies with context. In its visits to Palestinians *convicted* of security offenses by Israel and detained in the regular Israeli penal system, the ICRC has now become mostly a marginal social worker at that point in the detention process. Whatever the situation in the past, it can be said on this issue that Israel runs a modern, legalized penal system. The ICRC now winds up dealing with petty details of penal administration. In some ways, paradoxically enough, the ICRC objective is to exercise heroic leadership so it can become a marginal or routine social agency.

On the other hand, when visiting security prisoners in places like Chile or Argentina in the 1970s, or Colombia or Peru in the 1980s, among other

[28] Boegli, "Red Cross Man."
[29] Mandela, *Long Walk*, 409. Mandela's logic, in an otherwise wonderful book, is faulty here. He writes that South African authorities respected and feared the ICRC because they feared loss of international reputation. But if those authorities made relatively minor accommodation in detention conditions, the discreet ICRC would not resort to public denunciation.

places, ICRC visits constitute a basic life insurance policy. The issue is the life and death and fundamental mental health of prisoners. This is not a matter of petty penal administration. True, the ICRC takes no position on the causes of conflict and detention, but it winds up as a key player in trying to protect the right to life – hardly a matter of mere bureaucratic regulation.

All actors are comprised of contradictory elements and tendencies. Just as no one individual can be characterized with one simple summary label, so no organization is uni-dimensional. The ICRC is a heroic leader that has helped accomplish a number of important objectives over time; and it is also often a minor social worker operating on the margins of the great issues that confront humanity. On the general subject of limiting the damage to human beings because of conflict, its record is superb when viewed in historical perspective. On issues like the causes of peace and war, and whether genocide and other forms of crimes against humanity do in fact exist, and whether racist repression is pervasive, the ICRC is marginal – content with the morality of minor good deeds that mostly avoids the core of these big moral issues.

For those who wanted to save the Muslim males at Srebrenica, they should not have expected the ICRC to do this. First of all, that "safe area" was created by the United Nations, and UN officials promised protection to the civilians there. Secondly, the ICRC's humanitarian protection depended on cooperation from General Mladic, the immediate agent of the massacre. Moreover, the cautious ICRC, wedded to discretion by tradition and doctrine, often contents itself with incremental progress over time while continuing to search for discreet cooperation.[30]

Core dilemmas of humanitarian protection

What do contemporary policy choices by the ICRC tell us about the dilemmas of Red Cross neutral humanitarianism – and about the tensions between the roles of heroic leader for human dignity versus marginal social worker? Statistics about the number of detainees visited and tons of relief delivered do not tell us very much about the assertiveness of the ICRC, and the wisdom of its policy choices,

[30] Samantha Power, in "A Problem from Hell:" America and the Age of Genocide (New York: Perennial, 2002), is very critical of the ICRC for not denouncing the Serbs' non-cooperation at Srebrenica, see 409–11. She does not report on the dynamics of ICRC quiet diplomacy vis-à-vis Mladic.

when confronting grave violations of human rights and humanitarian standards.[31]

In chapter 2 Pierre Boissier was quoted to the effect that the organization was conscious of its need for cooperation from public authorities and therefore was careful not to proceed beyond the realm of their consent. Yet victims of war and of power politics are victimized precisely because of the policies of these same public authorities. It is precisely these governments that have killed millions in past decades.[32] That is why advocacy groups like AI and HRW believe in a more adversarial relationship with states featuring attempted public pressure – the naming and shaming game. They believe in the necessity of uncomfortable conflict, while the ICRC's neutral protection is based on hope for quiet cooperation.

So the ICRC locks itself into a complex situation in which it seeks cooperation from the very authorities that are causing most of the affronts to human dignity in the first place. On the one hand it is commendable to discuss violations of humanitarian standards with those directly responsible. The ICRC's Thierry Germond and François Bugnion did this with Mladic in the Balkans in the 1990s. Max Huber and Carl Burckhardt did not do this with Himmler and other Nazi leaders in the 1940s. On the other hand, how long does the ICRC wait for cooperation to manifest itself, and what does it do when serious cooperation is evidently not forthcoming.

What was the point of continuing to write politely to the German Red Cross in the 1930s about the concentration camps when that National Red Cross Society was part of the brutal totalitarian regime that instituted the camps in the first place? What was the point of continuing quietly to ask the Balkan parties for genuine cooperation in humanitarian matters, when especially the Serbs displayed a clear policy of stalling the ICRC so that they could continue with their ethnic cleansing on behalf of a chauvinistic nationalism? All of the Balkan belligerents might sign humanitarian agreements, but that meant nothing to ICRC humanitarian protection on the ground.

In the dialectic between "national security" and human security, between what passes for military and political "necessity" and humane

---

[31] Such macro-statistics may be important to donors, showing that goods and services are being delivered to beneficiaries. Too much focus on such macro-statistics may cause the humanitarian actor to lose sight of the needs of particular victims. See further John Pendergast, *Frontline Diplomacy: Humanitarian Aid and Conflict in Africa* (Boulder: Lynne Rienner, 1996).

[32] Readers may recall our early reliance in this regard on the work by R. J. Rummel, *Death by Government: Genocide and Mass Murder since 1900* (Somerset, NJ: Transaction, 1997).

values, how does the ICRC find and defend its synthesis? How does it justify the timing of its various policy options – discreet routine, high-level visits to officials, public denunciations?

The ICRC is the establishment humanitarian organization, officially recognized as such by states through their conferring rights on the organization in public international law. The ICRC is very proud of this special position, as noted with some irritation by President Sommaruga and his caustic comments about his colleagues who saw themselves as the high priests of humanitarianism. It is little wonder then that the ICRC likes to picture itself as the Good Samaritan engaging in service activities that have been approved by states. Given all of this, how could we logically expect the ICRC to be dynamic in protecting human dignity when that involves a certain challenge to the policies of public authorities?

Yet states did not tell the ICRC to start supervising prisoners of war, or to get involved in civil wars, or to start visiting detainees beyond situations of war, or – to use a very specific example from more recent years – to lobby for the Ottawa treaty banning anti-personnel landmines. The ICRC could not have become what it is today without state approval, but it also has a rich tradition of initiative and creativity as a private actor.[33]

In reality, the ICRC has a leg in two worlds – the world of state approval and the world of civil society initiative. Because of the organization's dual nature, there is a tension in ICRC actions between deferring to state views on military and political necessity, recorded in IHL, and pressing states in a timely fashion to do more for human dignity. Managing that tension wisely is the crux of humanitarian politics and diplomacy by the ICRC. How the ICRC manages that tension says a lot about whether the organization is more heroic humanitarian leader than marginal social worker.

Detention

For the contemporary ICRC and its attempts at traditional protection of detainees, we simply do not know how assertive and wise the ICRC has been overall. No outsider knows. The archives are closed under the forty-year disclosure rule. As for the larger historical record on this point, what we do know leads to a mixed conclusion. As already shown, on the one hand the ICRC was vigorous in dealing with the Greek junta in the

---

[33] The UNHCR, created by states and remaining an agency in an intergovernmental organization, also takes initiatives not preapproved by states. See Gil Loescher, *The UNHCR and World Politics: A Perilous Path* (Oxford: Oxford University Press, 2001).

1960s, French authorities in the war in Algeria, and so on. On the other hand it was silent on the question of Turkish treatment of the Armenians in the First World War, very cautious in dealing with fascist Germany and Italy in the 1930s and 1940s, not very assertive *vis-à-vis* Japan during the Second World War, not always assertive regarding the French in Indochina in 1945–54, and so on. But that was history, and the ICRC is not really the same organization now.

In the Cold War era we know[34] that, when confronting recalcitrant authorities, the ICRC would discreetly approach "patron" states and try to get the latter to bring effective pressure on the former. Some times this approach helped; other times it did not. The organization soon learned that it was fairly pointless to talk to Washington about Israel's many violations of IHL, although in early 2004 President Kellenberger was still trying.[35] After the Cold War, with the decline of the loose bi-polar structure of international relations, this approach proved less helpful in general. We noted that in the Balkan wars of the 1990s the ICRC delegates sometimes gave general information to journalists about the severity of certain detention conditions.

Some modern examples demonstrate dynamic efforts, within carefully calculated limits. In 2002 it was very clear that Israel was making the life of detained but unconvicted Palestinians very uncomfortable, one of several measures intended to convince Palestinian authorities, and Palestinian society in general, to control violence against the Jewish state. In that situation, the ICRC increased its material provisions to Palestinian detainees, thus trying to offset Israeli policies. In this case the organization did not hesitate to "get in the way of" the harsh policies of the detaining authority. Israel is a relatively wealthy and well-organized state. It certainly had the capability to provide for detainees what the ICRC wound up providing. For Israel it was not a matter of capability but of an intentional policy of deprivation. Geneva did not hesitate to take further action to buffer detainees from new deprivations.[36]

---

[34] From interviews, Geneva.

[35] An ICRC press release, no. 04/30, indicated that when Kellenberger visited Washington in early 2004, issues arising from the Israeli–Palestinian conflict were on his agenda.

[36] ICRC press release 02/30, 26 July 2002, "Israel and the Occupied/Autonomous Territories: ICRC Distributes Clothes to Detainees." On the other hand, in 2003 the ICRC reduced its assistance to certain Palestinian civilians under Israeli occupation in the West Bank area. The ICRC drew the conclusion that Israel was avoiding its responsibilities as occupying power to care properly for the civilian population. In other words, Geneva concluded that Israel was avoiding certain costs of occupation by trying to substitute the resources of the ICRC. See ICRC statement, 20 November 2003, "New Strategy for the West Bank."

Slow change and partial access remain problematical. In historical perspective, because the ICRC has been so reluctant on occasion to confront public authorities in a timely manner about their violations of humanitarian standards, a great deal of harm is done to individuals while the organization is probing the firmness and full meaning of governmental policy. At times in the past the ICRC has been "bought off" by brutal authorities willing to give the organization partial or inconsequential access to victims. The ICRC has accepted partial access in the hopes of proving its bona fides and expanding its operations over time. Sometimes this expansion transpires, as in Kosovo in the late 1980s. But, for example, it took the ICRC a very long time to suspend its detention visits in Peru. It continued with relatively meaningless visits for a considerable time before finally concluding that the authorities were not going to be serious about significantly improving very bad detention conditions. In the meantime, the Peruvian authorities could say that they were cooperating with the ICRC while they abused prisoners.

If one is an official in a repressive regime, like in the Bosnian Serb Republic in the 1990s, that official can offer the ICRC general promises of cooperation, and maybe access to some victims here and there, but can try to keep the organization away from any serious impact on policies of persecution and abuse. That official will be generally successful at least for a time, particularly if powerful outside actors do not intervene with force or economic coercion in behalf of humanitarian values, or if journalists do not publicize the situation, because the ICRC is committed to discreet and incremental change over time. This ICRC approach allows a repressive official to stall and continue with abuse of individuals. The ICRC will not quickly blow the whistle or declare non-cooperation. The ICRC is reluctant to reject or give up its access to some victims, and this allows the organization to be manipulated by inhumane authorities.[37] The decision to withdraw in protest is almost impossible to sustain if the detainees want a continuation of visits. The Mandela axiom of staying to prevent unspecified and unknowable harm in the future contributes to the same orientation. If the ICRC withdraws with a public denunciation, it loses its great comparative advantage over most other human rights and humanitarian organizations – its in-country presence. If it withdraws in

---

[37] In *Humanitarian Politics*, there is a discussion of the perils of "the one more blanket theory." The ICRC desire to bring in one more blanket allows it to be manipulated by unscrupulous authorities.

protest, having fired the last arrow in its humanitarian quiver, it is out of the game.[38]

In the last analysis, being discreet in the hopes of eventual, slow, incremental change at one and the same time is the defining feature of ICRC prison visits and the Achilles heel of ICRC detention policy.[39]

Delayed access is equally problematic. Everything considered, in the US "war" on terrorism after 11 September 2001, as well as concerning Israel after 1967, should the ICRC accept that "stress and duress" interrogation practices were going to occur, and that the best the ICRC could do was to try to ensure that the prisoner eventually emerged alive with as little damage to his physical and mental health as possible? Should the Geneva headquarters be more dynamic and assertive in addressing these matters discreetly with top national officials? Should there be a more timely and vigorous denouncement of such policies – at least in those situations in which such ICRC action held out prospect for beneficial change, which is in keeping with its doctrine on the question?

But if the ICRC goes public regarding detention by liberal democratic governments, in the hope that liberal public opinion will make a difference, does the organization arrive at a persistent double standard, denouncing democracies but not brutal authoritarians? On the other hand, was the ICRC too cautious in trying to mobilize support for a better protection of human dignity, given the broad outrage in the United States when the abuse of prisoners in Iraq became known in 2004?[40]

---

[38] The ICRC tends to refer obliquely and discreetly to the possibility of suspended visits, as Kellenberger did when he went to Washington in January 2004 to discuss prisoners under US control in the "war" on terrorism. The logic is similar to that in many foreign offices when discussing with another state the possibility of suspending foreign assistance. The main attempt is to get change by discussion of possible future action. Once aid is suspended, the one bullet in the gun has been used and one is out of the game. Moreover, actual suspension of aid can provoke intensified resistance on the other side. That is not an argument for never suspending aid, but like ICRC suspension of visits, it is an indication about the difficulty of generating influence from the process.

[39] Similar tendencies were visible in ICRC dealings with China. Beijing agreed to discuss ICRC detention visits, but stalled – seemingly forever. Rather than issue any kind of critical statement, the ICRC decided in 2003 to open a delegation in China for such things as humanitarian diplomacy in general and dissemination of IHL. No doubt the ICRC was hoping for a change in Chinese policy on the organization's access to political prisoners, based on increased familiarity with ICRC policies and personnel. But China then stalled regarding the opening of this office. Again, Geneva said it was on the road to progress, refusing any critical comment about China's procrastination.

[40] In the United States in 2004, after much attention to US abuse of prisoners in Iraq, Afghanistan, and Guantanamo, 66% of those sampled in a public opinion poll said the United States should respect legal prohibitions against torture; 58% objected to use of

After all, in that situation, as well as during the French-Algerian war, publicity from ICRC reports leaked by other parties brought about clear and rapid improvement on important humanitarian issues. (ICRC interlocutors like to recall the many times a press release failed to produce humanitarian progress. They almost never recall the 1962 publicity in Paris about French torture, which caused significant change in French policy.)

After the Cold War the ICRC developed some internal procedures that helped insure at least consistency of approach, and perhaps certain standards of assertiveness, regarding detention conditions. Letters to detaining authorities by those carrying out detention visits had to be approved by superiors in sub-delegations and then delegations. Everything had to be written down and recorded. These procedures made it possible for still-higher superiors in Geneva to compare the situation under review with what was being done in other regions. Thus any deviance from normal procedures had to be justified in writing on grounds of local context. It would be difficult under these procedures for a delegate in the field to be lax about the follow-up to a detention visit. In this case it was a good idea to bureaucratize the Good Samaritan.[41] Especially on detention visits, the ICRC wanted to be a known and predictable actor. This would enhance its access to prisoners and its image of neutrality.

But the big issue was the dynamism of Geneva in using the factual material compiled by delegates in the field. Our case study of the fate of prisoners in the US "war" on terrorism suggested much reasonable debate about whether the ICRC had been too slow and cautious in pressing Washington to correct problems at Guantanamo and in Afghanistan. If the ICRC had been ultra-cautious in the past, then relying on such precedent

---

dogs to terrify suspects, or forcing them to be naked (75%), even if the prisoner was not cooperative; 93% approved of Red Cross visits; 77% approved of Red Cross family messages. Program on International Policy Attitudes, School of Public Affairs, University of Maryland, 22 July 2004, listserv@americans-world.org.

[41] Compare Tony Waters, *Bureaucratizing the Good Samaritan: The Limitations of Humanitarian Relief Operations* (Boulder: Westview Press, 2000), 49–50. An ICRC delegate in the Sudanese conflict supposedly refused to take on board an airplane a young girl needing medical attention because she was not war wounded. She fell outside the mandate of the ICRC, and its bureaucratic instructions to its delegates. But even in this case, the ICRC decision could be defended. ICRC delegates were not to dissipate their energies in matters beyond conflict. The ICRC was not supposed to be an all-purpose do-gooder and development or relief agency. Whether this meant a delegate should never do an occasional good deed beyond the official mandate of the organization is another matter. But the ICRC does indeed need a clear and limited focus, leading to consistent policies.

still today for standards about going public tended to elevate concern
for perfect neutrality over stopping detention abuses in the shortest time
possible. Serious questions remained about how much improvement was
enough, during what time frame, in justifying continued ICRC discretion.
Moreover, it was not adequate for ICRC officials to say they were prepared
to give interviews about detention in places like Washington, but the media
were not much interested. Advocacy groups like AI and HRW knew that
one had to be assertive in attracting the attention of the press and public
officials. This the cautious ICRC had trouble doing.

An ICRC official with a knack for turning a good phrase in English
once said that "we have a very low profile with the press and quite a high
profile with the prisoners, and that's the way it should be."[42] But that is
not the last word in the analysis of ICRC detention efforts.

In the current era it might not be wrong to surmise that the ICRC is
discreetly assertive in detention visits in the field, "quietly demanding" in
the words of one delegate,[43] trying to chip away at obstacles thrown up
by detaining authorities.[44] The 2003 ICRC report on Abu Ghraib prison
in Iraq and the follow-on summary report of February 2004 show this
"quietly demanding" record. Whether the Geneva headquarters waits too
long to try, and has a bias against, both vigorous private diplomacy at top
levels and public pressure is a lingering question of considerable importance. Only historians with better access to facts, for example, can judge
whether the ICRC was too cautious regarding the way it dealt with US
abuse of humanitarian standards, particularly between 2002 and 2004.[45]

---

[42] Boegli, "Red Cross Man."   [43] Mercier, *Crimes sans châtiment.*
[44] Does it indicate excessive deference that an ICRC delegate is rarely declared *persona non
grata* by public authorities because of pushing hard for attention to humanitarian standards. The fact that Francis Amar was kicked out of Thailand in the 1979–80 period for
defending the rights of refugees not to be sent back to a dangerous situation in Cambodia
would seem to reflect well on him and the ICRC. His departure also sent a signal to others
about the inhumane policies then pursued by the Thai government. But context matters.
It may be pointless, even counter-productive, persistently to challenge authorities, even
discreetly, over a lost cause. If Saddam Hussein in 1990 was not going to agree that Kuwait
was occupied territory, then perhaps it was better not to argue over legal status and just
ask for extension of traditional activity. Of course this soft pragmatic approach did not get
the ICRC into occupied Kuwait either. But having a delegate declared *persona non grata*
for persistent devotion to the Geneva Conventions was no doubt not going to accomplish
humanitarian objectives either, at least not in Kuwait in 1990. And in some contexts, if
ICRC delegates pressed hard for immediate improvements in conditions, prisoners might
be killed or future ICRC access denied.
[45] As these words are being written in the summer of 2004, the ICRC is publicly stressing
again that the United States is apparently operating a secret system of detention centers for
prisoners related to conflict, to which the ICRC is being given no notification or access.
The ICRC seems to be more assertive in the public domain on this issue than in the past.

Relief

As for modern relief protection, we know that sometimes – but not often – the ICRC will proceed with relief in cross-border operations where it appears the authorities are not in a position physically to block that effort. The organization sometimes informs authorities at a given point in time about what is transpiring but does not always ask for advance permission. We noted that the ICRC did this for a time in the Ethiopian conflict in the mid-1980s (where its trucks, not marked with any Red Cross or Red Crescent emblem, sometimes came under ineffective military attack) and on the Thai–Cambodian border also in the 1980s, starting in September 1979.

One can recall that around 1980 in Cambodia and on the Thai–Cambodian border the ICRC was generally viewed as more assertive than UNICEF in dealing with the obstacles to humanitarian relief created by various governments.[46]

But in general, given that those with guns control humanitarian relief, whether one speaks of Nigeria in 1967–70 or Bosnia in 1992–95, the ICRC could only provide the relief allowed by the fighting parties. Somalia in the 1990s was very different, constituting one of the few places where outside parties (the United States, mostly) were willing to deploy military force in the service of relatively disinterested and therefore mostly neutral relief – at least for a time. And in that case, as noted in chapter 4, the ICRC took the historic decision to operate in tandem with state armed protection, in part because the military force was initially directed against bandits and not against the leading clans vying for power. In that fundamental sense UNITAF, or Operation Restore Hope, was neutral, at least initially.

We also know that in El Salvador, when the governmental side carried out aerial attacks on civilians trying to obtain ICRC relief, the organization confirmed the attacks with Human Rights Watch, which then tried to pressure the government on the issue.[47]

If we look at ICRC relief after the Cold War, we find an organization always present for relief in conflicts, and arguably as good as or better than the other major relief agencies like UNHCR, UNICEF, WFP, Oxfam, and so on. This was demonstrated in chapter 3 with case studies of the Balkans, Somalia, and Rwanda. Significant is the fact that in Nepal in 2003, scene of a Maoist uprising, the ICRC did not rush in with

---

[46] William Shawcross, *The Quality of Mercy: Cambodia, Holocaust and Modern Conscience* (New York: Simon and Schuster, 1984).

[47] Aryeh Neier, *Taking Liberties: Four Decades in the Struggle for Rights* (New York: Public Affairs, 2003), 209.

relief, fearing it would create unnecessary dependency by undermining "existing coping mechanisms," which were providing economic security at the time.[48] With regard to relief, often the ICRC was in the very center of conflict and combat, more heroic leader than marginal social worker. True, the organization did not address the root causes of displacement and distress, but keeping alive 1.5 million Somalis was hardly marginal action.

Relations with the Movement

A highly fragmented Red Cross Movement has been a fact of life, if not from the very beginnings, then certainly from the time of the First World War. It was from the latter conflict that, as we noted, the ICRC emerged as an important actor in the field. Subsequently its quest for independent and neutral humanitarianism, as an operational matter, caused it to give priority to its own position rather than to tightly coordinated action with the National Societies. It is probable that a general Swiss inclination toward unilateralism affected ICRC perspectives.

The organization certainly disliked the creation of the Federation, then tried to keep the Federation at arm's length in ICRC activities. From time to time there was some real cooperation in the Movement, including between the ICRC and the Federation, as during World War II and to a lesser extent during the Vietnam war and then in the Balkan wars. But it was only after the Cold War that the ICRC, under the press of an expanding workload and more competition from other relief agencies, saw that it would need to draw more on the resources of the entire Movement if it was to survive as an important humanitarian actor in conflicts.

Ironically, by late 2003 the problem for the ICRC was no longer an assertive and encroaching Federation, but rather a weak Federation (badly damaged by the withholding of dues by the American Red Cross), and unable to coordinate its National Societies. In the US invasion and occupation of Iraq, various National Societies implemented their own plans, either driven by the need for visibility at home or pushed into independence by their governments. The result was little coordination with the ICRC, regardless of the 1997 Seville Agreement confirming an ICRC lead role for the Movement in armed conflicts and occupation. Other fragmenting factors were at work. After the end of major combat in

---

[48] ICRC press release no. 03/06, 13 January 2003, "Nepal: Conflict Area Assessed."

2003, several of the more active National Societies were impatient to act in Iraq. The ICRC, unfortunately quite correctly, viewed the security situation on the ground as inhospitable to major relief projects. Several of the National Societies did not share this view and regarded the ICRC as unnecessarily cautious. This particular point of friction within the Movement was resolved by the violent attack on ICRC headquarters in Baghdad in October 2003, which confirmed the accuracy of ICRC views.

Many National Societies much of the time still do not see themselves as particularly linked to armed conflict and IHL.[49] Caroline Morehead is right when she writes, "The Committee did make a fundamental error in bothering too little about the national societies."[50] Even before the 1975 Tansley Report documented the disarray within the Red Cross family, the ICRC had teamed with the Federation at the 1973 International Red Cross Conference to suggest that the two Geneva bodies should have the right to review the statutes of National Societies to see if, beyond the stage of recognition by the ICRC and admission to the Federation, these national bodies remained in compliance with the rules of the Movement. This initiative, predictably, drew some opposition from important National Societies. But the Conference adopted a watered-down version of the original proposal anyway. All of this amounted to not very much at first, other than comprising a toe-hold for Geneva to question certain policies of the national units.

The dilemmas of trying to ensure that National Societies respected Red Cross principles, like impartiality toward individuals in need, or independence from politics, are well demonstrated by events concerning the Republic of South Africa during the apartheid era.

When, in 1986, the International Red Cross Conference voted to suspend the South African government because of apartheid, the ICRC declined to participate in the Conference vote. It objected to the process, arguing that Conference rules provided no grounds for suspension,

---

[49] For a somewhat legalistic but still interesting focus on relations among units of the Movement, see Christophe Lanord, "The Legal Status of National Red Cross and Red Crescent Societies," *International Review of the Red Cross*, 840 (December 2000), 1053–78. Given that the author is a former legal advisor to the Federation, this is a candid treatment. See also in general Ian Smillie, ed., *Patronage or Partnership: Local Capacity Building in Humanitarian Crises* (Bloomfield, CT: Kumarian Press, 2001), although unfortunately it has little information about the Red Cross network. At the time of writing the ICRC is much more attentive to local capacity within the Red Cross Movement.

[50] Morehead, *Dunant's Dream*, 372.

and it feared a backlash against its field operations. The latter concern proved accurate, as Pretoria responded by suspending for a time ICRC access to the detainees then being visited. While visits were eventually resumed (Pretoria revoked its suspension after one month), this sequence confirmed for the ICRC the wisdom of its policy of not raising the issue of racism, and violation of the Red Cross principle of impartiality, by National Societies.

Red Cross actors are supposed to be strictly humanitarian, avoiding controversies that are political, religious, racial, and so on. But this distinction generates competing views. It often proves controversial to try to draw a clear and firm boundary between a humanitarian issue and a political, religious, or racial one. The treatment of black prisoners in white-ruled South Africa was both humanitarian and political, both humanitarian and racial. The best that can be said is that when the ICRC gets involved in political, religious, or racial controversies, it is to focus only on the humanitarian dimensions of those disputes.

But when the ICRC refused to participate in the vote in 1986 (the Federation abstained), this meant that, as has been historically the case in the Red Cross world, once again there was no authoritative ICRC review of the National Society. There were no sanctions for violating Red Cross principles about impartial humanitarian concern for all individuals regardless of race, gender, ethnicity, religion, and so on. Even short of gross violations of principle, mere incompetence has never triggered withdrawal of National Society bona fides either. The ICRC has never withdrawn recognition from any National Society. Neither the Federation, nor its predecessor, the League, has ever disbarred any national society.[51]

Today the ICRC and the Federation, in the light of various resolutions by the Red Cross Conference, have carried on their attempted review of National Societies through a joint ICRC–Federation Commission. The approach is legalistic, focusing on statutes and rules for recognition and admission, but the attempt is to provide a central

---

[51] Lanord, "Legal Status." The ICRC, cautious as ever, likes to raise the point of whether it has the legal authority to withdraw recognition, once granted. Neither its own Statutes nor Movement Statutes explicitly mention withdrawal of recognition. No doubt practice now weighs heavily on this matter.

    For one point of comparison, note that in the United States, while two-thirds of the Senate must give its advice and consent for ratification of a treaty, the courts have held that the President alone can terminate a treaty. The rights of the Senate in formulating treaty obligations are not the same as in terminating treaty obligations. Logical, parallel rights have been said not to exist.

review of National Society policies. Still, in keeping with Red Cross traditions, there is an effort to avoid naming and shaming – and hence to avoid embarrassing either the National Society or its "patron" government. In current times the ICRC stresses, ironically enough, "constructive engagement" when dealing with wayward National Societies – at least most of the time. That is to say, the organization tries to work with the Society to improve its performance and adherence to Red Cross norms, rather than engage in any rebuke.[52] Each year now, the ICRC spends something like $25 million on National Society Development.

This approach may have merit in general, since most governments will rise to the defense of "their" National Society. But the policy of constructive engagement would have been pointless with the German Red Cross in the 1930s, and it will be pointless in similar "hard" cases in the future. If the Iranian Red Crescent discriminates against Iranian Bihai, there is not much that the ICRC, the Federation, or the Red Cross Conference is going to do about it. If the Iraqi Red Crescent during the era of Saddam Hussein discriminated against various opponents of the regime, and failed to come to their aid, Red Cross bodies were not going to address that violation of Red Cross principles.

So the Movement is likely to remain fundamentally fragmented. Universal humanitarianism has yet to triumph over nationalism. At least the ICRC and Federation are no longer trying to pretend that the problem does not exist, and in the Red Cross world that is a step forward. There are also efforts to improve the workings of the 1997 Seville Agreement and especially to fine tune the focus on the ICRC as lead actor for the Red Cross in conflicts.

Organizational culture

According to Gil Loescher, a leading scholar on the subject, the UNHCR manifests a very conservative organizational culture, resistant to change and inhospitable to new ideas, showing disdain for the view of outsiders, and with arrogance at the top that at least sometimes shows insensitivity

---

[52] See *International Review of the Red Cross*, 851 (September 2003). See also *Red Cross Red Crescent*, 4 (2003), 10–11, where the Presidents of the ICRC and Federation comment on the Movement and the International Conference. It was in some ways remarkable that the Red Cross network was addressing openly the defects of these institutions, even if they were circumspect in comments about how to effectuate beneficial change. It was clear that ICRC President Kellenberger was in favor of dialogue rather than sanctions.

to persons of concern within the mandate of that public humanitarian agency.[53] Is the same true for the ICRC?

The dominant ICRC culture has indeed been primarily conservative in the sense that Edmund Burke used the term. The organization believes that history has proven the validity of its traditions. The ICRC is well aware that proceeding slowly and cautiously in a discreet way on the basis of state consent has brought it a unique position in international relations – a position that others like the Red Cross Federation or various private relief groups might like to emulate if not replace with their own. Why change, if past policies have allowed access to numerous victims over the years? This is one reason why the organization keeps meticulous records of detainees visited, tons of relief delivered, number of family messages transmitted, and so on. It makes for an impressive general picture, presumably confirming the validity of ICRC policies as traditionally practiced. But all of the statistics about the ICRC in World War II failed to address the question of the organization's assertiveness and wisdom in dealing with German and Japanese authorities in particular.

Historically the ICRC has been slow to embrace change. The organization shares at least some of the conservative characteristics of the UNHCR. We have already observed that the ICRC Assembly is not known for coopting advocates of revolutionary change into Committee membership.[54]

It took almost thirty-five years for Geneva to create a CEO, or Director-General with personal responsibility, to improve the effectiveness of the organization in daily humanitarian affairs. This step took from 1970 and the end of the Nigerian civil war to July 2002. There were a number of half-steps during this transition, charted in chapter 6. Along the way various persons urged rapid movement in this direction, from Jacques Freymond through Cornelio Sommaruga. The ICRC Assembly, whose role was being reduced, took its time.

On yet another subject, the Tansley Big Study of the 1970s told the ICRC of the need to "open the windows" and not be such a secretive organization. It took decades for the organization to implement these

---

[53] Loescher, *A Perilous Path*, chapter 10.

[54] We noted in passing in chapter 6 that Swiss public figures who are political mavericks and prone to criticize past Swiss public policies and leaders, like Jean Ziegler, are not elected to the ICRC Assembly. But then Ziegler's position in Swiss society was roughly analogous to Noam Chomsky's in the United States. Both were academics with some recognized expertise in their original field, but who then spoke out in provocative ways beyond their expertise. Ziegler was no more likely to be coopted into the ICRC than Chomsky to be elected into the leadership of the American Red Cross.

recommendations by consulting more with outside parties and increasing the transparency of the House in other ways. The organization resisted change, but finally embraced at least some change on openness and transparency.

It was the pressure of events linked to reviews of Switzerland and the Holocaust that caused the organization finally to open its archives to the public from 1990, even if under the forty-year non-access rule.[55] This forced the organization to deal more candidly with its history, as researchers wrote independent and analytical studies rather than hagiography. Also, it was in 1996 that the ICRC opened up *The International Review of the Red Cross*, under the editorship of Hans-Peter Gasser, to more interesting content. The *Review* had been a stodgy, boring compendium of Red Cross in-house matters and legalistic studies, along with such breathtaking tidbits as which dignitary came to visit headquarters. Under Gasser's initiative, which was not mandated from the top but was supported by the top, the *Review* started to publish a wide range of views on various aspects of humanitarian affairs – even including from time to time some criticism of the organization.

The ICRC's annual report for 2002 noted, on the basis of a study by some outsiders, that the ICRC still faced many issues about its communication policy, and that its visibility in international relations was still problematic.[56] So again, as on the question of openness and transparency, the organization only moved with deliberate speed, if speed it was. As on other changes noted above, the ICRC finally moved to implement new policies when the realities of its environment left it little choice but to change if it was to remain important for humanitarianism in conflicts. At the end of chapter 6, using a Swiss source, we noted how the Swiss governing class, which overlaps with the ICRC Assembly, was risk averse.

Clearly, there are some similarities between ICRC and UNHCR organizational cultures, particularly in terms of conservatism and reluctance to take outsiders fully seriously.

While there is some arrogance at the top of the ICRC, which contributes to some friction with staff, it cannot be said that in general the organization is insensitive either to its delegates in the field or to the needs of those who benefit from its action. In the period 1996–2002 the ICRC undertook

---

[55] Interestingly, this historic decision by the Assembly was taken with almost no controversy or opposition. Apparently only one member of the Assembly objected to the policy adopted.

[56] ICRC, *Annual Report 2002* (Geneva: ICRC, 2003), 11–13.

the "Avenir" process, an effort to review its mandate, strategy, and tactics. Not surprisingly, it reaffirmed much in its basic mandate. Here we should note that it involved all levels of the House in its review, and it did prove open to a free discussion of many tactics.[57] Moreover, its budget process is a bottom-up process, starting with reports of sub-delegations and del-egations in the field. Each year this budget process generates something like 5,000–6,000 pages of documents. If contemplating a suspension of its detention visits, the organization usually consults with the detainees involved. When making tough decisions in the Balkans in the 1990s, it was aware that local civilians wanted to be moved out of harm's way even if that contributed to ethnic cleansing. Its project on "People in War" at the turn of the current century was designed to let war victims speak their views. Its project on "Women Facing War" (2001) and its manual on addressing the needs of *Women Affected by Armed Conflict* (2004) cer-tainly showed some sensitivity to the special plight of women and girls.[58] The doctrine of the House is certainly to "stay close" to the needs and views of the victims.

In general the organizational culture of the ICRC was better than the UNHCR. The organization created a new position to listen better to non-western opinion, and filled it with a woman interested in giving more attention to gender issues.[59] The organization also created an office for a female "political" advisor in the office of the Director-General.

Final thoughts

The ICRC at the start of the twenty-first century is decidedly more pro-fessional and less amateurish than ever before in its long history. It is more thoughtful about maximizing as much as possible its independence, neutrality, and impartiality. It has set in place performance-based evalua-tions to try to capture – measure if you like – the substance of its human-itarianism.[60] But many policy choices require contextual judgment, not quantified reports and guidelines.

---

[57] See further David P. Forsythe, "1949 and 1999: Making the Geneva Conventions Relevant after the Cold War," *International Review of the Red Cross*, 834 (June 1999), 265–76.

[58] Recall the article above by Harroff-Tavel, "L'action," regarding the ICRC's increased atten-tion to the long-term mental health of women in post-conflict situations.

[59] Harroff-Tavel, "L'action."

[60] See further A. Wood, R. Apthorpe, and J. Borton, eds., *Evaluating International Human-itarian Action* (London and New York: Zed Books, 2001), with a foreword by the ICRC's Wayne MacDonald.

One of the keys to this evolution is the necessity for the organization to look candidly at its past. It can no longer control what is known about the reality of its involvement with the world. In the past one knew mostly what ICRC publications and statements presented. This carefully nurtured hagiography was actually detrimental to the ICRC because it allowed the organization to cover-up various mistakes, lethargies, departures from neutrality, and so on. The hagiography allowed the ICRC to avoid taking a hard look at its self-proclaimed independence, neutrality, impartiality, and effectiveness.

One cannot stress too much how important it was in the 1970s for Donald Tansley to put some distasteful facts in the public arena, to show how dysfunctional ICRC hyper-secrecy and unilateralism was, to show how the Red Cross Movement was basically a dysfunctional family. Once he presented the Final Report of his "Big Study," the ICRC could not really ignore his findings and still retain a leadership position in the Movement. In 2004, almost thirty years after the Tansley Report, the ICRC Director-General wrote that the Tansley Report provided a useful benchmark for evaluating the organization and its changes.[61]

One also cannot stress too much how important it was for the ICRC itself to respond to renewed interest in the events of the 1930s and 1940s by opening up its archives to independent and serious research. Once those archives were opened in the 1990s, historians like John F. Hutchinson and journalists like Caroline Morehead raised serious questions about past events. No doubt high ICRC officials were too busy with pressing daily issues to read such works. But eventually the greater access to information would compel the ICRC to re-examine all sorts of questions.[62] Were close relations with the Swiss Confederation an asset or a liability? Had the ICRC in the past been much less independent, neutral, and impartial than widely

---

[61] Andrew Gnädiner and Wayne MacDonald, "The ICRC in a Changing World: Assessments, Ambitions and Priorities," in Liesbeth Lijnzaad, et al., eds., Making the Voice of Humanity Heard (Dordrecht: Brill, for Martinus Nijhoff, 2004).

[62] It is still the case that few ICRC officials at any level carefully read outside publications, or even The International Review of the Red Cross. Presidents Kellenberger and Sommaruga were more interested in operations than "doctrine." Lower-level officials, while impressive in intellect and historical knowledge, lack the time to read broadly, as is true of most governmental officials with operational responsibility. Hence publications by independent authors rarely get read, whether the author might be Hutchinson, Morehead, Forsythe, or whoever. It could be interesting for some part of the ICRC to compile a summary of the critiques of the organization by outside observers, indicating points of similarity and difference. Such a study might feed into future considerations – viz., things to emulate or avoid, policy to keep or reevaluate.

thought, or were there serious shortcomings that needed to be guarded against in the future? Was there reason to think that an integrated Red Cross Movement might offer more advantages than heretofore perceived, rather than just liabilities and threats, for humanitarian protection as led by the ICRC?

Since about 1970 the ICRC has increasingly grappled seriously with these and other questions. The spotlight of media coverage, from the Nigerian civil war through the latest war, complex emergency, and failed state, has made its contribution to this tougher thinking. Likewise, competition from other public and private actors, whether Joint Church Aid in Nigeria, Doctors Without Borders, the UNHCR and UNICEF, and so on, has compelled the ICRC to justify with facts its claim to be an important actor in humanitarian crises. Beyond emergency relief, even with regard to detention visits, the ICRC has to address carefully its role in comparison with European and UN agencies that are active in this area now. Various sectors of the ICRC did not always welcome competition to its role on detention, and were sometimes reluctant to admit that others could be responsible and competent with regard to detention visits.[63] But change did occur. Having Amnesty International and Human Rights Watch focus on humanitarian issues as well as human rights meant that the ICRC, as well as states, were scrutinized.

The results of a rather painful quarter of a century since about the end of the Nigerian war have been, on balance, positive. A more serious look at its past, a more searching spotlight by the media, more competition and scrutiny from other actors in international relations, have produced a better ICRC.

For example, the way the organization produces its budget projections for the following year is so thorough and impressive that it really constitutes an early warning system for humanitarian crises. Delegates in the field make a careful study of political context, which leads to predictions about refugee flows, displaced persons, scope of "political" detention, likelihood of major armed conflict, and so on. This information is then collated and reviewed at the Geneva headquarters, adjusted according to a Genevan perspective, and then fed into the international community in various ways. A close look at this process early in the twenty-first century confirmed that the delegates in the field were extremely well informed

---

[63] On this point see Hans-Peter Gasser, "The International Committee of the Red Cross," in Jurg Martin Gabriel and Thomas Fisher, eds., *Swiss Foreign Policy in a Changing World* (London: Palgrave, 2003).

about "political" trends. Alert diplomats in Geneva and elsewhere paid careful attention to these ICRC budgetary reports as an early warning indicator.

The ICRC might be neutral in the military struggles and strategic maneuvers and partisan competitions by "political" actors, but the organization paid great attention to them – and with much sophistication. Senior ICRC delegates in the field, who later became key officials in Geneva on the professional side of the House, were as "politically" astute as any political officer in any western embassy.

Crisis?

It has been said that "humanitarianism" is in crisis.[64] If one focuses on the ICRC in international humanitarian affairs, this crisis can be overstated. One component of the crisis is said to be a false sense of optimism on the part of humanitarian relief actors about what they can accomplish. But from Gustave Moynier to Jacob Kellenberger, the ICRC has been skeptical of states and mindful of the weakness of humanitarian actors. For example, Moynier in 1906 and Kellenberger in 2002 were skeptical about calling a new diplomatic conference to legislate more humanitarian law, fearing that states would seize the opportunity to reduce – not enlarge – humanitarian legal protections. For the same reasons, at the outset of the movement to add two new Protocols to IHL in the 1970s, the ICRC was suspicious of governmental motivation.[65] Beyond legal development efforts, ICRC delegates in the Balkans were certainly all too aware of how little power they had to affect the root causes of ethnic cleansing, crimes against humanity, and genocide. The ICRC has not been one to get caught up in Pollyannaish views of new world orders and dramatic improvements in human nature.

If part of the modern crisis of humanitarianism stems from discovery of the "political" side effects of humanitarian action, then the ICRC has long been aware of this dilemma and has long based its policy calculations precisely on wrestling with this problem. In Greece in the 1960s, as

---

[64] Rieff, *A Bed for the Night*. See also Michael Barnett, "What Is the Future of Humanitarianism," *Global Governance*, 9 (2003), 401–16. And Gil Loescher, "An Idea Lost in the Rubble," *New York Times*, 20 August 2004, A25.

[65] If one reads carefully 1977 Protocol II, Article 18, paragraph 2, it might be read as restricting the diplomacy of the ICRC compared to 1949 Common Article 3 for situations of internal war. Fortunately, in practice, reality may not have been much affected by such legal comparisons.

shown explicitly in chapter 2, the ICRC was aware that its presence for detention visits contributed to the legitimacy of the military government; the organization therefore satisfied itself that its defense of prisoners was vigorous enough to justify a continued presence in country. That defense was also vigorous enough for the government to terminate the organization's presence.

In Ethiopia in 1986, as noted, the ICRC refused to participate in governmental schemes for relocating civilians, believing that its contributions to the humanitarian needs of those civilians was not commensurate with the contribution it would necessarily provide to the strategic position of the government in its conflict with rebel/secessionist forces. The ICRC knows well that humanitarian action can have "political" consequences.

The ICRC has long been aware of the "difficult choices and moral quandaries"[66] inherent in much humanitarian work. The Balkan wars and other conflicts after about 1990 may have brought these difficult choices and moral quandaries back to center stage, but they certainly did not push the ICRC into a "twilight of hopelessness."[67] Even when intentional and deadly attacks, and other misfortunes like kidnappings, were visited upon ICRC delegates in the field, in Burundi, Chechnya, Democratic Republic of the Congo, Iraq, Somalia, and so on, the ICRC moved to a neighboring area and continued with both relief and detention visits to the original country, to the extent possible.

There *was* a serious problem for the ICRC in the sense that its emblem was not respected in many places, and that its humanitarian space in the midst of conflict often shrank to the point of disappearance. But this was because of the attitudes of others, their tendency toward total war, not because of the organization's naïve optimism. There *was* another serious problem in that patterns of conflict in the twenty-first century left the ICRC wondering who the fighting parties really were, and how to locate them. In Iraq in 2003, or Afghanistan in the same era, the ICRC did not know exactly with whom it should have dialogue in order to stop attacks on its personnel and facilities. In trying to deal with representatives of Al Qaeda and other amorphous networks, it was difficult to know who they were and where they were, in order to try to convince them of ICRC neutrality. Even in complicated situations like the Lebanese civil war, the situation had been easier.

For the ICRC early in the twenty-first century, the world was a lot different than desired, but on balance not all that different from past worlds

---

[66] Barnett, "What Is the Future of Humanitarianism," 406.   [67] *Ibid.*, 410.

already encountered. Was Russia in Chechnya all that different from Imperial Japan in China? Was Milosovic in Yugoslavia all that different from Mussolini in Abyssinia? Were the Americans, in their "war" on terrorism after 2001, totally different from the French when dealing with "Algerian terrorism" during 1954 to 1962? In the Geneva press of the 1970s, one could find high ICRC officials lamenting the total war that was practiced by all sorts of irregular fighters, not to mention the weaknesses of IHL in Southeast Asia in particular.[68] As ICRC President Kellenberger said in an interview in 2004, the problem of getting humanitarian restraints on total war thinking was an old problem, even if there were some new and "dramatic dimensions" to this old problem after 11 September 2001.[69]

If there was a profound crisis in humanitarianism circa 2005, it was in the eyes more of glib commentators and naïve relief workers than of in the experienced officials of the ICRC. The latter might have to take exceptional measures for physical security, or work harder at establishing a dialogue that could produce real security. The ICRC, however, doggedly continued with its strange but impressive combination of devotion to the humanitarian cause, on the basis of the neutral Red Cross model, mixed with appreciation of how limited was its contribution to humanity when confronting monstrous evil.

---

[68] André Naef, "Le CICR a-t-il encore un rôle à jouer dans une période de changements révolutionnaires?," *Tribune de Gèneve*, 9 May 1976, 2, based on interviews with Jacques Freymond and others.

[69] Vincent Bourquin, *Tribune de Genève*, 14 February 2004, downloaded from the Internet, no page number.

Annexe A
The ICRC and the Red Cross movement

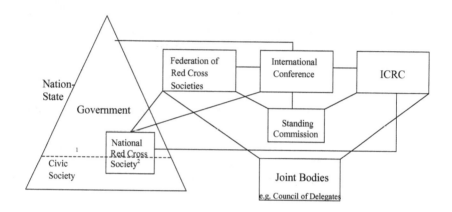

[1]The location of this line will vary, depending on whether the government is limited or totalitarian.
[2]The Red Cross or Red Crescent Society may be more or less within the governmental sector, varying with each case.

Adapted from David P. Forsythe, *Humanitarian Politics: The International Committee of the Red Cross*, (Baltimore: Johns Hopkins University Press, 1977), and from David P. Forsythe, "The Red Cross as Transnational Movement: Conserving and Changing the Nation-State System," *International Organization*, 30, no. 4 (Fall 1976), 607–31.

Annexe B
The ICRC and selected private relief agencies

	ICRC	CARE	World Vision	Oxfam	Doctors Without Borders
Created	1863	1945	1950	1942	1971
Headquarters	Geneva	Brussels (International Secretariat)	Seattle	Oxford (International Secretariat)	Brussels (International office)
Main activity	Protection of human dignity in conflicts	Emergency relief in developing countries	Child-focused emergency relief in disasters and armed conflict	General emergency relief and development	Emergency medical assistance and advocacy
Focus at start	War wounded	Food aid for Europe after WWII	Care for orphans in Asia	Famine in Greece during WWII	Same as main activity
Focus today	All victims of conflicts	General emergency aid	Child-focused emergency relief in disasters and armed conflict	Hunger and poverty in developing countries	Same as main activity
National influence at start	Swiss	American (began as cooperation among 22 US relief orgs.)	American	British	French
National influence today	Swiss at top, international staff	12 member-state organizations	Partnership of 7 National Offices	12 affiliate organizations	Confederation of 18 national sections
Accountability	Private committee, all Swiss (not more than 25 persons)	International Board of Directors (1 member from each state, plus chairperson and CEO)	International Board of Directors (24 members from 19 countries, 5 American members)	International Board of Trustees (members from affiliate orgs. w/ Executive Director)	International Board of Directors
Professional staff	2,000	N/A	N/A	N/A	Abot 1,000
Status	Private, but recognized in international law	Secular NGO	Faith-based NGO	Secular NGO	Secular NGO
Funding sources	80–85% governmental donations	(CARE USA) 67% governmental donations, 33% private donations	80% private/corporate donors, 20% government donations & investment income	N/A	80% private individual donations, 20% government/corporate
Annual Budget (2002)	Abot $600m	(CARE USA) abot $420m	about $820m (excludes gifts-in-kind)	abot $390m	abot $400m

Annexe C
The ICRC: one of the Big Four relief agencies

	ICRC	UNHCR	UNICEF	WFP
Created	1863	1950	1946	1963
Headquarters	Geneva	Geneva	New York	Rome
Main activity	Protection of human dignity in conflicts	Oversee and service rights of refugees	Advance child and maternal welfare in developing countries	Provide food aid and work for hunger prevention
Focus at start	Tending to war wounded	Diplomatic and legal advocacy for refugees	Aiding children after WWII	Providing food aid
Focus today	All victims of conflicts	Refugees and internally displaced persons	Women and children in need	Food aid provision and food hunger prevention
Accountability	Own private committee, all Swiss	UN General Assembly	UN General Assembly	UN General Assembly
Staff (2002)	2,000	5,245	6,000	2,570
Status	Private agency, but recognized in international law	Intergovernmental agency	Intergovernmental agency	Intergovernmental agency
Funding sources	80–85% governmental donations	About 95% governmental donations	About 65% governmental and IGO donations, 35% private sector and individuals	About 90% governmental and IGO donations
Annual budget (2002)	About $600m	About $880m	About $1.2b	About $1.7b

Annexe D
The ICRC and selected advocacy groups

(Some leading private groups, based in the west, concerned for victims of armed conflicts, complex emergencies, and domestic troubles, and victims of human rights violations)

AI = Amnesty International; HRW = Human Rights Watch

	ICRC	AI	HRW
Created	1863	1961	1978
National influence at start	Swiss	British	American
National influence at top today	Swiss	International	American
Focus at start	War wounded	Political prisoners	European communism
Focus today	Human dignity In conflicts	All human rights	All human rights
Mass membership?	No[1]	Yes	No
Professional staff	2000	350[2]	190
Government funds	Yes (85%)	no	no
Annual budget	$600m	$32.5m	$19.5m
Diplomatic style	discretion	publicity	publicity
Main activity	protective services, develop law	advocacy	advocacy
Status/character	unique	NGO	NGO

1. Loosely linked to National Red Cross and Red Crescent Societies which today number more than 180; these National Societies are mass membership organizations.
2. London Secretariat only; in addition, there is staff in the national offices of AI. AI has more than fifty-five such offices.

Annexe E
The ICRC organizational chart

INTERNATIONAL COMMITTEE OF THE RED CROSS

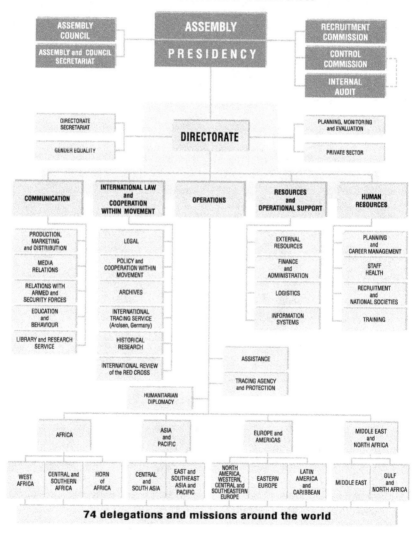

BIBLIOGRAPHY

Primary sources: reports, statements, archives, court cases

"*Bergier Report*": *Switzerland and Refugees in the Nazi Era*. Switzerland – Second World War. Berne: Independent Commission of Experts, 1999.

Code of Conduct for the International Red Cross and Crescent Movement and Non-Governmental Organisations (NGOs) in Disaster Relief. Geneva: Red Cross, 1993.

"*Fay Report*": *AR 15-6 Investigation of the Abu Ghraib Prison and 205th Military Intelligence Brigade*, MG George R. Fay, LTG Anthony R. Jones, http://news.findlaw.com/hdocs/docs/dod/fay82504rpt.pdf.

"Dissemination: Spreading Knowledge of Humanitarian Rules," Special Issue of *International Review of the Red Cross*, 319 (July–August 1997), 353–454.

General Comment 29, States of Emergency (article 4), UN Doc. Human Rights Committee, United Nations. CCPR/C/21/Rev.1/Add.11, 2001.

Human Rights Watch. *Uncertain Refuge: International Failures to Protect Refugees*. New York: Human Rights Watch, 1997.

"Prisoner Abuse: What About the Other Secret U.S. Prisons?" http://hrw.org.english/docs/2004/05/04/usint8542.htm.

"Afghanistan: Abuses by U.S. Forces," March 8, 2004, internet press release, referring to the longer report, *Enduring Freedom: Abuses by U.S. Forces in Afghanistan*.

"U.S. Investigate Civilian Deaths in Iraq Military Operations," hrw-news@topica.email-publisher.com, 18 June 2004.

Humanitarian Assistance in Conflict. Report prepared for the Norwegian Ministry of Foreign Affairs. Bergen, Norway: Chr. Michelsen Institute, 1997.

ICRC, *Rapport général du Comité International de la Croix-Rouge sur son activité de 1912 à 1920*. Geneva: ICRC, 1921.

Le conflit italo-éthiopien et la Croix-Rouge: rapport du Comité International de la Croix-Rouge. Geneva: ICRC, 1936.

Report of the International Committee of the Red Cross on Its Activities during the Second World War (3 vols. and annexes). Geneva: ICRC, 1948.

Le Comité International de la Croix-Rouge et le conflit de Corée, 2 vols. Geneva: ICRC, 1952.

Report on Relief Action in Hungary, October 1956–June 1957. Geneva: ICRC, 1957.

The ICRC and the Yemen Conflict. Geneva: ICRC, 1964.

Manuel du Delegue, 2nd edn. Geneva: ICRC, 1972.

Inter Arma Caritas: The Work of the International Committee of the Red Cross during the Second World War, 2nd edn, Geneva: ICRC, 1973. Original French edn 1947.

Documents Relating to the Work of the International Committee of the Red Cross for the Benefit of Civilian Detainees in German Concentration Camps between 1939 and 1945. Geneva: ICRC, 1975.

(and League). *The ICRC, the League, and the Tansley Report.* Geneva: ICRC and League, 1977.

Kampuchea, Back from the Brink. Geneva: ICRC, 1981.

Five Years of Activity 1981–1985. Geneva: ICRC, 1986.

The Gulf 1990–1991. Geneva: ICRC, 1991.

Annual Report. Various years.

"Human Rights and the ICRC: International Humanitarian Law." ICRC Home-page, 1 December 1993, www.icrc.org.

International Red Cross Handbook. Geneva: ICRC, 1994.

"What Treaties Make Up International Humanitarian Law?" Humanitarian Law, Humanitarian Law in Brief, 1999, ICRC Homepage, www.icrc.org.

ICRC Archives. CR 224, 13 May 1938, "Active Neutrality of Switzerland."

"General Correspondence with the Swiss Foreign Ministry," 1939–41, Box G.4, at 256.

Box G.3/12, G.3/13, No. 76 bis, 12 April 1940.

Box G.85/43–127, 23 August 1940.

Assembly meetings, 1942–1947, vol. 18, organized by dates of meetings; sup-plemented by other archival sources such as staff PTT consultations with Assembly members regarding a public protest, found in G.85/127, CR 73/8–/24.

Procès-verbal of Assembly Meetings, 1942–1947, vol. 18, PV 1, 19 January 1942.

Procès-verbal of Assembly meetings, 1942–1947, vol. 18, PV/2, 14 April 1942.

Note de dossier, 21 and 25 June 1943.

Box G.23, 20 February 1945.

InterAction. "Report of the Task Force on Protection from Sexual Exploitation and Abuse in Humanitarian Crises and Plan of Action," 20 August 2002, www.interaction.org.

International Court of Justice, advisory opinion about nuclear weapons, contain-ing a view on the relationship between human rights law and international humanitarian law: *Legality of the Threat or Use of Nuclear Weapons,* Advisory Opinion, 8 July 1996, para. 25.

Advisory opinion about Israeli Security Wall: "Legal Consequences of the Construction of a Wall in the Occupied Palestinian Territory," General List No. 31, 9 July 2004, www.icj-cij.org/icgwww.idocket/imwp/imwpframe.htm.

International Criminal Court for Yugoslavia, case concerning, in passing, definition of international humanitarian law: *Prosecutor v. Tadic*, Case No. IT-94-1-AR72, Decision on the Defence Motion for Interlocutory Appeal on Jurisdiction, 2 October 1995.

Case concerning ICRC refusal to provide a witness: *Prosecutor v. Simic et. al.*, Case No. IT-95-9-PT, Decision on the Prosecution Motion under Rule 73 for a Ruling Concerning the Testimony of a Witness, 27 July 1999.

Case concerning whether journalists can be compelled to testify: *Prosecutor v. Radoslav Brdjanin and Momir Talic*, Case No. IT-99-36-AR73.9, Decision on Interlocutory Appeal of Appeals Chamber on "Motion to Appeal the Trial Chamber's Decision on Motion on Behalf of Jonathan Randal to Set Aside Confidential Subpoena to Give Evidence," 11 December 2002.

Case concerning conviction for genocide at Srebrenica: *Prosecutor v. Krstic*, Case No. IT-98-33-A, Judgment, 19 April 2004.

Joint Evaluation of Emergency Assistance to Rwanda. *The International Response to Conflict and Genocide: Lessons from the Rwanda Experience* (5 vols.). Copenhagen: Steering Committee, 1996.

Kellenberger, Jacob. "Statement to the UN Human Rights Commission." ICRC Homepage, 28 March 2002, www.icrc.org.

Minear, Larry and Peter Walker, "The Strategy for the Red Cross and Red Crescent Movement: A Review of the Evolving Partnership," unpublished, 5 June 2003, Tufts University, New Medford, MA, commissioned by the Movement.

Office of the United Nations High Commissioner for Human Rights. *Training Manual on Human Rights Monitoring*, Professional Training Series No. 7. Geneva: United Nations, 2001.

Pitteloud, Jean-François, ed. *Procès-verbaux des séances du Comité International de la Croix-Rouge: 17 février 1863–28 août 1914*. Geneva: Henry Dunant Society and International Committee of the Red Cross, 1999.

The Responsibility to Protect: Report of the International Commission on Intervention and State Sovereignty. Ottawa: International Development Research Centre, 2001.

"*Schlesinger Report*": *Final Report of the Independent Panel to Review DoD Detention Operations*, August 2004, http://news.findlaw.com/nytimes/docs/dod/abughraibrpt.pdf.

Seville Agreement of 1997. Adopted by the Red Cross and Red Crescent Council of Delegates. Reprinted in *International Review of the Red Cross*, 322 (March 1998), 159–76.

"*Taguba Report.*" *On Treatment of Abu Ghraib Prisoners in Iraq: Article 15-6 Investigation of the 800th Military Police Brigade*, http: //news.findlaw.com/hdocs/doc/iraq/tagubarpt.html.

UN War Crimes Commission, *Law Reports of Trials of War Criminals: United Nations War Crimes Commission*. Buffalo, NY: William S. Hein and Co., 199.

UNHCR, "Note for Implementing and Operational Partners by UNHCR and Save the Children-UK on Sexual Violence and Exploitation," 26 February 2002, www.reliefweb.

US court case dealing with whether those in the Secret Service charged with protecting the President can be compelled to testify in judicial proceedings: *In re Sealed* (148 F.3d 1073 D.C. Cir., 1998)

US court cases dealing with detention of alleged "terrorists:" 542 U.S. *Hamdi v. Rumsfeld* 124 S. Ct. 2633, 72 USLW 4607 (2004); 542 U.S. *Rasul v. Bush* 124 S. Ct. 2686, 72 USLW 4596 (2004).

Winning the Human Race? The Report of the Independent Commission on International Humanitarian Issues. London: Zed Books, 1988.

Secondary sources

Abi-Saab, Georges. "The Specificities of Humanitarian Law," in Christophe Swinarski, ed., *Studies and Essays on International Humanitarian Law and Red Cross Principles.* Dordrecht: Martinus Nijhoff Publishers, 1984, 193–211.

Anderson, Mary. *Do No Harm: How Aid Can Support Peace – or War.* Boulder: Lynne Rienner, 1999.

An-Na'im, Abdullahi A. "The Legal Protection of Human Rights in Africa: How To Do More with Less," in Austin Sarat and Thomas R. Kearns, eds., *Human Rights: Concepts, Contests, Contingencies.* Ann Arbor: University of Michigan Press, 2001.

Arsenijevic, Drago. *Otages volontaires des SS.* Paris: Editions France Empire, 1974, 1984.

Balmer, Dres. *L'heure de cuivre.* Lausanne: Editions d'En Bas, 1984.

Barnett, Michael. *Eyewitness to a Genocide: The United Nations and Rwanda.* Ithaca: Cornell University Press, 2002.

"What Is The Future of Humanitarianism," *Global Governance*, 9 (2003), 401–6.

Beetham, David, ed. *Politics and Human Rights.* London: Blackwell, 1996.

Ben-Tov, Arieh. *Facing the Holocaust in Budapest.* Geneva: Henry Dunant Institute, 1988.

Benvenisti, Eyal. *The International Law of Occupation.* Princeton: Princeton University Press, 2004.

Bergier, Jean-François. *L'action du Comité International de la Croix-Rouge en Indochine (1946–1954).* Montreux: Editions Corbaz, 1982.

The Humanitarian Diplomacy of the ICRC and the Conflict in Croatia (1991–1992). Geneva: ICRC, 1995.

Bernadotte, Folke. *Instead of Arms.* London: Hodder and Stoughton, 1949.

Berry, Charles O. *War and the Red Cross: The Unspoken Mission.* New York: St. Martin's Press, 1997.

Berry, John A. and Carol Pott Berry, eds. *Genocide in Rwanda: A Collective Memory.* Washington, DC: Howard University Press, 1994.

Beschloss, Michael. *The Conquerors: Roosevelt, Truman and the Destruction of Hitler's Germany, 1941–1945.* New York: Simon and Schuster, 2002.

Best, Geoffrey. *Humanity in Warfare: The Modern History of the International Law of Armed Conflicts.* London: Methuen, 1983.

"Making the Geneva Conventions of 1949: The View from Whitehall," in Christophe Swinarski, ed., *Studies and Essays on International Humanitarian Law and Red Cross Principles.* Dordrecht: Martinus Nijhoff Publishers, 1984, 5–17.

War and Law since 1945. Oxford: Oxford University Press, 1994. Paperback edn 1997.

Blondel, Jean-Luc. "Rôle du CICR en matière de prévention de conflits armés: possibilités d'action et limites," *International Review of the Red Cross,* 844 (December 2001), 923–46.

Boissier, Pierre. *Histoire du Comité International de la Croix-Rouge: de Solferino à Tsoushima.* Paris: Plon, 1963.

"Henry Dunant," *International Review of the Red Cross,* 161 (August 1974), 395–419.

Boudreaux, Lise. "The Role of the International Committee of the Red Cross," in John A. Berry and Carol Pott Berry, eds., *Genocide in Rwanda: A Collective Memory.* Washington, DC: Howard University Press, 1999, 161–4.

Bowden, Mark. "The Dark Art of Interrogation," *Atlantic Monthly* (October 2003), 51–76.

Browning, Christopher R. *The Origins of the Final Solution: The Evolution of Nazi Jewish Policy, September 1939–March 1942.* Lincoln: University of Nebraska Press, 2004.

Bugnion, François. *L'emblème de la Croix-Rouge: aperçu historique* (Geneva: CICR, 1977).

Le Comité International de la Croix-Rouge et la protection des victimes de la guerre. Geneva: CICR, 1994. Revised French edition, 2000. English edition, 2003.

"Vers une solution globale de la question d'emblème," *International Review of the Red Cross,* 838 (June 2000), 427–65.

"Droit de Genève et droit de la Haye," *International Review of the Red Cross,* 844 (December 2001), 901–22.

"The Standing Commission of the Red Cross and Red Crescent: Its Origins, Role and Prospects for the Future," in Liesbeth Lignzaad *et al.,* eds., *Making the Voice of Humanity Heard: Essays on Humanitarian Assistance and International Humanitarian Law in Honour of HRH Princess Margriet of the Netherlands.* Leiden and Boston: Martinus Nijhoff Publishers, 2004, 41–59.

"The International Committee of the Red Cross and the Development of International Humanitarian Law," *Chicago Journal of International Law*, 5 no. 1 (Summer 2004).

Burgers, Jan Herman. "The Road to San Francisco: The Revival of the Human Rights Idea in the Twentieth Century," *Human Rights Quarterly*, 14 no. 4 (November 1992), 447–77.

Cahill, Kevin M., ed. *A Framework for Survival: Health, Human Rights, and Humanitarian Assistance in Conflicts and Disasters.* New York: Basic Books, for the Council on Foreign Relations, 1993.

    ed. *Basics of International Humanitarian Missions.* New York: Fordham, 2003.

Caratsch, Claudio. "Humanitarian Design and Political Interference: Red Cross Work in the Post-Cold War Period," *International Relations*, 11 (April 1993), 301–13.

Cardia, Isabelle Voneche. *Hungarian October.* Geneva: ICRC, 1999.

    "Les relations entre le Comité International de la Croix-Rouge et la Confédération Helvétique durant la Second Guerre Mondiale," unpublished paper, February 2000, read by permission.

Cassese, Antonio. *International Law.* Oxford: Oxford University Press, 2001.

Clark, Ann Marie. *Diplomacy of Conscience: Amnesty International and Changing Human Rights Norms.* Princeton: Princeton University Press, 2001.

Clark, Jeffrey. "Somalia," in Lori Fisler Damrosch, ed., *Enforcing Restraint: Collective Intervention in Internal Conflicts.* New York: Council on Foreign Relations, 1993, 205–40.

Clark, Roger S. and Madeleine Sann, eds. *The Prosecution of International Crimes.* New Brunswick: Transaction Books, 1995.

Clark, Wesley. *Waging Modern War: Bosnia, Kosovo, and the Future of Conflict.* New York: Public Affairs Press, 2002.

Collart, Yves. "L'affaire Grimm–Hoffmann et l'entrée de Gustave Ador au Conseil Fédéral," in Roger Durand, eds., *Gustave Ador: 58 ans d'engagement politique et humanitaire.* Geneva: Fondation Gustave Ador, 1996, 27–94.

Commanger, Henry Steele. *Churchill's History of the English-Speaking Peoples.* New York: Barnes and Noble, 1955, 1957.

Cornwell, John. *Hitler's Pope: The Secret History of Pius XII.* New York: Viking, 1999.

Coser, Lewis A. *Functions of Social Conflict.* Glencoe, IL: Free Press, 1964.

Coursier, Henri. *La Croix-Rouge Internationale.* Paris: Presses Universitaires de France, 1962.

Cowell, Alan. "Switzerland's Wartime Blood Money," *Foreign Policy*, 107 (Summer 1997), 132–44.

Cutts, Mark. *The Humanitarian Operation in Bosnia, 1992–1995: Dilemmas of Negotiating Humanitarian Access.* Geneva: UNHCR, New Issues in Refugee Research. Working Paper No. 8, May, 1999.

Damrosch, Lori Fisler, ed. *Enforcing Restraint: Collective Intervention in Internal Conflicts.* New York: Council on Foreign Relations, 1993.

Delorenzi, Simone. *ICRC Policy since the End of the Cold War.* Geneva: ICRC, 1999.

de Reynier, Jacques. *1948: à Jerusalem.* Neuchâtel: Editions de la Baconnière, 1969.

de St. Jorre, John. *The Nigerian Civil War.* London: Hodder and Stoughton, 1972.

de Waal, Alex, and Rakiya Omaar. *Humanitarianism Unbound? Current Dilemmas Facing Multi-Mandate Relief Operations in Political Emergencies.* London: African Rights, 1994.

Doswald-Beck, Louise and Sylvain Vite. "International Humanitarian Law and Human Rights Law," *International Review of the Red Cross,* no. 293 (April 1993), 94–119.

Doswald-Beck, Louise, *et al.*, eds. *Customary International Humanitarian Law: Rules.* Cambridge: Cambridge University Press, 2004.

Duffield, Mark. "The Political Economy of Internal War," in Joanna Macrae and Anthony Zwi, eds., *War and Hunger: Rethinking International Responses to Complex Emergencies.* London: Zed Books, 1994.

Dunant, Henry. *A Memory of Solferino.* Geneva: ICRC, 1986. French 1st edn 1862.

Durand, André. *The International Committee of the Red Cross.* Geneva: ICRC, 1981. *History of the International Committee of the Red Cross: From Sarajevo to Hiroshima.* Geneva: ICRC, 1984.

Durand, Roger, ed. *Gustave Ador: 58 ans d'engagement politique et humanitaire.* Geneva: Fondation Gustave Ador, 1996.

Editor, "Balance Sheet and Perspectives, Interview with George Weber," *Red Cross, Red Crescent* 1 (2000), 20–1.

Editor, "Etat des lieux: interview avec Jakob Kellenberger, Président du CICR," *Croix-Rouge, Croissant-Rouge,* 2 (2001), 20–1.

Egeland, Jan. *Humanitarian Initiative against Political "Disappearances."* Geneva: Henry Dunant Institute, 1982.

Egeland, Jan, ed. *Bulletin of Peace Proposals.* Special Issue: Humanitarian Organization-Building in the Third World, 18 no. 2 (1987).

Eizenstat, Stuart E. *Imperfect Justice: Looted Assets, Slave Labor, and the Unfinished Business of World War II.* New York: Public Affairs, 2003.

Evans, Malcolm D. *Preventing Torture: A Study of the European Convention for the Prevention of Torture and Inhuman or Degrading Treatment or Punishment.* Oxford: Oxford University Press, 1998.

Falk, Richard. "Human Rights, Humanitarian Assistance, and the Sovereignty of States," in Kevin M. Cahill, ed., *A Framework for Survival: Health, Human Rights, and Humanitarian Assistance in Conflicts and Disasters.* New York: Basic Books, 1996, 27–40.

"Assessing the Pinochet Litigation: Whither Universal Jurisdiction?" in Stephen Macedo, ed., *Universal Jurisdiction: National Courts and the Prosecution of Serious Crimes under International Law* (Philadelphia: University of Pennsylvania Press, 2004).

Fallows, James. "Blind into Baghdad," *Atlantic Monthly* (January–February 2004), 53–74.

Favez, Jean-Claude. *The Red Cross and the Holocaust*. Cambridge: Cambridge University Press, 1999. Original French expanded edition, 1988.

Fayet, Jean-François and Peter Huber. "La mission Wehrlin du CICR en Union soviétique (1920–1938)," *International Review of the Red Cross*, 849 (March 2003), 95–118.

Finnemore, Martha. *National Interests and International Society*. Ithaca: Cornell University Press, 1996.

Fiscalini, Diego. "Des élites au service d'une cause humanitaire: le Comité International de la Croix-Rouge," Mémoire de License, Université de Genève, Faculté des Lettres, Département d'Histoire, 1985.

Fischer, Thomas. "The ICRC and the 1962 Cuban Missile Crisis," *International Review of the Red Cross*, 842 (June 2001), 287–310.

Forsythe, David P. *Present Role of the Red Cross in Protection*. Geneva: Henry Dunant Institute, 1975.

"Political Prisoners: The Law and Politics of Protection," *Vanderbilt Journal of Transnational Law*, 9 no. 2 (Fall 1976), 295–322.

"The Red Cross as Transnational Movement: Conserving and Changing the Nation-State System," *International Organization*, 30 no. 4 (Fall 1976), 607–31.

"Who Guards the Guardians: Third Parties and the Law of Armed Conflict," *American Journal of International Law*, 70 no. 1 (January 1976), 41–61.

Humanitarian Politics: The International Committee of the Red Cross. Baltimore: Johns Hopkins University Press, 1977.

"Legal Management of Internal War: The 1977 Protocol on Non-International Armed Conflict," *American Journal of International Law*, 72 no. 2 (April 1978), 272–95.

"Humanitarian Mediation by the International Committee of the Red Cross," in I. William Zartman and Saadia Touval, eds., *The Theory and Practice of Mediation*. Boulder: Westview Press, 1984, 233–50.

"Human Rights and the International Committee of the Red Cross," *Human Rights Quarterly*, 12 no. 2 (May 1990), 265–89.

The Internationalization of Human Rights. Lexington, MA: Lexington Books, for D. C. Heath, 1991.

"Choices More Ethical than Legal: The International Committee of the Red Cross and Human Rights," *Ethics and International Affairs*, 7 (1993), 131–51.

"The International Committee of the Red Cross," in Michael A. Meyer and Helen Fox, eds., *Effecting Compliance: Armed Conflict and the New Law*, London: British Institute of International and Comparative Law, 1993, 83–106.

"Human Rights and US Foreign Policy: Two Levels, Two Worlds," in David Beetham, ed., *Politics and Human Rights*. Oxford: Blackwell, 1995, 111–31.

"The Politics of the Yugoslav War Crimes Court," in Roger S. Clark and Madeleine Sann, eds., *The Prosecution of International Crimes*. New Brunswick: Transaction Books, 1995, 185–206.

"Humanitarian Assistance: A Policy Analysis," *International Review of the Red Cross*, 314 (September–October 1996), 512–31.

"Human Rights and Humanitarian Operations: Theoretical Observations," in Eric Belgrad and Nitza Nachmias, eds., *The Politics of International Humanitarian Operations*. New York: Praeger, 1997, 37–52.

"Making the Geneva Conventions Relevant after the Cold War," *International Review of the Red Cross*, 834 (June 1998), 277–301.

"1949 and 1999: Making the Geneva Conventions Relevant after the Cold War," *International Review of the Red Cross*, 834 (June 1999), 265–76.

"Humanitarian Protection: The International Committee of the Red Cross and the United Nations High Commissioner for Refugees," *International Review of the Red Cross*, 843 (September 2001) 675–97.

UNHCR's Mandate: The Politics of Being Non-political, Working Paper No. 33, New Issues in Refugee Research, UNHCR. Geneva: UNHCR, Evaluation and Policy Analysis Unit, March 2001.

Human Rights in International Relations. Cambridge: Cambridge University Press, 2002.

"The United States and International Criminal Justice," *Human Rights Quarterly*, 24 no. 4 (2002), 974–91.

"Refugees and the Red Cross: An Underdeveloped Dimension of Protection," *Working Paper No. 76*, New Issues in Refugee Research, UNHCR. Geneva: UNHCR, Evaluation and Policy Analysis Unit, January 2003.

Freymond, Jacques. *Guerres, révolutions, Croix-Rouge: réflexions sur le rôle du Comité International de la Croix-Rouge*. Geneva: HEI, 1976.

"Humanitarian Policy and Pragmatism: Some Case Studies of the Red Cross," *Government and Opposition*, 11 (Autumn 1976), 408–25.

Fussell, Paul, "Hiroshima: A Soldier's View," *The New Republic*, 22 and 29 August 1981, 26–30.

Fux, Pierre-Yves and Mirko Zambelli. "Mise en œuvre de la Quatrième Convention de Genève dans les territoires palestiniens occupés: historique d'un processus multilatéral (1997–2001)," *International Review of the Red Cross*, 847 (September 2002), 661–97.

Gabbay, Rony E. *A Political Study of the Arab–Jewish Conflict: The Arab Refugee Problem*. Geneva: Librairie Droz, 1959.

Gabriel, Jurg Martin. "Switzerland and the European Union," paper presented at the CUNY European Union Studies Center, New York, 30 November 2000, http://web/gc.cuny.edu/Eusc/activities/paper/gabriel.htm.

"The Price of Political Uniqueness: Swiss Foreign Policy in a Changing World," in Jurg Martin Gabriel and Thomas Fischer, eds. *Swiss Foreign Policy in a Changing World*. New York and London: Palgrave Macmillan, 2003, 1–22.

Gabriel, Jurg Martin and Thomas Fischer, eds. *Swiss Foreign Policy in a Changing World*. New York and London: Palgrave Macmillan, 2003.

Gasser, Hans-Peter. "Respect for Fundamental Judicial Guarantees in Time of Armed Conflict – the Part Played by ICRC Delegates," *International Review of The Red Cross*, 287 (March–April 1992), 121–42.

"The International Committee of the Red Cross as a Humanitarian Actor in Conflict Situations: Development since 1945," in Jurg Martin Gabriel and Thomas Fischer, eds., *Swiss Foreign Policy in a Changing World*. New York and London: Palgrave Macmillan, 2003, 105–26.

Germond, Thierry. "NATO and the ICRC: A Partnership Serving the Victims of Armed Conflicts," *NATO Review*, 45 (May–June 1997), 30–2.

Gilpin, Robert. *War and Change in World Politics*. Cambridge: Cambridge University Press, 1981.

Girod, Christophe. *Tempête sur le désert: le Comité International de la Croix-Rouge et la Guerre du Golfe 1990–1991*. Brusseles: Bruylant, 1994.

Girod, Christophe and Angelo Gnaedinger, *Politics, Military Operations and Humanitarian Action: An Uneasy Alliance*. Geneva: ICRC, 1998.

Glenny, Misha. *The Fall of Yugoslavia*. London: Penguin, 3rd edn, 1996.

Gnädiger, Angelo, and Wayne MacDonald, "The ICRC in a Changing World: Assessments, Ambitions and Priorities," in Liesbeth Lignzaad, *et al.*, eds., *Making the Voice of Humanity Heard: Essays on Humanitarian Assistance and International Humanitarian Law in Honour of HRH Princess Margriet of the Netherlands*. Leiden and Boston: Martinus Nijhoff Publishers, 2004.

Goldstone, Richard J. *For Humanity: Reflections of a War Crimes Investigator*. New Haven: Yale University Press, 2000.

Goñi, Uki. *The Real Odessa: How Peron Brought the Nazi War Criminals to Argentina*. London: Granta Books, 2002.

Gourevitch, Philip. *We Wish To Inform You That Tomorrow We Will Be Killed with Our Families*. New York: Picador, for Farrar, Straus and Giroux, 1999.

Grossrieder, Paul. "Humanitarian Action in the Twenty-First Century: The Danger of Setback," in Kevin M. Cahill, ed., *Basics of International Humanitarian Missions*. New York: Fordham, 2003, 3–37.

Guest, Iain. *Behind the Disappearances: Argentina's Dirty War against Human Rights and the United Nations*. Philadelphia: University of Pennsylvania Press, 1990.

Gutman, Roy. *Witness to Genocide*. Middletown, WI: Lisa Drew, 1993.

Harroff-Tavel, Marion. "La guerre a-t-elle jamais une fin? L'action du Comité International de la Croix-Rouge lorsque les armes se taisent," *International Review of the Red Cross*, 851 (September 2003), 465–96.

Hawkins, Darren G. *International Human Rights and Authoritarian Rule in Chile.* Lincoln: University of Nebraska Press, 2002.

Hentsch, Thierry. *Face au blocus: la Croix-Rouge Internationale dans le Nigéria en guerre (1967–1970).* Genève: HEI, 1973.

Herrmann, Irene. "Le lien entre Genève et la Confédération," in Roger Durand, ed., *Gustave Ador: 58 ans d'engagement politique et humanitaire.* Geneva: Fondation Gustave Ador, 1996, 263–76.

Hersch, Seymour. "The Gray Zone," *The New Yorker,* 24 May 2004 posted at http://www.newyorker.com/printable/?fact/040524fa_ct;

"Torture at Abu Ghraib," *The New Yorker,* 30 April 2004, posted at http://www.newyorker.com/printable/?fact/040510fa_ct.

Chain of Command: The Road from 9/11 to Abu Ghraib. New York: HarperCollins, 2004.

Hertberg, Hendrik. "Unconventional War," *The New Yorker,* posted at www.newyorker.com/printable/?talk/040524_talk_hertberg

Hewins, Ralph. *Count Folke Bernadotte, His Life and Work.* London: Hutchinson and Co., 1949.

Holbrooke, Richard. *To End a War.* New York: Random House, 1998.

Hook, Steven W. and John Spanier. *American Foreign Policy since World War II.* Washington: CQ Press, 15th edn, 2000.

Howard, Michael, George J. Andreopolous, and Mark R. Shulman, eds. *The Laws of War: Constraints on Warfare in the Western World.* New Haven: Yale University Press, 1994.

Huber, Max. *The Red Cross: Principles and Problems.* Geneva: ICRC, no date [1941]. *Le bon samaritain.* Neuchâtel: Editions de la Baconnière, 1943.

Hubert, Don. *The Landmine Ban: A Case Study in Humanitarian Advocacy.* Watson Institute, Occasional Paper No. 42. Providence, RI: Brown University, 2000.

Hutchinson, John F. "Rethinking the Origins of the Red Cross," *Bulletin of the History of Medicine,* 63 (1989), 557–78.

Champions of Charity: War and the Rise of the Red Cross. Boulder: Westview, 1996.

"Disasters and the International Order: Earthquakes, Humanitarians, and the Ciraolo Project," *International History Review,* 22 no. 1 (January 2000), 1–36.

"Disasters and the International Order–II: The International Relief Union," *International History Review,* 23 no. 2 (June 2001), 253–504.

Ignatieff, Michael. "Television and Humanitarian Aid," in Jonathan Moore, ed., *Hard Choices: Moral Dilemmas in Humanitarian Intervention.* Lanham, MD: Rowman and Littlefield, 1998, 287–302.

The Warrior's Honor: Ethnic War and the Modern Conscience. London: Vintage, 1999.

Human Rights as Politics and Idolatry. Princeton: Princeton University Press, 2001.

Ingram, James. "The Future Architecture for International Humanitarian Assistance," in Thomas G. Weiss and Larry Minear, eds., *Humanitarianism across Borders: Sustaining Civilians in Times of War*. Boulder: Lynne Rienner, 1993, 171–94.

Jeannet, Stephane. "Recognition of the ICRC's Long-Standing Rule of Confidentiality," *International Review of the Red Cross*, 838 (June 2000), 403–25.

Johnson, James T. *Ideology, Reason, and the Limitation of War: Religious and Secular Concepts, 1200–1740*. Princeton: Princeton University Press, 1975.

Joyce, James Avery. *Red Cross International and the Strategy of Peace*. New York: Oceana Publications, 1959.

Junod, Dominique-D. *The Imperiled Red Cross and the Palestine– Eretz–Yisrael Conflict 1945–1952*. London: Kegan Paul International, 1996.

Junod, Marcel. *Warrior without Weapons*. Geneva: ICRC, 1982.

Junod, Sylvie-Stoyanka. *Protection of the Victims of Armed Conflict: Falkland–Malvinas Islands*. Geneva: ICRC, 1985.

Kalshoven, Frits. *Constraints on the Waging of War*. Geneva: ICRC and Martinus Nijhoff, 1987.

Keck, Margret and Kathryn Sikkink. *Activists beyond Borders: Transnational Advocacy Networks in International Politics*. Ithaca: Cornell University Press, 1988.

Kennan, George. *American Diplomacy 1900–1950*. Chicago: Mentor, for the University of Chicago, 1951.

Kennedy, David. *The Dark Sides of Virtue: Reassessing International Humanitarianism*. Princeton: Princeton University Press, 2004.

Knitel, Hans G. *Les Délégations du Comité International de la Croix-Rouge*. Geneva: HEI, 1967.

Lanord, Christophe. "The Legal Status of National Red Cross and Red Crescent Societies," *International Review of the Red Cross*, 840 (December 2000), 1053–78.

Laqueur, Walter. *The Terrible Secret: An Investigation into the Suppression of Information about Hitler's Final Solution*. London: Weidenfeld and Nicolson, 1980.

Lasswell, Harold D. *Psychopathology and Politics*. Chicago: University of Chicago Press, renewed edition in 1986.

Politics: Who Gets What, When and How. No place indicated: Peter Smith Publisher, 1990.

Laurence, John. *The Cat from Hue: A Vietnam War Story*. New York: Public Affairs, 2001.

Lauterpact, Hersch. "The Problem of the Revision of the Law of War," *The British Yearbook of International Law*, 29 (1952), 360–82.

Lavoyer, Jean-Philippe. "Refugees and Internally Displaced Persons: International Humanitarian Law and the Role of the ICRC," *International Review of the Red Cross*, 304 (March–April 1995), 162–91.

Leaning, Jennifer. "When the System Doesn't Work: Somalia 1992," in Kevin M. Cahill, ed., *A Framework for Survival: Health, Human Rights, and Humanitarian Assistance in Conflicts and Disasters*. New York: Basic Books, for the Council on Foreign Relations, 1993, 103–20.

Lebor, Adam. *Hitler's Secret Bankers: How Switzerland Profited from Nazi Genocide*. London: Simon and Schuster, 1997, 1999.

Leitenberg, Milton. "New Evidence on the Korean War Biological Warfare Allegations," Woodrow Wilson International Center for Scholars, Cold War International History Project, www.kimsoft.com.2000/germberia.htm.

Le Sueur, James. *Uncivil War: Intellectuals and Identity Politics during the Decolonization of Algeria*. Philadelphia: University of Pennsylvania Press, 2001.

Lieven, Anatol. *America Right or Wrong: An Anatomy of American Nationalism*. Oxford: Oxford University Press, 2004.

Lijnzaad, Liesbeth, *et al.*, eds. *Making the Voice of Humanity Heard*. Leiden: Brill Academic Publishers, 2004.

Lindsey, Charlotte. *Women Facing War*. Geneva: ICRC, 2001.

Loescher, Gil. *The UNHCR and World Politics*. Oxford: Oxford University Press, 2001.

Lorenzi, Massimo. *Le CICR, le cœur et la raison: entretiens avec Cornelio Sommaruga*. Lausanne: Favre, 1998.

McFarland, Neil. *Politics and Humanitarian Action*, Occasional Paper No. 41. Watson Institute for International Studies, Brown University, 2000.

Macrae, Joanna, *et al.*, eds. *War and Hunger: Rethinking International Responses to Complex Emergencies*. London: Zed Books, 1994.

Mandela, Nelson. *Long Walk to Freedom*. Boston: Little, Brown, 1995.

Mandelbaum, Michael. *The Ideas That Conquered the World: Peace, Democracy, and Free Markets in the Twenty–First Century*. New York: Public Affairs, 2003.

Mann, James. *Rise of the Vulcans: The History of Bush's War Cabinet*. New York: Penguin, 2004.

Marcus, David. "Famine Crimes in International Law," *American Journal of International Law*, 97 no. 2 (April 2003), 245–81.

Maresca, Louis and Stuart Maslen, eds. *The Banning of Anti-personnel Landmines: The Legal Contribution of the International Committee of the Red Cross*. Cambridge: Cambridge University Press, 2000.

Marti, Laurent. *Bonsoir mes victimes*. Geneva: Labor and Fides, 1996.

Martin, Eric. "An Enlightening Three-Year Episode," *International Review of the Red Cross*, 199 (October 1977), 434–8.

Mason, L. and R. Brown. *Rice, Rivalry and Politics: Managing Cambodian Relief*. South Bend, IN: University of Notre Dame Press, 1983.

Maxwell, Cameron A., Robert J. Lawson, and Brian W. Tomlin, eds. *To Walk without Fear: The Global Movement to Ban Landmines*. Oxford: Oxford University Press, 1998.

Mayall, James, ed. *The New Interventionism, 1991–1994*. Cambridge: Cambridge University Press, 1996.

Mazower, Mark. *Inside Hitler's Greece: The Experience of Occupation, 1941–1944*. New Haven: Yale University Press, 1993, 1995.

Megevand, Beatrice. "Between Insurrection and Government – ICRC. Action in Mexico (January–August 1994)," *International Review of the Red Cross*, 304 (January–February 1995), 94–108.

Mercier, Michèle. *Crimes sans châtiment: l'action humanitaire en ex-Yougoslavie 1991–1993*. Brussels: Bruylant, 1994. English edition 1995.

Meron, Théodore. *Human Rights and Humanitarian Norms as Customary Law*. Oxford: Oxford University Press, 1972.

"The Humanization of Humanitarian Law," *American Journal of International Law*, 94 no. 2 (April 2000): 239–78.

Meurant, Jacques, "The International Committee of the Red Cross: Nazi Persecutions and the Concentration Camps," *International Review of the Red Cross*, 271 (July–August, 1989), 375–97.

Michalak, Stanley. *A Primer in Power Politics* (Wilmington, DE: Scholarly Resources, 2001).

Minear, Larry. *The Humanitarian Enterprise: Dilemmas and Discoveries*. Bloomfield, CT: Kumarian Press, 2002.

Minear, Larry and Thomas G. Weiss. *Humanitarian Politics*. New York: Foreign Policy Association, 1995.

Mercy under Fire: War and the Global Humanitarian Community. Boulder: Westview, 1995.

Momtaz, Djamchid. "The Minimum Humanitarian Rules Applicable in Periods of Internal Tension and Strife," *International Review of the Red Cross*, 324 (September 1998), 455–62.

Monnier, Victor. "Les relations avec William E. Rappard," in Roger Durand, ed., *Gustave Ador: 58 ans d'engagement politique et humanitaire*. Geneva: Fondation Gustave Ador, 1996, 411–37.

Mooney, Erin D. "Presence, Ergo Protection? UNPROFOR, UNHCR, and the ICRC in Croatia and Bosnia and Herzegovina," *International Journal of Refugee Law*, 7 no. 3 (Summer 1995), 407–35.

Moore, Jonathan, ed. *Hard Choices: Moral Dilemmas in Humanitarian Intervention*. Lanham, MD: Rowman and Littlefield, for the ICRC, 1998.

Morehead, Caroline. *Dunant's Dream: War, Switzerland and the History of the Red Cross*. New York: HarperCollins, 1999.

Moreillon, Jacques. *Le Comité International de la Croix-Rouge et la protection des détenus politiques*. Geneva: Institut Henry Dunant, 1973.

Mossé, Claude. *Ces Messieurs de Berne, 1939–1945*, Paris: Stock, 1997.

Mueller, John. *Quiet Cataclysm: Reflections on the Recent Transformation of World Politics.* New York: HarperCollins, 1995.

Naik, A. "UN Investigation into Sexual Exploitation by Aid Workers: Justice Has Not Been Done," *Forced Migration Review*, 16 (2003), 46–7.

Neier, Aryeh. *Taking Liberties: Four Decades in the Struggle for Rights.* New York: Public Affairs, 2003.

Nunca Más: The Report of the Argentine National Commission on the Disappeared (New York: Farrar Straus Giroux, 1986).

Obradovic, Konstantin. "Que faire face aux violations du droit humanitaire? – Quelques réflexions sur le rôle possible du CICR," in Christophe Swinarski, ed., *Studies and Essays on International Humanitarian Law and Red Cross Principles.* Dordrecht: Martinus Nijhoff Publishers, 1984, 483–94.

Owen, David. *Balkan Odyssey.* New York: Harcourt Brace, 1995.

Pakenham, Thomas. *The Boer War* (London: Weidenfeld and Nicolson, 1979).

Patchett, Ann. *Bel Canto.* New York: Perennial, for HarperCollins, 2001.

Pavillon, Monique. *Les immobilisées: les femmes suisses durant la Second Guerre mondiale.* Lausanne: Editions d'En Bas, 1989.

Peleg, Ilan. *Human Rights in the West Bank and Gaza: Legacy and Politics.* Syracuse: Syracuse University Press, 1995.

Pelic, Jelena. "The Right to Food in Situations of Armed Conflict: The Legal Framework," *International Review of the Red Cross*, 844 (December 2001), 1097–1110.

Pendergast, John. *Frontline Diplomacy: Humanitarian Aid and Conflict in Africa* (Boulder: Lynne Rienner, 1996).

Penkower, Monty Noam. *The Jews Were Expendable: Free World Diplomacy and the Holocaust.* Urbana: University of Illinois Press, 1983.

Petitpierre, Max. *A Contemporary Look at the International Committee of the Red Cross.* Geneva: ICRC, 1971.

Pictet, Jean. *Le droit humanitaire et la protection des victimes de la guerre.* Leiden: Sijthoff, 1973.

   The Fundamental Principles of the Red Cross: Commentary. Geneva: Henry Dunant Institute, 1979.

Power, Samantha. *"A Problem from Hell": America and the Age of Genocide.* New York: HarperCollins, 2002.

Powers, Jonathan. *Like Water on Stone: The Story of Amnesty International.* Boston: Northeastern University Press, 2001.

Prendergast, John. *Frontline Diplomacy: Humanitarian Aid and Conflict in Africa.* Boulder: Lynne Rienner, 1996.

Prestowitz, Clyde. *Rogue Nation: American Unilateralism and the Failure of Good Intentions.* New York: Basic Books, 2003.

Probst, Raymond R. *"Good Offices" in the Light of Swiss International Practice and Experience*. Dordrecht: Martinus Nijhoff, 1989.

Reid, Ian. *The Evolution of the Red Cross*. Geneva: Henry Dunant Institute, 1975.

Rieff, David. *A Bed for the Night: Humanitarianism in Crisis*. New York: Simon and Schuster, 2002.

Risse, Thomas, Stephen C. Ropp, and Kathryn Sikkink, eds. *The Power of Human Rights: International Norms and Domestic Change*. Cambridge: Cambridge University Press, 1999.

Roberts, Adam. "Prolonged Military Occupation: The Israeli-Occupied Territories since 1967, *American Journal of International Law*, 84 no. 1 (January 1990), 44–103.

"Land Warfare: From Hague to Nuremberg," in Michael Howard, George J. Andreopolous, and Mark R. Shulman, eds., *The Laws of War: Constraints on Warfare in the Western World*. New Haven: Yale University Press, 1994, 116–139.

Humanitarian Action in War. London: Adelphi Paper No. 305, Oxford University Press, for the Institute for Strategic Studies, 1996.

Roberts, Adam and Richard Guelff, eds. *Documents on the Laws of War*. Oxford: Oxford University Press, 1989.

Rohde, David. *End Game: The Betrayal and Fall of Srebrenica, Europe's Worst Massacre since World War II*. Boulder: Westview, 1997.

Rufin, Jean-Christophe. *L'aventure humanitaire*. Paris: Gallimard, Collection Découvertes-Histoire, 2nd edn, 2001.

Rummel, R. J. *Death by Government: Genocide and Mass Murder since 1900*. New Brunswick: Transaction, 1997.

Ryfman, Philippe. *La question humanitaire: histoire, problématiques, acteurs et enjeux de l'aide humanitaire internationale*. Paris: Ellipses Editions, 1999.

Sadat, Leila Nadya. "International Legal Issues Surrounding the Mistreatment of Iraqi Detainees by American Forces," *American Society of International Law Insight* (May/July 2004), 5, 12, 13.

Sahnoun, Mohamed. *Somalia: The Missed Opportunities*. Washington, DC: US Institute of Peace Press, 1994.

Sandoz, Yves. "La notion de protection dans le droit international humanitaire et au sein du Mouvement de la Croix-Rouge," in Christophe Swinarski, ed., *Studies and Essays on International Humanitarian Law and Red Cross Principles*. Dordrecht: Martinus Nijhoff Publishers, 1984, 975–88.

The International Committee of the Red Cross as Guardian of International Humanitarian Law. Geneva: ICRC, 1998.

Sarat, Austin and Thomas R. Kearns, eds. *Human Rights: Concepts, Contests, Contingencies*. Ann Arbor: University of Michigan Press, 2001.

Schabas, William. *Introduction to the International Criminal Court*. Cambridge: Cambridge University Press, 2nd edn, 2004.

Schindler, Dietrich. "Significance of the Geneva Conventions for the Contemporary World," *International Review of the Red Cross*, 836 (December 1999), 715–29.

Schindler, Dietrich and Jiri Toman, eds. *The Laws of Armed Conflicts: A Collection of Conventions, Resolutions and Other Documents*. Dordrect: Martinus Nijhoff, 3rd edn, 1988.

Sella, Amnon. *The Value of Human Life in Soviet Warfare*. London: Routledge, 1992.

Sellars, Kirsten. *The Rise and Rise of Human Rights*. Phoenix Mill, UK: Sutton Publishers, 2002.

Senarclens, Jean de, *Gustave Moynier: le batisseur*. Geneva: Editions Slatkine, 2000.

Shaw, Martin. *War and Genocide*. Cambridge: Polity Press, 2003.

Shawcross, William. *The Quality of Mercy: Cambodia, Holocaust and Modern Conscience*. New York: Simon and Schuster, 1984.

Shue, Henry. *Basic Rights: Subsistence, Affluence, and U.S. Foreign Policy*. Princeton: Princeton University Press, 1980, 2nd edn, 1996.

Siegrist, Roland. *The Protection of Political Detainees: The International Committee of the Red Cross in Greece (1967–1971)*. Montreux: Corbaz, 1985.

Singer, P. W., *Corporate Warriors: The Rise of the Privatized Military Industry*. Ithaca: Cornell University Press, 2003.

Smillie, Ian, ed. *Patronage or Partnership: Local Capacity Building in Humanitarian Crises*. Bloomfield, CT: Kumarian Press, 2001.

Sogge, David, ed. *Compassion and Calculation: The Business of Private Foreign Aid*. London and Chicago: Pluto Press, for the Transnational Institute, 1996.

Sommaruga, Cornelio. "Humanitarian Law and Human Rights in the Legal Arsenal of the ICRC," ICRC Homepage, 16 March 1995, www.icrc.org.

Stella, Amnon. *The Value of Human Life in Soviet Warfare* (London: Routledge, 2002).

Stewart, James G. "Towards a Single Definition of Armed Conflict in International Humanitarian Law: A Critique of Internationalized Armed Conflict," *International Review of the Red Cross*, 850 (June 2003), 313–50.

Strasser, Steven, ed. *The Abu Ghraib Investigations*. New York: Public Affairs, 2004.

Swinarski, Christophe, ed. *Studies and Essays on International Humanitarian Law and Red Cross Principles*. Dordrecht: Martinus Nijhoff Publishers, 1984.

Sztuchlik, Rezso and Anja Toivola. *What Was the Impact of the "Tansley Report"?* (Geneva: Henry Dunant Institute, 1988).

Tansley, Donald D. *Final Report: Agenda for Red Cross*. Geneva: Henry Dunant Institute, 1975.

Tauxe, Jean-Daniel. "Faire mieux accepter le Comité International de la Croix-Rouge sur le terrain," *International Review of the Red Cross*, 833 (March 1999), 55–61.

Terry, Fiona. *Condemned To Repeat? The Paradox of Humanitarian Action*. Ithaca: Cornell University Press, 2002.

Thakur, Ramesh and William Maley. "The Ottawa Convention on Landmines: A Landmark Humanitarian Treaty in Arms Control?" *Global Governance*, 5 no. 3 (1999), 273–302.

Thomas, Hugh. *The Spanish Civil War*. London: Penguin Books, 1974.

Tolley, Howard B., Jr. *The International Commission of Jurists: Global Advocates for Human Rights*. Philadelphia: University of Pennsylvania Press, 1994.

Truninger, Florianne. "The International Committee of the Red Cross and the Indochina War," *International Review of the Red Cross*, 303 (November–December 1994), 564–94.

U Thant. *View from the UN*. Garden City, NY: Doubleday and Co., Inc., 1978.

van Boven, Theo. "Some Reflections on the Principle of Neutrality," in Christophe Swinarski, ed., *Studies and Essays on International Humanitarian Law and Red Cross Principles*. Dordrecht: Martinus Nijhoff Publishers, 1984, 643–54.

Walzer, Michael. "Prisoners of War: Does the Fight Continue after the Battle," *American Political Science Review*, 63 no. 3 (September 1969), 777–86.

Just and Unjust Wars: A Moral Argument with Historical Illustrations. New York: Basic Books, 1977, 1992.

Ward, Thomas. *The Ethics of Destruction: Norms and Force in International Relations*. Ithaca: Cornell University Press, 2001.

Waters, Tony. *Bureaucratizing the Good Samaritan: The Limitations of Humanitarian Relief Operations*. Boulder: Westview, 2000.

Weiss, Thomas G. *Military Civilian Interactions: Intervening in Humanitarian Crises*. Lanham, MD: Rowman and Littlefield, 1999.

Weiss, Thomas G., David P. Forsythe, and Roger A. Coate. *The United Nations and Changing World Politics*. Boulder: Westview, 4th edn, 2004.

Weiss, Thomas G. and Larry Minear, eds. *Humanitarianism across Borders: Sustaining Civilians in Times of War*. Boulder: Lynne Rienner, 1993.

White, William L. *The Captives of Korea: An Unofficial White Paper on the Treatment of War Prisoners*. New York: Scribner, 1957; reprinted Westport, CT: Greenwood Publishers, 1979.

Willemin, Georges and Roger Heacock. *The International Committee of the Red Cross*. Dordrecht: Martinus Nijhoff Publishers, 1984.

Wood, Adrian, Raymond Apthorpe, and John Borton, eds. *Evaluating International Humanitarian Action: Reflections from Practitioners*. London and New York: Zed Books, 2001.

Ziegler, Jean. *The Swiss, the Gold, and the Dead: How Swiss Bankers Helped Finance the Nazi War Machine*. London: Penguin, 1997, 1998.

Zimmermann, Warren. *Origins of a Catastrophe*. New York: Times Books, 1996.

War in the Balkans. New York: Council on Foreign Relations, 1999.

INDEX

cross-border relief 303
and landmines 265, 289
Cambone, Steven 150
Camp Cropper 148
Canada, ICRC funding 233
Cartigny 229
Catholicism 41, 176, 199, 204
Center of Human Rights and
Humanitarian Law, Washington
272
Central Intelligence Agency (US) *see*
CIA
Central Tracing Agency 83
charity, private 15
Chechnya 96, 98, 112, 219, 314
attacks on ICRC 229
Cherpitel, Didier 124
Chiapas 199
child soldiers 243, 248, 288
Chile 81–7, 176, 249, 294
China 54, 58, 176, 177, 300
Nationalist Party (Kuomintang) 53
Chinese 53–4
Chinese Manchuria 40–1
Chomsky, Noam 308
Christianity 2, 27, 28, 167, 218, 251
Christopher, Warren 109
CIA 130, 146, 182
at Bagram 141
legal cover 131
and prisoner abuse 150
civil war 33, 40
internationalized 40
civil-political rights 168
Clausewitz, K. M. von 160
Cold War 7, 22, 51–95, 159, 200, 208,
298
Colombia 81, 294
colonialism 60, 75, 151, 165, 256,
261
communism 51, 53–4, 58, 59, 75, 79,
159, 176, 200, 261
anti-communism 175
collapse of 96
complex emergencies 8
concentration camps 30, 44, 60, 186,
296
Buchenwald 187

German 170
Serbian 113
Congo 178, 291, 314
conservatism 20, 30, 41, 47, 58, 60, 69,
203, 240, 308
creative 171
definition 169
tactics 170
Convention on Civil and Political
Rights 254
Convention on the Rights of the Child
248
Costa Rica 158
Council of Europe 69, 70, 94
Council of ICRC 193, 201, 204, 215,
222
creation of 224–5
Courten, Jean de 211, 222, 230
Covenant of the League of Nations 33,
158
Cramer, A. 188
Cramer, Renée-Marguerite 41, 203–4
Crimean war 16
crimes
against humanity 249–50, 273, 313
outside armed conflict 249–50
see also genocide; war crimes
Croatia 108, 110
Croats 108, 111, 114
Cuba 3, 30, 134
Cuban missile crisis (1962) 53, 61–2,
160, 199, 205
Cuny, Fred 112
Cyprus 60
Czechoslovakia 54

Daccord, Yves 291
Davidson, Henry P. 33, 35, 36
Dayton Accords (1995) 115
Deluz, Guy 218, 224
democracy 51, 208
detainees
ghost 133, 152
legal basis for 198
non-war 62
release of 86–7
transferred 133
see also prisoners of war

CPSIA information can be obtained
at www.ICGtesting.com
Printed in the USA
LVHW03s1956260618
581962LV00002B/135/P

9 780521 612814